SLOVAKIA

Sena

Záhony

THE
NORTHERN
HIGHLANDS

Salgótarján

Miskolc

Nyíregyháza

Eger

Gyöngyös

Debrecen

Püspökladány

Szolnok

THE GREAT
PLAIN

Kecskemét

Békéscsaba

ROMANIA

Szeged

SERBIA

**The Northern
Highlands**
Pages 212–233

he Great Plain
Pages 234–259

0 kilometres

0 miles

D0273917

EYEWITNESS TRAVEL

HUNGARY

EYEWITNESS TRAVEL

HUNGARY

Main Contributors **Barbara Olszańska,**
Tadeusz Olszański, Craig Turp

LONDON, NEW YORK,
MELBOURNE, MUNICH AND DELHI
www.dk.com

Produced by Hachette Livre Polska Sp. z o.o.

Senior Graphic Designer Paweł Pasternak

Graphic Designers Paweł Pasternak, Paweł Kamiński

Senior Editor Agnieszka Trzebska-Cwalina

Photographers
Gábor Barka, Dorota and Mariusz Jarymowicz, Krzysztof Kur

Illustrators
Michał Burkiewicz, Gary Cross, Dorota Jarymowicz,
Paweł Marczak

Cartographers
Barbara and Jacek Gawrysiuk, Magda Polak

Printed in China

15 16 17 18 10 9 8 7 6 5 4 3 2 1

First published in Great Britain in 2007
by Dorling Kindersley Ltd.
80 Strand, London, UK, WC2R 0RL

Reprinted with revisions 2010, 2013, 2015

Copyright © 2007, 2015 Dorling Kindersley Limited, London
A Penguin Random House Company

All rights reserved. No part of this publication may be reproduced,
stored in a retrieval system, or transmitted in any form or by any
means, electronic, mechanical, photocopying, recording or otherwise
without the prior written permission of the copyright owner.

A CIP catalogue record is available from the British Library.

ISBN 978-0-24118-131-7

Floors are referred to throughout in accordance with
UK usage; i.e. the "first floor" is the floor above ground level.

MIX
Paper from
responsible sources
FSC
www.fsc.org   FSC™ C018179

**The information in this
DK Eyewitness Travel Guide is checked regularly.**
Every effort has been made to ensure that this book is as up-to-date as possible
at the time of going to press. Some details, however, such as telephone numbers,
opening hours, prices, gallery hanging arrangements and travel information are
liable to change. The publishers cannot accept responsibility for any consequences
arising from the use of this book, nor for any material on third party websites, and
cannot guarantee that any website address in this book will be a suitable source of
travel information. We value the views and suggestions of our readers very highly.
Please write to: Publisher, DK Eyewitness Travel Guides, Dorling Kindersley,
80 Strand, London, WC2R 0RL, UK, or email: travelguides@dk.com.

Front cover main image: The Református Nagytemplom (Great Reformed Church), Debrecen

◀ The glittering interior of Hungary's Parliament building, Budapest

Contents

How to Use This Guide **6**

Crest from the Esterházy Palace
in Fertőd *(see p171)*

Introducing Hungary

Neo-Gothic exterior of the Parliament
building, Budapest *(see pp84–5)*

Budapest Area by Area

Castle walls rising above a pretty square in Eger *(see pp220–23)*

Sailing on Lake Balaton, Hungary's largest freshwater lake *(see pp198–9)*

The library at Pannonhalma Abbey, a UNESCO World Heritage site *(see pp180–81)*

Budapest's grand State
Opera House *(see pp92–3)*

HOW TO USE THIS GUIDE

This travel guide helps you get the most from your visit to Hungary, providing detailed practical information as well as expert recommendations. *Introducing Hungary* maps the whole country and sets it in its historical and cultural context. The first section, on *Budapest*, gives an overview of the capital's main attractions. Hungary's regions are charted in the *Region by Region* section, which covers all the important towns, cities and places around the country, with photographs, maps and illustrations. Details of hotels, restaurants, shops and markets, entertainment and sports are found in *Travellers' Needs*, while the *Survival Guide* contains advice on everything from medical services and public transport to personal safety.

Budapest Area by Area

Budapest has been divided into four central areas and a Further Afield section. Each area is described in an individual section, giving the names of all main sights and attractions. The sights are numbered on the area map.

1 Area Map For easy reference, the sights in each area are numbered and plotted on a map. Sights in the city centre are also shown on the Budapest Street Finder on pages 122–7.

Sights at a glance lists the buildings in a particular area by category.

A locator map shows at a glance where you are in relation to the city plan.

A suggested route for a walk is shown in red.

2 Street-by-Street Map This bird's-eye view shows the heart of each sightseeing area. The sights carry the same numbers here as on the area map and the fuller description on subsequent pages.

Stars indicate the sights that no visitor should miss.

3 Detailed information All the important sights in Budapest are described individually. Practical information includes a map reference, opening hours and telephone numbers. The key to the symbols used can be found on the back jacket flap.

1 Introduction The landscape, history and character of each region are portrayed here, with a description of how the area has developed over the centuries and what it offers the visitor today.

Hungary Region by Region

The coloured areas shown on the map on the book's inside front cover show the five main sightseeing regions into which Hungary has been divided. Each is covered in a full chapter in *Hungary Region by Region (see pp128–259)*. The most interesting towns and places to visit have been numbered on Regional Maps throughout the book.

2 Regional Map This shows the road network and gives an illustrated overview of the whole region. The most interesting places to visit are numbered and there are also useful tips on getting around the region by car and train.

Each region of Hungary can be quickly identified using the colour coding on the inside front cover.

3 Detailed information All the important towns and other places to visit are described individually. They are listed in order, following the numbering on the Regional Map. Each entry has details of the main sights.

The visitors' checklist gives all the practical information needed to plan your visit.

4 Major Sights Historic buildings are dissected to reveal their interiors; museums and galleries have colour-coded floorplans to help you find the most important exhibits.

Story boxes highlight specific aspects relating to a top sight and explore these in more depth.

Ede Heinrich, *The Coronation of Franz Joseph I on 8 June 1867* ▶

INTRODUCING HUNGARY

DISCOVERING HUNGARY

The itineraries on the following pages have been designed to include as many of Hungary's highlights as possible, while keeping long-distance travel manageable. First comes a two-day tour of the country's exhilarating capital, Budapest. This is followed by a two-day tour of Lake Balaton, with suggestions for places to visit both along the shoreline itself and just inland. A one-week tour of the country covers many of Hungary's must-see sights, stopping off at the key towns and cities, as well as some of the areas of outstanding natural beauty. Lastly, there is a wonderful two-week tour of the whole country, which takes in all the sights of the one-week tour and much more besides. Extra suggestions are provided for those who wish to extend their stay by another day or so: add one, or perhaps two or three, or just dip in and out and take things at your own pace.

View across tiled rooftops from Sopron's Firewatch Tower to the Benedictine Church

A Week in Hungary

- Spend the day exploring noble Budapest, Hungary's great capital city.
- Head to Lake Balaton to chill out on the beach or try your hand at some watersports.
- Marvel at extraordinary pre-Christian and Turkish monuments in lively Pécs.
- Seek out ecclesiastical treasures in Szeged, including the Great Synagogue.
- Witness stunning horsemanship in the Hortobágy National Park on Hungary's Great Plain.
- Visit a UNESCO-listed village dedicated to indigenous folk culture, then continue onwards to the gorgeously Baroque town of Vác.

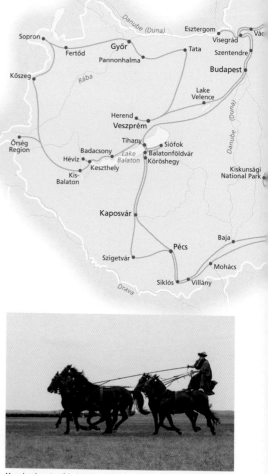

Marvel at the poise of the legendary csikós, or cowboys, of the Great Plain

The fairy-tale Parliament building in Budapest

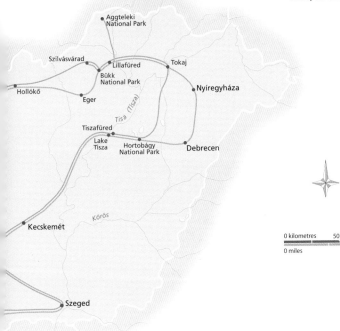

Key

— A Week in Hungary

— Two Weeks in Hungary

Two Weeks in Hungary

- Admire the architecture, wallow in steam baths, and enjoy the coffee houses of Budapest.

- Follow the dramatic sweep of the Danube Bend, taking in the architectural treasures found in charming towns along the route.

- Savour legendary Bull's Blood red wine in Eger, then sip a glass of golden sweet wine from Tokaj.

- Visit the forested Orség region, unspoiled rural Hungary at its finest.

- Marvel at the art of Csontváry and Art Nouveau master Rippl-Rónai, in Pécs and Kaposvár respectively.

- Explore the fabulously preserved old town of Sopron, and take a tour of the opulent Esterházy Palace, where Haydn once performed.

Two Days in Budapest

Straddling the Danube, Hungary's capital city offers two contrasting, but equally compelling, sides – Buda and Pest.

- **Arriving** Budapest Liszt Ferenc Airport is 20km (13 miles) southeast of the city. It's about 50 minutes by public transport to the centre.

Day 1
Morning Explore the **Castle District** *(pp56–69)*, the historic heart of Buda. Admire the fine 13th-century **Mátyás Church** *(pp66–7)* before taking in the superlative views across the Danube from the **Fisherman's Bastion** *(p64)*. Move on to the **Royal Palace** *(pp58–9)*, home to the engrossing **Hungarian National Gallery** *(pp62–3)*.

Afternoon After lunch on the Hill, take the Sikló funicular down to the majestic Chain Bridge. Cross the bridge to Pest and **St Stephen's Basilica** *(pp90–91)*, Budapest's most important ecclesiastical building. Ride the scenic no. 2 tram along the Pest embankment as far as the **Central Market Hall** *(p118)*, where you can indulge your senses and treat yourself to a few goodies. In the evening, take in a performance at the **Liszt Academy of Music** *(p105)*.

Day 2
Morning Absorb yourself in the atmospheric **Jewish Quarter** *(p104)*, dominated by the Great

Synagogue, the largest in Europe, before heading up Andrássy út to view – or even take a tour of – the opulent **Opera House** *(pp92–3)* and the striking eight-sided Oktogon square, beyond which lies the engrossing, but sobering, **House of Terror Museum** *(p105)*.

Afternoon Ride the beautifully preserved M1 metro line to **Heroes' Square** *(pp108–9)* and its mighty monuments. Then, either amble around the lake in **Városliget** park *(p110)* before visiting **Budapest Zoo** *(p121)*, whose Secessionist-style animal enclosures are a delight, or go for a blissful soak in the fabulous **Széchenyi Baths** *(p111)*.

Two Days on Lake Balaton

Holiday playground for many Hungarians, and the largest lake in central Europe, Balaton is packed with both active and cultural pursuits.

- **Arriving** From Budapest airport, you can hire a car, go by train from Budapest Déli station, or take a domestic flight to Keszthely – in which case, reverse the itinerary.

- **Getting Around** Public transport is feasible; a car gives you more flexibility.

Day 1
Morning Take to the beach in **Siófok** *(p198)*, and perhaps try your hand at some watersports,

Baroque statue supporting a window lintel at Festetics Palace near Keszthely

before enjoying a cultural fix at the village museum in **Zamárdi** *(p199)*. Board the ferry to the lake's northern shore, landing at the **Tihany Peninsula** *(p206)*, with its pleasing little village crowned by the Abbey Church. Lunch in one of the village's many traditional restaurants.

Afternoon Make the short trip to **Balatonfüred** *(p207)* for a walk along the shoreline of the lake's most graceful resort. Return back down along the coast to **Badacsony Mountain** *(p205)*, and follow the trail up into the vineyard-clad hills and the Kisfaludy Lookout Tower, where you can enjoy views of the lake with a glass of wine.

Day 2
Morning Heading inland, visit **Tapolca** *(p205)*, whose sublime setting is one of the best on the lake; do not miss the incredible Cave Lake. Back down on the shoreline, the pretty village of **Szigliget** *(p204–5)* lies in wait, with its atmospheric castle ruins.

Afternoon Venture round to the lake's western shore and **Keszthely** *(pp200–201)*, packed with great museums and the **Festetics Palace** *(pp202–3)*, notable for its remarkable Helikon library and gorgeous English gardens. Have a pit stop in one of the town's convivial cafés before the short trip to **Héviz** *(p204)* for a soak in one of the world's largest thermal lakes.

Budapest's Royal Palace atop Castle Hill, the historic heart of Buda

For practical information on getting around Budapest, see pp310–11

One Week in Hungary

- **Arriving** Arrive at Budapest Liszt Ferenc Airport. It's about 50 minutes by public transport to the centre.
- **Getting Around** A car is essential for this trip.

Day 1: Budapest

Pick a day from the city itinerary opposite; Day 1 takes in the city's major historical and cultural landmarks, or mix and match to suit your taste.

Tokaj wine ageing in underground rock-hewn cellars

Day 2: Lake Balaton

Head southwest from Budapest to **Lake Balaton** *(pp198–9)*. Start in **Tihany** *(p206)*, where you can nose around this pretty village, crowned by a glorious abbey church, or go off and explore the peninsula's inland lakes. After lunch, board the ferry to **Siófok** *(p198)* on the southern shore; try your hand at some beach activities, then, for a drop of culture, follow the shoreline down to **Balatonföldvár** *(p199)* and its exceptional Iron Age fortifications, or **Köröshegy** *(p199)* and its Gothic church.

To extend your trip…
Continue along the lake's western shore to cultured Keszthely *(pp200–201)* and the thermal lake at Hévíz *(p204)*.

Visegrád on the Danube Bend, at one of the river's narrowest points

Day 3: Kaposvár to the Villány-Siklós Wine Road

Due south of Balaton lies **Kaposvár** *(p189)*, which merits a visit by virtue of its links to József Rippl-Rónai, one of Hungary's most celebrated artists. Continue south again to **Pécs** *(pp190–91)*, a vibrant city noted for its splendid Turkish-influenced architecture. End the day with a short tour along the sunny wine road between **Villány** *(p187)* and **Siklós** *(p188)*, home to many of Hungary's most renowned vintners; dozens of cellars await for some impromptu tasting.

Day 4: Baja to Kecskemét

Cross the Danube near **Baja** *(p238)* – fish capital of Hungary – and push on towards **Szeged** *(pp246–7)*; here, an architectural treasure trove awaits, notably the Great Synagogue and Reök Palace, two Secessionist master-pieces. Drive north through **Kiskunság National Park** *(p239)* to **Kecskemét** *(pp240–41)* where you'll find fabulous museums.

Day 5: Across the Great Plain

Make your way into the heart of the Great Plain, the first stop of the day being **Lake Tisza** *(pp252–3)* where you can try your hand at some boating or birdwatching – or just chill out on the beach. After a picnic lunch, head east to **Hortobágy National Park** *(p256)*, classic Puszta territory, with its diverse range of wildlife (water buffalo, corkscrew-horned sheep and wild boar). It's also home to the

renowned csikós (the Plains cowboys) and their thrilling displays of horsemanship.

To extend your trip…
Drive to Hungary's second city, Debrecen *(pp254–5)*, in eastern Hungary, then on to Nyíregyháza *(pp258–9)*, whose church architecture is second to none.

Day 6: Through the Northern Highlands

No better way to start the day than by sampling some world-famous **Tokaj** wine, in the town of the same name *(p232)*. Take a trip through the beech-covered hills of **Bükk National Park** *(pp224–5)*, visiting either the Anna Cave in **Lillafüred** *(p225)* or the Lipizzaner horses in **Szilvásvárad** *(p228)*. In the far western reaches of the Highlands, explore **Hollókő** *(pp218–19)*, an extraordinary two-street village where traditional customs remain strong.

Day 7: Down the Danube

Spend a day by the Danube. Begin in **Vác** *(p137)* with a stroll around its gorgeous Baroque square, then board the ferry to **Visegrád** *(p145)* on the west bank, whose citadel and palace both merit a visit, as do the surrounding hills. Continue south along the river to **Szentendre** *(pp142–4)* and learn about the town's strong Serbian links and rich artistic legacy. From here, it's a short trip back to Budapest.

The town of Eger, famous for its robust red wine

Two Weeks in Hungary

- **Arriving** Arrive at Budapest Liszt Ferenc Airport. It's about 50 minutes by public transport to the centre.

- **Getting Around** A car is essential for this trip.

Day 1: Budapest
Pick a day from the city itinerary on page 12. Day 1 takes in the city's major landmarks, or mix and match to suit your taste.

Day 2: Along the Danube Bend
Head north out of Budapest to **Szentendre** *(pp142–4)*, a former Serbian enclave replete with fine ecclesiastical architecture, artistic treasures and the unmissable Hungarian Open-Air Museum. Further up the Danube, **Visegrád** *(p145)* hoves into view, defined by its two major historical ruins – the Royal Palace and the citadel. After a riverside lunch, track the course of the Danube round to **Esztergom** *(pp146–9)*, Hungary's most important religious centre; check out the mighty Basilica and the spooky crypt below.

Day 3: Vác to Eger
Having transferred to the Danube's east bank, enjoy the Baroque splendour of **Vác** *(p137)*, and the winsome National Botanical Gardens. Take some time to explore the charms of **Hollókő** *(pp218–9)*, where you can also learn about the customs of the local Palóc people. Spend the afternoon perusing the rich and varied sights of **Eger** *(p220–23)*, especially its fabulous castle (part of which can be explored underground) and graceful 16th-century minaret. Trying some of Eger's famous "Bulls Blood" wine is a must.

Day 4: Bükk National Park to Tokaj
In the morning, make for the forested heights of the Bükk hills in the **Bükk National Park** *(p224–5)*, whose abundant attractions include the magnificent Lipizzaner horses in **Szilvásvárad** *(p228)* and the Anna Cave in **Lillafüred** *(p225)*. There are, though, even more spectacular caves at Baradla in the **Aggtelek National Park** *(p228)* skirting the Slovakian border. Round off the day in **Tokaj** *(p232)*, Hungary's most celebrated wine region, with a glass of Tokaji Aszú.

Day 5: Nyíregyháza to the Hortobágy National Park
Moving eastwards onto the Great Plain, there's outstanding church architecture on show in **Nyíregyháza** *(pp258–9)*. From here, go south to **Debrecen** *(pp254–5)*, Hungary's second city and a Calvinist stronghold; enjoy, too, the city's modern thermal baths and fine restaurants. Next, drive to

Hortobágy National Park *(p256)*, distinguished by its superb nine-arched stone bridge, though the real highlight will be a breathtaking display of horsemanship by the blue-skirted csikós cowboys of the Plain.

Day 6: Lake Tisza to Kecskemét
The vast Plain extends west towards **Lake Tisza** *(pp252–3)* – the country's second-largest lake after Balaton and home to some stunning birdlife, including peregrine falcons. There are watersports available too, particularly around **Tiszafüred** *(p250)*, the lake's main resort. Turning south, **Kecskemét** *(pp240–43)* has an exceptional stock of Baroque and Secessionist masterpieces; don't miss the wildly colourful, Art Nouveau Cifrapalota palace, housing a wonderful gallery.

Day 7: Szeged
Second only in size to Hortobágy, the **Kiskunság National Park** *(p239)* has a similarly horsey vibe, thanks to the Bugac stud farm. Devote the rest of the day to sightseeing in **Szeged** *(pp246–7)*. Start in Dóm square, flanked by handsome arcades and overlooked by the mighty Votive Church, then cross town to the New Synagogue,

The Votive Church in Szeged, with its twin 100- m (328-ft) towers

Festetics Palace, housing a superb library and several unusual museums

which is distinguished by its magnificent blue stained-glass dome. For a spot of post-sightseeing refreshment, seek out Klauzál square and its buzzing outdoor cafés.

Day 8: Mohács to Pécs

Cross the Danube at **Mohács** (pp186–7) for the Memorial Park, site of the famous Battle of Mohács in 1526. The route west from here takes you along the lovely wine road between **Villány** (p187)and **Siklós** (p188), where it'd be remiss not to pause in one or two of the many cellars along the way. From here, take a sharp turn north to **Pécs** (pp190–91), as vibrant a city as any in Hungary; one place not to miss is the Csontváry Museum, containing the oeuvre of one of Hungary's greatest painters.

Day 9: Szigetvár to Lake Balaton

Travel north to **Szigetvár** (p194) to view the town's numerous Turkish relics, before continuing to **Kaposvár** (p189), whose most important sights revolve around the work of József Rippl-Rónai, the father of Hungarian Art Nouveau. Head due north again and you'll eventually reach the clean, shallow waters of **Lake Balaton** (pp198–9). Enjoy a sundown stroll before a fish supper at one of the lakeside restaurants.

Day 10: Lake Balaton

If the weather allows, hit the beach in **Siófok** (p198), then hop aboard the ferry to the northern shore. Disembark at **Tihany Peninsula** (p206) and walk up to exquisitely pretty Tihany village. After lunch, work your way along the shoreline to **Badacsony** (p205), where you can divide your afternoon between the village itself and Badacsony mountain, a stiff climb but well worth it for the marvellous lake views.

Day 11: Keszthely and Hévíz

The lake's western shore beckons this morning, and first up is **Keszthely** (pp200–201), Balaton's most charming town; take a guided tour of the stately **Festetics Palace** (pp202–3), then stroll around its fragrant rose gardens. A few miles out of town, while away an hour or so in **Hévíz** (p204), the world's second-largest thermal lake; note that hiring a rubber ring is de rigueur. Returning south, make for the reedy **Kis-Balaton** ("Little Balaton") nature reserve (p198), where you'll encounter an impressive range of migratory birds.

Day 12: The Őrség Region to Sopron

From Balaton, head west to the lush, thickly forested **Őrség Region** (p163), dotted with pretty villages. Turning north, take some time to amble around delightfully sleepy **Kőszeg** (pp168–9), the most attractive town in western Transdanubia. Continue north to **Sopron** (pp172–5), with, arguably, Hungary's finest medieval old town; climb its Firewatch Tower for superlative views.

Day 13: Győr and Pannonhalma Abbey

Leaving Sopron, visit the Esterházy Palace in **Fertőd** (p171), a Baroque and Rococo master-piece; you may even catch a lunchtime concert in the room where Haydn used to perform. The next major town heading east is **Győr** (p178–9), stuffed with Baroque churches and mansions. It's a short hop south to the sombre elegance of **Pannonhalma Abbey** (p180–81), with its awesome 330,000-volume Empire-style library.

Day 14: Tata to Lake Velence

Begin your last day in **Tata** (p177), a delightful lakeside town nestled around a moated castle. Then discover how some of the finest hand-painted porcelain in the world is made, touring the Herend factory with its tempting shop. From here, strike out for **Veszprém** (p208–9) and its beautifully preserved Castle District. Ornithologists will appreciate a stop at bird haven **Lake Velence** (p154) on the way back to Budapest.

The most famed landmark in Pannonhalma, the Benedictine Pannonhalma Abbey

Putting Hungary on the Map

The Republic of Hungary is one of the smallest states in Europe, with an area of 93,031 sq km (35,919 sq miles). From west to east it is 528 km (328 miles) at its widest point and from north to south is just 268 km (167 miles). Hungary has borders with Slovakia to the north, Ukraine to the northeast, Romania to the southeast, Serbia and Croatia to the south and Slovenia and Austria to the west. Entirely landlocked, it is split into three by the rivers Danube (Duna) and Tisa (Tisza), which traverse it from north to south. Lake Balaton, the main geographical feature, is central Europe's largest lake.

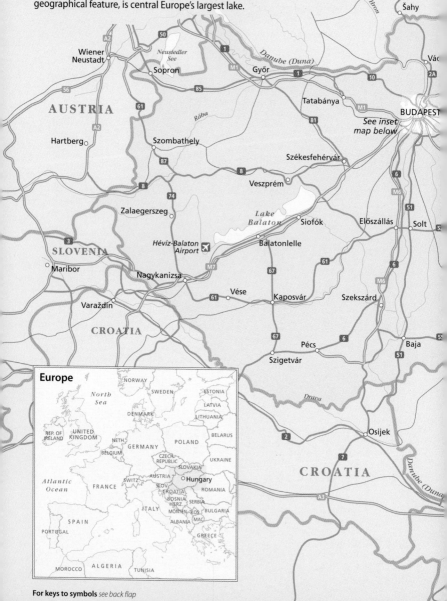

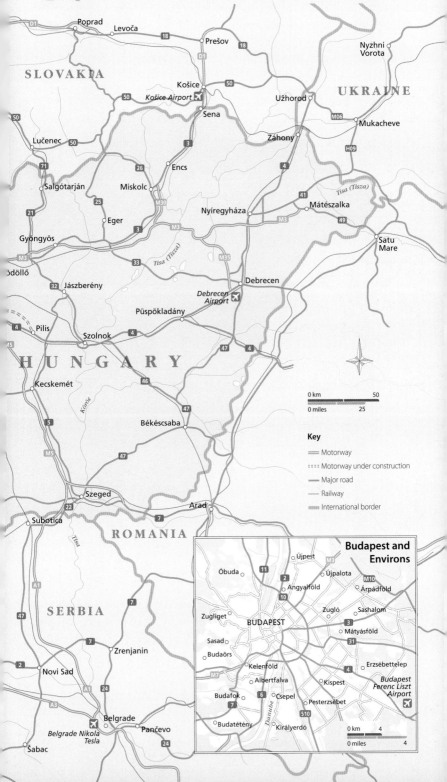

A PORTRAIT OF HUNGARY

Situated in the heart of Europe, at the centre of the continent, Hungary is a land with a rich history, a charming people and a culture that encompasses music and art, as well as fertile wine regions. Outside the romantic capital, Budapest, is a diverse landscape of lakes, forests and mountains, with enticing medieval cities and historic castles.

On paper Hungary's physical attractions look less than overwhelming; its tallest peak reaches just over 1,000 m (3,280 ft) and there is no sea coast. But it has got Balaton, Europe's largest lake outside Scandinavia and the nation's very own "inland sea", as well as the mighty Danube river, which makes a dramatic turn south before splitting Budapest in two. Furthermore, there is the endless Puszta, or Great Plain, where *csikósok* – Hungary's sturdy cowboys – still ride. In addition, there are the ancient castles, fascinating churches and cathedrals, historic spa baths, and numerous cities that can boast some of the finest Gothic, Baroque and Secessionist (Art Nouveau) architecture in Europe.

Hungary has been at the crossroads of both trade and cultures for as long as the continent has been inhabited. Many of the country's most enduring traditions predate the arrival of the Magyars in the Carpathian Basin in AD 896, and these are upheld and preserved in the hundreds of lively festivals held in towns and villages around the country each year.

Hungary remains the land of the Magyars nevertheless, a proud people and a nation that has spent more than a millennium both welcoming outsiders and fending off invaders. History has not always been kind to this land, but Hungary's historical legacy is rich and very well preserved.

Since abandoning Communism in 1989, the country has experienced rapid change

Hungary's vast Great Plain, covering one-third of the country and famous for its highly skilled cowboys

◀ Stained-glass window depicting St Leopold of Austria in Saint Stephen's Basilica, Budapest

The ruins of Csesznek castle, Bakony Mountains

10th century. Despite centuries of war, occupation and the ever-present fear of being swallowed up by its neighbours, Hungary and the Magyars survived and even flourished. Contemporary Hungarians remain extremely proud of their roots in the steppes of Asia, and they go to great lengths to preserve their traditions. The dramatic displays of horsemanship that take place on the Puszta may be primarily for the benefit of visitors but they also help retain a link with the past, as does the enormous panoramic painting that fills the replica tribal chieftain's tent at Ópusztaszer, near Szeged, commemorating the arrival of the Magyars. The painting is dismissed by some as kitsch and unworthy of our time, yet it plays an important role in preserving the spirit and memory of the nomadic Magyars. For better or worse, it is Hungarian nationalism that has kept the nation and the culture alive.

and (often uneven) economic growth. But while the scars of state socialism remain – most notably in the bland apartment blocks that encircle most cities – Hungarians are largely more affluent and optimistic than ever.

National Origins

Most modern Hungarians trace their ancestry to the Magyars, an Asiatic people of relatively obscure origins who arrived in the region shortly before the start of the

Culture and Society

Hungarians are very polite, formal people. Older men still kiss women's hands on meeting and even close friends shake hands when they get together. But while all this civility may help to oil the wheels

Young dancers in traditional folk costume performing at one of Hungary's many festivals

An indoor pool at the Gellért Hotel and Baths complex

found, most strikingly in the mosque at Pécs, now recycled as a Christian church, and in the towering minaret at Eger, as well as in the handful of wonderfully preserved 16th-century thermal bath houses in Budapest. Hungary also once had a thriving Jewish population, but it was decimated during World War II, when most Jews were sent to concentration camps. Neglected synagogues still found in many of Hungary's cities and towns are a testament to the numbers who died.

Most Hungarians who profess any religion at all say they are Roman Catholic (52 per cent). But religion in Hungary has often been a question of expediency. Under King Stephen I Catholicism, as opposed to Orthodoxy, was introduced to the country and, while the majority of Hungarians were quite happily Calvinists by the end of the 16th century, many donned a new mantle during the Counter-Reformation under the Habsburgs. As a result of these swings, Hungarians tend to have a pragmatic view of religion and there is very little bigotry. Today, however, both Catholicism and Calvinism appear to be losing their influence as the country becomes more and more secular.

that turn a sometimes difficult society, it can be interpreted as aloofness, a desire to keep "outsiders" (foreigners and other Hungarians) at a distance. This is not really the case; Hungarians simply need a while to make up their minds about people. There is also the language issue: Hungarian does not belong to the Indo-European language family, meaning that Russian and Hindi are closer to English than Magyar is. It is part of the Finno-Ugric group, and due to millennia of separation it is not even mutually intelligible with its closest cousins, Finnish and Estonian. As a result, visitors will recognize few words, and trying to order a glass of *vino* in a bar gets you nowhere; the word for wine is *bor*. Few foreigners ever master Hungarian completely, even after years of patient study, and Hungarians themselves are not particularly enthusiastic linguists. English is, however, becoming more popular as a second language, especially among younger people in the cities.

The Magyars are not the only people to have left their mark or helped form modern Hungarian society. Germans and Slovaks settled here as long ago as the reign of King Stephen I (István) from AD 1000 to 1038, and on the Great Plain Balkan influences in the form of the region's lively markets can still be seen. There are also Turkish footprints to be

The symphony orchestra and state choir, Budapest

A market stall selling fresh and dried produce

Politics and Economics

The social dislocation inherent in some post-Soviet societies has been avoided by an often shaky but relatively steady consensus among the political parties as to what Hungary needed in the wake of

Sunflowers, cultivated throughout the Hungarian countryside

Communism's collapse. A top priority was membership in the EU, for even the former Communists who initially opposed the idea realized that to remain outside Europe would be ruinous both politically and economically.

However, the economy was ailing and living standards started to deteriorate. In 2006, a controversial speech given by the newly re-elected Prime Minister Ferenc Gyurcsány to his inner party circles was leaked. In it he admitted they had been lying about the state of the economy and what measures were to be taken after the elections, and riots broke out in the streets of Budapest. Although demanded by many, even within his government coalition, Gyurcsány did not resign. Soon afterwards the global financial crisis hit Hungary's already weak economy. The austerity measures taken by Gyurcsány's government were nearly as unpopular as his style. Finally, in 2009, Gyurcsány resigned, and was replaced by his economic minister, Gordon Bajnai. Despite Bajnai's relative economic successes, in the subsequent elections of 2010, the Viktor Orbán-led Fidesz – Hungarian Civic Alliance – won with a landslide, taking two-thirds of the seats in Parliament. Orbán used this supermajority to change virtually all aspects of life in Hungary, including the country's constitution, election and judicial system. The Orbán government introduced unconventional new taxes and economic regulations, harshly criticized both in Hungary and internationally as probing the limits of democracy and as being a means of playing economic power into the hands of loyal friends. But despite this, in 2014 Fidesz again won all parliamentary, municipal and European Parliament elections with a landslide, maintaining its two-thirds majority in Parliament.

Economically Hungary is in the doldrums, its dream of adopting the euro any time soon not even on the agenda. In 2014, the average monthly net salary in Hungary was less than than 500 euros, while Hungary levies a world-record 27 per cent VAT on even basic commodities like

The ornate interior of a Budapest coffee house

A grape-picker with grapes ready for making into Tokaji wine

food. With jobs becoming rare and hopes fading away, there is a growing and unprecedented new tendency for Hungarians to leave the country.

But Hungary does have a long history of innovation and discovery, and boasts an enviable list of world-class scientists, engineers and inventors. Vitamin C, the biro, the safety match – not to mention the world-renowned Rubik's Cube – all originated here. Hungarians continue to tread new paths, and since 1989 Hungary has developed as a centre of scientific research; indeed, governments of all political persuasions have promoted their country as a knowledge-based economy.

Modern Life

If modern Hungary has one drawback, though, it is the dependence on the capital for everything. To borrow an old French expression about Paris, many people here believe that "when Budapest sneezes, Hungary catches cold". Although the country's geography and history may dictate in some ways that all roads lead to Budapest, it is often frustrating when the best way of travelling from one place to another is via the capital. Provincial Hungarians find it particularly galling and a constant reminder that their own cities,

towns and villages owe everything to Budapest. The imperial majesty of the capital is captivating but the rest of Hungary also has a wealth of history, character and architecture to offer. Several ongoing projects and development programmes – many co-founded by the EU – address this issue, and the Hungary outside of Budapest is developing fast. Yet central Hungary, with Budapest at its heart, is still home to one third of the population and produces nearly half of the country's GDP.

Outdoor dining at one of Szentendre's restaurants

Landscape and Wildlife of Hungary

The Great Plain, a rich and fertile land and one of the first in Europe to be cultivated, covers almost half of Hungary. It is traversed by two major rivers: the Tisa (Tisza) in the east, and the majestic Danube (Duna) in the west. The gentle but scenic mountains of the Mátra range mark the nation's northern borders, while the forests of Transdanubia and the great lakes of Balaton and Fertő enhance what is – for a relatively small country – a varied and attractive landscape.

The Danube river, Hungary's defining natural feature

The Great Plain

Grassland covers 12 per cent of Hungary, and almost all of it is in the treeless Great Plain. Modern irrigation has enabled much of the original plain to become agricultural land, but in the protected areas of Hortobágy and Kiskunság the pale green vegetation of the region is preserved.

Herds of horses define the Great Plain and are regarded as a sacred part of the nation's soul. Hungarians have traditionally made great horsemen and cowboys or *csikósok* still exist.

Racka sheep are bred for their milk, wool and sometimes their meat, and are unique to the Great Plain region of Hungary. They are characterized by their long, thin, corkscrew-like horns.

Mangalica pigs are hairy, almost sheep-like, and are bred for their meat. Look out for sausages made from Mangalica pork.

Lakes and Rivers

The Danube is the greater river, but for many Hungarians the Tisza river is more important. All of the country's other rivers are tributaries of these two. Hungary's abundance of lakes makes it a favoured destination of migrating birds. In the northwest, Lake Fertő is also popular with bird-watchers.

The Great Bustard is Europe's largest land bird, with males weighing up to 14 kg (31 lb). It is found throughout Hungary and is especially common around the Tisza lake. Catching sight of its intricate spring courtship ritual is a rare treat for bird-watchers.

The Hungarian iris or *Iris variegata* is fond of damp soil and marshland and thrives on the floodplains of the Danube.

Night herons are particularly active in the evening, when they leave their woodland nests to feed. Thick-billed, and with shorter legs than typical herons, the birds are most commonly found in Northern Transdanubia, close to the Danube river.

Hungarian Conservation

Magyars were once considered one of the great hunting peoples of Europe, but in recent times their efforts have been directed into conservation. As a result, all sorts of species that were once teetering on the brink of extinction are being preserved. Deer, wild boar, wolves and lynxes are again commonly spotted in the Northern Mountains. The National Forest Plantation Programme of 1997 has enhanced the spread of forests and the saving of vulnerable wild flowers. Hungary's wetlands are a preferred destination for migrating birds and the protection of their habitat has become a source of national pride.

The lynx, inhabitant of the Northern Mountains of Hungary

The Northern Mountains

Three different mountain ranges, the Mátra, Bükk and Zemplén, are usually grouped together as the Northern Mountains. As the only alpine region in Hungary, they are home to some unique species. In the Mátra range, the country's highest peaks reach a meagre height of 1,015 m (3,330 ft).

Brown bears are commonly found in the Carpathian arc that stretches from northern Hungary to Romania.

Horned eagle owls are one of the largest owl species, often measuring 70 cm (28 in) in height. Superb predators, they feed mostly on rodents and rabbits, though they occasionally devour game birds.

Great spotted woodpeckers are a frequent sight in the gardens, parks and woodlands of northern Hungary. They are one of nine woodpecker species native to the country.

Forests

A fifth of Hungary is covered in forest, and this is set to increase by 2035. The country's existing forests, of which the main areas are the Northern Mountains, the Buda Hills *(see p115)* and the Bakony Forest *(see pp160–61)* are increasingly protected by conservationist legislation.

The Dolomite flax, once Hungary's common national flower, survives today only in the forests of the Buda Hills around the capital. Both the flower and its habitat are fiercely protected.

Lesser purple butterflies emerge from a deep green chrysalis at the beginning of every July. Widespread in forested areas, they spend much of their time on treetops defending their territory against unwelcome rivals.

The black stork stands about 1 m (3 ft) tall. Mainly black, it has a white spot on its front and a red bill and legs. This long-distance migrant winters in southern Africa.

Thermal Springs and Baths

Hungary has been one of Europe's great spa destinations for hundreds of years. Natural hot springs pour out over 80 million litres (18 million gallons) of richly mineralized water every day. There are more than 1,300 hot springs in the country, of which 300 are used for bathing and medicinal purposes. A third of these are in Budapest, which has the greatest concentration of natural springs. Baths have existed since Roman times but it was the Turks who exploited the natural waters for healing all sorts of ailments.

Best Thermal Baths

- Aquaticum *see p255*
- Bükfürdő *see p167*
- Gellért Hotel and Baths Complex *see pp74–5*
- Hajdúszoboszló Medicinal Spa *see p256*
- Lake Hévíz *see p204*
- Miskolctapolca *see p229*
- Nagyatád *see p194*
- Parádfürdő *see p217*
- Sárvár Spa *see p167*
- Széchenyi Baths *see p111*

A Visit to the Baths

The Széchenyi Baths complex in Budapest (illustrated here) is in many ways the archetypal classic Hungarian bathhouse, from the complicated pricing system to the vast network of indoor and outdoor baths. Built on the site of a thermal spring first discovered in 1879, Széchenyi is as popular with locals as it is with visitors.

Unisex changing rooms make the baths ideal for families. An attendant provides a locker key and towel, and expects a tip.

The ticket office displays every conceivable price on a board.

The Main Entrance and grandiose exterior of the Széchenyi Baths are splendid examples of Neo-Baroque architecture. The complex, designed by Győző Cziegler and Ede Dvorzsák, was constructed in 1909–13.

Wellness Hotels

Wellness centres, dedicated to finding a healthy balance of mind and body, have had a long history in Hungary, ever since, in fact, the discovery of the healing properties of thermal waters. While the roots of the wellness movement lie in alternative medicine, modern wellness centres are based around large, often luxury bathhouses, which, besides thermal spas, offer a wide range of medical, dietary and even psychiatric treatments. Massage, mud packs and electrotherapy may also be available. Some of the best wellness hotels have golf courses attached, such as the Greenfield Hotel at Bükfürdő *(see p293)*. Arthritis, rheumatism and skin disorders are just a few of the ailments that wellness centres claim to cure, and as such attract a large number of visitors who return year after year.

Bathing in the healing waters of a heated outdoor pool

Outdoor Pools are open all year round, even in the depths of winter. Taking a bath in the steaming water when the air temperature is below zero is a unique experience. In summer, the outdoor pools can get very busy.

The terrace at the rear of Széchenyi Baths serves refreshing cold drinks to bathers.

Chess being played is a common sight at baths in Hungary. Matches take place at outdoor pools all year round, even when there is snow on the ground.

Saunas and steam rooms are used by bathers after taking a hot bath, before bathing again in cooler water.

The spacious and elegant interior of the Széchenyi entrance hall, like that of many baths in Hungary, is in stark contrast to the changing rooms, which can be a little cramped.

At pools used for medicinal purposes water temperatures are clearly displayed at the edge of the pool. The hotter the water, it is said, the stronger its healing powers.

Hungarian Architecture

It is difficult to separate the development of Hungarian architecture from the country's history. Of the Romanesque and Gothic constructions built during the reign of the first Magyar kings, little survived the Mongol invasion of the 13th century. Of the Renaissance era, only remnants and reconstructions remain, though there is more of the Baroque period to admire. The Secession (the struggle for a national style at the end of the 19th century) mirrored the nation's political fight for independence. After World War II, Soviet utilitarianism took over, and surrounded fine cities with its unsightly apartment blocks.

Budapest's Secession Post Office Savings Bank

Roman (AD 200–450)

The first master builders in Hungary were the Romans, much of whose capital, Aquincum, in the suburbs of present-day Budapest, survives. Amphitheatres, fortifications and giant statues were erected making use of *opus cimenticum* (concrete), a Roman invention that enabled great loads to be supported by giant pillars.

Aquincum, originally a heavily fortified military base, was home to as many as 40,000 people in its heyday at the end of the 2nd century.

Heavy granite stone was used in the construction of round arches.

The use of stone to reinforce concrete walls lent an aesthetic quality to Roman constructions. Ceramic tiles were also used to decorate concrete walls.

Colonnades were often used to mask heavy, load-bearing walls.

Romanesque and Gothic (1000–1450)

Also referred to as Norman architecture, the Romanesque period was one of the most energetic phases of church building ever witnessed in Europe. On becoming king of Hungary, István ordered a church to be built for every 10 villages in the land. Many followed the same construction model, with a large single nave supported by round arches known as piers – the medieval equivalent of Roman columns. Towers did not become commonplace until the 12th century, as superior masonry facilitated their construction. Romanesque façades were usually simple, and it was only as architects became more confident in the 13th century that more decorative elements such as rose and stained-glass windows, flying buttresses and gargoyles appeared, creating a new style that would become known as Gothic. The 13th-century church at Ják, with its exquisite *porta speciosa* (a stepped portal of rounded, barrel and pointed arches) is one of the finest remaining examples of medieval architecture in Europe, and marks the transition from Romanesque style to Gothic.

The tower is four-sided at its base and octagonal at the top.

The portal was recreated using fragments of the original.

Mátyás Church is considered to be a Gothic masterpiece. However, little of what remains today is part of the 14th-century original, having been extensively rebuilt in Neo-Gothic style in the 1880s.

Gothic arches precede cross-ribbed vaults in Esztergom Cathedral.

Renaissance and Baroque (1450–1800)

Renaissance architecture was a successful attempt to incorporate the grandeur of Rome into the contemporary world. Led by the Italians Brunelleschi and Bramante, the concept of art for art's sake became paramount, with buildings being designed around their façades. In Hungary the movement found royal favour from King Mátyás, who was greatly influenced by his Italian wife, Beatrice. The Hungarian Renaissance was brought to an end by the Turks, who destroyed many of its greatest achievements.

Sarospatak Castle's 15th-century Renaissance tower is a copy of Palazzo Vecchio in Florence.

After they were expelled from Hungary in 1690, the Baroque era began, characterized by grand designs which reflected a shift away from the proto-humanism of the Renaissance. Most Baroque mansions were built to showcase the wealth of their patrons.

The elaborate Bishop's Palace in Szekes-fehérvár is representative of Baroque style.

Neo-Classical (1800–90)

In Hungary, the Neo-Classical movement was considered a statement of intent: that this was a heroic nation worthy of statehood. The National Museum *(see pp102–3)* and the Opera House *(see pp93–3)* were built with independence in mind.

Budapest's National Museum, built to signify national consciousness, is where Sándor Petőfi read *National Song* and sparked the 1848 Revolution.

Secession (1890–1930)

The Secessionist era saw an ornamental style of art (also known as Art Nouveau) flourish in Europe at the end of the 19th century. In architecture, the movement initially made use of elaborate ironwork, tiles and bright colours to decorate linear buildings, while in the latter part of the Secession period ever more daring architects created curving, bulbous and organic constructions.

The Cifra Palota, Kecskemét, is typical of Secession design, with a curved, tiled roof, ironwork balconies and intricate arabesque decoration.

Utilitarian (1950–90)

At the end of World War II, art was relegated to a distant second behind necessity, as Hungary's Communist regime set about constructing hundreds of thousands of new homes on the outskirts of the country's cities. Designed to accommodate the workers taking part in Hungary's massive industrialization programme, vast estates of identical high-rise apartment blocks were rapidly built. Though generally very small and by no means luxurious, the apartments all came with central heating, running water and electricity, which was a first for many of the occupants who were allocated one.

Prefabrication facilitated the swift building of many apartment blocks.

Access to apartments was often via a long balcony.

Built in haste and at low cost, most Communist-era apartment blocks are still in excellent condition, though they are somewhat bleak-looking.

Famous Hungarians

For a relatively small nation, a surprisingly large number of Hungarians have made a name for themselves worldwide. They include inventor László Bíró, who gave the world the ballpoint pen, and composer Ferenc Liszt, a Hungarian so famous that it was once quipped "he must be Austrian". His namesake, the late Ferenc Puskás, remains the country's greatest sports star, revered by football fans. In recent years, numerous Hungarian sports stars, inventors, actors and artists have received international acclaim.

Tony Curtis playing escapologist Harry Houdini in the 1953 film

Music and Literature

In music, the most prominent Hungarian is Ferenc (Franz) Liszt, born in 1811. His repertoire of beautiful yet technically complicated melodies betray his first love: playing the piano. While Liszt is regarded by most Hungarians as a composer first and foremost, outside Hungary he is known simply as the greatest pianist of all time. After spending much of his life touring France, Germany, Austria and Britain, Liszt retired at the age of 50 to Rome, where he joined the Franciscan order and spent the rest of his life teaching the piano. He died in 1896, while in Germany attending the Bayreuth Music Festival.

Liszt was succeeded as Hungary's finest musician by a man whom he inspired from afar: Béla Bartók. Born in 1881, Bartók was one of the founders of ethnomusicology, the study of the ethnography of music, as well as being a pianist and composer. Less celebrated internationally is the work of Ferenc Erkel, who wrote *Bánk Bán* (1861), Hungary's rarely performed national opera. It was made into a film in 2002, and featured Éva Márton, Hungary's highly acclaimed soprano. Márton achieved fame at Budapest's State Opera in the 1970s before embarking on a

Soprano Éva Márton

sensational international career. She regularly headlines at the opera houses of London and New York and often performed under the baton of Budapest-born Sir Georg Solti, one of the greatest operatic conductors of the 20th century.

Hungarian literature has barely made an impression on the world, a result of its often impenetrable language. The 19th-century poets Mihály Vörösmarty and Sándor Petőfi are celebrated more for their activity as revolutionaries than for their poetry. In the 20th century, while Hungarian-born novelist Imre Kertész received the Nobel prize for literature in 2002, only Ferenc Molnár, whose work *Liliom* (1909) was adapted into the musical *Carousel* (1945), has achieved anything resembling worldwide fame.

Ferenc Molnár (1878–1952), Hungary's best-known novelist

Film and Visual Arts

Hollywood has been a successful stamping ground for Hungarians since before the advent of the talking picture. Indeed, two of the great pioneers of cinema were both born and raised in Budapest. Adolph Zukor founded Paramount Pictures and produced the first full-length feature film, *The Prisoner of Zenda* (1937), and Vilmos Fried fled Hungary for Hollywood, changed his name to William Fox and founded Fox Studios. Silver-screen heroes Johnny Weissmuller, the first cinematic Tarzan; Béla Lugosi, the original screen Dracula; and Leslie Howard, whose most renowned role was his portrayal of Ashley Wilkes in *Gone with the Wind* (1939) – all had Hungarian roots to one degree or another. So too did the late Hollywood legend Tony Curtis. One of Curtis's best remembered films is *Houdini* (1953), a biopic of another Hungarian, escapologist Harry Houdini.

Arguably the greatest Hungarian in Hollywood, however, was Manó Kertész Kaminer, who, under the anglicized name Michael Curtiz, directed the legendary *Casablanca* (1942), a film in which Peter Lorre, master of the sinister and another Hungarian, played a film-stealing cameo. Less celebrated for their work, but notorious for their countless marriages to leading Hollywood men, are Zsa Zsa Gábor and her late sister, Éva.

Other Hungarian film stars have also found international fame. István Szabó, who has spent his entire career living and working in Hungary, resisting the lure of Hollywood, won an Oscar for his film *Mephisto* (1981).

Hungarian visual artists have often attracted international acclaim, from architects Miklós Ybl and Imre Steindl – responsible for Budapest's stunning Opera House *(see pp92–3)* and Parliament *(see pp84–5)* respectively – to the trio of Secessionist painters Lajos Gulácsy, János Vaszary and József Rippl-Rónai, whose works inspired a generation of Post-Impressionists worldwide. More latterly, contemporary painters Margit Anna, Lajos Sváby, Tibor Palkó and Zoltán Szabó have been making waves on the international art scene.

Ferenc Puskás, the greatest Hungarian footballer of all time

Sport

For a period in the 1950s Hungary was the greatest footballing nation on earth, although it never actually won the World Cup. Defeat in the 1954 final to West Germany remains a national tragedy. The team captain was the legendary Ferenc Puskás, nicknamed "the Galloping Major". Officially an amateur, he had the rank of major in the Hungarian army and possessed a prolific left foot. His three goals against England at Wembley in 1953 were crucial to his side's 6–3 win – only the second time England had ever lost on home soil. Puskás was on a tour of Spain with Honvéd football club during the 1956 revolution *(see p49)* and refused to go back to Hungary. He signed to Real Madrid, and led them to three European Cup triumphs. He became a Spanish national and played a number of international matches for Spain.

Before football brought Hungary to the world's attention, athlete Alfréd Hajós had been the country's finest sporting ambassador. Hajós won Hungary's first ever modern Olympic gold medal for swimming at the 1908 Olympic Games in London. Several swimming pools and thermal baths in Hungary are named after him. More recently, Krisztina Egerszegi has excelled in swimming for her country, winning five Olympic gold medals between 1988 and 1996.

László Papp was the first boxer to win gold medals at three consecutive Olympic Games, a feat he achieved from 1948 to 1956. In 1965 Papp was on the verge of competing for the world middleweight title when the Communist government revoked his permit to travel abroad, thus ending his career.

Hungary has a long history of producing chess champions. The most recent is the prodigious Judit Polgár, who, aged 15, became a grandmaster in 1982. Polgár is the highest-rated female chess player in the world (a title once held by her sister, Zsuzsa). She beat Anatoly Karpov in a speed-chess tournament in 1992, an achievement that makes her the only female ever to defeat a reigning world champion.

Chess champion Judit Polgár

Hungarian Inventors

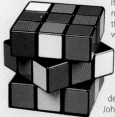

It is perhaps in science and technology that Hungarians have most excelled, and the ballpoint pen (invented in 1938) is probably the best known of their inventions. Known as the biro, the pen was named after its inventor, László Bíró. A more controversial inventor was John von Neumann, a child genius who worked as a binary theoretician before becoming a member of the US government's atomic bomb programme, the Manhattan Project. The mathematical projections von Neumann computed with another Hungarian, Edward Teller, were crucial in the development of the hydrogen bomb. A third project member, John Kemény, was co-inventor of BASIC computer language.

Other Hungarian inventors include Tivadar Puskás, who built the first European telephone exchange, and Ernő Rubik, who in 1977 gave the world the fiendish Rubik's Cube.

The colourful Rubik's Cube puzzle, renowned the world over

The Wines of Hungary

With warm, dry summers and highly fertile soil, Hungary has the ideal conditions for winemaking. It has produced wine since the 3rd century BC, although its industry was badly neglected during the Communist regime. Large-scale private investment has recently revived wine production in some areas, most notably in Tokaj, which is famous for its wines. Quality reds and whites, as well as sparkling wines, are produced all over the country. In Aszú, the golden wine of Tokaj, Hungary has one of the world's most fêted dessert wines; in Bull's Blood – a full-bodied red from Eger – it has one of the most legendary *(see p223)*.

Volcanic red soil typical of the Balatonfüred-Csopak vineyards gives the wines made here – especially the world-class Pinot Gris – a unique flavour with a hint of vanilla.

The wines of northwestern Hungary are characterized by their rich and vivid colours. The dessert wines of the Sopron region are light and refreshing, and the relatively high humidity of Ászár-Neszmély is perfect for growing Chardonnay and Sauvignon Blanc grapes.

Villány-Siklós is dotted with cellars and wine-press houses, many of which date back to the end of the 18th century.

Kiskunság specializes in fine table whites made from Chardonnay and Sauvignon Blanc grapes.

Tokaj Wine Region

Immigrant Italian farmers introduced viticulture to the Tokaj-Hegyalja region in the 12th century, after finding outstanding conditions for growing grapes on the slopes of Mount Tokaj. The golden Aszú wine that made the area famous was first produced in the 16th century, using overripe grapes infected with Botrytis cinerea (noble rot). After pressing, the wine is left to ferment slowly over several years, producing an intensely sweet taste.

Tokaj's landscape – ideal for winemaking

Overripe grapes with noble rot, used to make Aszú

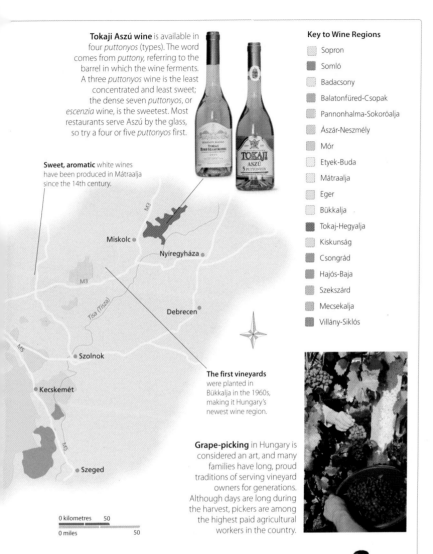

Tokaji Aszú wine is available in four *puttonyos* (types). The word comes from *puttony*, referring to the barrel in which the wine ferments. A three *puttonyos* wine is the least concentrated and least sweet; the dense seven *puttonyos*, or *escenzia* wine, is the sweetest. Most restaurants serve Aszú by the glass, so try a four or five *puttonyos* first.

Sweet, aromatic white wines have been produced in Mátraalja since the 14th century.

Key to Wine Regions

- Sopron
- Somló
- Badacsony
- Balatonfüred-Csopak
- Pannonhalma-Sokoróalja
- Ászár-Neszmély
- Mór
- Etyek-Buda
- Mátraalja
- Eger
- Bükkalja
- Tokaj-Hegyalja
- Kiskunság
- Csongrád
- Hajós-Baja
- Szekszárd
- Mecsekalja
- Villány-Siklós

The first vineyards were planted in Bükkalja in the 1960s, making it Hungary's newest wine region.

Grape-picking in Hungary is considered an art, and many families have long, proud traditions of serving vineyard owners for generations. Although days are long during the harvest, pickers are among the highest paid agricultural workers in the country.

Hungarian Sparkling Wine

Much as Reims competes with Epernay, so the wineries of Pécs and Etyek-Buda vie for the title of best Hungarian *Méthode Champenoise*. Sparkling wine was first made in Hungary in 1859 at the Pannonia winery in Pécs. Three of its brands – Pannonia, Hungaria and Törley (perhaps the best known) – offer a broad range of excellent sparkling wines, including extra-dry, semi-sweet and rosé. Hungary's sparkling wine is today widely regarded as one of the finest non-vintages produced outside the Champagne region in France.

Hungarian Grande Cuvée sparkling wine

Aszú ageing for several years in barrels in cellars

HUNGARY THROUGH THE YEAR

Hungary is subject to climate extremes, with winters usually bitterly cold and summers stiflingly hot. This does have its advantages – Christmas is often white, while summer evenings are long, sunny and warm. Spring and autumn also have their charms: spring is welcomed by bathers, who beset the country's outdoor pools, beaches and thermal baths as soon as the bitter cold makes way for spring. Autumn is the favourite season of bird-watchers, who flock to Hungary to observe the southward migration of the birds, while the late summer harvest is a popular time for festivals in many towns, especially on the Great Plain, as winter preparations are made.

Spring

Spring festivals, often musical events, take place in almost every town and city, to celebrate the passing of winter. Often coinciding with Easter, these festivals offer a chance to taste the many sweet treats – such as gingerbread – that Hungarians prepare in spring.

March

Budapest Spring Festival (end Mar–Apr), various venues, Budapest. Hungary's cultural year starts with this celebration of classical music. For more than two weeks, renowned performers from the world of opera, music and dance converge on various venues in Budapest, including the State Opera House (see pp92–3).
Pécs Spring Festival (mid-Mar–Apr), Pécs. Symphonic and chamber concerts, theatre and literary evenings, folklore shows, exhibitions and craft markets make this the largest spring festival held outside Budapest.
Revolution Day (15 Mar) The anniversary of the revolution of 1848, and the beginning of the revolt against the Habsburgs, is commemorated with a re-enactment of Sándor Petőfi's reading of the Twelve Points on the steps of the National Museum in Budapest.

April

Easter is a major event in devoutly Catholic Hungary, and a large number of people attend Easter Mass. Palm Sunday services, too, are interesting events, as people take bright flowers to church to be blessed. Visitors should also make sure they do not miss the brightly decorated gingerbread that can be found in sweet shops and supermarkets all over Hungary in the run-up to Easter.
Hollókő Easter Festival (Easter Sun & Mon) The UNESCO World

Boys throwing water over the girls at the Hollókő Easter Festival

Heritage village of Hollókő (see pp218–19) showcases Palóc traditional crafts, including fine, delicately hand-painted Easter eggs and masses of tasty gingerbread.

May

Gizella Days (first/second weekend), Veszprém. The May Bank Holiday sees Veszprém honour Gizella of Bavaria, St István's wife, with a colourful procession led through the heart of the city's old town.
Sailing Day (first/second weekend), Balatonfüred. The opening of the sailing season on Lake Balaton is marked with a colourful regatta of thousands of sailing boats. Sailing Day has been celebrated since 1935 and continues to grow in size. Supporting events include exhibitions, concerts, street parties and firework displays.

The Budapest Spring Festival, ringing in the performance season

Average Daily Hours of Sunshine

Hours

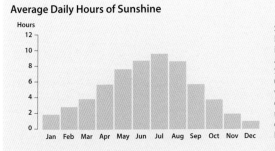

Sunshine Chart
Hungary enjoys most of its sunshine hours in July and August, although September and even October can often still be very sunny. The southwest of the country sees the most sunshine, the town of Pécs being officially Hungary's sunniest city.

Summer

Summer is the most enjoyable season, and every town and village has its festival week. Lake Balaton comes alive when the entire country seems to decamp here, while folklore, music and artistic events tempt visitors (and residents) to stay in the capital.

June

Miskolc Opera Festival *(mid-Jun)*, National Theatre, Miskolc *(see p230)*. Hungary's premier opera festival is held for a week in June. Each year, one or more Hungarian operas and the work of one great foreign composer are performed at the festival.
Danube and Chain Bridge Carnival *(throughout Jun)*, Budapest. The completion of Chain Bridge is celebrated in a number of river-based activities, which climax in the powerboat races on the final Sunday. There are also concerts and street performances, many of which take place on Chain Bridge itself.

Sopron Festival Weeks *(mid-Jun–mid-Jul)*, Sopron. Hungary's largest town festival outside Budapest showcases everything from gastronomy and architecture to classical music and children's theatre. The Early Music Days at the end of June are a highlight.
Hortobágy Equestrian Days *(late Jun–early Jul)*, Hortobágy National Park. Horsey pursuits include competitions in carriage-driving and horse-herding, displays of horseman-ship, and a large market selling equestrian goods.

July

Jazz Days *(Jul)*, Debrecen. Attracting world-renowned jazz musicians, this is the most important jazz event in the country. Running now for more than 30 years, it brings together a range of jazz styles.
Visegrád Palace Games *(Jul)*. Hungary's best castle festival, with jousting contests, archery displays, mock battles and a festival of medieval arts to be enjoyed.

Floats parading in the Debrecen Flower Carnival on 20 August, a national holiday

Sziget Festival *(end Jul–early Aug)*, Budapest. The biggest music festival in central Europe, the three-day event on a Danube island attracts the very biggest names in pop and rock.

August

Hungarian Grand Prix Formula 1 *(Aug)*, Budapest. Hungary has hosted motor races since the 1920s. For three days the F1 circus rolls into Mogyoród.
Flower Carnival, Debrecen *(Virágkarnevál, 20 Aug)*, Debrecen. St István's Day is celebrated in Debrecen by decorating the entire city centre with flowers. A large flower market takes place on Piac utca, and flower-bedecked floats parade through the city's streets. In the evening there is a free pop concert that is usually well attended.
Fireworks over the Danube *(20 Aug)*, Budapest. Pyrotechnics to celebrate St István's Day.

Formula 1 race at the Hungarian Grand Prix, Mogyoród near Budapest

Average Monthly Rainfall

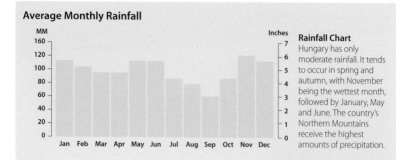

Rainfall Chart
Hungary has only moderate rainfall. It tends to occur in spring and autumn, with November being the wettest month, followed by January, May and June. The country's Northern Mountains receive the highest amounts of precipitation.

Autumn

Harvest fruits dominate the calendar in autumn, with wine and food festivals taking centre stage. Many of the towns along the Danube and Tisza hold fish soup festivals, the largest in Baja. The capital, meanwhile, attracts runners and sports enthusiasts for the Budapest Marathon.

September

Pécs Days *(mid-Sep)*, Pécs. Brass band concerts and wine tastings are the highlights of this week-long festival.
Wine Festivals *(Sep–Oct)* Major wine harvest festivals are held in all of Hungary's wine-producing regions *(see pp32–3)*, the largest in the Badacsony, and at Eger, Balatonfüred and Sopron. Vintage wines are cele-brated at Szekszárd on 14 September.
Goulash Festival *(second Sun of Sep)*, Szolnok. Hungary's national dish *(see pp272–3)* is the star of

this one-day festival. There are goulash cooking competitions, traditional handicraft fairs and recitals of poetry dedicated to the national dish. Most years there is also an attempt to break the "world's largest goulash" record, with the end product shared freely among all.
Winesong Festival *(end of Sep)*, Pécs and Villány. Wine-makers in Pécs and on the Villány-Siklós wine road celebrate the harvest by bringing in the best choirs in Hungary for 10 days of wine and song. There are concerts all along the wine road, with the biggest and best held in the main square in Pécs.
Budavári Borfesztivál *(International Wine Festival, Sep)*, Royal Palace, Budapest. Hungary's largest wine festival features more than 100 marquees, many offering a chance to sample the best Hungarian wines from all of the wine-producing regions.

The Budapest Marathon, one of the largest in Europe

October

Budapest Marathon *(early Oct)*, Budapest. Taking in the city's main sights, including Buda Castle, Margaret Island and Chain Bridge, on its 42-km (26-mile) route, the Budapest Marathon has been run every year since 1985. The start is in Hősök tere, and the finish in Városliget *(see p110-11)*.
Gödöllő Harp Festival *(mid-Oct)*, Royal Palace, Gödöllő. Every year Baroque musicians from all over the world converge on the perfect setting of Gödöllő Royal Palace *(see pp138–9)* for this renowned series of chamber concerts.

November

Szombathely St Martin Week *(1st week Nov)*, Szombathely. The town celebrates its patron saint, St Martin of Tours, with a variety of musical and theatrical events.

Music and dance at the Tihany Wine Festival

Average Monthly Temperature

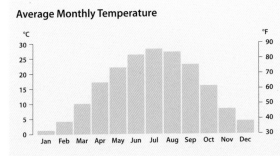

Temperature Chart
July and August can boast up to 10 hours of warm sunshine per day, with average summer temperatures a comfortable 22 °C (71.6 °F). Winters are cold, especially on the Great Plain, where bitter winds tend to blow in from the east.

Winter

Snows can arrive as early as November, and by Christmas the country is often covered in a blanket of snow. The big freeze does not, however, stop the outdoor fun, and natural ice rinks, such as that in Városliget park, Budapest *(see p110-11)*, are very popular.

December

Christmas Eve *(24 Dec)*, countrywide. In Hungary this is the main, most intimate day for Christmas celebration, when close family members have their festive dinner and exchange presents. Life in Hungary therefore normally comes to a halt at noon on the 24th, but in many cases the whole day is taken as a holiday.
Mikulás *(6 Dec)*. As in many countries in central Europe, Mikulás (aka St Nicholas or Santa Claus) visits children on this day. Traditional presents given on St Nicholas' Day tend to be of the edible and sugary variety, with larger toys now reserved for Christmas.

Christmas Gift Markets *(Dec)*, Sopron and Budapest. Throughout December, Fő tér in Old Sopron and Vörösmarty tér in Budapest are the enchanting settings for Christmas Gift Markets, attracting shoppers from afar as well as locals.

January

Szilveszter *(New Year's Eve)*
New Year's Eve in Hungary is traditionally celebrated on the streets. People eat early, grab a bottle of sparkling wine and head for the free concerts in most city centres. The largest is in Vörösmarty tér, Budapest, while there is also a massive street festival in Szentendre.

February

Kapos Carnival Days *(early Feb)*, Kaposvár. The whole of Kaposvár *(see p189)* appears to take part in this festival of Kapos culture, the highlight of which is the parade of costumed stilt-walkers.
Renaissance Carnival Gyula *(2nd weekend of Feb)*, Gyula. The grounds of Gyula Castle *(see p245)* play host to this medieval-style pageant yearly.

Revellers in menacing costumes at the Busójárás Carnival, Mohács

Busójárás Carnival *(end Feb)*, Mohács. During the occupation of Mohács by the Turks, the citizens would dress in menacing masks and costumes in an attempt to frighten the occupiers away. Today, people still dress up in spooky outfits for Carnival, which is now a far wider event, featuring performers of traditional and modern music alongside the costume parade.

Public Holidays

New Year's Day (1 Jan).
Anniversary of the Revolution of 1848 (15 Mar)
Easter Monday (Mar/Apr)
Whit Monday (May/June)
May Day (1 May)
National Day (St István's Day) (20 Aug)
Anniversary of the 1956 Hungarian Uprising and the proclamation of Hungary's democratic constitution in 1989 (23 Oct)
All Saints' Day (1 Nov)
Christmas (25–26 Dec)

Christmas Gift Market, Budapest

THE HISTORY OF HUNGARY

Most modern histories give little space to pre-Magyar Hungary but, given the importance of the region both then and now, this is a shame. Hungary's geographical location, at the heart of the European continent, has made it pivotal in invasions and empire-building from a time long before the notion of Europe – or Hungary – had ever been contemplated.

There is evidence that the Great Plain has been inhabited since the Bronze Age. Horsemen from the steppes eventually destroyed the existing culture in the 13th century BC. Celts later occupied parts of the land, and in AD 10 to 35, in its final push for expansion, Rome conquered Transdanubia, renaming it Pannonia, and later adding Dacia.

The Romans developed an urban infrastructure, including paved roads, city forums, stadiums and baths, in Northern Transdanubia, still visible today in the ruined remains of Aquincum, Óbuda, Szombathely and Sopron.

Barbarian tribes finally put an end to the rule of Rome. In 271 Dacia was abandoned as too expensive and troublesome to defend; Pannonia was similarly left to its fate in 403. Gothic, Hun, Avar and Slav tribes by turns filled the void; indeed, the Hun king Attila ran his powerful but short-lived empire from here.

The Magyars

The Magyars, a nomadic, pagan, Finno-Ugric tribe whose ancient homeland is thought to have been an area east of the Urals, rolled into the region in 895 or 896. It was at this time that Hungarian history first became entangled in conflict. The Magyars claim to have arrived in a desolate, sparsely populated land (the Slavs having moved south into the Balkans at the end of the 8th century); meanwhile, Romanian historians – to support their claim on Transylvania – insist that the Carpathian basin was in fact inhabited by direct descendants of the Romans.

The Magyars first settled on Csepel Island, in the middle of the Danube just south of present-day Budapest, before quickly occupying much of the surrounding area. Tradition holds that once the entire Carpathian basin had been occupied – and what little resistance there was had been quelled – the Magyar clan leaders chose a chieftain named Árpád to lead them, and that they swore an oath by sipping from a cup of their mixed blood to accept Árpád's male descendants as the Magyars' hereditary chieftains. Estimates suggest that Árpád ruled over some 400,000 people, made up of seven Magyar, one Kabar, and other smaller tribes.

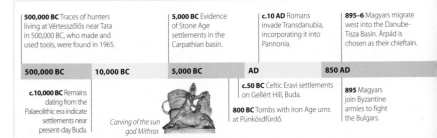

500,000 BC	10,000 BC	5,000 BC	AD	850 AD
500,000 BC Traces of hunters living at Vértesszőlős near Tata in 500,000 BC, who made and used tools, were found in 1965.		**5,000 BC** Evidence of Stone Age settlements in the Carpathian basin.	**c.10 AD** Romans invade Transdanubia, incorporating it into Pannonia.	**895–6** Magyars migrate west into the Danube-Tisza Basin. Árpád is chosen as their chieftain.
c.10,000 BC Remains dating from the Palaeolithic era indicate settlements near present-day Buda.		*Carving of the sun god Mithras*	**c.50 BC** Celtic Eravi settlements on Gellért Hill, Buda. **800 BC** Tombs with Iron Age urns at Pünkösdfürdő.	**895** Magyars join Byzantine armies to fight the Bulgars.

◀ Gyula Benczúr's *The Baptism of Vajk*, in the Hungarian National Gallery

Altarpiece with Saints István, Imre and Gellért

The Birth of the Hungarian Kingdom

Europe in the 10th century was weak and Magyar bands roamed the land and looted the towns for decades. They were routed in the west in 955 by King Otto I, and in the east in 970 by the Byzantines. Chieftain Géza (972–97), Árpád's great-grandson, was baptized into the Christian Church, and missionaries began the process of converting the Magyars. Géza established a strong central authority.

István I

Géza's son, István (Stephen, ruled 997–1038), was educated in Prague, baptized at some point in his early life, and in 996 he married Gisela, a Bavarian princess and sister of Emperor Henry II. István became chieftain when Géza died. He ousted rival clan chiefs, confiscating their lands. István then asked Pope Sylvester II to recognize him as king of Hungary. The pope agreed, and – with a crown sent by the pope himself –

Holy Crown of Hungary, or Crown of St István

István was crowned on Christmas Day 1000. István now held absolute power. He ordered that every tenth village build a church and donated land to bishoprics and monasteries. He required all persons, Christian or pagan – but not the clergy – to marry. Foreign monks worked as teachers and introduced Western agricultural methods.

István's Successors

István died in 1038 and was canonized in 1083. Hungary continued to grow stronger, having conquered Transylvania in 997–1006. In 1090, László I (1077–95) occupied Slavonia and Kálmán I (1095–1116) became King of Croatia in 1103. Under Béla III (1173–96) Hungary dominated in southeastern Europe.

The good times came to an end with King András II (1205–35). A big spender on foreign military adventures and domestic luxuries, he gave huge land grants to friendly foreign nobles. They soon made up a class of magnates whose wealth was far greater than that of the Magyar lesser nobles. When he tried to raise taxes, the people rebelled. In 1222 he was forced to sign the Golden Bull, limiting his power and leading to the creation of Parliament.

Béla IV (1235–70), András's son, tried with little success to regain lost crown lands in order to re-establish royal pre-eminence, but instead this created a rift between king and nobles just as the Mongols were sweeping towards Europe. He ordered his armies to mobilize, but few did,

King Géza I, father of King István

972–97 Chieftain Géza becomes king. He is baptized as a Christian in 975.

1090 László I (1077–95) occupies Slavonia.

1103 Kálmán I (1095–1116) takes the title of King of Croatia.

| 900 | 950 | 1000 | 1050 | 1100 | 1150 |

997 István I (997–1038) succeeds his father Géza; Pope Sylvester II recognizes him as King of Hungary.

1077–95 Latin alphabet adapted for Hungarian. Magyars occupy Transylvania.

10th-century Magyar belt buckle

1173–96 Under Béla III, Hungary becomes a leading power in southeastern Europe.

and the Mongols routed Béla's army at Muhi on 11 April 1241. Béla fled to Austria. The Mongols utterly destroyed Hungary, killing half the population. After the mysterious death of their leader in 1242, however, the superstitious Mongols withdrew.

Renaissance

On his return to power, Béla transformed royal castles into towns, encouraging Germans, Italians and Jews to populate them. Mining restarted, farming methods improved, and crafts and commerce flourished. Béla died in 1270, and the Árpád line expired in 1301, when András III died without a male heir.

Confronted by succession disputes, Hungary's nobles chose foreign kings. These, Charles I (1309–42) and his son and successor Louis I (1342–82), both from the House of Anjou, ruled during a time of peace. Louis I confirmed the Golden Bull again in 1351, and in 1367 founded Hungary's first university, at Pécs. However, he also fought costly wars, becoming king of Poland in 1370. During

Árpád, sculpture in Mátyás Church, Budapest

one of his foreign excursions the Turks made their first inroads into the Balkans. After Louis's death in 1382, Sigismund of Luxemburg bankrupted the country, amid the expansion of the Ottoman empire. Sigismund led a crusade against the Turks in 1396, but was routed at Nicopolis. He died in 1437, and his successors, Albrecht V of Austria (1437–9) and Władysław III of Poland (1439–44), known in Hungary as Ulászló I, both died during campaigns against the Turks.

Hungary's noblemen now chose the infant king László V and appointed a regent, János Hunyadi, to run the country. Hunyadi was a gifted warrior, defeating the Ottomans in Transylvania in 1442 and in the Battle of Belgrade in 1456, but he died of the plague soon after, and after two years of struggle for the succession his son Mátyás was proclaimed king.

King Mátyás

Mátyás enlisted 30,000 foreign mercenaries and built fortresses along the southern frontier, but instead of a direct anti-Turkish policy, he launched attacks on Bohemia, Poland and Austria, hoping to forge a unified front against the Turks. Mátyás was a modernizer, reforming the legal system and promoting development. A Renaissance man, he made his court a centre of humanism; under his rule Hungary began printing and established a second university. However, he failed in his quest for a Western alliance and, with it, the Holy Roman crown.

The Renaissance main altar in Mátyás Church, Budapest

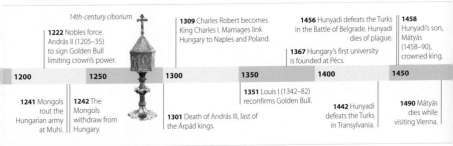

14th-century ciborium

1222 Nobles force András II (1205–35) to sign Golden Bull limiting crown's power.

1309 Charles Robert becomes King Charles I. Marriages link Hungary to Naples and Poland.

1456 Hunyadi defeats the Turks in the Battle of Belgrade. Hunyadi dies of plague.

1458 Hunyadi's son, Mátyás (1458–90), crowned king.

1367 Hungary's first university is founded at Pécs.

1200	1250	1300	1350	1400	1450

1241 Mongols rout the Hungarian army at Muhi.

1242 The Mongols withdraw from Hungary.

1301 Death of András III, last of the Árpád kings.

1351 Louis I (1342–82) reconfirms Golden Bull.

1442 Hunyadi defeats the Turks in Transylvania.

1490 Mátyás dies while visiting Vienna.

Mátyás Corvinus and the Hungarian Renaissance

Although St Stephen (István) is Hungary's patron saint, Mátyás Corvinus had a much greater impact on the country, and is generally far more celebrated than his canonized predecessor. Mátyás was one of the original Renaissance men: at once a king, military leader, warrior and patron of the arts. During his 32-year reign from 1458 to 1490, and at his often brutal behest, Hungary evolved rapidly from its feudal past to become the greatest kingdom in Middle Europe. Much of this progress came from the influence of Mátyás's equally visionary second wife, Queen Beatrice, daughter of the King of Naples. Her powers of persuasion over Mátyás, and subsequently on Hungary, should not be underestimated.

Gold seals were indicative of the affluence enjoyed by Hungary while Mátyás was on the throne.

This illuminated letter from the Philostratus Codex formed part of the *Codex Heroica*, the most valuable volume in Mátyás's library. It featured tracts by the Athenian philosopher Philostratus, and was translated into Latin by humanist Antonio Bonfini in 1497. It is housed at the Széchényi National Library *(see p60)*.

King Matthias and the Daughter of the Mayor of Breslau

Painted by Mihály Kovács, this famous 19th-century work depicts a carousing Mátyás (Matthias) wooing Barbara Krebs, the daughter of the Mayor of Breslau (present-day Wrocław). Mátyás wanted to marry Krebs, but as she was not of noble blood he was not permitted to do so. Instead, Mátyás took Krebs as his mistress. She bore him an illegitimate child, Johannus, who, when Mátyás failed to produce a legitimate son, became his chosen heir, although Władysław II (Ulászló II) was his successor.

Barbara Krebs was Mátyás's mistress for six years.

These marble engravings of Queen Beatrice and Mátyás, held at the Hungarian National Museum *(see pp102–3)*, are believed to be the work of Gian Cristoforo Romano, and were probably a wedding gift from a rich courtier.

Inscribed with the date 1470, the Crest of Mátyás Corvinus commemorates the building of significant additions to Mátyás Church in Budapest *(see pp66–7)*. Originally called the Parish Church of Our Lady Mary, the church was renamed after the king.

Manuscripts from Mátyás's library are on display at the Széchényi Library *(see p60)*. Mátyás set up the first national library, *Bibliotheca Corviniana*, and sanctioned the first printing press in the country. The earliest book published in Hungary (written in Latin) was the *Chronica Hungarorum*, printed in Buda in 1473.

Renaissance Hungary

The full bloom of the Renaissance period took place in Hungary in the late 15th and early 16th centuries, having reached the country via a procession of Italian master craftsmen and masons brought by Mátyás's second wife, Queen Beatrice. The Turkish occupation, which changed the course of Hungarian art and history, destroyed much evidence of Renaissance splendour, but Sárospatak Castle *(see pp232–3)* is a fine example of the style.

Foot soldiers in Mátyás's army would have carried shields like this one. It bears part of an early coat of arms of the Hunyadi family, and is exhibited at the Hungarian National Museum *(see pp102–3)*.

The globe, depicted alongside mathematical instruments, books and a telescope, reinforces the idea of Mátyás as a humanist, scientist and man of the arts.

The fabulous architectural detail of Mátyás Church in Budapest

Representing a man and woman, these wine cups date from the 16th century and are designed to fit together to form one covered receptacle. The cups would have been used in elaborate wedding celebrations during the Renaissance.

Győr Cathedral *(see p178)* was destroyed by the Mongols in the 13th century, and Mátyás viewed its reconstruction as one of his most sacred and important duties.

Mátyás was a generous king, known for his equity and his admiration for the Italian Renaissance.

Carved by an unknown sculptor in 1526, this Virgin and Child marks the zenith of Hungarian Renaissance art. Today it forms part of the Andras Bathory collection at the Hungarian National Museum *(see pp102–3)*.

Siklós Castle was first constructed in the late medieval period (about 1190) but is best known for its Renaissance-era modifications. It hosts a summer Renaissance Arts Festival.

Austrian Siege of Buda, 1602–3

Partition

After Mátyás, oligarchs took control of Hungary and crowned a puppet king, Władysław Jagiello, known in Hungary as Ulászló II (1490–1516), to nominally rule the country. In 1492 the Diet once again limited the serfs' freedom of movement, and in 1514 serfs attacked estates across Hungary. The rebellion was brutally crushed.

Shaken by the peasant revolt, the Diet of 1514 passed laws that condemned the serfs to eternal bondage. Corporal punishment became widespread, and one noble even branded his serfs like livestock. The laws were included in the Tripartitum of 1514, a document that gave Hungary's king and nobles, or magnates, equal shares of power: the nobles recognized the king as superior, but in turn they had the power to elect and remove him. The Tripartitum also freed the nobles from taxation, and many of their military obligations.

When Ulászló II died in 1516, his 10-year-old son Louis II (1516–26) became king, though a royal council in effect ruled the country. Endless quarrels among the noblemen of the Diet weakened the country, however, and the Turkish ruler Sultan Suleyman the Magnificent attacked Hungary

in August 1526, annihilating the Hungarian army and Louis II at the Battle of Mohács *(see p187)*. Rival factions of nobles then elected two kings, János Szapolyai (1526–40), supported by Eastern nobles and the Turks, and Habsburg king Ferdinand (1526–64), supported by Western nobles and the Holy Roman Empire. Hungary's partition became final in 1541, when the Turks put an end to Habsburg attempts at reuniting the throne by occupying Buda and Pest.

A 16th-century Ottoman coat

The Three States of Hungary

Western Hungary officially became part of the Habsburg Empire. The Austrian king directly controlled Habsburg Hungary's financial, military and foreign affairs, and imperial troops guarded its borders. Central Hungary became a province of the Ottoman Empire. The Turks ruling in Buda were interested mainly in squeezing as much wealth from the land as quickly as possible. However, the

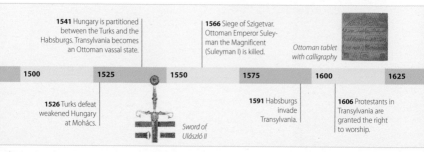

The liberation of Buda in 1686, painting by Gyula Benczúr (1896)

1541 Hungary is partitioned between the Turks and the Habsburgs. Transylvania becomes an Ottoman vassal state.

1566 Siege of Szigetvar. Ottoman Emperor Suleyman the Magnificent (Suleyman I) is killed.

Ottoman tablet with calligraphy

| 1500 | 1525 | 1550 | 1575 | 1600 | 1625 |

1526 Turks defeat weakened Hungary at Mohács.

Sword of Ulászló II

1591 Habsburgs invade Transylvania.

1606 Protestants in Transylvania are granted the right to worship.

Turks practised religious tolerance, giving Hungarians living within the empire significant autonomy.

Transylvania became an Ottoman vassal state. It functioned as an independent country, ruled by local princes who paid a tribute to the Turks. But the princes' increasing autonomy angered the Turks, who routed their armies in 1660 and took control of Transylvania.

Ottoman Campaign Tent, taken during the Siege of Vienna, 1683

Reunification

Hungary's aristocracy was increasingly dominated by Protestants and opposition to Catholic Habsburg rule grew. Angered by the persecution of Protestants and insufficient action against the Turks, an outright rebellion in 1664 failed to overthrow the Habsburgs. Instead, Emperor Leopold I suppressed the Hungarian constitution, and ruled Habsburg Hungary from Vienna. Protestantism was viciously repressed. Hungarian discontent deepened still further, until 1681, when Imre Thököly, a Transylvanian nobleman, led a more successful rebellion against the Habsburgs, forcing Leopold to restore Hungary's constitution. It was during these internal conflicts that the Turks attacked Austria, only to be almost wiped out entirely near Vienna in 1683. A Western campaign then gradually drove the Turks from all of Hungary, and the Ottoman government finally surrendered its Hungarian possessions at the Peace of Karlowitz in 1699.

Habsburg rule

After the expulsion of the Turks, the Austrians colonized Hungary with Germans, which led to an anti-Habsburg revolt in 1703–11. It was put down and the leader, Transylvanian prince Ferenc Rákóczi, was forced into exile, yet the Habsburgs guaranteed constitutional independence for Hungary and restored noble privileges.

Peace and prosperity followed, first under Empress Maria Theresa (1740–80) and later her son, Joseph II (1780–90). Enlightened absolutists, they strengthened their empire by pursuing a more humane social policy. Maria Theresa had Buda and Pest rebuilt, and built most of the Habsburg Royal Palace (see pp58–9) and a floating yet permanent bridge across the Danube.

Joseph II was even more radical. He curbed the power of the Church, disbanding monastic orders, and introduced tax reforms that limited the powers of the Hungarian aristocracy. He also made German the official language, but he died young, in 1790, and many of his reforms died with him.

The return of the Crown to Buda (1790)

1650	1675	1700	1725	1750	1775

1664 Habsburgs rout a Turkish army at St Gotthard in Hungary.

1683 Turks attack Habsburgs but are routed near Vienna.

1686 Christian troops enter Buda. Turkish rule in Hungary ends.

Order created by Maria Theresa

1780 Joseph II (1780–90) succeeds his mother, Maria Theresa; he enacts further reform.

1681 Hungarians rebel against Habsburg rule.

1684 Start of ultimately successful Siege of Buda by Habsburgs.

1699 Turks lose almost all Hungarian possessions in Peace of Karlowitz, which formally ends partition.

1740 Maria Theresa (1740–80) becomes Habsburg Empress, and institutes social reform.

1792 Coronation of Ferenc I (1792–1835), who repeals many of the reforms carried out by his predecessors.

The Founding of the Academy, bas-relief by Barnabás Holló

National Revival

Ferenc I (1792–1835) was far more conservative than Joseph II. It was during his reign, however, that the Hungarian aristocracy first began to promote the ideas of liberalism, and with them a national consciousness. The donation of a substantial arts collection to the state at this time enabled the foundation of a Hungarian national library and museum. Many noblemen supplemented their income from civil occupations, and formed a genuine political movement. Probably their greatest champion was István Széchenyi, a liberal nobleman who believed that the prime cause of Hungary's relative backwardness was the feudal system rather than subordination to Vienna. Széchenyi was also associated with the foundation of the Hungarian Academy of Sciences, the advent of rail transport and the construction of the first

Lajos Kossuth's speech during the revolution of 1848

permanent bridge across the Danube, the Chain Bridge. Lajos Kossuth, another outstanding Hungarian of the era, called Széchenyi the greatest Hungarian.

In 1847, Kossuth formally established the Opposition Party, an umbrella organization that sought Hungarian independence. On 15 March 1848, during a tumultuous spring – when the whole of Europe seemed to explode in revolution – Sándor Petőfi, one of the greatest Hungarian poets, read his Twelve Points manifesto for liberal reform from the steps of the National Museum. Vienna initially agreed to talks, but after the Austrians had quelled their own revolt in September, they confronted the Hungarian reformers, and armed conflict lasting almost a year ensued. The fate of the reformers was finally sealed by an alliance between Emperor Franz Joseph I and Russian Tsar Alexander II. A 200,000-strong Russian force quickly defeated the Hungarians, who surrendered on 13 August 1849.

Absolutism and Compromise

Hungary was now entirely subsumed by the Habsburg Empire. The political elite, led by diplomat Ferenc Deák, could offer little more than passive resistance. Deák managed to keep the dialogue with Vienna open. By 1866, when Austria had become isolated internationally after a series of wars, Vienna was ready to talk about some kind of compromise.

Deák led the Hungarian delegation, and the Habsburg Empire agreed to transform itself into a federation. The parts of the federation, Austria and Hungary, would be equal and separate, with the emperor at

1802 Count Ferenc Széchényi donation forms the basis of the Széchényi National Library and Hungarian National Museum.

1817 The first steamboat sails on the Danube.

1847 Lajos Kossuth forms the Opposition Party, which openly calls for independence.

1846 Hungary's first railway links Pest with Vác.

1867 After defeat by Russia a weak Austria accepts a compromise, and Hungarian independence in the Dual Monarchy.

1800

1825

1850

1808 The Embellishment Commission is established, led by Governor Archduke Joseph.

1809 The Habsburg Royal Court moves to Buda as Napoleon advances across Europe. He offers independence but the Hungarians side with Vienna.

Poet Sándor Petőfi (1823–49)

1848 The Hungarian Uprising against the Habsburgs begins on 15 March after poet Sándor Petőfi reads his Twelve Points from the steps of the National Museum.

once Emperor Franz Joseph of Austria, and King Ferenc József of Hungary. Half a century of progress followed, crowned when Budapest hosted the Millennium Exhibition in 1896.

War, Regency and Holocaust

In World War I, hundreds of thousands of Hungarians died fighting with the Germans and Austrians. After defeat in 1918, a revolution broke out in Budapest in October. A republic was proclaimed, headed by Count Mihály Károlyi. He was overthrown by Bolsheviks, led by Béla Kun, in March 1919. Kun proclaimed the Communist Hungarian Republic of Councils, and killed all those who opposed its policies. Only the intervention of Romanian troops, led by Hungarian Admiral Miklós Horthy, ended the "Red Terror".

In the Treaty of Trianon in 1920, vast areas of Hungary were awarded to Romania, the new state of Yugoslavia and Czechoslovakia. Horthy became regent. His two decades in power were marked by economic and social stagnation, as well as fierce anti-Semitism. When war broke out in 1939, Hitler offered Hungary half of Transylvania as reward for siding with Germany, and in 1941

Deportation of Hungarian Jews in World War II

Horthy committed forces to the invasion of first Yugoslavia, then the Soviet Union. Many Hungarians were killed on the Eastern Front. When Horthy tried to negotiate a separate peace with the Allies, Hitler replaced him with the Hungarian Nazi Arrow Cross party.

The first Hungarian Jews had been deported in June 1941, on the orders of prime minister László Bárdossy de Bárdos, who believed that this act would keep German troops out of Hungary. In the summer of 1942, however, Horthy replaced Bárdossy with the less viciously anti-Semitic Miklós Kállay. Kállay did not repeal any of Bárdossy's legislation, but he prevented any further large-scale deportations of Jews. After the German invasion of March 1944, Kállay was himself sent to Dachau concentration camp in one of the last deportations of Jews, Gypsies and political criminals. SS chief Adolf Eichmann oversaw the deportations in Hungary. By August 1944, when Horthy put a stop to them, 440,000 Jews had gone, mainly to Auschwitz, despite the efforts of Raoul Wallenberg and others (see p79). Indeed, a third of all those killed at Auschwitz throughout the war were Hungarian Jews.

Signing of the Treaty of Trianon at Versailles, 1920

1896 Continental Europe's first underground railway opens in Budapest. The city hosts a massive exhibition to celebrate the Hungarian Millennium.

1920 Hungary signs the Treaty of Trianon, and is at a stroke stripped of more than half its territory.

1916 Charles IV is crowned King of Hungary.

1941 Hungary joins the war on the side of the Axis Powers, ostensibly to recover territory lost in 1920.

1939 Hungary declares neutrality at the outbreak of World War II.

1875

1900

1925

1873 Buda, Óbuda and Pest merge to form a single city: Budapest.

Béla Kun, politician and revolutionary

1919 Brief Bolshevik rule under Béla Kun is ended by Admiral Miklós Horthy.

1944 Germany invades Hungary, Horthy is replaced by Ferenc Szalasi, the leader of the Arrow Cross, a Hungarian Nazi organization. The subsequent Holocaust costs nearly half of all Jews their lives.

Cardinal Mindszenty accused of treason and espionage

Sovietization

The parliamentary elections in 1945 were won by the Independent Smallholders' Party, supported by a wide spectrum of Hungarian society. However, the occupying Soviet Union enforced a coalition with the Social Democrats, the National Peasant Party and the Communists. New elections in 1947 were rigged, the Communists claiming a massive victory. By the end of 1948 all other political parties had been outlawed, or forced to merge with the Communists in the Hungarian Workers Party (HWP). In 1949, after an election in which only HWP candidates were allowed, Hungary was declared a People's Republic.

The Church became the main source of opposition to the HWP. The government confiscated church property and nationalized church schools. Protestant church leaders reached a compromise with

Mátyás Rákosi,
Hungarian prime minister

the government, but the head of the Roman Catholic Church, Cardinal József Mindszenty, resisted. The government arrested him in December 1948 and sentenced him to life imprisonment. Shortly after, the regime disbanded most Catholic religious orders and secularized Catholic schools.

Between 1948 and 1953 Mátyás Rákosi led a brutal regime that reorganized the economy. In a campaign reminiscent of the Soviet Union's forced collectivization in the 1930s, the regime compelled most peasants to join collective farms and required them to make deliveries to the government at prices lower than the cost of production. Hundreds of thousands were deported, arrested and executed.

Revolution

The terror eased slightly after Stalin's death in 1953, when Rákosi was ousted and Imre Nagy became prime minister. Nagy embarked on reform until the return of Rákosi in 1955. Rákosi attempted to reinstitute a Red Terror. He was forced to resign in July 1956 and replaced by Ernő Gerő. On 23 October anti-Soviet crowds protested in Budapest. Nagy was reappointed. He dissolved the state security police, abolished the one-party system and promised free elections. On 1 November Hungary announced neutrality and withdrawal from the Warsaw Pact. On 4 November the Soviet Union invaded and crushed the revolution.

1947 The Communists win rigged elections, and outlaw all other political parties.

1953 The reform-minded Imre Nagy becomes prime minister, but lasts only two years before being dismissed. In November Hungary's football team is the first from mainland Europe to defeat England in London; the score is 6–3.

1955 Hungary is a founding member of the Warsaw Pact.

1957 János Kádár becomes Hungarian leader.

1945

1950

1955

1945 The Germans abandon Hungary to the Russians in April 1945.

Imre Nagy
(1896–1958)

1956 Nagy is reinstated. When he announces Hungary's withdrawal from the Warsaw Pact, Soviet forces invade and arrest him. He is executed in 1958.

The 1956 Hungarian Revolution

On the morning of 23 October, students and workers unhappy with falling living standards marched on Radio Hungary in Budapest, in a bid to broadcast a list of demands, which included the immediate withdrawal of all Soviet troops stationed in Hungary. Actively supported by sections of the Hungarian army, the revolutionaries attacked the AVH (secret police) and Soviet soldiers, and the revolt spread nationwide. The Hungarian Communist Party, fearing total collapse, gave in to a number of demands, and on 27 October invited Imre Nagy to form a new government. However, on 4 November, thousands more Soviet troops invaded Hungary and, despite fierce resistance, quickly crushed the revolution.

Revolutionaries with Captured Soviet Tank

For a short time, the revolutionaries unquestionably had the upper hand and initially Soviet troops stationed in Hungary offered little resistance. It is thought that some troops even sided with the revolution. However, when the Soviet army invaded on 4 November, it did so to brutal effect, and an estimated 200,000 Hungarians fled the country as refugees.

The enormous statue of Stalin that stood in Budapest's City Park (Városliget) was iconoclastically torn down on 24 October by revolutionaries and perhaps defines the finest moment of the revolution.

Bronze statue of Imre Nagy, Budapest

Imre Nagy

Captured by the Russians in World War I, Imre Nagy (1856–1958) fell in with Russian Communists and emigrated to Russia at the war's end. Avoiding Stalin's purges of the 1920s and 1930s, he became a leading figure in the Communist international, the Comintern, and in 1944 was sent to accompany the Red Army as it invaded Hungary. He became the Hungarian prime minister in 1953 and pursued a reformist agenda during his two-years in office. Following the uprising, Nagy briefly returned to office in 1956, but after the Soviet invasion he was betrayed by one of his closest friends, Romanian Communist Walter Roman. He was arrested and taken to Snagov Monastery, near Bucharest in Romania, where he was questioned, tried on camera, and then executed in Budapest in 1958.

Goulash Communism, with limited collectivization

The Long, Slow Process of Reform

In 1957 the Soviets appointed nominally hardliner János Kádár as head of the HWP, but the experience of the 1956 revolution had convinced Kádár that a return to Rákosi's methods of the early 1950s would be counterproductive. He therefore eased restrictions imposed by the Soviets, announcing an amnesty for political prisoners in 1960 and calling a halt to forced collectivization. The economy was reorganized to accommodate a limited amount of private enterprise, and living standards duly improved. By the end of the 1960s Hungarians enjoyed easily the highest standard of living in the Soviet bloc.

Yet, as the Soviet invasion of reformist Czechoslovakia in 1968 demonstrated, there was a limit to the economic and political reforms that Moscow would tolerate. The HWP's monopoly on power, and its subservient relationship with the Soviet Union, remained taboo subjects.

The Hungarian road to socialism became known – only slightly tongue-in-cheek – as "Goulash Communism". An increasingly relaxed approach to censorship reduced the number of banned works, and expanded the number of intellectual works that were supported and tolerated. Uniquely among Eastern Europeans, Hungarians were relatively free to travel abroad, though only after thorough background checks. Currency regulations further restricted foreign travel to the privileged.

While the Kádár regime must be given some credit for successfully walking a very thin line between acceptable and unacceptable reform, by the 1980s the limitations of Goulash Communism had become far too apparent. Economic reforms proved insufficient to ensure decent levels of growth, meaning that foreign loans were needed in an attempt to prop up falling living standards.

Reformers in the HWP who believed only further economic reform could preserve its grip on power removed Kádár from office in May 1988. Shortly afterwards, opposition groups that had operated in semi-secrecy

Soviet soldiers participating in a ceremony to mark the withdrawal of troops from Hungary

1963 Kádár grants freedom to most remaining political prisoners in a widespread amnesty.

1968 Kádár announces formal, limited free-market reform, a policy that becomes known as "Goulash Communism".

1981 Director István Szábo receives an Oscar for his film *Mefisto*.

| 1960 | 1965 | 1970 | 1975 | 1980 | 1985 |

János Kádár (1912–89)

1968 Hungary takes part in the Warsaw Pact invasion of Czechoslovakia.

1974 Economist Nyers is forced out of the Politburo. A return to central planning brings economic disaster, and Nyers is reinstated.

1987 Buda's entire Castle District is placed on UNESCO's list of protected historical monuments.

Proclamation of the Republic of Hungary in 1989

for years organized themselves into political parties. In 1989 they organized mass demonstrations throughout the country against the HWP's monopoly on power. Led by the Hungarian Democratic Forum (MDF), the Alliance of Free Democrats (SZDSZ) and the Federation of Young Democrats (Fidesz), the opposition held talks with the government in March 1989, and, although no agreement was reached until autumn, the days of the one-party state were numbered. On 23 October 1989, the country's name was changed from Hungarian People's Republic to the Republic of Hungary, a symbolic move confirming the replacement of the one-party system with a multi-party democracy.

Hungary Since 1990

Hungary's first post-Communist elections, held in 1990, were won by the MDF. The HWP took part as the Hungarian Socialist Party (MSZP), but fared poorly. Árpád Göncz, who had been sentenced to death for his part in the 1956 revolution, was elected president; he was to serve two five-year terms.

The 1990–94 government enacted tough economic reform, including a massive privatization programme. Living standards for many people dropped, and unemployment reached almost 16 per cent in early 1994. As a result, the Socialists, promising a less dramatic transition to a market economy, easily won the election in 1994. Since then Hungary has seen its governments yo-yo between left and right. In 1998 Fidesz replaced the Socialists, only for the latter to return to power in 2002. They narrowly won the 2006 general election, though Prime Minister Ferenc Gyurcsány's admission of lying during the campaign provoked weeks of protests. Gyurcsány refused to resign, however, and the protests eventually died down.

A member of both NATO (2001) and the European Union (2004), the 2008 global financial crisis hit Hungary hard. In 2010, Fidesz swept to victory with a two-thirds majority – the first party to govern outright since the fall of Communism – and, despite introducing deeply unpopular austerity measures to rescue the ailing economy, won emphatically again in 2014.

Hungary's accession to the European Union, 2004

1990	1995	2000	2005	2010	2015

1988 Kádár is forced to resign by his own party.

Hungarian national emblem after 1989

2004 Hungary joins the European Union on 1 May.

2006 Gyurcsány and the Socialist Party (MSZP) win the elections.

2010 Fidesz wins elections with a two-thirds majority in Parliament.

2012 A new constitution is introduced on 1 Jan 2012.

1989 In March a series of talks begins that will see the HWP renounce its monopoly in October. On 23 October, the Republic of Hungary becomes the country's official name.

1999 Hungary is admitted to NATO.

2002 Imre Kertész receives a Nobel prize for literature.

Ferenc Gyurcsány

2009 Ferenc Gyurcsány resigns and Gordon Bajnai becomes prime minister.

2014 Fidesz wins all parliamentary, municipal and EP elections with a landslide.

BUDAPEST AREA BY AREA

Budapest at a Glance

The centre of town includes Buda's Castle Hill (district I) on the western bank of the Danube and districts V, VI, VII, VIII and IX of Pest on the river's eastern bank, bounded by the city's original tram line. The Roman numerals denote the official administrative districts. For the purposes of this guide, the centre of Budapest is divided into four areas. Each area has its own chapter containing a selection of the most interesting sights that convey its character and history. Sights on the outskirts of the city are covered in a separate chapter.

Royal Palace
The Royal Palace has been destroyed and painstakingly rebuilt many times. It was last meticulously reconstructed after World War II, to the form that the Habsburgs had given it *(see pp44–5)*.

Liberation Monument
This statue of a woman holding aloft the palm of victory was created by the Hungarian sculptor Zsigmond Kisfaludi Strobl. Situated in a park on Gellért Hill, the monument is visible from all over the city, and so it has become one of the symbols of Budapest *(see p76)*.

◄ Hungary's Parliament, the largest building in the country

Map labels:
Danube (Duna)
Országház Parliament
Kossuth Lajos tér
SZABO ILONKA U.
MÁTRAY U.
VÁRFOK U.
SZABO ILONKA U.
KAPISZTRÁN TÉR
CASTLE DISTRICT
ATTILA ÚT
Mátyás templom Mátyás Church
ÚRI U.
LOGODI U.
Déli pályaudvar
Vérmező
MIKÓ U.
KRISZ-TINA TÉR
DÍSZ TÉR
TÁRNOK U.
SZENT GYÖRGY U.
HUNYADI J. U.
CLARK ÁDÁM TÉR
Széchenyi lánchid
FESTY A. U.
KOSCIUSZKO T. U.
AG U.
ALAGÚT U.
ATTILA ÚT
VÁRALJA U.
LÁNCHID
BUDAI
GYÖZÖ U.
RÓKA U.
FENYÖ U.
NAPHEGY U.
ÚSZNYAU.
KRISZTINA ÚT
Budavári Palota Royal Palace
ALSÓ RAKPART
MÉSZÁROS U.
TIGRIS U.
DEREK U.
CZAKÓ U.
KÖRÚT
SZARVAS TÉR
DÖRENTEI U.
DÖB-RENTEI TÉR
ZSOLT U.
ALSÓHEGY U.
OROM U.
SAKC U.
HEGYALJA ÚT
GELLÉRT HILL AND TABÁN
MIHÁLY U.
GYULA U.
SZÁMA DÓ U.
SZIRTES U.
SZIRTES ÚT
Gellért hegy
SOMLÓI ÚT
KELENHEGYI ÚT
SOMLÓI ÚT
KELENHEGYI ÚT
MÉNESI ÚT
SOMLÓI ÚT
SZÜRET U.
MÉNESI ÚT
BALOGH LEJTO
VILLÁNYI ÚT

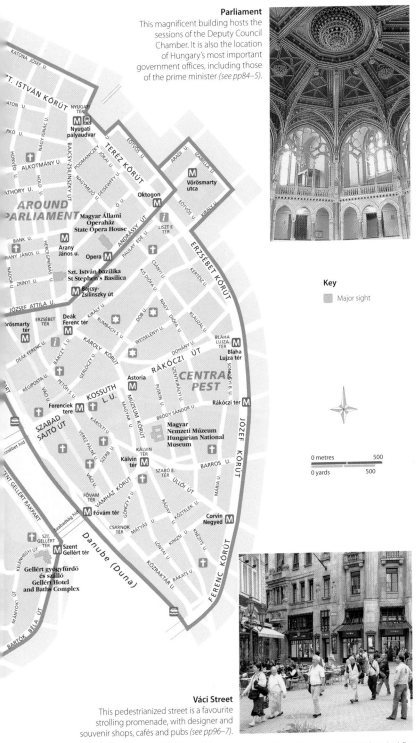

Parliament

This magnificent building hosts the sessions of the Deputy Council Chamber. It is also the location of Hungary's most important government offices, including those of the prime minister *(see pp84–5)*.

KATONA JOZSEF U.

'T. ISTVÁN KÖRÚT

ATON U.

RKÓ U.

NYUGATI TÉR

Nyugati pályaudvar

HONVÉD U.

ALKOTMÁNY U.

NAGY IGNÁC U.

BAJCSY-ZSILINSZKY ÚT

PODMANICZKY U.

TERÉZ KÖRÚT

EÖTVÖS U.

JÓKAI U.

NAGYMEZÓ U.

DESSEWFFY U.

ARADI U.

IZABELLA U.

ATHORY U.

Oktogon

Vörösmarty utca

AROUND PARLIAMENT

BANK U.

Magyar Állami Operaház State Opera House

ANDRÁSSY ÚT

PAULAY EDE U.

LISZT F. TÉR

EÖTVÖS U.

KIRÁLY U.

ERZSÉBET KÖRÚT

RANY JÁNOS U.

Arany János u.

HERCEGPRÍMÁS U.

Opera

NÁDOR U.

ZRÍNYI U.

Szt. István bazilika St Stephen's Basilica

Bajcsy-Zsilinszky út

GYÁNTÚ U.

KIS DIÓFA U.

NAGY DIÓFA U.

KERTÉSZ U.

JÓZSEF ATTILA U.

KIRÁLY U.

DOB U.

KLAUZÁL U.

örösmarty tér

ERZSÉBET TÉR

Deák Ferenc tér

RUMBACH S. U.

WESSELÉNYI U.

BLAHA LUJZA TÉR

Blaha Lujza tér

Key

Major sight

DEÁK FERENC U.

BARCZY U.

KÁROLY KÖRÚT

GERLÓCZY U.

DOHÁNY ÚT

SZENTKIRÁLYI U.

SÓMOGYI B. U.

DEÁK FERENC U.

RÉGIPOSTA U.

PETÓFI S. U.

Astoria

RÁKÓCZI ÚT

CENTRAL PEST

PUSKIN U.

Rákóczi tér

VÁCI U.

Ferenciek tere

KÁROLYI U.

KOSSUTH L. U.

MÚZEUM KÖRÚT

MAGYAR U.

JÓZSEF KÖRÚT

SZABAD SAJTÓ ÚT

VITÉZ PÁLNÉ U.

SZERB U.

BRÓDY SÁNDOR U.

Magyar Nemzeti Múzeum Hungarian National Museum

0 metres 500

0 yards 500

rzsébet híd

VÁCI U.

KÁLVIN TÉR

Kálvin tér

SZABÓ E. TÉR

BARROS U.

FÓVÁM TÉR

VÁMHÁZ KÖRÚT

GÓNCZY P. U.

ÜLLÓI ÚT

MÁRIA U.

RÁDAY U.

KÓZTELEK U.

Corvin Negyed

ENT GELLÉRT RAKPART

Fóvám tér

CSARNOK TÉR

MÁTYÁS U.

KINIZSI U.

KNÉZITS U.

FERENC KÖRÚT

KELENHEGYI ÚT

SZT GELLÉRT TÉR

Szent Gellért tér

LÓNYAI U.

KÓZRAKTÁR U.

BÁKÁTS U.

Danube (Duna)

Szabadság híd

Gellért gyógyfürdó és szálló **Gellért Hotel and Baths Complex**

MANYOKI U.

BARTÓK BÉLA ÚT

Váci Street

This pedestrianized street is a favourite strolling promenade, with designer and souvenir shops, cafés and pubs *(see pp96–7)*.

For additional keys to symbols see back flap

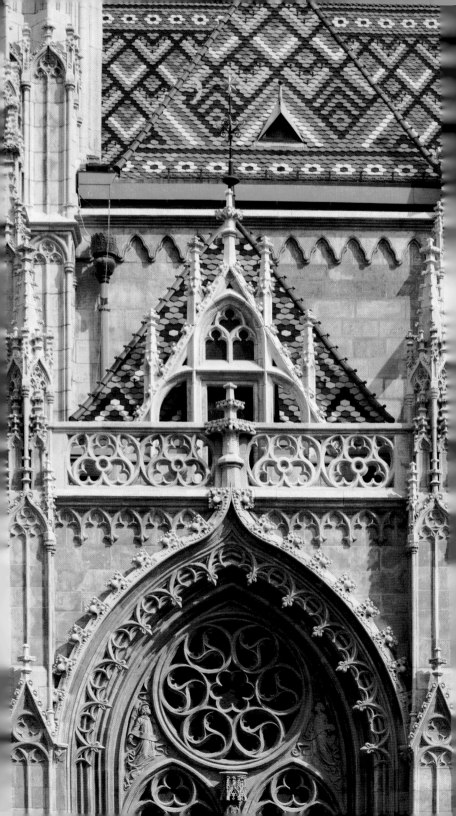

CASTLE DISTRICT

The hill town of Buda grew up around its castle and Mátyás Church from the 13th century onwards. The hill's fine strategic position, at 60 m (197 ft) above the Danube, and its natural resources made it a prize site. In the 13th century, a large settlement arose when King Béla IV decided to build his own defensive castle and establish his capital here. The reign of King Mátyás Corvinus in the 15th century was an important period in the evolution of Buda but it was neglected under Turkish rule and then destroyed by Christian troops. Under the Habsburgs, the town was reborn, however, and assumed an important role during the 18th and 19th centuries. By the end of World War II, the old town had been almost utterly destroyed and the Royal Palace burned to the ground. Since the war, both the district and the palace have been restored to their former glory.

Sights at a Glance

Churches
⓬ Mátyás Church pp66–7
⓱ Buda Lutheran Church
⓲ Church of St Mary Magdalene

Museums and Galleries
❶ Budapest History Museum
❷ National Széchényi Library
❹ Hungarian National Gallery see pp62–3
❽ Golden Eagle Pharmacy Museum

⓾ The Hungarian House
⓴ Museum of Military History
㉒ Hospital in the Rock

Historic Streets and Squares
❼ Parade Square
❾ Holy Trinity Square
⓮ András Hess Square
⓯ Mihály Táncsics Street
⓰ Vienna Gate Square
⓳ Parliament Street
㉑ Lords' Street

Palaces, Historic Buildings and Monuments
❸ Mátyás Fountain
❺ Sándor Palace
❻ Tunnel
⓫ Fisherman's Bastion
⓭ Hilton Budapest Hotel

See also Street Finder maps 1 & 3

Street-by-Street: The Royal Palace

The Royal Palace has experienced many incarnations during its long life. Even now it is not known exactly where King Béla IV began building his castle, though it is thought to be nearer the site of Mátyás Church (*see pp66–7*). The Holy Roman Emperor Sigismund of Luxembourg built a Gothic palace on the present site, from which today's castle began to evolve. In the 18th century, the Habsburgs built their monumental palace here. The current form dates from the rebuilding of the 19th-century palace after its destruction in February 1945. During this work, remains of the 15th-century Gothic palace were exposed and Hungarian archaeologists decided to reveal the recovered defensive walls and royal chambers in the reconstruction.

❺ Sándor Palace

An ornamental gateway, dating from 1903, leads to the Habsburg Steps and the Royal Palace. Nearby, a bronze sculpture of the mythical turul bird guards the palace. This statue marked the millennium anniversary of the Magyar conquest in 896.

❸ ★ Mátyás Fountain
In the northern courtyard of the Royal Palace stands the Mátyás Fountain. It was designed by Alajos Stróbl in 1904 and depicts King Mátyás Corvinus and his beloved Ilonka.

The Lion Gate, leading to a rear courtyard of the Royal Palace, gets its name from the four lions that watch over it. These sculptures were designed by János Fadrusz in 1901.

1255 First written document, a letter by King Béla IV, refers to building a fortified castle	**c.1400** Sigismund of Luxembourg builds an ambitious Gothic palace on this site	**1541** After capturing Buda, the Turks use the Royal Palace to stable horses and store gunpowder	**1719** The building of a small palace begins on the ruins of the old palace, to a design by Hölbling and Fortunato de Prati	**1881** The architect Miklós Ybl begins programme to rebuild and expand the Royal Palace
1200	**1400**	**1600**		**1800**
c.1356 Louis I builds a royal castle on the southern slopes of Castle Hill	**1686** The assault by Christian soldiers leaves the palace completely razed to the ground		**1849** Royal Palace is destroyed again, during an unsuccessful attack by Hungarian insurgents	*Turul bird*
1458 A Renaissance palace evolves under King Mátyás	**1749** Maria Theresa builds a vast palace comprising 203 chambers			

The dome of the Royal Palace was rebuilt in the Neo-Classical style after the Neo-Baroque dome, designed by Alajos Hauszmann, was destroyed in the razing of the palace during World War II.

Locator Map
See Street Finder map 1

A statue of Prince Eugene of Savoy, by József Róna, was unveiled in 1900. It commemorates the Battle of Zenta in 1697, victory at which was a turning point in the Turkish war. The bas-reliefs on the base depict scenes from the battle. Two Turkish prisoners cower by the feet of the prince.

❹ ★ **Hungarian National Gallery**
Artworks depicting Hungary's turbulent history are displayed here. Periods of both foreign domination and patriotic home rule are brought to life through the gallery's extensive collection.

```
0 metres        50
0 yards         50
```

❷ National Széchényi Library

❶ Budapest History Museum

Key

— Suggested route

Building the Royal Palace

In the early 15th century, a Gothic Royal Palace was built on the site, but it was rebuilt in the Renaissance style by King Mátyás in 1458. After the Turkish occupation it was razed and reborn on a smaller scale. Maria Theresa further developed the palace and it was rebuilt again after World War II to a design originally completed in 1905.

☐ 15th century   ☐ 1749
◼ 1719   ☐ 1905

Fifteenth-century Renaissance majolica floor, uncovered during excavations on Castle Hill and displayed at the Budapest History Museum

❶ Budapest History Museum
Budapesti Történeti Múzeum

Szent György tér 2, Royal Palace Building "E". **Map** 3 C1. **Tel** (1) 487 88 71. 🚌 5, 16, 16A, 116, 178. 🚋 18. **Open** Mar–Oct: 10am–6pm Tue–Sun; Nov–Feb: 10am–4pm Tue–Sun. ♿ fee 🌐 btm.hu

Since Budapest's unification in 1873, historic artifacts relating to the city have been collected and many are on show at the Budapest History Museum.

During the rebuilding that followed the destruction suffered in World War II, chambers dating from the Middle Ages were uncovered in the south wing (Building "E") of the Royal Palace. They provide an insight into the character of a much earlier castle within today's Habsburg reconstruction.

These rediscovered chambers, including a tiny prison cell and a chapel, were recreated in the basement of the palace. They now house an exhibition, the Royal Palace in medieval Buda, which displays various interesting items, including authentic weapons, seals, tiles and other early artifacts.

On the ground and first floor, exhibits testify to the history of Buda castle from 1686 to the present. On the ground floor are Gothic statues from the Royal Palace and a tapestry with the Hungarian–Angevin coat-of-arms, dating from the 14th and 15th centuries. On the first floor, the permanent exhibition "Budapest – Light and Shadow" leads the visitor through the millennia that formed the Hungarian capital, the River Danube acting as a guide through periods of war and peace, prosperity and decline.

❷ National Széchényi Library
Országos Széchényi Könyvtár

Szent György tér 6, Royal Palace Building "F". **Map** 3 C1. **Tel** (1) 224 37 00. 🚌 5, 16, 16A, 116, 178. 🚋 18. **Open** 9am–8pm Tue–Sat. **Closed** mid-Jul–mid-Aug. 🌐 oszk.hu

A superb collection of books, manuscripts, maps, engravings, posters, photographs and sheet music has been housed, since

Corvinian illuminated manuscript in the National Széchényi Library

1985, in the Royal Palace Building "F", built in 1890–1902 by Alajos Hauszmann and Miklós Ybl (*see p93*). Among the national library's most precious treasures are 35 pieces from the Bibliotheca Corviniana, a collection of ancient books and manuscripts that originally belonged to King Mátyás Corvinus (*see pp40–41*). His collection was one of the largest Renaissance libraries in Europe. Also of importance are the earliest-surviving records in the Hungarian language, dating from the early 13th century.

The library was established by Count Ferenc Széchényi in 1802, who endowed it with 35,000 books and manuscripts. Now comprising nine million items, the library's primary task is to collect everything published in Hungary, in the Hungarian language, by a Hungarian author, or that refers to Hungary.

Crest on the Lion Gate, adjacent to the Mátyás Fountain

❸ Mátyás Fountain
Mátyás kút

Royal Palace. **Map** 1 B5. 🚌 5, 16, 16A, 116, 178. 🚋 18.

The ornate fountain in the northernmost courtyard of the Royal Palace (between Buildings "A" and "C") was designed by Alajos Stróbl in 1904. The statue is dedicated to the great Renaissance king, Mátyás, about whom there are many legends and fables.

The Romantic design of the bronze sculptures takes its theme from a 19th-century ballad by the poet Mihály Vörösmarty. According to the tale, King Mátyás, while on a hunting expedition, meets a beautiful peasant girl, Ilonka, who falls in love with him, but their love is doomed. This representation shows King Mátyás disguised as hunter, standing proudly with his kill. He is accompanied by his chief hunter and several hunting dogs in the central part of the fountain. Below the left-hand columns sits Galeotto Marzio, an Italian court poet, and the figure of the young Ilonka is below the columns on the right.

In keeping with the romantic reputation of King Mátyás, a new tradition has grown up concerning this statue. The belief is that anyone wishing to revisit Budapest should throw a coin into the fountain to ensure their safe return.

The imposing entrance to the tunnel on Clark Ádám tér

❹ Hungarian National Gallery

Magyar Nemzeti Galéria

See pp62–3.

❺ Sándor Palace

Sándor-palota

Szent György tér 1–3. **Map** 1 B5. 🚌 16, 16A, 116. **Open** only on special occasions. **W** keh.hu

By the top of the cog-wheel railway stands the grand Neo-Classical mansion, Sándor Palace. It was commissioned in 1806 by Count Vincent Sándor from architects Mihály Pollack and Johann Aman.

The bas-reliefs that decorate the palace are the work of Richárd Török, Miklós Melocco and Tamás Körössényi. The decoration on the western

elevation depicts Greek gods on Mount Olympus. The south side shows Count Sándor being knighted, and the northern façade features a 1934 sculpture of St George by Zsigmond Kisfaludi Strobl.

Sándor Palace functioned as the prime minister's official residence from 1867 to 1944, when it was severely damaged in World War II. It has been completely restored and is now the official residence of the President of Hungary.

❻ Tunnel

Alagút

Clark Ádám tér. **Map** 1 C5. 🚌 16, 86.

The Scottish engineer Adam Clark settled in Hungary after completing the Chain Bridge. One of his later projects, in 1853–7, was the construction of the tunnel that runs right through Castle Hill, from Clark Ádám tér to Krisztinaváros. The tunnel is 350 m (1,150 ft) long, 9 m (30 ft) wide and 11 m (36 ft) in height.

The entrance on Clark Ádám tér is flanked by two pairs of Doric columns. The square in front of the tunnel is the city's official centre because of the location here of the Zero Kilometre Stone, from which all distances from Budapest are calculated.

The tunnel's western entrance was originally ornamented with Egyptian motifs. However, it was rebuilt without these details after it was damaged in World War II.

❼ Parade Square

Dísz tér

Map 1 B5. 🚌 16, 16A, 116.

In the past, Parade Square was a marketplace and a site of execution. It is named after the military parades that were held here in the 19th century. At the northern end of the square is the Honvéd Monument, built in 1893 by György Zala. It honours and commemorates those who died during the recapture of Buda from Austria in the 1848 revolution.

The two-floor Baroque palace at No. 3 was the home of the Batthyány family until 1945. It was built between 1743 and 1748 by József Giessl, and, although it has been frequently remodelled, the façade remains intact.

A few houses on Parade Square incorporate medieval remains. Examples can be seen at Nos. 4–5 and No. 11, built by Venerio Ceresola. The former has seat niches dating from the 13th century.

The western elevation of the Neo-Classical Sándor Palace

❹ Hungarian National Gallery

Established in 1957, the Hungarian National Gallery houses a comprehensive collection of Hungarian art from medieval times to the 20th century. Gathered by various groups and institutions since 1839, these works had previously been exhibited at the Hungarian National Museum *(see pp102–3)* and the Museum of Fine Arts *(see p110)*. The collection now occupies four wings (A, B, C and D) of the Royal Palace. There are eight permanent exhibitions, which present the most valuable and critically acclaimed Hungarian art in the world.

St Anne Altarpiece (c.1520)
This elaborately decorated folding altarpiece from Kisszeben is one of the gallery's Gothic highlights.

Madonna of Toporc (c. 1420)
This is a captivating example of medieval wood sculpture in the Gothic style. It was originally crafted for a church in Spiz (now part of Slovakia).

First floor

Madonna of Bártfa
(1465–70)
This painting of Virgin and Child is from a church in Bártfa (now in Slovakia). It is thought to have been painted in Krakow, Poland.

Wing D

Ground floor

Wing C

Main entrance

★ **The Visitation**
(1506)
This painting by Master MS is a delightful example of late Gothic Hungarian art. It is a fragment of a folding altarpiece from a church in Selmecbánya in modern-day Slovakia.

Key

- Medieval and Renaissance stone carvings
- Panel paintings and wooden sculptures from the Gothic period
- Late Gothic winged altarpieces
- Late Renaissance and Baroque art
- 19th-century paintings, sculptures and medals
- Paintings, sculptures and medals 1900–1945
- Hungarian art post-1945
- Mihály Munkácsy and The Realism of the End of the 19th Century
- Temporary exhibition space

Luischen (1884)
One of the earliest works by the sculptor Alajos Stróbl is this marble bust of a young girl who was to become his wife.

Third floor

Woman Bathing (1901)
This painting by Károly Lotz is the finest example of Neo-Classical painting in Hungary. It reflects his fascination for the work of the French painter, Ingres.

Gallery Guide

Early stone and Gothic exhibits are on the ground floor. Late Gothic, Renaissance and Baroque works and 19th-century works share the first floor. Works from the early 20th century are on the second floor, and the most modern pieces are on the third floor.

Second floor

Churning Woman (1872–3)
This painting is by Mihály Munkácsy, Hungary's most internationally celebrated artist. The tiredness of the woman's features with her worn hands show the reality of a life of poverty.

Wing B

Wing A

★ **Picnic in May** (1873)
The captivating colours of this landscape scene were painted by Pál Szinyei Merse. He was influenced by two works of Edouard Manet and Claude Monet, both entitled *Le Déjeuner sur l'Herbe*.

❽ Golden Eagle Pharmacy Museum
Arany Sas Patikamúzeum

Tárnok utca 18. **Map** 1 B5.
Tel (1) 375 97 72. 🚌 16 from Deák tér, 16, 16A & 116 from Széll Kálmán tér.
Open Mar–Oct: 10am–5:30pm Tue–Sun; Nov–Feb: 10am–3:30pm Tue–Fri, 10am–5:30pm Sat & Sun.

This pharmacy was opened in 1688 by Ferenc Ignác Bösinger and traded under the name "The Golden Eagle" from 1740. It moved to this originally Gothic building, with a Baroque interior and Neo-Classical façade, in the 18th century. The museum opened in 1974 and displays pharmaceutical items from the Renaissance and Baroque eras.

❾ Holy Trinity Square
Szentháromság tér

Map 1 B5. 🚌 16 from Deák tér, 16, 16A & 116 from Széll Kálmán tér.

This square is the central point of the old town. It takes its name from the Baroque Holy Trinity Column, originally sculpted by Philipp Ungleich in 1710–13 and restored in 1967. The column commemorates the dead of two outbreaks of plague that struck the people of Buda in 1691 and 1709.

The pedestal of the column is decorated with bas-reliefs by Anton Hörger, depicting the horrific fate Buda's citizens suffered during these epidemics. Further up the ornate column are statues of holy figures and at the summit is a magnificent composition of the figures of the Holy Trinity. The central section of the column is decorated with angelic figures surrounded by clouds.

Buda's Old Town Hall, a large Baroque building with two courtyards, was also built on the square at the beginning of the 18th century. It was designed by the imperial court architect, Venerio Ceresola, whose architectural scheme incorporated the remains of medieval houses. In 1770–74, an east wing was built, and bay windows and a stone balustrade with Rococo urns, by Mátyás Nepauer, were also added. The corner niche, opposite Mátyás Church, houses a small statue of the Greek goddess Pallas Athene by Carlo Adami.

❿ The Hungarian House
Magyarság Háza

Szentháromság tér 6. **Map** 1 B5.
Tel (1) 795 26 19. 🚌 16 from Deák tér, 16, 16A & 116 from Széll Kálmán tér.
Open 10am–6pm Tue–Sat. 📷 🎥
📶 🌐 **magyarsaghaza.net**

On the north side of Holy Trinity Square, this cultural institute houses an exhibition that celebrates all manner of Hungarian achievements in the arts, sciences, engineering and sport. The building looks medieval but in fact was only built in the early 20th century, in a Neo-Gothic style. The beautiful interior is also used for cultural events and, while parts of the exhibition may be unfamiliar to non-Hungarians, the regular performances of music and dance held here need no translation.

A statue of St István in front of the Fisherman's Bastion

⓫ Fisherman's Bastion
Halászbástya

Szentháromság tér. **Map** 1 B5. 🚌 16 from Deák tér, 16, 16A & 116 from Széll Kálmán tér. **Open** 1 May–15 Oct: 9am–8pm (16 Mar–30 Apr: to 7pm).

Frigyes Schulek designed this Neo-Romanesque monument to the Guild of Fishermen in 1895. It occupies the site of Buda's old defensive walls and a medieval square where fish was once sold. The bastion is a purely aesthetic addition to Castle Hill and boasts fine views of the Danube. In front of it is a statue of St István.

⓬ Mátyás Church
Mátyás templom

See pp66–7.

Buda's Old Town Hall, its clock tower crowned with an onion-shaped dome, on Holy Trinity Square

For hotels and restaurants see pp264–269 and pp276–285

Bas-relief depicting King Mátyás on the Hilton Budapest Hotel's façade

⓭ Hilton Budapest Hotel

Hilton Szálloda

Hess András tér 1–3. **Map** 1 B4. **Tel** (1) 889 66 00. 🚌 16 from Deák tér, 16, 16A & 116 from Széll Kálmán tér. ♿

Built in 1976, the Hilton Budapest Hotel is a rare example of modern architecture in the old town. Controversial from the outset, the design by the Hungarian architect Béla Pintér combines the historic remains of the site with contemporary materials and methods.

From 1254 a Dominican church, to which a tower was later added, stood on this site, followed by a late Baroque Jesuit monastery. The remains of both buildings are incorporated into the new hotel. The ruins of the medieval church, for example, uncovered during excavations in 1902, form part of the Dominican Courtyard, where concerts and operettas are staged in summer.

The main façade comprises part of the façade of the Jesuit monastery. To the left of the entrance is St Nicholas's Tower. In 1930, a replica of a 15th-century German bas-relief of King Mátyás, considered to be his most authentic likeness, was added to this tower.

⓮ András Hess Square

Hess András tér

Map 1 B4. 🚌 16 from Deák tér, 16, 16A & 116 from Széll Kálmán tér.

This square is named after the Italian-trained printer who printed the first Hungarian book, *Chronica Hungarorum*, in a printing works at No. 4 in 1473. The house was rebuilt at the end of the 17th century, amalgamating three medieval houses, with quadruple seat niches, barrel-vaulted cellars and ornamental gates.

The former inn at No. 3 was named the Red Hedgehog in 1696. This one-floor building has surviving Gothic and Baroque elements.

The square also features a statue by József Damkó of Pope Innocent XI, who was involved in organizing the armies that recaptured Buda from the Turks. It was built to mark the 250th anniversary of the liberation, in 1936.

⓯ Mihály Táncsics Street

Táncsics Mihály utca

Táncsics Mihály utca 7. **Map** 1 A/B4. 🚌 16 from Deák tér, 16, 16A & 116 from Széll Kálmán tér. Museum of Musical History: **Tel** (1) 214 67 70. **Open** 10am–4pm Tue–Sun. 🌐 zti.hu

Erdődy Palace was built in 1750–69 for the Erdődy family by Mátyás Nepauer, the leading architect of the day. It features outstanding Baroque façades

The Museum of Musical History on Mihály Táncsics Street

on three sides. Like many houses on this street, it was erected on the ruins of medieval houses. In 1800, Ludwig van Beethoven, who was then giving concerts in Budapest, resided here for a short time.

The palace now houses the Museum of Musical History and the Béla Bartók archives. A permanent exhibition illustrates musical life in Budapest from the 18th to 20th centuries, and includes some of the oldest-surviving Hungarian musical instruments.

The Royal Mint stood on the site of No. 9 during the Middle Ages and, in 1810, the Joseph Barracks were built here. These were later used by the Habsburgs to imprison leaders of the 1848–9 rebellion, including Mihály Táncsics.

Relics of Buda's Jewish heritage can be found at Nos. 23 and 26. The remains of a 15th-century synagogue stand in the garden of No. 23. During excavations, tombs and religious items were found in the courtyard of No. 26.

King István I

Born in Esztergom in 975, Vajk (Hero), the son of Géza, was baptized at the age of 10 and chose the name István (Stephen). He succeeded his father as Prince and in 1000 was crowned Catholic king of Hungary – the Vatican signalled its approval by sending what became known as the crown of St István. A devout man, István set about Christianizing Hungary, founding bishoprics, cathedrals and abbeys. He died in 1038, and was canonized by Pope Gregory VII as St István of Hungary in 1083.

⑫ Mátyás Church

The Parish Church of Our Lady Mary was built on this site between the 13th and 15th centuries. Some of the architectural style dates from the reign of Sigismund of Luxembourg, but the church's name refers to King Mátyás Corvinus, who greatly enlarged and embellished it. Much of the original detail was lost when the Turks converted the church into the Great Mosque in 1541. With the liberation of Buda, modifications were made by the Jesuits as part of the restoration process, largely in the Baroque style. The church again sustained damage in 1723, and was restored in the Neo-Gothic style by Frigyes Schulek in 1873–96. The gallery rooms house the Museum of Ecclesiastical Art.

Rose Window
Frigyes Schulek faithfully reproduced the medieval stained-glass window that was in this position during the early Gothic era.

Béla Tower
This tower is named after the church's founder, King Béla IV. It has retained several of its original Gothic features.

★ **Baroque Madonna**
According to legend, the original statue was set into a wall of the church during the Turkish occupation. When that wall was destroyed in 1686, the Madonna miraculously appeared. The Turks took this as an omen of defeat.

KEY

① **The roof** is decorated with multicoloured glazed tiles.

② **The main altar**, created by Frigyes Schulek, was based on Gothic triptychs.

Main Portal
Below the arches of the west entrance is a 19th-century bas-relief of the Virgin and Child between two angels. The pyrogranite ceramics were made by Zsolnay.

★ Tomb of King Béla III and Anne de Châtillon

The remains of this royal couple were transferred from Székesfehérvár Cathedral to Mátyás Church in 1860. They lie beneath an ornamental stone canopy in the Trinity Chapel.

Pulpit

The richly decorated pulpit includes the carved stone figures of the four Fathers of the Church and the four Evangelists.

Stained-Glass Windows

Three arched windows on the south elevation have beautiful 19th-century stained glass. They were designed by Frigyes Schulek, Bertalan Székely and Károly Lotz.

★ Mary Portal

This depiction of the Assumption of the Blessed Virgin Mary is the most magnificent example of Gothic stone carving in Hungary. Frigyes Schulek reconstructed the portal from fragments.

c. 1370 Church redesigned as Gothic hall-church under Louis I

1464 Thanksgiving Mass following the election of Mátyás Corvinus as king

1541 Turks convert church into a mosque

1686 After liberation of Buda from Turkish rule, the church is restored with a Baroque interior

Holy figures on the pulpit

2014 Full reconstruction of the building completed

1250	1350	1450	1550	1650	1750	1850	1950	2050

1309 Coronation of the Angevin king Charles Robert

1255 Church originally founded by King Béla IV after the Mongol invasion

1526 Cathedral burned in the first attack by Turks

1470 Mátyás Tower is completed after its collapse in 1384

1896 Frigyes Schulek completes the reconstruction of the church in the Neo-Gothic style

1945 Church is severely damaged by German and Russian armies

1970 Final details are completed in postwar rebuilding programme

Vienna Gate, rebuilt in 1936, commemorating the liberation of Buda

⑯ Vienna Gate Square

Bécsi kapu tér

Map 1 A4. 🚌 16 from Deák tér, 16, 16A & 116 from Széll Kálmán tér.

The square takes its name from the gate that once led from the walled town of Buda towards Vienna. After being damaged several times, the old gate was demolished in 1896. The current gate, based on a historic design, was erected in 1936 on the 250th anniversary of the liberation of Buda from the Turks.

The square has a number of interesting houses. Those at Nos. 5, 6, 7 and 8 were built on the ruins of medieval dwellings. They are Baroque and Rococo in design and feature sculptures and bas-reliefs. The façade of No. 7 has medallions with the portraits of Classical philosophers and poets; Thomas Mann, the German novelist, lodged here in 1935–6. No. 8, however, is differentiated by its bay windows, attics and the restored medieval murals on its façade.

On the left-hand side of the square is a vast Neo-Romanesque building with a beautiful multicoloured roof, built in 1913–20 by Samu Pecz. This building houses the National Archive, which holds documents dating from before the battle of Mohács in 1526, and others connected with the Rákóczi and Kossuth uprisings (*see pp44–5*).

Behind the Vienna Gate Square is a monument built in honour of Mihály Táncsics, the leader of the Autumn Uprising. It was unveiled in 1970.

⑰ Buda Lutheran Church

Budavári Evangélikus templom

Táncsics Mihály utca 28. **Map** 1 A4. **Tel** (1) 356 97 36. 🚌 16 from Deák tér, 16, 16A & 116 from Széll Kálmán tér. ♿

The Neo-Classical Lutheran Church was built in 1896 by Mór Kallina. A plaque commemorates the evangelical pastor Gábor Sztéhló, who saved some 2,000 Jewish children and adults during World War II.

At one time, a painting by Bertalan Székely, called *Christ Blessing the Bread*, adorned the altar, but unfortunately it was destroyed during the war.

⑱ Church of St Mary Magdalene

Mária Magdolna templom

Kapisztrán tér 6. **Map** 1 A4. 🚌 16 from Deák tér, 16, 16A & 116 from Széll Kálmán tér.

Now in ruins, this church was built in the mid-13th century. During the Middle Ages, Hungarian Christians worshipped here because Mátyás Church was only for use by the town's German population.

The church did not become a mosque until the second half of the Turkish occupation, but it was severely damaged in 1686, during the liberation of Buda from the Turks. An order of Franciscan monks

subsequently took possession and during their time added a Baroque church and a tower.

After suffering serious air-raid damage in World War II, all but the Franciscan tower and gate were pulled down. These now stand in a garden, together with the reconstructed single Gothic window.

⑲ Parliament Street

Országház utca

Map 1 A4–B4/5.

This street was once inhabited by the Florentine artisans and craftsmen who were working on King Mátyás's Royal Palace (*see pp58–9*), and so it was known for a time as Italian Street. Its present name comes from the building at No. 28, where the Hungarian State Parliament and Budapest High Court met from 1790 to 1807. This building was designed in the 18th century by the architect Franz Anton Hillebrandt as a convent for the Poor Clares. However, Emperor Joseph II dissolved the order before the building was completed. The Great Hall is beautifully restored.

Numerous buildings on Parliament Street have retained Gothic and Baroque features. No. 2 Országház utca, now with a Neo-Classical façade, is the site of the Alabárdos restaurant, but the building's history dates back to the late 13th century. In the 15th century, Sigismund of Luxembourg built a Gothic mansion here, and some details, such as the colonnade around the courtyard and the murals on the second floor, have survived until today. The entrance to No. 9 features the Gothic traceried seat niches that were popular in Buda at this time. In front of the Neo-Classical house at No. 21 stands a statue of the famous actor Márton Lendvay (1807–58).

The reconstructed Baroque tower of the Church of St Mary Magdalene

The façade of the Museum of Military History

⑳ Museum of Military History

Hadtörténeti Múzeum

Kapisztrán tér 2–4. **Map** 1 A4. **Tel** (1) 325 16 00. 🚌 16 from Deák tér, 16, 16A & 116 from Széll Kálmán tér. **Open** 10am–6pm Tue–Sun. 🖬 **W militaria.hu**

The museum is located in a wing of the former Palatine barracks. It houses a wide range of military items relating to the skirmishes and wars that have afflicted Budapest from before the Turkish occupation to the 20th century. Uniforms, flags, weapons, maps and ammunition from as far back as the 11th century give an insight into the long, turbulent history of Budapest.

Of particular interest is the exhibition concerning the 1956 Revolution. Photographs illustrate the demonstrations that ended in a Soviet invasion, the execution of the prime minister and a great number of civilian deaths *(see pp48–9)*.

㉑ Lords' Street

Úri utca

Map 1 A4 – B5. 🚌 16 from Deák tér, 16, 16A & 116 from Széll Kálmán tér. Telephone Museum: **Tel** (1) 201 81 88. **Open** 10am–4pm Tue–Sun. 🖬 **W postamuzeum.hu**

The buildings in Lords' Street, or Úri utca, were destroyed first in 1686 and again in 1944. Reconstruction in 1950–60 restored much of their original medieval character. Almost all have some remnant of a Gothic gateway or hall, while the façades are Baroque or Neo-Classical.

An excellent example of a Gothic façade can be seen on Hölbling House at No. 31. Enough of its original features survived the various wars and renovations to enable architects to reconstruct the façade in considerable detail. The first-floor window is a particularly splendid Gothic feature. The houses opposite are also examples of restoration work.

The building at No. 53 was rebuilt between 1701 and 1722 as a Franciscan monastery, but in 1789 it was restyled for use by Emperor Joseph II. In 1795, Hungarian Jacobites, led by Ignác Martinovics, were imprisoned here; a plaque records this event. A well, featuring a copy of a sculpture by Praxiteles of Artemis, the Greek goddess of hunting, was set in front of the house in 1873.

The **Telephone Museum**, at No. 49, is housed in the city's first telephone exchange, established in 1881. It is an enjoyable interactive museum, centred around a huge switchboard with exhibits on the history of telephony.

㉒ Hospital in the Rock

Sziklakórház

Lovas út 4/c. **Map** 1 A5. **Tel** (70) 701 01 01. 🚌 16 from Deák tér, 16, 16A & 116 from Széll Kálmán tér. **Open** 10am– 8pm daily. 🖬 🖬 **W sziklakorhaz.hu**

Connected to the network of caves under Buda Castle, the Hospital in the Rock is an atmospheric sight where visitors can learn about the history of Hungary through-out the mid-20th century. In 1944–5 the caves were used as an emergency military hospital and air-raid shelter, providing treatment and refuge for thousands of people during the siege of Budapest. During the revolution in 1956 it was again used as a hospital. A nuclear bunker was added during the Cold War, the existence of which was only made public in 2010.

Many pieces of the original medical equipment are on display. There are presentations on the history of the city, information on the 1956 Revolution and the Cold War, along with wax figures, all bringing this unique sight to life. The guided tour (approx. 60 mins) is compulsory.

Lords' Street, or Úri utca, which runs the full length of the old town

GELLÉRT HILL AND TABÁN

Rising steeply beside the Danube, Gellért Hill is one of the city's most attractive areas. From the top, at a height of 140 m (460 ft), a beautiful view of the whole of Budapest unfolds. The Celtic Eravi, who preceded the Romans, formed their settlement on the hill's northern slope (see p78). Once called simply Old Hill, many superstitions and tales are connected with it. The hill's present name

recalls the fate and martyrdom of Bishop Gellért, who tried to convert the unwilling locals to Christianity. In 1046, they threw the bishop from the hill to his death in a sealed barrel. Gellért Hill bulges out slightly into the Danube, which narrows at this point. This made the base of the hill a favoured crossing place, and the settlement of Tabán evolved as a result.

Sights at a Glance

Museums
11 Semmelweis Museum of Medical History

6 Rudas Baths
9 Rác Thermal Spa

Churches
2 Cave Church
10 Tabán Parish Church

Districts, Squares and Monuments
3 Liberation Monument
5 Statue of St Gellért
7 Queen Elizabeth Monument
8 Tabán

Historic Buildings
4 Citadel
12 Golden Stag House

Hotels and Baths
1 *Gellért Hotel and Baths Complex pp74–5*

See also Street Finder maps 1, 3 & 4

0 metres 300
0 yards 300

◀ Stylized Classical statue and Secessionist mosaics at the Gellért Baths

For keys to map symbols *see back flap*

Street-by-Street: Gellért Hill

The hill to the south of Castle Hill was long regarded as a notorious spot. In the 11th century Prince Vata, brother of King István, incited a heathen rebellion here that resulted in the death of Bishop Gellért. During the Middle Ages, witches were even reputed to celebrate their sabbath here. Under the Turks, a small stronghold was first built on the hill to protect Buda. In 1851, the Austrians placed their own bleak and intimidating Citadel at the summit. Not until the end of the 19th century did the popular image of Gellért Hill begin to change, when it became a venue for picnicking parties. In 1967, the area around the Citadel was made into an attractive park.

❼ Queen Elizabeth Monument
Close to the entrance to Elizabeth Bridge stands this statue of Austrian Emperor Franz Joseph's wife, who was popular with the Hungarians.

Elizabeth Bridge

HEGYALIA ÚT

❺ ★ Statue of St Gellért
Blessing the city with his uplifted cross, the martyred Bishop Gellért is known as the patron saint of Budapest.

❹ Citadel
Once a place to inspire terror, the Citadel now hosts a hotel, restaurant and wine bar, where people can relax and enjoy the splendid view.

Key

— Suggested route

❸ Liberation Monument
At the foot of the Liberation Monument, towering above the city, are two sculptures, one representing the battle with evil.

0 metres   500
0 yards   500

❻ Rudas Baths
These famous Turkish baths, which date from the 16th century, have a characteristic Ottoman cupola.

The Observation Terraces on Gellért Hill reward those who climb up to them with a beautiful panorama over the southern part of Buda and the whole of Pest.

Locator Map
See Street Finder map 3

The Reservoir

In 1978, a new reservoir to supply the capital with drinking water was built near the Uránia Observatory to the northwest of Gellért Hill. The surface of the reservoir is covered over and provides a point from which to observe the Royal Palace *(see pp58–9)* to the north. A sculpture by Márta Lesenyei decorates the structure.

Sculpture by Márta Lesenyei on Gellért Hill's reservoir

❷ Cave Church
This church was established in 1926 in a holy grotto. Under the Communists, the Pauline order of monks was forced to abandon the church, but it was reopened in 1989.

SZENT GELLÉRT RAKPART

Liberty Bridge

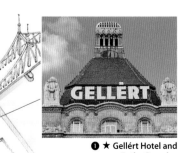

❶ ★ Gellért Hotel and Baths Complex
One of a number of bath complexes built at the beginning of the 20th century, this magnificent spa hotel was erected here to exploit the natural hot springs.

❶ Gellért Hotel and Baths Complex

Between 1912 and 1918, this hotel and spa was built in the modernist Secession style *(see p87)* at the foot of Gellért Hill. The architects of the hotel were Ármin Hegedűs, Artúr Sebestyén and Izidor Sterk. The earliest reference to the existence of healing waters at this spot dates from the 13th century. During the reign of King András II and in the Middle Ages a hospital stood on the site. Baths built here by the Ottomans were mentioned by the renowned Turkish travel writer of the day, Evliya Çelebi. Severely damaged in 1945, the hotel was restored and modernized after World War II. Today it has several restaurants and cafés. The baths complex includes an institute of water therapy, set within Secession interiors but with modern facilities.

Outdoor Wave Pool
An early swimming pool with a wave mechanism, built in 1927, is situated at the back of the complex, looking towards Gellért Hill behind.

★ Baths
Two separate baths, one for men and one for women, are identically arranged. In each there are three plunge pools, with water at different temperatures, a sauna and a steam bath.

Balconies
The balconies fronting the hotel's rooms have fanciful Secession balustrades that are decorated with lyre and bird motifs.

★ Entrance Hall
The interiors of the hotel, like the baths, have kept their original Secession decor, with elaborate mosaics, stained-glass windows and statues.

KEY

① Hot pool with medicinal spa water

For hotels and restaurants see pp264–269 and pp276–285

Sun Terraces
Situated in the sunniest spot, these terraces are a popular place for drying off in summer.

VISITORS' CHECKLIST

Practical Information
Szent Gellért tér. **Map** 4 D3.
Tel (1) 466 61 66. ✉ ♿ ▭
✐ 🏠 Baths: Kelenhegyi út.
Open 6am–8pm daily. ♿ ✉
♿ 🌐 budapestspas.hu

Transport
Ⓜ Szent Gellért tér. 🚌 7, 86.
🚃 18, 19, 47, 49.

Eastern-Style Towers
The architects who designed the hotel gave its towers and turrets a characteristically Oriental cylindrical form.

Main Staircase
The landings of the main staircase have stained-glass windows by Bozó Stanisits, added in 1933. They illustrate an ancient Hungarian legend about a magic stag, recorded in the poetry of János Arany.

Restaurant Terrace
From this first-floor terrace, diners can appreciate a fine view of Pest. On the ground and first floors of the hotel there is a total of four cafés and restaurants.

★ Main Façade
Behind the hotel's imposing façade are attractive recreational facilities and a health spa that is also open to non-guests. The entrance to the baths is around to the right from the main entrance, on Kelenhegyi út.

Entrance to the Cave Church, run by the Pauline order of monks

The monument's central figure is a woman standing on a pedestal, reaching a height of 14 m (46 ft). At the base of the monument there are two allegorical compositions, representing progress and the battle with evil.

The arrival of the Russians in Budapest was a liberation, but it also signalled the beginning of Soviet rule. After the fall of Communism, a figure of a Russian soldier was removed from the monument to Memento Park (see p116).

❷ Cave Church
Sziklatemplom

Szent Gellért rakpart 1. **Map** 4 D3. Ⓜ Szent Gellért tér. 7, 86. 18, 19, 47, 49. **Tel** (1) 385 15 29. **Open** 9am–8pm daily.

Based on Lourdes, this grotto church on the southern slope of Gellért Hill was established in 1926 by Kálmán Lux for the Pauline order of monks, which originated in Hungary in the 13th century. The church was sealed in the late 1950s by the Communist authorities, but it and the adjoining monastery were reopened in 1989, when a papal blessing was conferred on its new granite altar.

To the left of the grotto is a copy of the Black Madonna of Czestochowa and a depiction of a Polish eagle. A painting commemorates the Polish monk St Kolbe, who died helping inmates at Auschwitz. At the entrance stands a statue of St István. In the monastery, Béla Ferenc's exquisite wooden sculptures are worth seeing.

❸ Liberation Monument
Felszabadulási emlékmű

Map 4 D2. 27.

Positioned high on Gellért Hill, this imposing monument towers over the rest of the city. It was designed by the outstanding Hungarian sculptor Zsigmond Kisfaludi Strobl and set up here to commemorate

the liberation of Budapest by the Russian army in 1947 (see pp48–9). The monument was originally intended to honour the memory of István, son of the Hungarian Regent Miklós Horthy, who disappeared in 1943 on the Eastern Front. However, after the liberation of the city by Russian troops, Marshal Kliment Voroshilov spotted the work in the sculptor's workshop and reassigned it to this purpose.

The Liberation Monument, standing at the top of Gellért Hill

❹ Citadel
Citadella

Map 3 C2. 27.

After the suppression of the uprising of 1848–9 (see pp46–7), the Habsburgs constructed a fortification on this strategically important site. Built in 1850–54, the Citadel housed 60 cannons, which could, in theory, fire on the city at any time. In reality, from its very inception the Citadel did not fulfil any real military requirements, but served rather as a means of intimidating the population.

The Citadel is some 220 m (720 ft) long by 60 m (200 ft) wide, and has 4-m- (12-ft-) high walls. After peace was agreed with the Habsburgs, Hungarians continually demanded the destruction of the Citadel but it was not until 1897 that the Austrian soldiers left their barracks here and a section of its entrance was symbolically ripped out.

Saint Gellért

Bishop Gellért was born Giorgio di Sagredo, near Bologna, Italy, around 980. He became a Benedictine monk and made a pilgrimage to the Holy Land, where he met the Raslan, Abbot of Pannonhalma Abbey (see pp180–81), who invited him to Hungary. After a period preaching in pagan areas of the country, he was asked by King St István to tutor his son, Prince Imre. István later made him a Bishop. Gellért was killed in 1046 during a pagan revolt – sealed in a barrel, he was thrown off the hill that today takes his name, Gellért Hill.

A hotel window depicting St Gellért

After much debate in the early 1960s, the Citadel became a leisure complex. A restaurant, a hotel and a nightclub here used to tempt customers up Gellért Hill, but are now closed, with no information available on when, or whether, they will reopen. However, the walk up to the old walls of the Citadel is rewarded with spectacular views of the entire city below.

The main plunge pool at the Rudas Baths, covered by a Turkish cupola

❺ Statue of St Gellért
Szent Gellért emlékmű

Map 3 C2. 🚌 27 (and a long walk; go via the steps by Elizabeth Bridge).

In 1904 a vast monument was established on the spot where, in the 11th century, Bishop Gellért was said to have been thrown off the hill in a sealed barrel, by a mob opposed to the adoption of Christianity. St Gellért holds a cross in his outstretched hand, and a Hungarian convert to Christianity kneels at his feet.

The statue was designed by Gyula Jankovits; the semi-circular colonnade behind it is by Imre Francsek. A spring that bubbles up here was used to create the fountain.

Overlooking the Elizabeth Bridge, the larger-than-life monument of the bishop can be seen from all over the city.

❻ Rudas Baths
Rudas Gyógyfürdő

Döbrentei tér 9. **Map** 3 C2. **Tel** (1) 356 13 22. Spa Baths: **Open** (men only) 6am–8pm Mon, Wed–Fri; (women only) 6am–8pm Tue; (mixed) 10pm–4am Fri, 6am–8pm, 10pm–4am Sat, 6am–7pm Sun. Swimming pool: **Open** 6am–6pm Mon–Fri, 6am–5pm Sat & Sun. 🌐 spasbudapest.com

Dating originally from 1550, these baths were greatly extended in 1566 by Sokoli Mustafa, an Ottoman pasha. The main part of the baths, which comprises an octagonal plunge pool and four small corner pools with water of varying temperatures, dates from this period.

In recent years the baths have been extensively modernized and now include a covered swimming pool. This pool is for mixed bathing.

❼ Queen Elizabeth Monument
Erzsébet királyné szobra

Döbrentei tér. **Map** 3 C1/2.

This monument to Queen Elizabeth, wife of Habsburg Emperor and king of Hungary Franz Joseph, was created by György Zala. The statue was erected in its present location in 1986. It stands close to the Elizabeth Bridge, which was also named after the empress and queen, who showed great friendship to the Hungarians. The statue stood on the opposite side of the river from 1932 until 1947, when the Communists ordered it to be taken down.

The landmark Gellért Monument, overlooking the Elizabeth Bridge

❽ Tabán

Map 3 B/C1. 🚋 18, 19. 🚌 5, 112.

The Tabán now consists of a pleasant park and a few historic buildings, but it was once very different. In the early 20th century this district, nestling in between Castle Hill and Gellért Hill, was a slum which was cleared as part of a city improvement programme. Only a few buildings survived, including Tabán Parish Church.

Natural conditions ensured that this was one of the first places in the area where people chose to live. The Celtic Eravi were the first to make a settlement here, while the Romans later built a watch-tower from which they could observe people using a nearby crossing point over the river. The first reference to the thermal waters in Tabán dates from the 15th century. The Turks took advantage of this natural asset and built two magnificent baths here, the Rác Baths and the Rudas Baths (see p77). Around them a blossoming town was soon established. Apart from the baths, virtually everything was destroyed in the recapture of Buda in 1686.

In the late 17th century, a large number of Serbs, referred to in Hungarian as Rác, moved into the Tabán after fleeing from the Turks. They were joined by Greeks and Gypsies. Many of the inhabitants of the Tabán at this stage were tanners or made their living on the river. On the hillside above, grapevines were cultivated. In the early 20th century, though picturesque, the district was still without proper sanitation. The old, decaying Tabán, with its bars and gambling dens, was demolished and the present green space established in its place.

Gardens with terraces, decorative stairways and arcades designed by Miklós Ybl were established in Tabán to connect the Royal Palace (see pp58–9) with the banks of the Danube.

Several Ottoman tombstones stand here. They are the remnants of a cemetery in which the Turks who died defending Buda in 1686 were buried.

A statue of Miklós Ybl, the 19th-century architect, was erected here in 1894. It was designed by Ede Mayer.

Golden Stag House

YBL MIKLÓS TÉR

ÁRPÁD UTCA

DÖBRENTEI UTCA

GROZA PÉTER RAKPART

0 metres 150
0 yards 150

❾ Rác Thermal Spa
Rác Gyógyfürdő

Hadnagy utca 8–10. **Map** 3 C2. 18, 19. **Closed** until further notice.

The Rác Spa dates from 1550 and boasts an original thermal Turkish pool, a hammam bath and a historical dome. This significant piece of heritage is now privately owned, and has been renovated with a five-star luxury hotel adjoining it, with modern facilities for guests and visitors to indulge in the latest spa treatments. Unfortunately, the opening of the hotel and thermal spa complex has been delayed by unresolved financial issues.

Turkish bath area, Rác Thermal Spa

❿ Tabán Parish Church
Tabáni plébánia templom

Attila út 11. **Map** 3 C1. **Tel** (1) 375 54 91. 18, 19.

A temple is thought to have stood on this site even in the reign of Prince Árpád. In the Middle Ages a church was built here, which was converted to a mosque by the Turks and subsequently destroyed. In 1728–36, after the Habsburgs had taken control of the city, a new church was erected to a design by Keresztély Ober-gruber. Mátyás Nepauer added the tower in 1750–53. In 1881 the façade was extended and the tower was crowned by a fine Neo-Baroque dome.

Inside the church, on the right-hand side under the choir gallery, is a copy of a 12th-century carving entitled *Christ of Tabán*; the original is

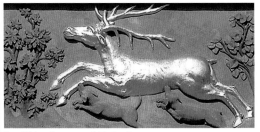

Bas-relief above the entrance to Golden Stag House

now in the Budapest History Museum *(see p60)*. The nave and side chapels are Baroque; the altar, pulpit and several paintings adorning the walls all date from the 19th century. The church hosts regular organ concerts.

⓫ Semmelweis Museum of Medical History
Semmelweis Orvostörténeti Múzeum

Apród utca 1–3. **Map** 3 C1. **Tel** (1) 375 35 33. 18, 19. **Open** Mid-Mar–Oct: 10:30am–6pm Tue–Sun; Sep–mid-Mar: 10:30am–4pm Tue–Sun. semmelweis.museum.hu

This museum is located in the 18th-century house where Dr Ignáz Semmelweis was born in 1818. He is renowned for his discovery of the cause and cure for puerperal fever, a fatal condition frequently contracted by women during or shortly after childbirth.

The history of medicine from ancient Egypt onwards is portrayed in the museum, which includes the replica

of a 19th-century pharmacy. Semmelweis's surgery can also be seen with its original furniture. In the courtyard stands a monument called *Motherhood* by Miklós Borsos.

⓬ Golden Stag House
Szarvas ház

Szarvas tér 1. **Map** 3 C1. **Tel** (1) 375 64 51. 18, 19. aranyszarvas.hu

Standing at the foot of Castle Hill is this distinctive early 18th-century house. Its name recalls the inn that opened here in 1704, "Under the Golden Stag" (Aranyszarvas) – a bas-relief above the door depicts a golden stag pursued by two hunting dogs. Much reworked over the past three centuries, the house today is a classy, whitewashed Neo-Baroque building, as famous for its uniquely slim chimney pots as for its façade. It is now occupied by the Aranyszarvas restaurant, which serves game dishes, and has a popular terrace with a nice view.

Raoul Wallenberg

The celebrated Swedish diplomat Raoul Wallenberg saved more than 7,000 Hungarian Jews from deportation. Born in Sweden in 1912, Wallenberg was assigned to the Swedish Embassy in Budapest in 1944 and immediately began certifying Jews threatened with deportation as Swedish subjects awaiting repatriation. Arrested (as a US spy) by the Soviet Army in 1945, Wallenberg was taken to Moscow and probably executed in 1947. He is honoured in Budapest with a statue depicting a man slaying a snake.

Bas-relief of Raoul Wallenberg

AROUND PARLIAMENT

Towards the end of the 18th century and throughout the 19th century, Pest underwent a series of huge changes. In 1838 a flood destroyed most of the rural dwellings that had occupied the area. The Chain Bridge, the city's first permanent Danube crossing, was built in 1839–49. The unification of Budapest in 1873 and the 1,000-year anniversary, in 1896, of the Magyar conquest also boosted the city's

development. The medieval walls that originally marked Pest's limits were crossed as the area expanded and was urbanized. This period produced some of the most important buildings in Hungary, including St Stephen's Basilica, Parliament and the Hungarian Academy of Science. Many Neo-Classical residences were also built, particularly on Nádor utca, Akadémia utca and Október 6 utca.

Sights at a Glance

Historic Buildings and Palaces
- ❶ Parliament pp84–5
- ❸ Ministry of Agriculture
- ❻ Gresham Palace
- ❼ Hungarian Academy of Sciences
- ❿ Drechsler Palace
- ⓬ Radisson Blu Béke Hotel

Theatres
- ❾ State Opera House pp92–3
- ⓫ Budapest Operetta Theatre

Museums
- ❷ Museum of Ethnography

Squares
- ❹ Liberty Square
- ❺ Széchenyi Square

Churches
- ❽ St Stephen's Basilica pp90–91

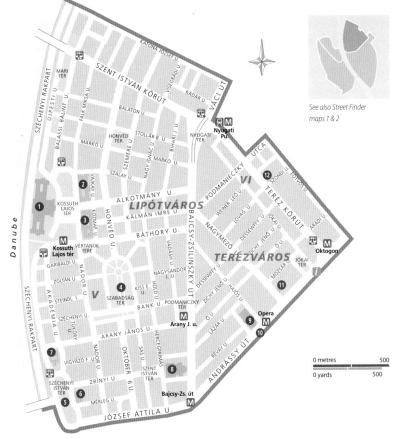

See also Street Finder maps 1 & 2

◄ Magnificent Neo-Gothic craftsmanship in the Hungarian Parliament building

For keys to map symbols see back flap

Street-by-Street: Kossuth Square

This square expresses well the pomp and pride with which Pest was developed during the 19th and early 20th centuries. Parliament dominates the square on the Danube side, but equally imposing are the Ministry of Agriculture and the Museum of Ethnography on the opposite side. Several monuments commemorate nationalist leaders and provide a visual record of Hungary's recent political history.

❷ **Museum of Ethnography**
Among 250,000 exhibits amassed in the museum's collection is a captivating collection of folk costumes representing the various nationalities and ethnic groups in Hungary.

❶ **Parliament**
This building has become the recognized symbol of democracy in Hungary, despite the fact that the dome was crowned by a red star during the Communist period.

Attila Jòzsef was a radical poet whose work sensitively explored the human condition. In 1937 he committed suicide, aged 32. This statue by László Marton dates from 1980.

BALASSI BALINT U

KOSSU LAJOS TÉR

Lajos Kossuth (1802–94)

Lajos Kossuth, after whom this square is named, is still immensely popular in Hungary today. Kossuth led the 1848–9 uprising against Austrian rule (see pp42–6) and was one of the most outstanding political figures in Hungary. A member of the first democratic government during the uprising, he briefly became its leader before being exiled after the revolt was quashed in 1849. He died in Turin in 1894.

Stained-glass window depicting Lajos Kossuth

0 metres 150
0 yards 150

Ferenc Rákóczi II, the prince of Transylvania, led one of the earliest uprisings for national independence against the Habsburgs in 1703–11. This bronze equestrian monument, standing in front of Parliament, was created by János Pásztor in 1937.

Locator Map
See Street Finder maps 1 & 2

❸ Ministry of Agriculture
A massive Corinthian colonnade supporting an entablature lends this Neo-Classical building a dignified character.

This monument to Imre Nagy symbolizes the pro-reform Communist prime minister who rose up with the people against Soviet rule in 1956 – a protest that cost him his life two years later.

The former headquarters of Hungarian TV, this elegant Secessionist building was designed by Ignác Alpár and constructed in 1905. It originally housed the Stock Exchange.

Plaque commemorating Brigadier Woroniecki, hero of the uprising of 1848–9

Z A L A Y U

V E C S E Y U

G A R I B A L D I U

N A D O R U

Key
— Suggested route

❶ Parliament

Hungary's Parliament, the country's largest building, has become a symbol of Budapest. A competition held to choose its design was won by Imre Steindl, who based his plans on the Houses of Parliament in London, built by Charles Barry in 1837–47. Steindl's rich Neo-Gothic masterpiece, constructed between 1885 and 1904, is 268 m (880 ft) long and 96 m (315 ft) high, and contains 691 rooms.

Parliament Visitor Centre
The Neo-Gothic northern façade of the parliamentary building overlooks the contemporary Visitor Centre's entrance, which houses educational exhibitions in state of the art surroundings.

★ Domed Hall
Adorning the massive pillars that support Parliament's central dome are figures of some of Hungary's rulers.

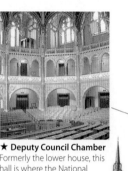

★ Deputy Council Chamber
Formerly the lower house, this hall is where the National Assembly now convenes. Two paintings by Zsigmond Vajda, specially commissioned for the building, hang on either side of the Speaker's lectern.

Gables
Almost every corner of the Parliament building features gables with pinnacles based on Gothic sculptures.

Lobby
Lobbies, the venues for political discussions, are to be found along corridors beneath the stained-glass windows.

Dome
The ceiling of the 96-m-(315-ft-) high dome is covered in an intricate design of Neo-Gothic gilding combined with heraldic decoration.

Tapestry Hall
This room, on the Danube side of the Domed Hall, has a tapestry depicting Prince Árpád, with seven Magyar leaders under his command, as he signs a peace treaty and takes an oath.

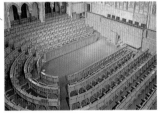

Old Upper House Hall
This vast hall is virtually a mirror image of the Deputy Council Chamber. Both halls have public galleries running around a horseshoe-shaped interior.

The main entrance on Kossuth Lajos tér

KEY

① **South wing**

② **Danube façade**

③ **The Royal Insignia**, excluding the Coronation Mantle *(see p102)*, is kept in the Domed Hall.

④ **North wing**

⑤ **Tickets can be bought at gate 10**

Main Staircase
The best contemporary artists were invited to decorate the interior. The sumptuous main staircase features ceiling frescoes by Károly Lotz and sculptures by György Kiss.

The magnificent façade of the Museum of Ethnography

❷ Museum of Ethnography

Néprajzi Múzeum

Kossuth Lajos tér 12. **Map** 2 D3.
Tel (1) 473 24 42. 🚌 2, 70. Ⓜ Kossuth Lajos tér. **Open** 10am–6pm Tue–Sun.
📷 🎫 ♿ Ⓦ neprajz.hu

This building, designed by Alajos Hauszmann and constructed between 1893 and 1896, was built as the Palace of Justice and, until 1945, served as the Supreme Court.

The building's design links elements of Renaissance, Baroque and Classicism. The façade is dominated by a vast portico crowned by two towers. A gable features the figure of the Roman goddess of justice in a chariot drawn by three horses, created by Károly Senyei. The grand hall inside the main entrance boasts a marvellous staircase and frescoes by Károly Lotz.

The building was first used as a museum in 1957, housing the Hungarian National Gallery *(see pp62–3)*, which was later transferred to the Royal Palace. The Museum of Ethnography has been here since 1973.

The museum's collection was established in 1872, in the Department of Ethnography at the Hungarian National Museum *(see pp102–3)*. There are now around 240,000 exhibits, although most are not on display. The collection includes artifacts reflecting the rural folk culture of Hungary from the prehistoric era to the 20th century. A map dating from 1909 shows the settlement areas of the various groups who came to be included in Hungary. Ethnic items relating to these communities, as well as early artifacts of the peoples of North and South America, Africa, Asia and Australia, can also be seen.

❸ Ministry of Agriculture

Földművelésügyi Minisztérium

Kossuth Lajos tér 11. **Map** 2 D4.
Ⓜ Kossuth Lajos tér.

On the southeastern side of Kossuth Square is a huge building, bordered by streets on all four sides, which was built for the Ministry of Agriculture by Gyula Bukovics at the end of the 19th century.

The façade is designed in a typical late Historicist style, drawing heavily on Neo-Classical motifs. The columns of the colonnade are echoed in the well-proportioned pedimented windows above.

On the wall to the right of the building, two commemorative plaques can be seen. The first is dedicated to the commanding officer of the Polish Legion, who was also a hero of the 1848–9 uprising *(see pp46)*. Brigadier Woroniecki, renowned for his bravery, was shot down on this spot by the Austrians in 1849. The second plaque honours Endre Ságvári, a Hungarian hero of the resistance movement, who died when fighting the Fascists in 1944.

The metal balls studding one part of the wall are set into bullet holes and form a memorial for the civilian victims of the shooting at Kossuth tér on 25 October 1956, when a peaceful demonstration during the revolution turned violent. The two sculptures in front of the building are by Árpád Somogyi: the *Reaper Lad* (1956) and the *Female Agronomist* (1954).

❹ Liberty Square

Szabadság tér

Map 2 D4. Ⓜ Kossuth Lajos tér, Arany János utca.

After the demolition of the Neugebäude Barracks in 1886, Liberty Square was laid out in their place. The barracks, built for the Austrian troops, once dominated the southern part of Lipótváros (Leopold Town). It was here that Hungary's first independent prime minister, Count Lajos Batthyány, was executed on 6 October 1849. Since 1926, an eternal flame has been burning at the corner of Aulich utca, Hold utca and Báthory utca to honour all who were executed.

Two impressive buildings by Ignác Alpár stand on opposite sides of the square. The former Stock Exchange dates from 1905 and shows the influence of the Secession style. The Hungarian National Bank (Magyar Nemzeti Bank), also from 1905, is decorated in Historicist style. An obelisk by Károly Antal at the northern end of the square commemorates the Red Army soldiers who died during the siege of Budapest in 1944–5. A second statue honours US General Harry Hill Bandholtz, who foiled the looting of the Hungarian National Museum.

Bas-reliefs on the former Stock Exchange in Liberty Square

Secession Architecture

Visitors to Budapest are often impressed by its wonderful range of late 19th- and early 20th-century buildings. The majority of these are found in central Pest and around the Városliget district *(see pp110–11)*; Buda was already developed at this stage and so boasts few examples. The Secession Movement started among groups of avant-garde artists in Paris and Vienna, from where the term "Secession" comes. In Budapest, the Secessionist style was also the inspiration for what would develop into the Hungarian National style. Secessionist architecture is characterized by decorative forms, glazed ceramics and the artistic implementation of modern technical solutions.

Ödön Lechner (1845–1914), Hungary's most influential Secessionist architect, combined modern functionalism and characteristically decorative forms.

The former Post Savings Bank has a splendid main staircase designed by Ödön Lechner. It is embellished by fine balusters, spherical lamps and decorative window frames.

The Geological and Geophysical Institute of Hungary is characterized by its stunning blue Zsolnay ceramic roof tiles. Designed by Ödön Lechner, the building dates from 1898–9. The central pitched roof is topped by four human figures bent under the weight of a large globe.

Finely crafted peacocks, a classic Secession motif, adorn the wrought-iron gates of Gresham Palace. This former office block, now a luxury hotel *(see p88)*, was built by Zsigmond Quittner in 1905–7.

This vase by István Sovánák stands in the Museum of Applied Arts. Its plain shape and Oriental flower motif hint at the many Eastern elements that crept into later Secessionist works of art.

This window at the Hungarian National Bank was created by Miksa Róth in 1905. Róth (1865–1944) was Hungary's leading exponent of stained-glass windows. His windows also adorn Budapest's Parliament.

Reinforced concrete, steel and glass were often used together to create large, light interiors. The foyer of the Gellért Hotel and Baths Complex is a perfect example of this technique.

Monument to Ferenc Deák, dating from 1887, in Széchenyi Square

❺ Széchenyi Square

Széchenyi István tér

Map 1 C5. 🚌 16. 🚋 2.

Széchenyi Square has been known by several different names – Franz Joseph Square, Unloading Square and, until 2011, Roosevelt Square – a title given to it in 1947. It leads into the Pest side of the **Chain Bridge**, which was designed by Englishman William Tierney Clark and built by the Scot Adam Clark in 1839–49. It was the city's first permanent Danube bridge and a major feat of engineering.

At the beginning of the 20th century the square was lined with hotels, the Diana Baths and the Lloyd Palace designed by József Hild. The only building from the previous century still standing today is the Hungarian Academy of Sciences. All other buildings were demolished and replaced by the Gresham Palace and the Bank of Hungary, on the corner of József Attila utca.

There is a statue to Baron József Eötvös (1813–71), a reformer of public education, in front of the InterContinental Budapest. In the centre of the square are monuments to two politicians with quite different ideologies: Count István Széchenyi (1791–1860), the leading social and political reformer of his age and initiator of the Chain Bridge, and Ferenc Deák (1803–76), who was instrumental in the Compromise of 1867, which led to the Dual Monarchy *(see p46)*.

❻ Gresham Palace

Gresham palota

Széchenyi István 5–7. **Map** 2 D5. **Tel** (1) 268 60 00. 🚌 16. 🚋 2. 🌐 **fourseasons.com/budapest**

This Secession palace aroused both controversy and praise from the moment it was built. One of Budapest's most distinctive pieces of architecture, it was commissioned by the London-based Gresham Life Assurance Company from Zsigmond Quittner and the brothers József and László Vágó, and completed in 1907.

The enormous edifice enjoys an imposing location directly opposite the Chain Bridge. The façade features classic Secession motifs *(see p87)*, such as curvilinear forms and organic themes. The ornately carved window surrounds appear as though they are projecting from the walls, blending seamlessly with the architecture. The bust by Ede Telcs, at the top of the façade, is of Sir Thomas Gresham. The founder of the Royal Exchange in London, he came up with Gresham's Law: "bad money drives out good".

On the ground floor of the palace there is a T-shaped arcade, covered by a multi-coloured glazed roof, which is occupied by shops and a restaurant. The entrance to the arcade is marked by a beautiful wrought-iron gate with peacock motifs. Still the original

Bust of Sir Thomas Gresham on the façade of the Gresham Palace

gate, it is widely regarded as one of the most splendid examples of design from the Secession era. Inside the building, the second floor of the Kossuth stairway has a stained-glass window by Miksa Róth, featuring a portrait of Lajos Kossuth *(see p82)*.

In 2004 the palace was restored and reopened as a Four Seasons Hotel, the second in central Europe and the first in Hungary. Visitors are welcome to admire its splendours.

Miklós Izsó's sculptures inside the Hungarian Academy of Sciences

❼ Hungarian Academy of Sciences

Magyar Tudományos Akadémia

Széchenyi István tér 9. **Map** 1 C5. **Tel** (1) 411 61 00. 🚌 16. Academy and Collection of Art: **Open** 11am–4pm Mon–Fri. **Closed** Jun–Aug. 🌐 **mta.hu**

Built in 1862–4, this Neo-Renaissance building was designed by the architect Friedrich August Stüler.

Six statues, representing the disciplines of knowledge – law, history, mathematics, sciences, philosophy and linguistics – and the works of Emil Wolf and Miklós Izsó, adorn the façade. On the Danube side, allegories of poetry, astronomy and archaeology can be seen, while the building's corners have statues of renowned thinkers including Newton and Descartes. Inside, there is a library and the Academy's Collection of Art.

The Neo-Renaissance façade of the Drechsler Palace

❽ St Stephen's Basilica
Szent István bazilika

See pp90–91.

❾ State Opera House
Magyar Állami Operaház

See pp92–3.

❿ Drechsler Palace
Drechsler palota

Andrássy út 25. **Map** 2 E4/5.
Ⓜ Opera.

Formerly the State Ballet Institute, the Drechsler Palace was originally built as Neo-Renaissance apartments for the Hungarian Railways Pension Fund in 1883. It was designed by Gyula Pártos and Ödön Lechner to harmonize with the façade of the State Opera House *(see pp92–3)*, and is of great architectural importance to the area.

The palace's name derives from the Drechsler Café, which occupied the ground floor towards the end of the 19th and in the early 20th century.

⓫ Budapest Operetta Theatre
Budapesti Operettszínház

Nagymező utca 17. **Map** 2 E4.
Tel (1) 472 20 30. Ⓜ Oktogon.
🚊 4, 6, 70. Ⓦ operettszinhaz.hu

Budapest has long enjoyed a good reputation for musical entertainment, and its operetta scene is over 100 years old. Operettas were first staged on this site in the Orfeum Theatre, designed in the Neo-Baroque style by the Viennese architects Fellner and Helmer in 1898. In 1922, the US entrepreneur Ben Blumenthal redeveloped the building and opened the Capital Operetta Theatre, which then specialized in the genre. After 1936, this theatre became the only venue for operetta in Budapest.

The theatre presents light opera by international and Hungarian composers, such as Imre Kálmán, Ferenc Lehár and Pál Ábrahám.

⓬ Radisson Blu Béke Hotel
Radisson Blu Béke Hotel

Teréz körút 43. **Map** 2 E3. **Tel** (1) 889 39 00. Ⓜ Oktogon.
Ⓦ **danubiushotels.com/beke**

This elegant, historic hotel was built in 1896 as an apartment building, and in 1912 was restyled by Béla Málnai as the Hotel Britannia. A mosaic of 16th-century general György Szondi was added to the façade at this time.

In 1978 the hotel was taken over by the Radisson group, which restored the rich interiors to their former splendour. Notable features are the fine stained-glass windows and frescoes by Jenő Haranghy in the Szondi Lugas Restaurant, which illustrate the works of Richard Wagner. The Romeo and Juliet Conference Room and the Shakespeare Restaurant are named after the murals that decorate them. The Zsolnay Café serves cake and coffee on porcelain from the Pécs factory *(see p190)*.

Entrance to the Budapest Operetta Theatre on Nagymező utca

❽ St Stephen's Basilica

Dedicated to St Stephen, or István, the first Hungarian Christian king (see p65), this church was designed by József Hild in the Neo-Classical style, using a Greek cross floorplan. Construction began in 1851 and was taken over in 1867 by Miklós Ybl (see p93), who added the Neo-Renaissance dome after the original one collapsed in 1868. József Kauser completed the church in 1905. It received the title of Basilica Minor in 1938, the 900th anniversary of the death of Prince Imre (St Emeric), István's son.

Dome
Reaching 96 m (315 ft), the dome is visible from all over Budapest.

St Matthew
St Matthew is one of the four Evangelists represented in the niches on the exterior of the dome. They are all the work of the sculptor Leó Feszler.

Tower
A bell, weighing 9,250 kg (9 tons) is housed in this tower. It was funded by German Catholics to compensate for the original bell, which was looted by the Nazis in 1944.

Main Portal
The massive door is decorated with carvings depicting the heads of the 12 Apostles.

KEY

① Observation point

② **Figures of the 12 Apostles,** by Leó Feszler, crown the outer colonnade at the back of the church.

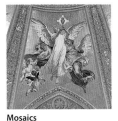

Mosaics
The dome is decorated with mosaics designed by Károly Lotz.

VISITORS' CHECKLIST

Practical Information
Szent István tér. **Map** 2 D5.
Tel (1) 338 21 51. **Open**
9am–5pm Mon–Fri, 9am–1pm
Sat, 1–5pm Sun.

Transport
Ⓜ Deák Ferenc tér.

★ Main Altar
In the centre of the altar there is a marble statue of St István by Alajos Stróbl. Scenes from the king's life are depicted behind the altar.

★ Holy Right Hand
Hungary's most unusual relic is the mummified forearm of St István. It is kept in the Chapel of the Holy Right Hand.

St Gellért and St Emeric
This portrayal of St Gellért and his pupil, St Emeric, is the work of Alajos Stróbl.

★ Painting by Gyula Benczúr
This image shows King István, left without an heir, dedicating Hungary to the Virgin Mary, who became *Patrona Hungariae*, the country's patron.

❾ State Opera House

Opened in September 1884, the State Opera House in Budapest was built to rival those of Paris, Vienna and Dresden. Its beautiful architecture and interiors were the life's work of the great Hungarian architect, Miklós Ybl. The interior contains ornamentation by Hungarian artists, including Alajos Strobl and Károly Lotz. During its lifetime, the State Opera House has seen some influential music directors, including Ferenc Erkel, composer of the Hungarian opera *Bánk Bán*, Gustav Mahler and Otto Klemperer.

Façade
A musical theme underlies the decoration of the symmetrical façade. In niches on either side of the main entrance there are figures of two of Hungary's most prominent composers, Ferenc Erkel and Ferenc (Franz) Liszt. Both were sculpted by Alajos Stróbl.

Murals
The vaulted ceiling of the foyer is covered in magnificent murals by Bertalan Székely and Mór Than. They depict the nine Muses.

★ Foyer
With its marble columns, gilded vaulted ceiling, murals and chandeliers, the foyer gives the State Opera House a feeling of opulence and grandeur.

Main Entrance
Wrought-iron lamps illuminate the wide stone staircase and the main entrance.

★ Main Staircase
Going to the opera was a great social occasion in the 19th century. A vast, sweeping staircase was an important element of the opera house, as it allowed ladies to show off their new gowns.

KEY

① **The side entrance** has a loggia that reflects the design of the main entrance.

Chandelier
The main hall is decorated with a bronze chandelier that weighs 3,050 kg (3 tons). It illuminates a magnificent fresco by Károly Lotz of the Greek gods on Olympus.

VISITORS' CHECKLIST

Practical Information
Andrássy út 22. **Map** 2 E4.
Tel (1) 332 81 97 or 353 01 70
(box office). 🎭 ✉ ♿ 🏠 📷
3pm & 4pm daily. 🌐 **opera.hu**

Transport
Ⓜ Opera. 🚌 4, 70. 🚋 4, 5, 6.

Central Stage
This proscenium arch stage employed the most modern technology of the time. It featured a revolving stage and metal hydraulic machinery.

★ Royal Box
Located centrally in the three-storey circle, the royal box is decorated with sculptures symbolizing the four operatic voices – soprano, alto, tenor and bass.

Miklós Ybl (1814–91)
The most prominent Hungarian architect of the second half of the 19th century, Miklós Ybl had an enormous influence on the development of Budapest. He was a practitioner of Historicism, and tended to use Neo-Renaissance forms. The State Opera House and the dome of St Stephen's Basilica are examples of his work. Ybl also built apartment buildings and palaces for the aristocracy in this style. A statue of the architect stands on the western bank of the Danube, in Miklós Ybl Square.

Bust of Miklós Ybl

CENTRAL PEST

At the end of the 17th century much of Pest was in ruins and few residents remained. Within the next decades, however, new residential districts were established – today's midtown suburbs. In the 19th century, redevelopment schemes introduced grand houses and apartment blocks, as well as secular and municipal buildings. Perhaps the

most prominent example of this work is the Hungarian National Museum. At this time Pest surpassed Buda as a centre for trade and industry. This was partly due to the Jewish community, who actively helped develop the area. Today it combines commerce and culture with beautiful architecture, elegant shopping arcades and plentiful cafés and restaurants.

Sights at a Glance

Museums

⓫ Museum of Applied Arts
⓬ Hungarian National Museum *pp102–3*
⓲ House of Terror Museum

Historic Buildings and Monuments

❸ Turkish Bank
❹ Pest County Hall
❼ Klotild Palaces
❽ City Council Chamber
❿ Ervin Szabó Library
⓯ New York Palace
⓰ Liszt Academy of Music
⓱ New Theatre

Churches and Synagogues

❻ Inner City Parish Church
❾ University Church
⓭ Great Synagogue

Streets and Squares

❶ Vigadó Square
❷ Mihály Vörösmarty Square
❺ Váci Street
⓮ Jewish Quarter

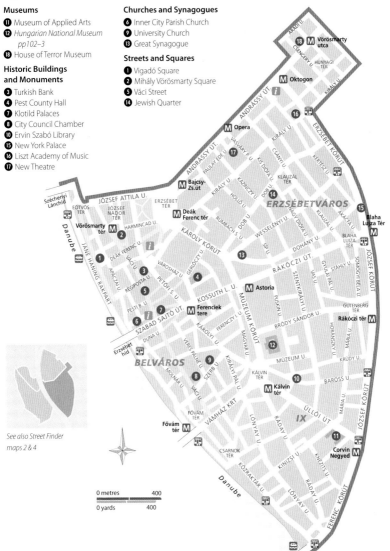

See also Street Finder maps 2 & 4

0 metres 400
0 yards 400

◀ Ornate façade on Váci Street, which like much of central Pest is pedestrianized   For keys to map symbols *see back flap*

Street-by-Street: Around Váci Street

The northern section of Váci Street has been Budapest's fashionable area for walking, meeting in cafés and shopping in elegant boutiques since the early 19th century. Its attractive promenade is an enjoyable place for a stroll in the evening, when it is stylishly illuminated.

Gerbeaud Cukrászda is one of the best patisseries in town.

Vigadó concert hall

Holy Figures adorn the 19th-century façade of the Baroque Servite Church.

❸ Turkish Bank

DOROTTYA U

VIGADÓ U

DEÁK FERENC U

VÁCI UTCA

RÉGIPOSTA UTCA

PESTI U

❷ Mihály Vörösmarty Square A Carrara marble monument to the poet Mihály Vörösmarty stands in this square. The statue was created by Ede Telcs and symbolizes the Hungarian nation united in the poet's words: "Your homeland, Hungary, serve unwaveringly".

Thonet House was built in 1888–90 by Ödön Lechner (*see p87*) and Gyula Pártos. The building stands today in its original form, featuring Zsolnay ceramics from Pécs.

Péterffy Palace, now the Százéves Étterem, is one of Pest's few remaining Baroque mansions. Built by András Mayerhoffer in 1755 for the magistrate János Péterffy, above the gateway there is a beautiful balcony supported by atlantes.

Remains of Contra Aquincum

5 ★ Váci Street
Budapest's most elegant promenade and shopping area is lined with fashion boutiques, cafés, fountains and statues. Off the street there are old courtyards and shopping arcades.

Locator Map
See Street Finder map 4

Párizsi Udvar is found on the corner of Kígyó utca and Petőfi Sándor utca. The arcade, which features shops, bookshops and a café, is decorated with attractive wrought-iron work.

7 ★ Klotild Palaces
These beautifully decorated twin buildings, designed as elegant apartment blocks in the Historicist style, flank each side of the approach to the Elizabeth Bridge.

0 metres 50
0 yards 50

Key

— Suggested route

6 ★ Inner City Parish Church
This limestone and marble tabernacle, in the church, dates from the early 16th century

Inside the elegant Gerbeaud patisserie, on Mihály Vörösmarty Square

❶ Vigadó Square
Vigadó tér

Map 4 D1. 🚊 2.

The Vigadó concert hall dominates the square with its mix of eclectic forms. Built to designs by Frigyes Feszl from 1859 to 1864, it replaces a predecessor destroyed by fire during the uprising of 1848–9 (*see pp46–7*). The façade has arched windows and includes features such as folk motifs, dancers on columns and busts of former monarchs, rulers and other Hungarian personalities. An old Hungarian coat of arms is also visible in the centre.

The Budapest Marriott Hotel, located on one side of the square, was designed by József Finta in 1969. It was one of the first modern hotels to be built in Budapest.

On the Danube promenade is a statue of a childlike figure sitting on the railings: *Little Princess*, by László Marton. Vigadó Square also has numerous craft stalls, cafés and restaurants.

❷ Mihály Vörösmarty Square
Vörösmarty Mihály tér

Map 2 D5. Ⓜ Vörösmarty tér.

In the middle of this splendid pedestrianized square stands a monument depicting the poet Mihály Vörösmarty (1800–55), after whom the square is named. Unveiled in 1908, it is the work of Ede Telcs. Behind the monument, on the eastern side of the square, is the Luxus department store. It is located in a three-storey corner building dating from 1911 and designed by Kálmán Giergl and Flóris Korb.

The main attraction on the northern side of the square is the renowned patisserie, Gerbeaud Cukrászda, first opened by Henrik Kugler in 1858. It was taken over by his business partner, the Swiss *pâtissier* Emil Gerbeaud, who was responsible for the richly decorated interior which survives to this day. It features fine woods, marble and bronze; ceiling stucco-work in Louis XIV style; chandeliers, lamps and Secession-style chairs brought from Paris. A tempting selection of frothy coffees, cakes, pastries and desserts is on offer. In summer, refreshments can be taken on a terrace overlooking the square.

❸ Turkish Bank
Török Bankház

Szervita tér 3. **Map** 4 D1.
Ⓜ Deák Ferenc tér.

Dating from 1906 and designed by Henrik Böhm and Ármin Hegedűs, the building that formerly housed the Turkish Bank is a wonderful example of the Secession style.

Modern construction methods were used to create the glass façade, which is set in reinforced concrete. Above the fenestration, in the gable, is a magnificent colourful mosaic created by Miksa Róth. Entitled *Glory to Hungary,* it depicts the country paying homage to the Virgin Mary, its patron saint, *Patrona Hungariae* (*see p91*). Angels and shepherds surround the Virgin, along with figures of Hungarian political heroes, such as Prince Ferenc Rákóczi (*see p45*), István Széchenyi (*see pp46*) and Lajos Kossuth (*see p82*).

Glory to Hungary, the mosaic on the façade of the Turkish Bank

❹ Pest County Hall
Pest Megyei Önkormányzat

Városház utca 7. **Map** 4 E1. **Tel** (1) 485 68 00 or 485 68 26. Ⓜ Ferenciek tere. **Open** 8am–6pm Mon–Fri.

Built in several stages, this is one of Pest's most beautiful, monumental Neo-Classical civic buildings. It was erected during the 19th century, as part of the plan for the city drawn up by the Embellishment Commission.

A seat of the Council of Pest has existed on this site since the late 17th century. By 1811, the building comprised two conference halls, a prison and a prison chapel. Between 1829 and 1832, a wing designed by József Hofrichter was added on Semmelweis utca.

In another development phase, in 1838–42, Mátyás Zitterbarth Jr completed the impressive façade, which overlooks Városház utca. It features a portico with six Corinthian columns that support a prominent tympanum.

County Hall was rebuilt and enlarged after destruction during World War II. Three internal courtyards were added. The first of these is surrounded by cloisters; summer concerts are often held here.

In the small adjoining street, Kamermayer Károly tér, stands an aluminium monument, designed in 1942 by Béla Szabados, to Budapest's first mayor, Károly Kamermayer (1829–97), who took office in 1873 after the unification of Óbuda, Buda and Pest.

❺ Váci Street
Váci utca

Map 4 D1–E2. Ⓜ Ferenciek tere.

Once two separate streets, which were joined at the beginning of the 18th century, the two ends of Váci Street still have distinct characters, the northern end being perhaps the more elegant. The whole street is pedestrianized, making this a popular visitor destination for shopping and strolling. Most of the buildings lining the street date from the 19th and early

Thonet House, with Zsolnay tile decoration, at No. 11 Váci Street

20th centuries. More recently, however, modern department stores, banks and shopping arcades have sprung up along the street among the older original buildings.

Philantia, a Secession-style florist's shop opened in 1905, now occupies part of the Neo-Classical block at No. 9, built in 1840 by József Hild. No. 9 also houses the Pest Theatre, where classic plays by Anton Chekhov, among others, are staged. The building was once occupied by the "Inn of the Seven Electors", which had a large ballroom and concert hall. It was here that a 12-year-old Ferenc (Franz) Liszt performed in 1823.

Crest of Pest in Inner City Parish Church

Thonet House, at No. 11, is most notable for the Zsolnay tiles from Pécs that adorn its façade. No. 13 is the oldest building on Váci Street and was built in 1805. In contrast, the Post-Modern Fontana department store at No. 16 was built in 1984. Outside there is a bronze fountain with a figure of the Greek god Hermes, dating from the mid-19th century.

The Nádor Hotel once stood at No. 20 and featured a statue of Archduke Palatine József in front of the entrance. Today the Taverna Hotel, designed by József Finta and opened in 1987, stands here. It has a popular coffee shop.

In a side street off Váci Street, at No. 13 Régiposta utca, stands a Modernist-style building. An unusual sight in Pest, this Bauhaus-influenced building dates from 1937 and is by Lajos Kozma.

❻ Inner City Parish Church
Belvárosi Plébánia templom

Március 15 tér 2. Map 4 D1. **Tel** (1) 318 31 08. Ⓜ Ferenciek tere. **Closed** until further notice.

Currently closed for archaeological excavations and reconstruction, this is the oldest building in Pest. The church was first established during the reign of St István, on the burial site of the martyred St Gellért. In the 12th century it was replaced by a Romanesque church, of which a wall fragment remains in the façade of the South Tower. In the 14th century it became a large Gothic construction, and subsequently a mosque. Damaged by the Great Fire of 1723, the church was partly rebuilt in Baroque style by György Paur in 1725–39. The interior also contains Neo-Classical elements by János Hild, as well as 20th-century works. The main altar (1948) is one such piece, replacing the original. It was painted by Károly Antal and Pál Molnár.

The Baroque nave of the Inner City Parish Church, dating from the 1730s

❼ Klotild Palaces
Klotild paloták

Szabadsajtó út. **Map** 4 D1.
Ⓜ Ferenciek tere.

On either side of Szabadsajtó utca, on the approach to the Elizabeth Bridge, stand two massive apartment blocks built in 1902. The buildings were commissioned by the daughter-in-law of Emperor Franz Joseph, Archduchess Klotild.

The palaces were designed by Flóris Korb and Kálmán Giergl in the Historicist style, with elements of Rococo decoration. Once they comprised entirely rented apartments; now only the upper floors remain in residential use. The ground floor is occupied by shops, a café and the Budapest Gallery; the right wing of the palace houses the Buddha-Bar Hotel.

A detail from the decorative façade of the City Council Chamber

Neo-Renaissance design in brick, with grotesques between the windows, while the interior features cast-iron Neo-Gothic motifs. The Great Debating Hall is decorated with mosaics designed by Károly Lotz.

Fashionable bars, restaurants and cafés, all assembled along a pedestrianized road, make the area around the Council Chamber a charming part of the city. There are some antiquarian bookshops and galleries located here, as well as fashion boutiques, and high-end designer shops.

❾ University Church
Egyetemi templom

Papnövelde utca 5–7. **Map** 4 E1/2.
Tel (1) 318 05 55. Ⓜ Kálvin tér.
Open 7am–7pm daily.

This single-aisle church is considered one of the most impressive Baroque churches in the city. It was built for the Pauline order between 1725 and 1742, and was probably designed by András Mayerhoffer. The tower was added in 1771. The Pauline order, founded in 1263 by Canon Euzebiusz, was the only religious order to be founded in Hungary. The magnificent

exterior features a tympanum and a row of pilasters that divide the façade. Figures of St Paul and St Anthony flank the emblem of the Pauline order, which crowns the exterior. The carved-wood interior of the main vestibule is also worth seeing.

Inside the church a row of side chapels stand behind unusual marble pilasters. In 1776 Johann Bergl painted the vaulted ceiling with frescoes depicting scenes from the life of Mary. Sadly, these frescoes are now in poor condition. The main altar dates from 1746, and the carved statues behind it are the work of József Hebenstreit. Above it is a copy of the painting *The Black Madonna of Czestochowa*, which is thought to date from 1720. Much of the Baroque interior is the work of the Pauline monks; for example the balustrade of the organ loft, the confessionals and the carved pulpit on the right.

The church – which is the property of Budapest University's Law Faculty – today often hosts concerts of choral and classical music, to raise funds for a massive programme of renovation.

One of the twin Klotild Palaces, by the approach to Elizabeth Bridge

❽ City Council Chamber
Új Városháza

Váci utca 62–64. **Map** 4 E2.
Tel (1) 235 17 00. Ⓜ Deák tér. 🖼

This three-storey edifice was built between 1870 and 1875 as offices for the newly unified city of Budapest. Its architect, Imre Steindl, was also responsible for designing the Parliament *(see pp84–5)*.

The building displays a mix of styles. The exterior is a

Magnificent sculptures decorating the pulpit in the University Church

Spiral staircase in one of the rooms of the Ervin Szabó Library

❿ Ervin Szabó Library
Fővárosi Szabó Ervin Könyvtár

Reviczky utca 1. **Map** 4 F2. **Tel** (1) 411 50 00. Ⓜ Kálvin tér. **Open** 10am–8pm Mon–Fri, 10am–4pm Sat.

In 1887, the wealthy industrialist Wenckheim family commissioned the architect Artur Meining to build a palace in the Neo-Baroque and Rococo style. The result was Wenckheim Palace, regarded as one of the most beautiful palaces in Budapest.

In 1926, the city council acquired the palace and converted it into a public lending library, which focuses on the city itself and social sciences.

It was named the Ervin Szabó Library after the politician and social reformer Ervin Szabó (1877–1918), who was the library's first director. The library has over 100 branches throughout Budapest and houses some three million books.

Beautifully renovated, the library boasts one of the most elegant reading rooms anywhere. It features glorious stucco decoration with gold tracery, enormous chandeliers and finely worked wooden staircases. Also worth particular attention are the richly gilded salons on the first floor and the dome above an oval panel of reliefs. Outside, the magnificent wrought-iron gates, dating from 1897, are the work of Gyula Jungfer.

⓫ Museum of Applied Arts
Iparművészeti Múzeum

Üllői út 33–7. **Map** 4 F2. **Tel** (1) 456 51 07. Ⓜ Ferenc körút. **Open** 10am–6pm Tue–Sun. ⓦ **imm.hu**

The Museum of Applied Arts was opened in 1896 by Emperor Franz Joseph as part of the Millennium Celebrations (*see p108*). The collection is housed not within a Neo-Classical building, but within an outstanding Secession building designed by Gyula Pártos and Ödön Lechner. The exterior incorporated elements inspired by the Orient as well as the Zsolnay ceramics characteristic of Lechner's work. Damaged in 1945 and again in 1956, the building has been restored to its original magnificence.

The building is set around a glorious, arcaded courtyard, surrounded by cloisters and designed in an Indian-Oriental style. The museum, established in 1872, comprises many superb examples of arts and crafts workmanship.

Among the museum's permanent collections is furniture from the 14th to the 20th centuries, including the furnishings of entire historic buildings in Hungary, fine French pieces and Thonet

A 17th-century dress in the Museum of Applied Arts

bentwood furniture. The fine metalwork collection comprises watches, jewellery and other items made by foreign and Hungarian craftsmen. The extensive ceramics and glassware collection contains early Haban ware, Bohemian glass, as well as glassmaking in Hungary. In the textiles section, superb European silks, including many from the 13th and 14th centuries, can be seen. It also traces the history of Hungarian lacemaking.

Amphitrite and triton pendant

The museum holds regular temporary exhibitions. The first-floor library, also dating from 1872, contains around 50,000 books, making it one of the largest in Hungary.

The Oriental-style inner courtyard of the Museum of Applied Arts

⑫ Hungarian National Museum

The Hungarian National Museum is the country's richest resource of art and artifacts relating to its own turbulent history. Founded in 1802, the museum owes its existence to Count Ferenc Széchényi, who bequeathed his collection of coins, books and documents to the nation. The museum's constantly expanding collection of art and documents is exhibited in an impressive Neo-Classical edifice built by Mihály Pollack.

Placing the Cornerstone (1864)
This painting by Miklós Barabás shows the ceremony that marked the beginning of construction of the Chain Bridge in 1842.

Silk Corset of Queen Elisabeth
This black silk corset was worn by Queen Elisabeth of Hungary and still bears the mark of the stab wound that killed her in Geneva on 10 September 1898.

First floor

★ **Funeral Crown**
This magnificent 13th-century golden crown was found in the ruins of the Dominican Church and Convent on Margaret Island in the Danube (see pp112–13).

★ **Coronation Mantle**
This textile masterpiece, made of Byzantine silk, was donated to the church in Székesfehérvár by St István in 1031. It became the Coronation Mantle in the 12th century.

Main entrance

Right Hand of Stalin
This hand is all that remains of the 8-m-(26-ft-) high statue of Stalin that stood in the Városliget in Budapest. A symbol of the Communist regime, the statue was destroyed in the Hungarian Revolution of 1956.

Second floor

Pelisse
This short jacket, dating from around 1620, is typical of Hungarian national costume. It belonged to Gábor Bethlen, a prince of Transylvania.

Gothic Well
These reconstructed fragments are part of a well from the Royal Palace at Visegrád. The well dates from the 14th-century rule of the Angevin dynasty.

Museum Guide
On the first floor is the Coronation Mantle and the archaeological exhibition. Second-floor exhibits comprise Hungarian artifacts from the 11th to the 20th centuries. The lapidaries are on the ground floor and in the basement.

★ Golden Stag
This hand-forged Iron Age figure dates from the 6th century BC. It was originally part of a Scythian prince's shield.

Key
- Coronation Mantle
- Archaeological exhibition
- 11th- to 17th-century exhibition
- 18th- to 19th-century exhibition
- 20th-century exhibition

⓭ Great Synagogue

Zsinagóga

Dohány utca 2. **Map** 4 E1. **Tel** (1) 462
04 77. Ⓜ Astoria. 🚋 74. Jewish
Museum: **Open** Mar–Oct: 10am–6pm
Mon–Thu & Sun, 10am–4:30pm Fri;
Nov–Feb: 10am–4pm Mon–Thu &
Sun, 10am–2pm Fri. ♿ 📷

The Great Synagogue is the
largest in Europe. Built in a
Byzantine-Moorish style by the
Viennese architect Ludwig
Förster in 1854–9, it has three
naves and, according to
orthodox tradition, separate
galleries for women. Together
the naves and galleries can
accommodate up to 3,000
worshippers. Some features,
such as the position of the
reading platform, reflect
elements of Judaic reform. The
interior has valuable decorative
fittings, particularly those on the
Ark of the Law, by Frigyes Feszl.

A large rose window is
flanked by two richly
decorated towers crowned
by distinctive onion domes.

A Hebrew inscription
from the Second Book of
Moses is situated under
the rose window.

The façade has white
and red bricks and
intricately designed
ceramic friezes.

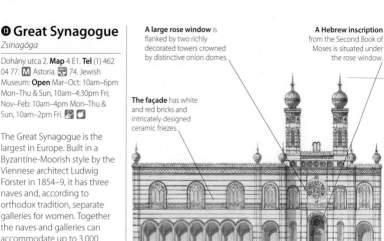

In 1931, a museum was
established, and a vast
collection of historical relics,
Judaic devotional items and
everyday objects, from ancient
Rome to the present day, has
been assembled. It includes the
book of Chevra Kadisha from
1792. There is also a haunting
Holocaust Memorial Room.

⓮ Jewish Quarter

Zsidó Negyed

Király utca, Rumbach Sebestyén
utca, Dohány utca & Akácfa utca.
Map 2 E5 & 2 F5. Ⓜ Deák Ferenc
tér, Astoria.

Jews first came to Hungary in
the 13th century and settled
in Buda and Óbuda. In the
19th century, a larger Jewish
community was established
outside the Pest city boundary,
in a small area of Erzsébetváros.
   In 1251, King Béla IV gave the
Jews of Buda certain priviliges,
including freedom of religion.
The Jewish community became
well integrated into Hungarian
society until, in 1941, a series of
anti-Semitic laws was passed by

Holocaust Memorial

Imre Varga's weeping willow sculpture was unveiled in 1991 in the
rear courtyard of the Synagogue, in memory of the 600,000
Hungarian Jews killed by the Nazis in World War II. It was part funded
by the late US-Hungarian actor Tony Curtis.

**Detail of the Orthodox Synagogue,
built in Byzantine-Moorish style**

Hungary's regent, Miklós Horthy,
and the wearing of the Star of
David was made compulsory. In
1944, a ghetto was created in
the area around the Great
Synagogue and the deportation
of thousands of Jews to camps,
including Auschwitz, was
implemented. After heavy
fighting between the Russian
and German armies, the Soviet
Red Army liberated the ghetto
on 18 January 1945. In total,
600,000 Hungarian Jews were
victims of the Holocaust.
A plaque on the Orthodox

Synagogue on Rumbach utca
commemorates the thousands
of Jews sent from Budapest.
   In the late 19th century,
three synagogues were built
and many Jewish shops and
workshops were established.
Kosher businesses, such as
the Hanna Étterem in the
courtyard of the Orthodox
Synagogue, and the butcher
at No. 41 Kazinczy utca, were
a common feature. Shops,
galleries and cafés are now
springing up, attracting young
locals and tourists.

The Liszt Academy's Grand Hall, with gilding restored to its 1907 magnificence

⓯ New York Palace
New York palota

Erzsébet körút 9–11. **Map** 2 F5.
Tel (1) 886 61 11. Blaha Lujza tér.
🖥 budapest.boscolohotels.com

Built in 1891–5 to a design by
the architect Alajos Hauszmann,
the New York Palace was once
the offices of an American insurance firm. Today it is a luxurious
5-star hotel. The building
displays an eclectic mix of Neo-
Baroque and Secession motifs.
The decorative sculptures that
animate the façade are the work
of Károly Senyei.

On the ground floor is the
renowned New York Café. Its
walls are adorned with paintings
by Gusztáv Mannheimer and
Károly Lotz. The beautiful, richly
gilded Neo-Baroque interior,
with its grand chandeliers and
marble pillars, was once the
favourite haunt of literary and
artistic circles, though today it
tends to attract mainly tourists.

⓰ Liszt Academy of Music
Liszt Ferenc Zeneakadémia

Liszt Ferenc tér 8. **Map** 2 F4.
Tel (1) 321 06 90. 🚌 4, 6 to Király
utca. 📷 by prior arrangement.
🖥 lisztacademy.hu

The Academy is housed in a late
Historicist palace, built in 1904–
7 by Kálmán Giergl and Flóris
Korb. Above the main entrance
there is a statue of Ferenc
(Franz) Liszt, by Alajos Stróbl.
The six bas-reliefs above its base
are by Ede Telcs, and depict the
history of music.

Restoration has recreated
the Secessionist interior in
all its original splendour,
while also outfitting the performance spaces with
21st-century technology.
The jewel is the ornate Grand
Hall, a world-famous concert
venue – not only for its
beauty, but also because of
its superb acoustics.

⓱ New Theatre
Új Színház

Paulay Ede utca 35. **Map** 2 E5.
Tel (1) 269 60 21. 🅜 Opera.

Originally completed in 1909,
this building has undergone
many transformations. It was
designed by Béla Lajta in the
Secession style, and, as the
home of the cabaret troupe
Parisian Mulató, became a
shrine to frivolity.

In 1921 the building was
completely restyled by László
Vágó, who turned it into a
theatre. After World War II, the
theatre gained a glass-and-steel
façade, and a children's theatre
company was based here.

Between 1988 and 1990 the
building was returned to its
original form, using Lajta's plans.
Gilding, stained glass and
marble once more adorn this
unusual building. Today,
Hungary's New Theatre is in
residence here.

⓲ House of Terror Museum
Terror Háza Múzeum

Andrássy út 60. **Map** 2 F4. **Tel** (1) 374
26 00. 🅜 Vörösmarty utca. 🚌 4, 6 to
Oktogon. **Open** 10am–6pm Tue–Sun.
📷 🖥 terrorhaza.hu

The museum records in graphic
detail the grim events that took
place here from 1936 – when
the Arrow Cross (the Hungarian
Nazi Party) took over the
building as its headquarters –
until 1956, when it was
turned into a club for Young
Communists. Set over three
floors, the most chilling part of
the museum is the basement,
where the various types of
prison cell have been recreated.

The House of Terror Museum, documenting
tragic 20th-century events

FURTHER AFIELD

Many of Budapest's greatest treasures are out of the city centre. The city's Art Nouveau zoo is found in the beautiful Városliget City Park. The vast Heroes' Square opposite has two outstanding art collections: the Museum of Fine Arts and the Műcsarnok Palace of Art. East of here a new museum honours the victims of Hungary's Holocaust, while to the west Margaret Island makes for a tranquil day out. North of Buda are the extensive ruins of the Roman city of Aquincum, founded around AD 100. To the west of the city, the beautiful Eagle Hill nature reserve and, further out, the wooded Buda Hills attract nature-lovers. Out to the east of Pest, the Jewish Cemetery is a reminder of the vibrant Jewish community in prewar Hungary, and the Memento Park to the south is a surreal relic from Soviet days.

Sights at a Glance

Museums

❷ Museum of Fine Arts
❸ Műcsarnok Palace of Art
❽ Aquincum
❿ Budapest Holocaust Memorial Centre
⓫ Palace of Arts

Historic Buildings and Monuments

❺ Vajdahunyad Castle
❻ Széchenyi Baths
⓮ Memento Park (pp116–7)

Churches

❶ St Anne's Church

Parks and Recreation Areas

❹ Városliget
❼ Margaret Island (pp112–3)
⓬ Eagle Hill Nature Reserve
⓭ Buda Hills

Cemeteries

❾ Jewish Cemetery

Key

═══ Motorway
▬▬ Main road
═══ Other road
── Railway

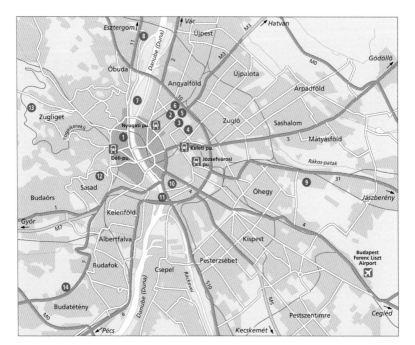

◀ Turtles basking in the Japanese Garden on peaceful Margaret Island

For keys to map symbols see back flap

Street-by-Street: Around Heroes' Square

Heroes' Square is a relic of a proud era in Hungary's history – it was here that the Millennium Celebrations opened in 1896. A striking example of this national pride is the Millennium Monument. Its colonnades feature statues of renowned Hungarian leaders and politicians, and the grand central column is crowned by a figure of the Archangel Gabriel. Vajdahunyad Castle was built in Városliget, or City Park, adjacent to the square. Probably the most flamboyant expression of the celebrations, it is composed of elements of the finest archi-tectural works found throughout Hungary.

❷ ★ Museum of Fine Arts
This monumental museum building has an eight-pillared portico supporting a tympanum.

Entrance to the zoo

Millennium Monument
Dominating Heroes' Square, this chariot is one of a pair of monuments symbolizing "War" and "Peace", by György Zala.

❸ Műcsarnok Palace of Art
The crest of Hungary decorates the façade of this building – the country's largest venue for artistic exhibitions.

Secession pavilion

The Hungarian Millennium Celebrations

The Millennium Celebrations in 1896 marked a high point in the development of Budapest and in the history of the Austro-Hungarian monarchy. The city underwent modernization on a scale unknown in Europe at that time. Hundreds of houses, palaces and civic buildings were constructed, gas lighting was introduced and continental Europe's first underground transport system was opened.

Archangel Gabriel

Key

— Suggested route

❻ ★ Széchenyi Baths
This is the largest complex of spa baths in Europe. Its hot springs, discovered in 1876, bubble up from a depth of 970 m (3,180 ft) and are reputed to have considerable healing properties.

❹ Városliget

Ják Chapel
This chapel faithfully reproduces the portal of a Benedictine church, dating from 1214, which can be found in the area of Ják (see p166), near the border with Austria. It is part of the Vajdahunyad Castle complex.

Statue of Anonymus
Completed in 1903 by Miklós Ligeti, this is one of Budapest's most famous monuments.

| 0 metres | 200 |
| 0 yards | 200 |

❺ ★ **Vajdahunyad Castle**
This Baroque section of the castle houses the Museum of Agriculture.

❶ St Anne's Church

Szent Anna templom

Batthyány tér 7. **Map** 1 B4. **Tel** (1) 201 34 04. Ⓜ Batthyány tér. **Open** Only for services. ✝ daily. Angelika Café: **Open** 9am–12pm daily.

Budapest is home to many churches, but the twin-towered Baroque parish church of the Víziváros district is one of the finest. Begun in 1740 by Kristóf Hamon and completed after his death by Mátyás Nepauer, it was seriously damaged by an earthquake in 1763. The dissolution of the Jesuit order – which had commissioned it – further delayed completion. It remained unconsecrated until 1805.

The church's façade features Buda's coat of arms on the tympanum, set between the magnificent Baroque spires. Inside, the High Altar (1773) depicts Mary as a child with St Anne, her mother.

High Altar in St Anne's Church, one of Károly Bebo's finest works

❷ Museum of Fine Arts

Szépművészeti Múzeum

Dózsa György út 41. **Tel** (1) 469 71 00. Ⓜ Hősök tere. 🚋 75, 79. 🚌 4, 20, 30, 105. **Open** 10am–5:30pm Tue–Sun. 📷 ♿ 📶 🅦 **szepmuveszeti.hu**

The origins of the Museum of Fine Arts' comprehensive collection date from 1870, when the state bought a magnificent collection of paintings from the aristocratic Esterházy family. The museum's collection was

A magnificently decorated ceiling at the Museum of Fine Arts

enriched by donations and acquisitions, and in 1906 it moved to its present location, a stunning Neo-Classical building with Italian Renaissance influences designed by Fülöp Herzog and Albert Schickedanz. The tympanum crowning the portico is supported by eight Corinthian columns. It depicts the Battle of the Centaurs and Lapiths, and is copied from the Temple of Zeus at Olympia, Greece.

The museum's collection encompasses a wide range of art from antiquity to the 20th century. Among the exhibition of Egyptian artifacts, most of which were unearthed by Hungarian archaeologists during 19th-century excavations, the collection of bronze figures from the New Kingdom of Ptolemy is the most fascinating. The collection of Greek vases is the highlight of the classical artifacts, along with the famous Grimani jug, which dates from the 5th century BC.

Grimani jug, Museum of Fine Arts

A small bronze figure by Leonardo da Vinci is the highlight of the sculpture gallery, while the rich collection of Dutch and Flemish art features the sublime *St John the Baptist's Sermon*, painted by Pieter Bruegel the Elder in 1566. Other collections of note include Italian and Spanish art with works by Raphael, El Greco and Goya, drawings and graphics with items by Dürer, and 19th- and 20th-century works by Pablo Picasso as well as gems from the French Impressionists.

❸ Műcsarnok Palace of Art

Műcsarnok

Dózsa György út 37. **Tel** (1) 460 70 00. Ⓜ Hősök tere. **Open** 10am–6pm Tue–Sun, noon–8pm Thu. 📷 ♿ 📶 🅦 **mucsarnok.hu**

Situated on the southern side of Heroes' Square, opposite the Museum of Fine Arts, is the largest exhibition space in all of Hungary. Temporary exhibitions of mainly contemporary painting and sculpture are held here.

Designed by Albert Schickedanz and Fülöp Herzog in 1895, the imposing Neo-Classical building is fronted by a vast six-columned portico. The mosaic, depicting St István as the patron saint of fine art, was added to the tympanum in 1938–41.

Behind the portico is a fresco by Lajos Deák-Ébner in three parts entitled *The Beginning of Sculpture, The Source of Arts* and *The Origins of Painting*.

❹ Városliget

Városliget

Városliget. Ⓜ Hősök tere, Széchenyi fürdő.

Városliget, or City Park, was once an area of marshland used as a royal hunting ground. Drained and planted during the reign of Maria Theresa, the park was designed and laid out in the English style in the late 19th century.

City Park was the centre for the 1896 Millennium Celebrations *(see p108)*, when the Museum of Fine Arts, Vajdahunyad Castle and the Heroes' Square Monument were built.

Today, attractions include a lake – an ice rink in winter and a boating lake in summer – overlooked by a Secession Pavilion. The park is also home to the Széchenyi Baths, Budapest's zoo and Gundel Restaurant, which opened in 1910 and where the Gundel *palacsinta*, a pancake, was invented.

One of the outdoor pools at the beautiful Széchenyi Baths

❺ Vajdahunyad Castle

Vajdahunyadvár

Városliget. **Tel** (1) 363 19 73. Ⓜ Széchenyi fürdő. 🚋 70, 72, 75, 79. 🚌 4, 20, 30. Museum of Agriculture: **Tel** (1) 363 11 17. **Open** Mid-Mar–mid-Oct: 10am–5pm Tue–Sun; mid-Oct–mid-Mar: 10am–4pm Tue–Fri, 10am–5pm Sat & Sun. 🅿 ♿ 📷 Ⓦ **mmgm.hu**

This fairytale-like building is located among the trees at the edge of the lake in Városliget. Not a genuine castle but a complex of buildings reflecting various architectural styles, it was designed by Ignác Alpár for the 1896 Millennium Celebrations *(see p108)*.

Alpár's creation illustrated the history of architecture in Hungary. Originally intended as temporary exhibition pavilions, the castle proved so popular with the public that, between 1904 and 1906, it was rebuilt using brick to create a permanent structure.

The pavilions are grouped chronologically by style, with individual styles linked together to give the impression of a single, cohesive design. Each of the pavilions uses authentic details copied from Hungary's most important historic buildings or is a looser interpretation of a style inspired by a specific architect of that period. The complex reflects more than 20 of Hungary's most renowned buildings. The medieval period, often considered a glorious time in Hungary's history, is emphasized, while the controversial Habsburg era is not.

The Romanesque complex features a copy of the portal from a church in Ják *(see p109)* as well as a monastic cloister and palace. The details on the Gothic pavilion are taken from castles such as that in Segesvár (now in Romania). The architect Fischer von Erlach inspired the Renaissance and Baroque complex. The façade copies part of the Bakócz chapel in the Esztergom cathedral *(see pp148–9)*.

The **Museum of Agriculture**, in the Baroque section, has interesting exhibits on cattle-breeding, wine making, hunting and fishing.

❻ Széchenyi Baths

Széchenyi Strandfürdő

Állatkerti körút 11. 🚋 72. **Tel** (1) 363 32 10. Ⓜ Széchenyi fürdő. Swimming pool: **Open** 6am–10pm daily; Thermal pool: **Open** 6am–7pm daily. 📷 Ⓦ **spasbudapest.hu**

A statue stands at the main entrance to the Széchenyi Baths, depicting geologist Vilmos Zsigmondy, who discovered a hot spring here while drilling a well in 1879.

The Széchenyi Baths are among the deepest and hottest in Budapest – the water reaches the surface at a temperature of 74–5° C (165° F). The springs, rich in minerals, are known for their alleged healing properties and are recommended for treating rheumatism and disorders of the nervous system, joints and muscles. The spa, housed in a Neo-Baroque building by Győző Czigler and Ede Dvorzsák, was constructed in 1909–13. In 1926, three open-air swimming pools were added. These are popular all year due to their high water temperatures.

View across the lake of the Gothic (left) and Renaissance (right) sections of Vajdahunyad Castle

⦿ Margaret Island

Inhabited as far back as Roman times, Margaret Island (Margitsziget) is a car-free, tranquil oasis in the middle of the Danube, a beautiful green space that has been open to the public since 1869. The 3-km (2-mile) long island served as a popular hunting ground for medieval kings, while monks were drawn to its peaceful setting. During Turkish rule it was used as a harem. In the 1200s Princess Margaret, daughter of Béla IV, spent most of her life as a recluse in the former convent here, and the island is named after her. Today Margaret Island still offers the perfect escape after sightseeing in the busy city.

Palatinus Strand
Opened in 1919, this is the largest outdoor swimming pool in Budapest. Its lush, grassy sunbathing areas and playgrounds make it especially popular with families.

Franciscan Church
Little remains of this early 14th-century church, which was abandoned in the 16th century. Yet the ruins, which include a glorious arched window and staircase, hint at its former size.

Margaret Island's Bicycles
There is no better way to explore the car-free island than hiring one of these family-sized bicycles.

KEY

① Margit Bridge
② Music fountain
③ Hajós Olympic Pool Complex
④ Margitsziget Small Zoo
⑤ St Michael's Church
⑥ Árpád Bridge

★ **Centenary Monument**
This monument was erected in 1973 to celebrate a century of united Budapest, the cities of Buda, Pest and Óbuda having merged in 1873. It was designed by István Kiss.

★ Japanese Garden
One of three landscaped parks on Margaret Island, the Japanese Garden features a wide range of flora as well as ponds and waterfalls, rock gardens and playgrounds.

VISITORS' CHECKLIST

Practical Information
Margitsziget, Budapest.
Map 2 D1. Danubius Grand Hotel Margitsziget: **Tel** (1) 889 47 00. Palatinus Strand Baths: **Tel** (1) 236 00 40. **Open** May–Aug: 9am–7pm; Sep: 10am–6pm. 🚹

Transport
🚃 4, 6. 🚌 26 from Nyugati Station.

Bodor Well
This musical well, built in 1936, is a copy of the original which stood in Târgu Mureş (today in Romania). On the hour, it plays gentle music.

Danubius Grand Hotel Margitsziget
This plush hotel, built in Neo-Renaissance style to designs by Miklós Ybl, was opened in 1873. For almost four decades it was the most fashionable hotel in the city, attracting aristocracy from all over Europe.

0 metres   150
0 yards   150

★ Water Tower
This unique 57-m (187-ft) tower was built in 1911 to provide clean water for the island's hotel. Protected by UNESCO, it offers great views from its Lookout Gallery.

Princess Margit

King Béla IV *(see p40)* swore that if he succeeded in repelling the Mongol invasion of 1241, he would offer his daughter to God. He kept his oath, sending his nine-year-old daughter Margit (Margaret) to the St Michael's Church and convent, which he built on the island. She led a pious and ascetic life, and at the age of 29 died on the island, which today carries her name.

The ruin of the 13th-century convent in which Margit spent 20 years of her life is probably the most important monument on the island. A marble plaque in the nave of the convent church ruins marks the spot where she is buried.

St Margit – stained-glass window, Gellért Hotel

View of the excavations of the Roman town Aquincum and the museum

❽ Aquincum
Aquincum

Szentendrei út 135. **Tel** (1) 250 16 50.
🚆 Aquincum. 🚌 34, 42, 106. Ruins:
Open Apr–Oct: 9am–6pm. **Closed**
Nov–Mar. Museum: **Open** Apr–Oct:
10am–6pm; Nov–Mar: 10am–4pm.
📷 ♿ 🅆 aquincum.hu

The remains of the Roman
town of Aquincum were
excavated at the end of the
19th century. Visitors today are
free to stroll along its streets,
viewing the outlines of
temples, baths, shops and
houses, in what was once the
centre of the town.
    The civilian town of Aquincum,
capital of the Roman province
of Pannonia Inferior, was
founded at the beginning of the
2nd century AD, a couple of
decades after a legionary fortress
had been established to its
south. For centuries, it was the
largest city in central Europe.
    In the centre of the site a
museum is housed in a Neo-
Classical lapidarium displaying
the most valuable Roman
archaeological finds from the
area. The items on display
include weapons and various
inscribed stone monuments.
    Only a fraction of the
former town is open to visitors
today, but it is nonetheless
impressive with its remarkable
central heating system based
on hot air circulated under
mosaic floors. A drain cover is
evidence that there was a good
water supply and drainage

system. The sanctuaries of the
goddesses Epona and Fortuna
can also be seen.
    On the other side of the hév
railway line, the remains of an
amphitheatre are visible, where
the town's inhabitants once
sought entertainment.

❾ Jewish Cemetery
Zsidó temető

Kozma utca 6. 🚌 37.

Next door to the Municipal
Cemetery is the Jewish
Cemetery, opened in 1893.
The many grand tombs here
are a vivid reminder of the
vigour and
success of
Budapest's
prewar
Jewish

Schmidl family tomb at the Jewish Cemetery

community. At the end of
the 19th century, nearly a
quarter of the city's inhabitants
were Jewish. Tombs to look
out for as you stroll among
the graves include that of the
Wellisch family, designed in
1903 by Arthur Wellisch, and
that of Konrád Polnay, which
was designed five years later
by Gyula Fodor. Perhaps the
most eyecatching of all tombs
belongs to the Schmidl family.
The startlingly flamboyant
edifice, designed in 1903
by Hungary's prominent
architects Ödön Lechner and
Béla Lajta, is covered in vivid
turquoise ceramic tiles. The
central mosaic in green and
gold tiles represents the
Tree of Life.

❿ Budapest Holocaust Memorial Centre
Holokauszt Emlékközpont

Páva utca 39. **Tel** (1) 455 33 33.
Ⓜ Ferenc körút. 🚌 4, 6, 30, 30A.
Open 10am–6pm Tue–Sun.
🅆 hdke.hu

This outstanding memorial
centre is dedicated to the tens
of thousands of Hungarians
deported from the Budapest
Ghetto to Auschwitz in the
latter stages of World War II.
Housed in a former synagogue,
the exhibition tells of the fate
suffered by Hungarian Jews,
Gypsies and other victims.
    The most moving part of
the memorial is the former
main prayer hall, given over
to the photos of members
of the congregation who
once worshipped here.
The 8-m- (24-ft-) high
glass wall around the
centre, designed by
László Zsótér, is
inscribed with the
names of all Hun-
garians known to
have died in the
Shoah. It allows
new names to be
added; the goal is
one day to have a
complete list of all
who perished in
the Holocaust.

Foyer in the Palace of Arts, a multi-arts performance venue

⑪ Palace of Arts

Művészetek Palotája (MÜPA)

Komor Marcell utca 1. 🚋 1, 2, 2A, 24. Ticket office (for all events): **Tel** (1) 555 33 00 or online. **Open** 10am–6pm daily. 📷 **W** mupa.hu
Museum of Contemporary Art:
Tel (1) 555 34 44. **Open** 10am–8pm Tue–Sun. **W** ludwigmuseum.hu

The Palace of Arts, located in the Millennium City Centre on the Pest side of the Danube, between Lágymányos Bridge and the new National Theatre, brings together all the arts under one roof. Permanent residents in the palace include the Ludwig Museum of Contemporary Art, the Béla Bartók National Concert Hall, the Festival Theatre and the National Dance Theatre.

⑫ Eagle Hill Nature Reserve

Sas-hegy Természetvédelmi Terület

Tájék utca 26. **Tel** (1) 319 67 89. 🚌 8, 8A. **Open** 10am–6pm Tue, Fri–Sun & pub hols, or by arrangement. 📷 compulsory.

A nature reserve such as this that is close to the centre of a large city is a remarkable phenomenon.
    Access to the summit of this steep, 266-m- (872-ft-) high hill to the west of Gellért Hill *(see pp73)* is strictly regulated to protect the extremely rare animal and plant species found here. A smart residential quarter of attractive bourgeois villas, which lies on the lower slope of Eagle Hill, extends almost to the

fence of the wild and craggy 300-sq-m (360-sq-yd) reserve that it encloses. It is worth taking the guided walk in the reserve, particularly in spring or early autumn. This is one of the only places to see the endangered *Centaurea sadleriana*, a flower that resembles a cornflower but with a much larger flower head. The reserve is also home to a blue grass and a spider found nowhere else in the world, as well as extraordinary, colourful butterflies and a rare lizard.

⑬ Buda Hills

Budai-hegység

Ⓜ Széll Kálmán tér, then 🚋 56, then cog-wheel railway and chair lift.

To the west of the city centre are the wooded Buda Hills. There are many caves here, including Szemlőhegyi and Pálvölgyi-barlang.
    The first station of a cog-wheel railway, built in 1874, is on Szilágyi Erzsébet fasor. This runs up Sváb Hill – named after the Germanic Swabians, who settled here under the Habsburgs *(see pp44–5)* – and then Széchenyi Hill.
    From Széchenyi Hill a narrow-gauge railway covers a 12-km (7-mile) route to the Hűvös Valley. As in the days of the Soviet Young Pioneers movement, the railway is staffed by children, apart from the adult train drivers. At the top of János Hill stands the Erzsébet Look-Out Tower, designed by Frigyes Schulek in 1910. A chair lift connects János Hill with Zugligeti út and this is a good way of making the descent.

The Erzsébet Look-Out Tower at the summit of János Hill, Buda Hills

⑭ Memento Park

During Communist rule, Socialist Realism was the artistic movement, resulting in some of the most striking sculpture of the 20th century. While most of the other former Soviet-bloc countries iconoclastically toppled their Socialist statuary as soon as they had toppled their Socialist leaders, the more reflective Hungarians decided to preserve these unique public works of art, which until 1989 had stood in the country's major public squares. The propagandist statues, some of which were erected as late as the mid-1980s, are now displayed in this, Europe's most unusual theme park of Communism.

Béla Kun Memorial
Béla Kun was a Hungarian Communist who briefly ran the country in 1919 after leading a Russian-backed Communist coup. Kun's regime was quickly overthrown by nationalist forces led by Admiral Horthy, however, and Kun fled to Russia.

Hungarian-Soviet Friendship Memorial
A Hungarian worker greets a Red Army officer with a handshake in this classic piece of Soviet agitprop.

Karl Marx and Friedrich Engels
The authors of *The Communist Manifesto* stand together in a large archway.

Stalin's tribute

★ **Main Entrance**
The monumental main entrance and the austere wall that surrounds the park are designed to remind visitors of the restrictive nature of the Iron Curtain.

KEY

ⓘ Souvenir shop

Captain Steinmetz
In December 1944, the Hungarian-born Soviet Red Army Captain Miklós Steinmetz delivered the *Ultimátum* with the proposed terms for surrender from the Soviet troops to the Germans occupying Budapest. He was shot while returning to Soviet lines.

VISITORS' CHECKLIST

Practical Information
Balatoni út & Szabadkai utca, Budapest. **Road Map** D3. **Tel** (1) 424 75 00. **Open** Apr–Oct: 10am–dusk daily; Nov–Mar: 10am–4pm daily. 🅿️ ♿ 📷
W **mementopark.hu**

Transport
🚌 101, 150 from Kelenföld

★ Republic of Council's Monument
This monument honours the many European revolutionaries of all nationalities who flocked to Spain to fight there in the 1936–9 Civil War.

★ Workers' Movement Memorial
Two monstrously large hands are about to clasp a globe, and with it the working class of the world.

Souvenir Shop
There are hawkers and street sellers all over the former Eastern Bloc selling souvenirs of the Communist period, and much of this – two decades on – is not likely to be genuine. At the unique Statue Park souvenir shop some original memorabilia of Soviet Hungary, as well as quality reproductions, are on sale. There are Soviet-era flags and banners, excellent Soviet Army watches and kitsch Trabant keyrings. Also available on CD are the Communist anthem, "The Internationale", in many languages, as well as recordings of the incomparable Red Army Choir.

Reproduction Soviet flags, on sale in the souvenir shop

Lenin
Vladimir Lenin (1870–1924), leader of the 1917 Revolution and first head of the Soviet state, points the way to a bright Socialist future.

SHOPPING IN BUDAPEST

Shopping in Budapest has changed dramatically in recent years. Despite price rises since the return to a free-market economy, many Hungarian goods still represent good value for visitors. Major shopping streets include elegant, pedestrianized Váci Street *(see pp96–7)*, good for folk art, and the less fashionable but better-value Nagykörút, where locals do their shopping. For local goods, a visit to one of Budapest's many markets is recommended. These range in style from stunning 19th-century food halls, such as the Great Market Hall (Nagy Vásárcsarnok), to second-hand markets, such as the huge and lively Ecseri Flea Market, where everything from bric-a-brac to furniture and antiques can be found.

Opening Hours

Most shops in Budapest open 9am–5:30pm or 6pm Monday to Friday, and 9am–1pm on Saturday. Department stores open at 10am, while green-grocers, bakeries and super-markets are open 7am–8pm. Indoor markets and depart-ment stores currently open on Sunday, although a ban on Sunday opening is a regular topic for political debate. Many small shops selling groceries are open 24 hours a day, although in many districts alcohol can only be sold until 10pm.

Department Stores and Shopping Centres

Since the late 1990s, more than 20 department buildings and malls have opened in Budapest. Origin-ally drawing scepticism, depart-ment stores, such as **Arena Plaza**, have proved popular with the Hungarian populace. Providing a wealth of well-established European and international brands, the shopping centres normally sell men's and women's clothing, accessories and perfumes.

Smoked sausages on display at the Central Market Hall

WestEnd City Center, with over 350 stores, near the centre of the city, is worth a visit. Locals tend to shop at out-of-town malls, where parking is easier, although stylish **Mammut** on Széll Kálmán tér is frequented by more affluent Buda residents.

Markets

Markets are an essential part of life in Budapest. Perhaps the most spectacular are the five cavern-ous market halls around the city. All were built in the late 19th cen-tury and several are still used as

markets. The three-level **Central Market Hall** (Nagy Vásárcsarnok) on Fővám tér is the largest. Here, more than 180 stalls display a huge range of foods under a gleaming roof of coloured Zsolnay tiles. The market opens from 6am to 6pm Monday–Friday and 6am to 3pm Saturday. Other markets to explore are in **Fehérvári út** and **Fény utca**.

Beginning at 156 Nagykőrösi út in district XIX, tables at the vast outside **Ecseri Flea Market** are covered in Communist artifacts, second-hand clothes and bric-a-brac.

Food and Drink

Hungarian paprika, a wide varie-ty of spicy salamis and other fine foodstuffs, such as goose liver pâté, are widely available in the city's many lively markets, supermarkets and smaller deli-catessens. Visitors wishing to buy – and sample – Hungary's regional wines, including the golden Tokaji, should head for **Borház** in Pest's Jókai tér or **La Boutique des Vins** in József Attila utca, which stock a superb selection from all over the coun-try. Hungary's apricot and plum liqueurs and brandy *(pálinka)* can be purchased at **House of Hungarian Pálinka** in Rákóczi út.

Folk Art

Hungarian folk art such as embroidered peasant blouses and wooden carvings are still produced in many rural areas and sold in the capital. These can be found at flea markets around Moszkva tér and Parliament or the top floor of the Central Market Hall. If you

A small wine merchant, selling wines from Hungary's regions

are looking for handmade items in particular, head for **Tekla Folklór**.

Porcelain and Antiques

Dominated by 18th- and 19th-century pieces in the Habsburg style, the Budapest antiques scene is concentrated in the Castle District, around Falk Miksa utca and on Váci utca (Váci Street, *see pp96–7*). **Moró Antik** is a tiny shop specializing in 18th-century weapons. The huge **Nagyházi Gallery** sells everything from jewellery to furniture. Budapest's flea markets are good places to hunt for collectibles.

If looking to buy genuine **Herend** and **Zsolnay** porcelain, there are several outlets in Budapest. The **Hollóházi** porcelain factory also has a shop.

Clothes and Shoes

Made-to-measure clothes and shoes, as well as ready-made designer clothes, offer some of the best deals to be had in the capital. Clothes can be made up by a local designer in a choice of fabrics – often for a modest fee. At the top end, **Naray Tamas Atelier** is the showcase for one of Hungary's most celebrated designers. Shoemakers **Vass** offer handmade men's shoes, but they are expensive and can take some time to make.

WestEnd City Center, central Europe's largest shopping mall

Music

Hungary's rich musical traditions make for tempting low-priced items to buy. Good-quality CDs and music DVDs are mostly now found in bookshops, both new and second-hand, although the specialist **Rózsavölgyi Zeneműbolt** remains, and is great for traditional gypsy and village folk music, as well as orchestral works. The **Alexandra Book House** (and its palatial café) is in Párisi Nagyáruház, once a stylish department store with a wonderful Art Nouveau façade.

Traditional folk costumes, on sale from a street vendor

DIRECTORY

Department Stores and Shopping Centres

Arena Plaza
Kerepesi út 9.
Tel (1) 880 70 10.
🌐 arenaplaza.hu

Mammut I–II Mall
Lövőház utca 2–6 & Széll Kálmán tér. **Map** 1 A3.
Tel (1) 345 80 20.
🌐 mammut.hu

WestEnd City Center
Váci út 1–3.
Map 2 E3.
Tel (1) 238 77 77.

Markets

Budapest Flea Market
Zichy Mihály utca 14.
Tel (20) 933 39 79.

Central Market Hall
Vámház körút 1–3
(Fővám tér). **Map** 4 E2.
Tel (1) 366 33 00.

Ecseri Flea Market
Nagykőrösi út 156.
Tel (1) 282 95 63.

Fehérvári út Market
Fehérvári út 20.

Fény utca Market
Near Széll Kálmán tér.
Map 1 A4.

Food and Drink

Borház
Jókai tér 7.
Map 2 E4.
Tel (1) 353 48 49.

La Boutique des Vins
József Attila utca 12.
Map 2 D5. **Tel** (1) 317 59 19.

House of Hungarian Pálinka
Rákóczi út 17. **Map** 4
E1/2. **Tel** (1) 338 42 19.

Folk Art

Tekla Folklór
Váci utca 58. **Map** 4 D1.
Tel (1) 486 00 58.

Porcelain

Herend Shops
József Nádor tér 11.
Map 2 D5. **Tel** (1) 317 26 22.
Szentháromság utca 5.
Map 1 B5.
Tel (1) 225 10 50/51.
Andrássy út 16. **Map** 2 E4.
Tel (1) 374 00 06.

Hollóházi Shop
Rákóczi út 31.
Map 4 E1.
Tel (1) 413 14 63.

Zsolnay Shop
Kecskeméti utca 14.
Map 4 E2.
Tel (1) 318 26 43.

Antiques

Moró Antik
Falk Miksa utca 13. **Map** 2
D3. **Tel** (1) 311 08 14.

Nagyházi Gallery
Balaton utca 8. **Map** 2 D3.
Tel (1) 475 60 00.

Clothes and Shoes

Naray Tamas Atelier
Hajós utca 17. **Map** 2 E4.
Tel (1) 266 24 73.

Vass Shoes
Haris köz 2. **Map** 4 D1.
Tel (1) 318 23 75.

Music

Alexandra Book House
Párisi Nagyáruház ,
Andrássy út 39. **Map** 2 E4.
Tel (1) 484 80 00.

Rózsavölgyi Zeneműbolt
Szervita tér 5. **Map** 4 D1.
Tel (1) 318 35 00.

ENTERTAINMENT IN BUDAPEST

Budapest has been known as a city of entertainment since the late 19th century, when people would travel here from Vienna in search of a good time. Its buzzing nightclubs were frequented for their electric atmosphere and the beautiful girls that danced the spirited *csárdás* and the cancan.

Between the wars the city was as famous for its glittering society balls as for its more decadent delights. The half-century of Communist rule dampened the revelry, but since 1990 the Budapest music scene has flourished and theatres, cabarets, festivals, cinemas and discotheques are all buzzing.

Practical Information and Tickets

Two monthly cultural listings magazines, the *Programme* and the *Budapest Panorama*, contain information in English. Both are free and available in hotels and tourist information centres. Pamphlets and bulletins are often issued for festivals and other special events, and it is worth keeping an eye out for the poster pillars throughout the city.

Tickets for plays and concerts can be purchased in advance from the booking offices, such as **Ticket Express**, or the relevant venue. The best way of securing a seat for concerts at the **Liszt Academy of Music** (*see p105*) or major opera productions is via the **Cultur-Comfort Central Ticket Office**.

Opera, Classical and Sacred Music

The standard of opera in Budapest is very high. The **State Opera House** (*see pp92–3*) has a mainly classical repertoire, sung with Hungarian surtitles. The large hall of the Liszt Academy of Music (magnificently renovated) is the city's leading venue for classical music. Another venue for concerts and theatre is the **Palace of Arts (MÜPA)**. Classical concerts may also be held in the domed hall of Parliament (*see pp84–5*), where the acoustics are excellent. Other important venues for organ or choral music are **Mátyás Church** (*see pp66–7*), **St Stephen's Basilica** (*see pp90–91*) and the Great Synagogue (*see p104*).

Jazz, Traditional Hungarian and Rock Music

Jazz was very late in reaching Hungary. The best-known and revered Hungarian jazz band is the Benkó Dixieland Band, which during spring festivals (*see p34*) plays in various theatres and large halls. For

August Rock Festival on Óbudai-sziget

nightly performances (Sundays excepted), check out the well-regarded **Budapest Jazz Club**.

For traditional Hungarian music and dance, head to the **Hungarian Heritage House**, where authentic Hungarian dance evenings are held along with lessons for the young and old.

For fans of rock and pop, the biggest event of the year is the three-day **Sziget Festival** in August on Óbudai-sziget. Big names in rock and pop also play at the modern **Papp László Budapest SportArena**. For more live rock, try the party boat **A38** and **Fat Mo's**, a legendary live music venue.

Theatre and Cinema

Budapest has many theatres, which are worth visiting not only for their great repertoires, but also because most are located in beautiful historic buildings. Cinemas show the latest films soon after their world premieres, and most foreign films in Hungary are dubbed and subtitled into Hungarian. Visitors who do not speak Hungarian should choose the *angol nyelvű* (English soundtrack) version.

The main stage at the opulent Opera House, in Budapest

Corvintető nightclub, a lively rooftop venue with great views

Nightlife

The dynamic Budapest club scene changes from month to month, often week to week. For a great night with live DJs head to **Corvintető**, a roof garden on top of a 1926 department store. **LÄRM** is a suberb venue notable for its top DJs who play cutting-edge

music. **A38** also hosts lively club nights. Budapest's gay scene is legendary. **Action Bar** lives up to its name, with go-go dancing and more, while **Coxx Club** is a huge multi-level place that attracts a more mainstream crowd.

Despite strict new gaming laws in Hungary that have closed many gambling venues and may, eventually, close them all, a few **casinos** remain open, largely attracting gamblers from Europe and the Middle East.

Sign for Bahnhof music club

Children's Entertainment

The Royal Palace (see pp58–9) and the Castle District generally are good places to start, while a must is the ride up or down Castle Hill by funicular railway. The **Children's Railway** (Gyermekvasút) runs through

the woods in Buda Hills and is staffed mostly by children. The **Museum of Military History** enthrals older children with weapons, armour and battle scenes.

Most children enjoy the **Zoo**, and Budapest's is one of the largest in Europe. The **Great Capital Circus** is another ideal venue for family entertainment.

Façade of the vast Great Capital Circus building

DIRECTORY

Tickets

Cultur-Comfort Central Ticket Office
Paulay Ede utca 46. **Map 2** E5. **Tel** (1) 322 00 00.

Ticket Express
Andrássy út 18. **Map 2** E4.
Tel (1) 303 09 99.
w tex.hu

Opera, Classical and Sacred Music

Liszt Academy of Music
Liszt Ferenc tér 8. **Map 2** F4. **Tel** (1) 462 46 00.

Mátyás Church
Szentháromság tér 2.
Map 1 B4.
Tel (1) 355 56 57.

Palace of Arts (MÜPA)
Komor Marcell utca 1.
Tel (1) 555 33 00.
w mupa.hu

St Stephen's Basilica
Szent István tér 2. **Map 2** D5. **Tel** (1) 317 28 59.

State Opera House
Andrássy út 22. **Map 2** E4.
Tel (1) 331 25 50.
w opera.hu

Jazz, Traditional Hungarian and Rock Music

A38
Petőfi híd Budai hídfő.
Tel (1) 464 39 40. w a38.hu

Budapest Jazz Club
Hollán Ernő utca 7. **Map 2** D2. **Tel** (1) 798 72 89.

Fat Mo's
Nyáry Pál u. 11.
Tel (1) 266 80 27.

Hungarian Heritage House
Corvin tér 8, District 1 (Castle District).
Tel (1) 225 60 49.

Papp László Budapest SportArena
Jfjúság utca 4. Tickets from Ticketa **Tel** (1) 422 26 82.
w budapestarena.hu

Sziget Festival
w szigetfestival.com

Theatre and Cinema

Cinema City Westend
Váci út 1–3. **Map 2** E2.
Tel (40) 60 06 00.
w funzine.hu

József Katona Theatre
Petőfi Sándor utca 6.
Map 4 D1.
Tel (1) 266 52 00.

Margitsziget Openair Stage
Margitsziget Island.
Tel (1) 340 41 96.

Nemzeti Theatre
Bajor Gizi Park 1.
Tel (1) 476 68 00.

Casinos

Las Vegas Casino
Roosevelt tér 2. **Map 1** C5.
Tel (1) 266 20 83.
w lasvegascasino.hu

Tropicana Casino
Vigadó utca 2. **Map 4** D1.
Tel (1) 266 30 62.
w tropicanacasino.hu

Nightlife

Corvintető
Blaha Lujza tér 1–2.
Tel (20) 772 29 84.
w corvinteto.com

LÄRM
Akácfa utca 51.
w larm.hu

Gay Clubs

Action Bar
Magyar utca 42. **Map 4** E1. **Tel** (1) 266 91 48.
w action.gay.hu

Coxx Club
Dohány utca 38. **Map 2** F5. **Tel** (1) 344 48 84.
w coxx.hu

Children's Entertainment

Children's Railway
Széchenyi-hegy Station.
Tel (1) 395 54 20.
w gyermekvasut.hu

Great Capital Circus
Állatkerti körút 12/A.
Tel (1) 343 83 00.
w fnc.hu

Museum of Military History
Kapisztrán tér 2–4.
Map 1 A4.
Tel (1) 325 16 47.

Zoo
Állatkerti körút 6–12.
Tel (1) 273 49 00.
w zoobudapest.com

BUDAPEST STREET FINDER

The map references given for all the sights, hotels, bars, restaurants, shops and entertainment venues in Budapest refer to the maps in this section. Opposite is a complete index of street names marked on the maps. The map below shows the area of Budapest covered by the Street Finder; it is colour-coded by area. The Street Finder shows bus and tram routes and major sights together with other useful information listed in the key below. As an aid to navigation, all street names on the Street Finder and in the index are in Hungarian. Terms that may be confusing are *utca* (often abbreviated to *u*), which means "street", and *út* meaning "avenue", usually wide, busy roads. Other commonly used terms are *körút* (*krt*, ring road), *tér* (square), *köz* (lane), *körtér* (circus) and *híd* (bridge).

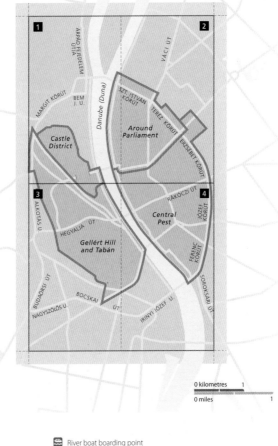

Scale of Map Pages	
0 metres 200	1:14,000
0 yards 200	

Key

 Major sight
Place of interest
Other building
Main bus stop
M Metro station
Funicular
hév station
Train station
Tram route
River boat boarding point
i Tourist information point
Hospital with casualty unit
Police station
Church
Synagogue
Railway line
Pedestrianized street

Street Finder Index

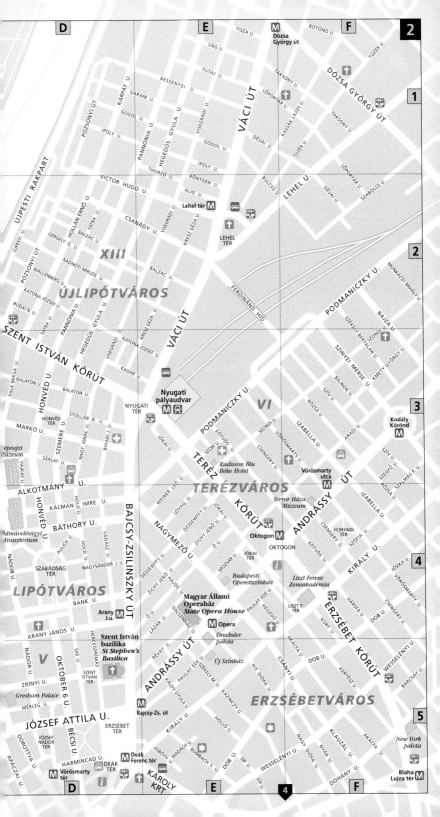

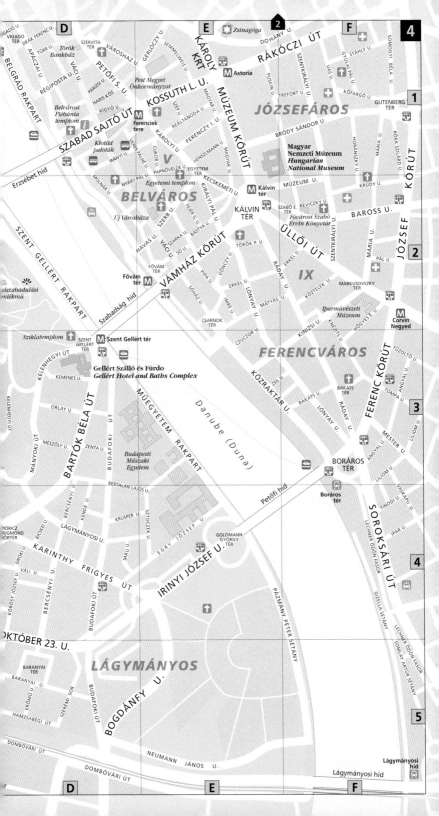

HUNGARY REGION BY REGION

Hungary at a Glance

Hungary was traditionally divided into four regions – the Great Plain, the Northern Highlands, Transdanubia and Transylvania – but since 1918, with the exception of a short period at the beginning of World War II, Transylvania has been a part of Romania. In this guide, the vast region of Transdanubia is divided into a northern and a southern half. While each region has its own traditions and values, culture and habits, Hungary is one of the most homogenous countries in the world. It is also one of the least urban countries in Europe: outside Budapest, no city has more than 200,000 inhabitants. The population is concentrated in small towns and thousands of villages, and it is the traditions of these smaller places that give the country its charm.

Firewatch Tower in Sopron
Located in the far northwest of the country, the attractive town of Sopron has a well-preserved medieval centre.

Royal Palace of Gödöllő
Franz Joseph's wife, "Sisi", loved staying here at the Habsburgs' fine summer residence in Gödöllő. The town also has a renowned local artists' colony.

Vác

Sopron

Győr

Gödöllő

Tatabánya

NORTHERN TRANSDANUBIA
(see pp150–81)

BUDAPEST
(see pp52–127)

Szombathely

AROUND
BUDAPEST
(see pp132–49)

Székesfehérvár

Veszprém

Zalaegerszeg

Siófok

Előszállás

Solt

Balatonlelle

Nagykanizsa

SOUTHERN
TRANSDANUBIA
(see pp182–211)

Vése

Kaposvár

Szekszárd

Baja

Szigetvár

Pécs

Pécs Cathedral
The ornate St Peter's Cathedral stands at the historic centre of this sunny town, while busy Széchenyi tér is dominated by a former mosque.

◄ View from the citadel of Visegrád, on the Danube Bend

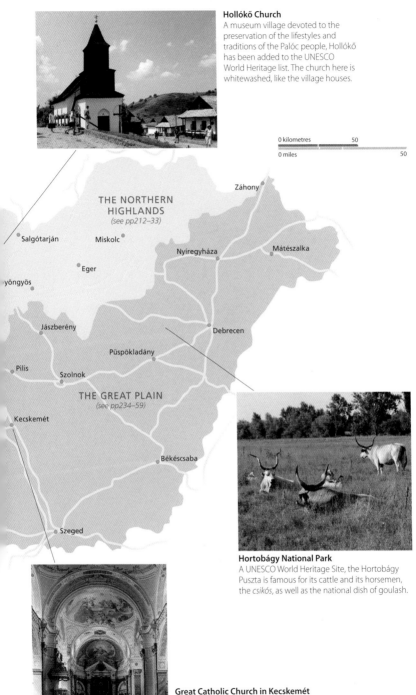

Hollókő Church
A museum village devoted to the preservation of the lifestyles and traditions of the Palóc people, Hollókő has been added to the UNESCO World Heritage list. The church here is whitewashed, like the village houses.

0 kilometres 50

0 miles 50

THE NORTHERN
HIGHLANDS
(see pp212–33)

Záhony

Salgótarján   Miskolc

Nyíregyháza

Mátészalka

Eger

yöngyös

Jászberény

Debrecen

Püspökladány

Pilis

Szolnok

THE GREAT PLAIN
(see pp234–59)

Kecskemét

Békéscsaba

Szeged

Hortobágy National Park
A UNESCO World Heritage Site, the Hortobágy Puszta is famous for its cattle and its horsemen, the *csikós*, as well as the national dish of goulash.

Great Catholic Church in Kecskemét
A centre of the arts and education, Kecskemét boasts some fine architecture, including this large Baroque edifice. Older buildings have been skilfully integrated into the modern cityscape.

AROUND BUDAPEST

Strategically sited castles and vast cathedrals, including Hungary's largest, look out over the pleasure boats navigating the Danube Bend. The unique evening sunlight here has always attracted artists to the region, and evidence of a rich cultural heritage is everywhere. Gödöllő boasts the stunning Royal Palace, while the Duna-Ipoly National Park offers a superb habitat for native wildlife.

With its darting twists and turns, steep banks and deep valleys, the Danube Bend has been a site of refuge for almost 2,000 years. Rome built garrisons here, and there are remnants of that great empire everywhere. The natural fortress that is the Danube's west bank was later the chosen site for the construction of the historic towns of Visegrád and Esztergom, both built with protection and defence in mind. Esztergom was the scene of the Hungarian conversion to Christianity, and Visegrád was the impenetrable seat of royal power. Later still came Szentendre, which, like Ráckeve to the south of the capital, was founded by Serbs fleeing persecution at home and, though few Serbs remain, traces of their culture and their religion are evident everywhere. Those who come

seeking respite today are the thousands of Budapest residents who keep holiday homes in the area, and the legions of visitors on short trips from the capital – a fact that is reflected in local prices.

Over on the east bank the rolling hills of the Börzsöny and the Duna-Ipoly National Park – home to more than half of Hungary's native bird species – make for sensational hiking, walking and birdwatching.

This is perhaps the most cosmopolitan part of Hungary, where visitors can expect warm, welcoming and multilingual hosts, but in summer it can be very hot and busy. As autumn usually brings plenty of rain and winter can be very cold, the early spring – March, April and May – may be the best time for exploring these historic places.

Magnificent frescoes in the Serbian Orthodox Church in Ráckeve

◄ Statue of István, the first Hungarian king, at Esztergom – the site of his coronation

Exploring Around Budapest

The countryside and villages around Budapest have always been a major draw for visitors to the capital. To the north is the Danube Bend (Dunakanyar), and in the middle of it the art-loving village of Szentendre. Further upriver are the Baroque town of Vác and Hungary's most sacred city, Esztergom. Beyond, the Duna-Ipoly National Park offers countless hiking and nature trails. The Royal Mansion in Gödöllő to the east is worth seeing, and south of Budapest are the pretty town of Ráckeve and the Ócsa Nature Reserve, a unique habitat of reedy bogs.

Beautiful waterlilies in the marshes around Ócsa

Getting Around

Budapest has an international airport, and from here destinations such as Szentendre, Gödöllő and Ócsa are best reached by train, on the Budapest suburban rail network (HÉV, *see p310*). Other sightseeing areas can be visited by train or car. During the summer months, the most relaxing way to reach the Danube Bend is by Mahart Passnave motorboat, departing northwards from Vigadó tér in Budapest. Services run to Esztergom and stop at most towns along the way. Other services go to Szentendre and Vác.

Inside Esztergom Basilica, centre of Catholicism in Hungary

For hotels and restaurants see pp264–269 and pp276–285

Sights at a Glance

The Royal Palace in Gödöllő, built by Count Antal Grassalkovich

Key

— Motorway
— Major road
····· Major road under construction
— Secondary road
···· Minor road
—·— Main railway
— Minor railway
▬▬ International border
— Regional border

A statue of Justice, crowning the Baroque town hall in Vác

For additional keys to symbols see back flap

Magnificent frescoes in the Serbian Orthodox Church in Ráckeve

❶ Ráckeve

43 km (27 miles) southwest of Budapest. **Road Map** C4. 🏙 8,500. 🚍 from Budapest. 🚤 from Budapest. 🚶 Tourinform, Eötvös utca 1, (24) 42 97 47.

The small town of Ráckeve has for centuries been considered the capital of Csepel Island, which extends 54 km (34 miles) south along the middle of the Danube from Budapest. Ráckeve (*Rác* means "Serb" in Hungarian) was founded in the 15th century by Serbs from Keve, who fled Serbia after the Turkish invasion.

The oldest building in the town is the **Serbian Orthodox Church** on Viola utca, built by some of the first Serbs to arrive here. Dating back to 1487, this is the oldest Orthodox church in Hungary. Its walls are covered in well-preserved frescoes, the first telling the story of the Nativity and the last depicting the Resurrection. A vast, colourful iconostasis separates the sanctuary from the nave. Two side chapels with Renaissance elements were added in the 16th century.

Ráckeve's peaceful and convenient situation made it the country home of one of Europe's greatest military strategists, Prince Eugene of Savoy. Credited with the expulsion of the Turks at the end of the 17th century, Prince Eugene built himself a country mansion known as the **Savoyai Castle**, on what is now Kossuth Lajos utca. Used as a hotel today, the interior has been modernized, but the elegant, very early Baroque façade has been preserved. The formal gardens of the mansion can be admired from the river.

❷ Ócsa

30 km (19 miles) west of Budapest. **Road Map** D3. 🏙 8,500. 🚍 from Budapest. 🚤 from Budapest. 🚶 Tourinform, Bajcsy-Zsilinszky utca 2, (29) 57 87 50.

The part-Romanesque, part-Gothic **Calvinist Church** at Ócsa was originally built in the 13th century by the Premonstratensian Order, about which there is a small exhibition in one of the church's side rooms. Used as a mosque during the Turkish invasion, it was converted back into a church during the 18th century, and thorough restoration in 1920 (following damage by a fire) has ensured that this is one of the best-preserved Romanesque churches in the country.

Many of the houses that surround the church date from the 18th century, and all are protected buildings. One contains a small ethnographic museum, with collections of folk costumes, tools and dolls. The house also serves as the visitors' centre for the **Ócsa Nature Reserve** (Ócsai Tájvédelmi Körzet), one of the most accessible nature reserves in Hungary. The reserve surrounds the village, and apart from one small area visitors can freely explore it. Much of the reserve consists of reedy bog or marsh, known as *turjános*, which once covered a vast area here. The marshes are home to rare plant and animal species, including tortoises, lizards and a number of birds, such as harriers and corncrakes. Guided tours depart from the visitors' centre.

🏞 **Ócsa Nature Reserve**
Dr. Békési Panyik Andor utca 4–6.
Open Mar–Oct: 9am–6pm Tue–Sun. 🅿 ♿

Romanesque façade of the Calvinist Church in Ócsa

❸ Gödöllő

35 km (22 miles) northeast of Budapest. **Road Map** D3. 🏙 29,000. 🚍 HÉV from Budapest. 🚶 Tourinform, Királyi Kastély, (28) 41 54 02.

Gödöllő is most famous for its restored Baroque palace, the **Antal Grassalkovich Mansion** (*see pp138–9*), built in 1741.

Opposite the mansion, on the other side of the railway tracks, is what is left of old Gödöllő, mainly the cluster of buildings around Szabadság tér. At No. 5 is the oldest building in the town, dating from 1661. Once the home of local landowner Ferenc Hamvay, it is today the excellent **Gödöllő Town Museum** (Gödöllő Városi Múzeum). Besides displays telling the story of the town and of its greatest patron, Antal Grassalkovich, there is a colourful exhibition focusing on the works of the Gödöllő Artists' Colony. This group of artists, active between 1901 and 1920, was inspired by William Morris and John Ruskin and pursued ideals of communal rural living. Behind the museum is the Calvinist Church, built here in 1745 with money donated by Grassalkovich, who had demolished the town's original Calvinist church to make way for his palace.

Rock garden at the National Botanical Garden, Vácrátót

🏛 **Gödöllő Town Museum**

Szabadság tér 5. **Tel** (28) 42 20 03.
Open 10am–4pm Wed–Sun. 📷

❹ Vácrátót

35 km (22 miles) from Budapest.
Road Map D3. 🚉 1,700. 🚌 from Budapest. 🚌 from Budapest, Vác.

The **National Botanical Garden** (Nemzeti Botanikuskert) at Vácrátót is among the oldest in Hungary, and at present the largest. Founded in 1870 by Count Sándor Vigyázó, the gardens have been open to the public since 1961. Among the 12,000 different kinds of plant covering over 2 sq km (0.8 sq miles) are more than 1,000 species that are native to Hungary, as well as plants of the Russian steppes, Central Asia, the Rocky Mountains in the US, and trees and shrubs from the Far East. Waterfalls, rock gardens, lakes and many statues add to the enjoyment, while frogs are a frequent sight along the paths and walkways of the gardens.

Inside the greenhouses are a further 2,800 different types of plant and flower, as well as a fascinating exhibition on the flora of the tropics.

🌿 **National Botanical Garden**

Alkotmány utca 2–4. **Tel** (28) 36 01 22.
Open Gardens: Apr–Oct: 8am–6pm daily; Nov–Mar: 8am–4pm daily. Greenhouses: Apr–Oct: 8am–3:45pm Tue–Sun (to 1:45pm Fri). 📷 📷 ♿

❺ Vác

40 km (25 miles) north of Budapest.
Road Map D3. 🚉 33,000. 🚌 from Budapest. 🚌 from Budapest.
ℹ Tourinform, Március 15 tér 17, (27) 31 61 60. 🛒 daily, behind Március 15 tér. 🌐 www.visitvac.hu

Vác has stood on the eastern bank of the Danube since the year 1000. Destroyed by war in the late 17th century, the town was rebuilt. Its centre, around Március 15 tér, dates from the 18th century and was a thriving marketplace until 1951. The market itself survives, though it is now hidden behind the town hall, a Baroque masterpiece from 1680. The façade – with two Corinthian half-columns guarding the entrance – is adorned with an intricate wrought-iron balcony. Next door is the Sisters of Charity Chapel and Hospital, built in the 17th century and still a functioning hospital to this day (a more modern section was recently incorporated into the back of the hospital building, cleverly kept out of view from the square).

The pink Neo-Renaissance building opposite the hospital was for a short time the Bishop's Palace, then the Vác residence of Habsburg Empress Maria Theresa, who adored the town. Since 1802 the building has been the home of Hungary's Deaf and Dumb Society.

On the southern side of the square stands the **Dominican Church of Our Lady of Victory**, on which construction began in 1699. Due to the War of Independence, however, work on the interior decoration only began in 1755. As a result the façade is sober, while the interior is rich in Rococo artwork.

At the northernmost end of the old town, on Köztársaság út, stands the only triumphal arch in Hungary. This was built in 1764, ostensibly to honour Maria Theresa.

The Dominican Church in Vác, with its simple exterior belying the riches within

Royal Palace of Gödöllő

Seemingly lifted directly from a fairytale, the Baroque
Gödöllő Royal Palace is as enchanting now as it was
the day it was completed in 1748. Designed by András
Mayerhoffer, the palace was commissioned by the
flamboyant Hungarian aristocrat Antal Grassalkovich I,
a confidant of Empress Maria Theresa. Home to Hungarian
rulers from Emperor Franz Joseph to Governor Horthy,
it is Franz Joseph's wife, the beautiful Sisi, who has left
the most indelible mark on the palace.

★ Franz Joseph's Reception Room
The walls of the Emperor's suite
are covered in the finest red silks.
The wooden floor is the original,
from the 18th century.

★ Chapel
The Chapel, consecrated
in 1749, replaced the original
Calvinist village church. It features
two Rococo pulpits and a mosaic
portrait of Antal Grassalkovich I.

KEY

① **Bath and Orangerie**

② **The Oratory** has a full-size
portrait of Antal Grassalkovich I
above the marble fireplace.

③ **The Wardrobe of Franz Joseph I**
contains replicas of his vast
collection of uniforms, with which
the Emperor was obsessed – he was
rarely seen out of uniform.

④ **Below the Dressing Room of
Queen Elizabeth** is a secret room in
which key negotiations leading to
the Austro-Hungarian Compromise
of 1867 (see p46) were held.

⑤ **The Queen Elizabeth Memorial
Exhibition** suite has been restored
to its original violet, the Queen's
favourite colour. On display are her
most cherished paintings.

Minor Coronation Hall
Originally the king's
bedroom, an oversized
and stunning depiction of
Franz Joseph's coronation
in 1867, commissioned by
himself, is the centrepiece
of this room.

**The Palace
from the Park**
Used as an old
people's home and to
house Soviet troops
after World War II, the
palace was rebuilt and
renovated in 1986–91.

★ Grand Hall
A vast ballroom, with marble and gilded stucco decoration on walls and ceiling, the Hall also has a hidden music room above the entrance.

Grand Staircase
The elegant double staircase features stucco decoration and Rococo motifs. The balustrade is a simple, open design in painted stone.

Main entrance

Baroque Painted Room
This informal room, its walls covered with paintings, is today furnished with items from Queen Elizabeth's private waiting room at Budapest Nyugati railway station.

★ Queen Elizabeth's Reception Room
A symbolic portrait here depicts Elizabeth as a Hungarian queen, dressed in traditional Hungarian costume and mending the coronation robe.

Bridge over the Drina at Visegrád, close to the present-day Serbian border ▶

❻ Szentendre

For any visitor, Szentendre is a delight. Its Baroque architecture, Orthodox churches, galleries, cobbled streets and riverside setting make it an idyllic place to visit. A horse-drawn carriage ride along the Danube at sunset will be an unforgettable experience.

Although known as the largest Serb settlement in Hungary – Serbs fled here from the Turks after the Battle of Kosovo Polje in 1389, and again after the Battle of Belgrade in 1690 – it was the Romans who founded the town in the 4th century. Many Serbs moved away in the 1920s and artists moved in, attracted by the town's air and light; it remains popular with artists today.

The Szamos Marzipan Museum, a homage to confectionery

🏢 Fő Square
Fő tér

Fő tér is the bustling heart of Szentendre, which is packed with hawkers and street artists in summer. Its wrought-iron cross was raised in 1763 by survivors of the last major outbreak of bubonic plague.

On the Danube side of Fő tér is its tallest building, the **Blagovestenska Church**, built from 1752 to 1754 to designs by András Mayerhoffer. Its elegantly curved balcony and tall, split-level belfry are models of late Baroque simplicity. Inside, the choir, frescoes of Emperor Constantine and a large, colourful iconostasis depicting the Annunciation vie for the visitor's attention.

Next door is the pastel pink **Szentendre Gallery**, featuring the works of local artists. The building was once a terrace of six identical merchants' houses. It was converted into a gallery in 1987.

Opposite, in an early 19th-century Saxon-style house, is the **Kmetty Museum**, devoted to the life and works of the painter János Kmetty (1889–1975), a pioneering Cubist who lived here for 45 years, from 1930 until his death.

🏛 Kmetty Museum
Fő tér 21. **Tel** (26) 92 09 90. **Open** Apr–Sep: 10am–2pm Wed–Sun. 🐾 📷 ♿

🏛 Szentendre Gallery
Fő tér 2–5. **Tel** (26) 92 09 90. **Open** 10am–5pm Wed–Sun (to 5:30pm Apr–Sep). 🐾 ♿

🏛 Szamos Marzipan Museum
Dumtsa Jenő utca 12. **Tel** (26) 31 05 45. **Open** May–Sep: 9am–8pm; Oct–Apr: 9am–7pm.
🌐 szamosmarcipan.hu

Since 1935, Szamos has been making marzipan and other sweet treats; today, the name is nothing short of legendary in the world of Hungarian confectionery.

The museum in Szentendre opened in 2003. There is a shop and small café on the ground floor offering pastries, bonbons and cakes. These can be enjoyed immediately or be boxed up for later indulgence. Upstairs in the museum,

children of all ages will delight in the exhibition of a wide range of objects, including flowers, buildings and figurines – all meticulously and skilfully crafted from marzipan.

🏢 Templom Square
Templom tér

At the top of a small hill above Fő tér, this walled square, the centre of the town in the Middle Ages, stands on the site of the original Roman fort of Ulcisia.

The Catholic church in the middle of the square was first built in Romanesque style in the 14th century and was renovated in Baroque style in the 18th century. A few original features remain, including the sundial on the right-hand side.

Opposite the church is a charming building, home to the **Czóbel Museum**. Béla Czóbel, a painter famous for landscapes and nudes, lived in Szentendre from 1946 to his death in 1976.

🏛 Czóbel Museum
Templom tér 1. **Tel** (26) 92 09 90. **Open** Apr–Sep: 2–6pm Wed–Sun 🐾 📷 ♿

🏛 Belgrade Church and Museum of Serbian Orthodox Ecclesiastical Art
Szerb Ortodox Egyházművészeti Gyűjtemény, Könyvtár és Levéltár
Pátriárka utca 5. **Tel** (26) 31 23 99. **Open** May–Sep: 10am–6pm Tue–Sun; Mar, Apr, Oct–Dec: 10am–4pm Tue–Sun; Jan & Feb: 10am–4pm Fri–Sun. 🐾 ♿

Built by Serbs (but often known as the Greek Church) the Belgrade Church is the Hungarian

Monument and pretty coloured houses in Fő Square

seat of the Serbian Orthodox Patriarch and so officially a cathedral. Built in 1756–64, it is a sublime mix of Baroque and Rococo styles, its clock tower topped by a tall spire. Inside it contains icons of Orthodox saints by Vasili Ostoic and a red marble altar.

In the gardens, the Museum of Serbian Orthodox Ecclesiastical Art has some 2,000 icons, vestments, treasures and art objects, all brought here in the 19th century after the closure of their original host churches: testament to the demise of the Serb population of Hungary (*see p144*).

Icons of Orthodox saints in the Belgrade Church

🏛 Bogdányi Street
Bogdányi utca

Winding its way north from Fő tér, Bogdányi utca is a lively thoroughfare lined with historical buildings, and packed with many shops, stalls and portrait painters.

The **Imre Ámos/Margit Anna Museum** at No. 10 commemorates the life and work of painters Imre Ámos and Margit Anna, who married in 1936 and moved to Szentendre in 1937. Ámos, a Jew, was taken to a labour camp in Vojvodina in 1940, where he continued to paint. He was deported to Germany in 1944, where he died, probably in a concentration camp. His wife Margit lived until 1991. Her Cubist paintings are on the ground floor, while Ámos's work, including his accounts of life in a labour camp, is on the first floor.

A cross on the corner of Bogdányi utca and Lázár tér stands where the body of the legendary Serb ruler Prince Lázár once lay in a church. He

A wine barrel sign in Bogdányi Street

was killed by a traitor at the Battle of Kosovo Polje in 1389. His body was taken back to Serbia in the 19th century, and the church was later destroyed in a fire.

Preobrazenska Church, at the top of the street, built in 1741–6, is another fine Baroque Serbian Orthodox church. The annual Serb Folk Festival takes place here on 19 August.

🏛 Imre Ámos/Margit Anna Museum
Bogdányi utca 10. **Open** Apr–Sep: 2–6pm Wed–Sun. 🗺 🗂 ♿

VISITORS' CHECKLIST

Practical Information
25 km (16 miles) north of Budapest. **Road Map** D3.
🗺 22,000. 🛈 Tourinform, Dumtsa Jenő utca 22, (26) 31 79 65.
🔲 szentendreprogram.hu

Transport
🚃 Szentendre (hév). 🚌 Dunakanyar Körút. 🚢 Dunakorzó (summer only).

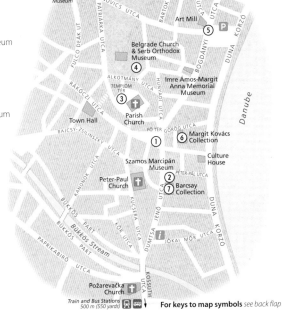

Szentendre City Centre

① Fő Square
② Szamos Marzipan Museum
③ Templom Square
④ Belgrade Church and Museum of Serbian Orthodox Ecclesiastical Art
⑤ Bogdányi Street
⑥ Margit Kovács Collection
⑦ Barcsay Collection
⑧ Hungarian Open-Air Museum

0 metres 100
0 yards 100

For keys to map symbols *see back flap*

🏛 Margit Kovács Ceramics Collection

Kovács Margit Kerámiagyűjtemény
Vastagh György utca 1. **Tel** (26) 92 09 90. **Open** 10am–5pm daily (to 6pm Apr–Sep). 🅿 &

This 18th-century building (whose entrance is somewhat hidden at the back of a courtyard) was originally a salt storage facility, and became a vicarage for the Blagovestenska Church a century later. Since 1973 it has been Szentendre's best gallery, devoted to the eclectic work of Margit Kovács (1902–77), a ceramic artist. Kovács attended Budapest's School of Applied Arts before learning the fundamentals in the pottery workshop of Herta Bücher in Vienna, from 1926 to 1928. She developed her skills further in the State School for Applied Arts in Munich, before returning to Hungary, where she produced most of her best-known works.

Nursing (1948) is an example of Kovács's obsession with the Madonna, a common theme in many of her early works, while the later *Bread Cutter* (1962) is a witty satire of the idealized Hungarian peasant woman from a feminist perspective.

Margit Kovács Collection, Szentendre

🏛 Barcsay Collection

Barcsay Gyűjtemény
Dumtsa Jenő utca 10. **Tel** (26) 92 09 90. **Open** Apr–Sep: 2–6pm Wed–Sun. 🅿 &

This museum, located in a fine 19th-century Saxon house, is dedicated to Jenő Barcsay (1900–88), who settled in Szentendre in 1926 after studying art in Budapest and Paris, where he was influenced by the work of Cézanne. Widely regarded as the first Hungarian Constructivist, he strongly affected his contemporaries. Barcsay's finest works are on display here. Among the most representative are *Street at Szentendre* (1932), *Landscape at Szentendre* (1934) and *Female Portrait* (1936).

A thatched building in the Hungarian Open-Air Museum in Szentendre

🏛 Hungarian Open-Air Museum

Szabadtéri Néprajzi Múzeum
Sztaravodai út. **Tel** (26) 50 25 00. **Open** Apr–Oct: 9am–5pm Tue–Sun; Nov–Mar: 10am–4pm Sat & Sun. 🎬 & 🆆 **skanzen.hu**

Hungary's largest and best open-air village museum is 4 km (2 miles) from Szentendre; buses depart every 30 minutes (every hour at weekends) from the bus station on Dunakanyar körút (stop No. 7). The museum, opened in 1967, is spread over 5.5 sq km (0.2 sq miles) and features a reconstructed village from each of Hungary's five historic regions. Each of the five villages is complete and self-contained, comprising houses, churches, schools, mills, wine presses, forges and stables. Worth looking out for in particular are the three huge outdoor ovens in the village of the Great Plain (brought to the museum from the village of Kisbodak), the roadside crucifixes in the Central Transdanubian village, and the flint-stone walls of the Bakony region houses.

All of the buildings in the museum are open to the public, and some are working museums, with artisans demonstrating traditional skills from pottery to wine making to visitors. At various times of the year special courses are organized for visitors who want to acquire traditional skills.

The Skanzen Nostalgia Train takes in the main sights of Skanzen. Visitors should allow plenty of time for a visit here.

Hungary's Serbs

The development of the towns and cities of the Danube Bend, especially Szentendre *(see pp142–3)*, was marked by two major waves of Serb migrations to the region. The first, when around 10,000 Serbs fled north following a defeat by the Turks at Kosovo Polje in 1389, was followed by a larger migration in 1690 after another defeat at the hands of the Turks. This second time more than 30,000 Serbs fled north, with as many as 6,000 Serbs settling in Szentendre, founding churches and schools. In the 18th century, Empress Maria Theresa sent many of Hungary's Serbs to settle in the border lands of the Vojvodina, rewarding them with large parcels of land. Today, just 3,800 Serbs officially remain in Hungary.

Crucifix from the Serb Orthodox Museum in Szentendre

❼ Visegrád

40 km (25 miles) north of Budapest. **Road Map** C3. 🏰 1,700. 🚍 🚌 from Budapest. 🚢 from Budapest, Esztergom; from Szentendre (summer only). 🌐 **visitvisegrad.hu**

Set on the narrowest stretch of the Danube, Visegrád is a popular village with visitors dominated by its spectacular ruined **Citadel**. Built in the 13th century by King Béla IV, this was once one of the finest royal palaces in Hungary. The massive outer walls are still intact, and offer the visitor superb views.

Halfway down the hill, in the Salamon Tower, is the **Mátyás Museum**, a collection of items excavated from the ruins of the **Royal Palace**. Built by King Sigismund in the 14th century, it was renovated a century later, in magnificent Renaissance style, by Mátyás Corvinus *(see p41)*. It fell derelict in the 16th century after the Turkish invasion and was then buried in a mudslide. The ruins were not rediscovered until 1934, when excavations took place. Now largely reconstructed and whitewashed, several rooms recreate life in the Renaissance Palace.

🏰 Citadel
Tel (26) 39 81 01. **Open** Mar–Oct: 9am–5pm; May–Sep: 9am–6pm; Nov: 9am–4pm daily; Dec–Feb: 10am–4pm Fri–Sun (daily 25 Dec–11 Jan).

🏛 Mátyás Museum
Salamon-torony utca. **Tel** (26) 59 70 10. **Open** May–Oct: 9am–5pm Wed–Sun. 🖼

🏛 Royal Palace
Fő utca 23. **Tel** (26) 39 80 26. **Open** Mar–Oct: 9am–5pm; Nov–Feb: 10am–4pm. 🖼 🗾

Zebegény's Roman Catholic church, built in Secessionist style

❽ Zebegény

30 km (19 miles) east of Vác. **Road Map** C3. 🏰 1,200. 🚍 from Budapest. 🚢 from Budapest.

Famous for fine views of the Danube Bend, the tiny village of Zebegény also boasts one of Hungary's few Catholic churches in Secession style. Designed by Károly Kós, Dénes Györgyi and Béla Jánszky and built from 1910 to 1914, its plain façade has Neo-Romanesque traits. It is its sharply angled and tiered, Christmas-tree-like roof that sets the church apart, while the tall adjoining spire adds elegance. Inside, the colourful frescoes of St Constantine are the last major works by the master painter Kriesch Aladár Körösfői (1863–1920).

Behind the church is the **István Szőnyi Memorial Museum**. One of the most prominent Hungarian Expressionist painters, Szőnyi lived here most of his life until his death in 1960. The museum displays personal artifacts, family photos and some of his works, including *A Bench in the Garden* (1943).

🏛 István Szőnyi Memorial Museum
Bartóky utca 7. **Tel** (27) 62 01 61. **Open** Mar–Oct: 9am–5pm Tue–Sun; Nov–Feb: 10am–4pm Fri–Sun, or by appointment. 🖼 🗾 Hungarian and German. ♿

❾ Nagybörzsöny & Duna-Ipoly National Park

24 km (15 miles) north of Visegrád. **Road Map** C2/3. 🚌 from Szob (to Nagybörzsöny). 🌐🚠 **dinpi.hu**

Home to the fine 14th-century stone Romanesque Church of St Stephen, a working mid-19th-century water mill (open to the public) and a mining museum, Nagybörzsöny is best known as the gateway to the Duna-Ipoly National Park, one of the largest in the country. The Buda Hill caves and the Sas-hegy nature trail outside Budapest are also within its borders.

The park is home to more than 70 protected plants and more than half of Hungary's native bird species (including black and white-backed woodpeckers).

A narrow-gauge railway runs at weekends from Nagybörzsöny to Nagyirtás across the Börzsöny Hills, from where well-marked hiking trails fan out across the park. There is also a long trail from Nagybörzsöny itself, leading up to Nagy Hideg Hegy peak, which offers views across to Slovakia.

A second narrow-gauge railway, from Kismaros to Királyrét, opens up the southern part of the park. There are hiking trails from Királyrét across the hills, and on to Nógrád, where there is a spectacular ruined castle.

Signpost in Duna-Ipoly National Park

The spectacular ruins of the citadel, towering over Visegrád

⑩ Esztergom

St István, Hungary's first king, was baptized in Esztergom, and crowned here on Christmas Day in the year 1000. Almost completely destroyed by the Mongol invasion 250 years later, the town was gradually rebuilt during the 18th and 19th centuries. Esztergom today is still Hungary's most sacred city, the seat of the Archbishop of Hungary. Although it is dominated by the huge Basilica *(see pp148–9)*, Esztergom has much to offer besides its mighty cathedral, including one of Hungary's oldest castles, the picturesque and eclectic district of Vízíváros (Watertown), the fascinating Danube Museum and Hungary's finest collection of ecclesiastical art.

🏠 Esztergom Basilica
See pp148–9.

🏰 Royal Palace and Castle Museum
Vár & Vármúzeum
Szent István tér 1. **Tel** (33) 41 59 86.
Open Apr–Oct: 10am–6pm Tue–Sun; Nov–Mar: 10am–4pm Tue–Sun. 📷 🎧 compulsory.

Opposite Esztergom Basilica are the partly reconstructed remains of the Royal Palace, one of the oldest buildings in Hungary. The southern walls date back to the 10th century. From 1256 onwards it was the palace of Esztergom's archbishops, and improvement was continuous right up until the Turkish invasion, when it was sacked. Much of the palace remained, however, and is open today as the Castle Museum.

A guided tour of the palace takes in the study of King Mátyás's tutor, with frescoes based on Florentine Renaissance

Statue of Queen Elizabeth in Vízíváros

palaces, and the 12th-century Royal Chapel, with an original rose window and 13th-century portraits of the Apostles.

To the south and north are well-preserved remains of the ramparts and steps back into the town. The Esztergom Castle Theatre stages plays in summer, and the castle also hosts the History Days festival in September.

🎭 Vízíváros
Berényi utca

Vízíváros (Watertown) is a district of mainly Baroque buildings, narrow streets, single-storey houses and tiny well-kept gardens. The area was developed during the regeneration of Esztergom after the withdrawal of the Turks in the early 18th century. Vízíváros Parish Church, consecrated by Jesuits in 1728, is a perfect example of the Baroque architecture of the time with its

rounded façade and high nave. The twin spires were added much later, in the middle of the 19th century. The Baroque interior was unfortunately lost during World War II, and has yet to be replaced. The statue in front of the church was raised in 1740 by the people of Esztergom, grateful for having survived an outbreak of the plague. A bridge behind the church leads to Prímás Sziget, an island of gardens and parks in the Danube, from where another bridge crosses the river into Slovakia.

The Lord's Coffin of Garamszentbenedek, in the Christian Museum

🏛 Christian Museum
Keresztény Múzeum
Mindszenty tér 2. **Tel** (33) 41 38 80.
Open Mar–Nov: 10am–5pm Wed–Sun. **Closed** Dec–Feb. 📷 🎧

The Roman Catholic Primate of All Hungary, János Simor, resided in this grand Neo-Renaissance palace after it was completed in 1882, and immediately opened the palace and its vast collection of paintings, including works by early Italian Renaissance artists Migazzi and Bertinelli, to the public. The building has been a dedicated museum since 1924, and its collection of church art, bolstered by many subsequent purchases, is now the finest in Hungary.

The splendid, wheeled Lord's Coffin of Garamszentbenedek (now in Slovakia), dating from 1480, is decorated with carved figures and is still used in Easter

The domed Basilica, iconic building of Esztergom

processions. It is thought not to contain any human remains: its purpose has always been symbolic. The room devoted to altarpieces, some dating back to the 14th century, is stunning in its colour and historical import. Tamás Koloszvári's *Ascension* is considered the most significant medieval painting in Hungary.

Besides the picture gallery, there are equally stunning sculpture and icon galleries.

🏛 Bálint Balassa Museum
MNM Balassa Bálint Múzeum

Mindszenty tér 5. **Tel** (33) 50 01 75.
Open Mar–Oct: 10am–6pm Tue–Sun;
Nov–Feb: 10am–4pm Tue–Sun.

Situated opposite the Víziváros Parish Church, the Bálint Balassa Museum is named after a Renaissance poet who died in 1594 while fighting the Turks. The over 120-year-old museum underwent a major refurbishment in 2014 and exhibits now showcase archaeological artifacts, weapons from the 18th to the 20th centuries, ship models, antique furniture and a rich book collection. Also displayed are 18th-century tableware and other interesting ethnographic items.

The Danube Museum, devoted to life with the river

🏛 Danube Museum and Lower Esztergom
Duna Múzeum & Belváros

Kölcsey utca 2. **Tel** (33) 50 02 50.
Open Feb, Nov & Dec: 10am–4pm Wed–Mon; Mar–Oct: 9am–5pm Wed–Mon. **Closed** Tue and Jan.

The role of the Danube in the history and development of Esztergom is given due importance in this outstanding museum close to the city centre. The building itself is a gem. It was built in the 18th century in Baroque style and was a crumbling wreck until renovated in 1973, when the museum moved here from its previous home on the Danube. The museum houses all sorts of hydraulic equipment from the past century, as well as exhibits devoted to damming the Danube and navigation, water supply and purification. There is a collection of engineering tools, as well as a history of water management since Roman times. Children will enjoy the many hands-on displays, which enable them to get very wet indeed.

A 5-minute walk south along Vörösmary utca leads to Széchenyi tér, centre of the Lower Town and surrounded on all sides by a mixture of Baroque and Neo-Classical houses, many of which are now cafés. Its focal point is the town hall, an immaculately preserved Rococo building from 1729.

VISITORS' CHECKLIST

Practical Information
Road Map C3. 🚩 28,357.
🎭 Castle Theatre (Jul–Aug); History Days Festival (Sep).

Transport
🚉 Bem József tér. 🚌 Simor János utca. 🚤 Nagy-Duna sétány (summer only).

Esztergom City Centre

① *Basilica pp148–9*
② Royal Palace and Castle Museum
③ Víziváros
④ Christian Museum
⑤ Bálint Balassa Museum
⑥ Danube Museum and Lower Esztergom

SZENTGYÖRGYMEZŐ

St. Adalbert Center

SZENT ISTVÁN TÉR

Basilica
Dark Gate
①

ISKOLA UTCA

BÁNOM

BERÉNYI

Danube

③

VÍZIVÁROS

Christian Museum ④

Víziváros Parish Church

② Royal Palace and Castle Museum

Rondella

MAJER ISTVÁN UTCA

BASA UTCA

⑤ Bálint Balassa Museum

PÁZMÁNY UTCA

MINDSZENTY TERE

BATTHYÁNY UTCA

BAJCSY-ZSILINSZKY UTCA

SZENT TAMÁS-HEGY

🏛 Chapel

TÖRÖK UTCA

VASVÁRI PÁL UTCA

Kossuth híd

Kis-Duna

ATTILA TÉR

IMAHÁZ UTCA

Mária Valéria híd

NAGY-DUNA SÉTÁNY

Customs House

TÁNCSICS MIHÁLY UTCA

Outdoor Pool

KIS-DUNA SÉTÁNY

Danube Museum and Lower Estergom ⑥

Bottyán híd

LŐRINCZ UTCA

VÖRÖSMARTY UTCA

RÁKÓCZI TÉR

🚉 Train Station
1.2 km (0.7 miles)
🚌 Bus Station
1 km (0.6 miles)

0 metres   200
0 yards   200

For keys to map symbols *see back flap*

Esztergom Basilica

Rising high above the Danube, its bright blue cupola visible from afar, the cathedral at Esztergom has been a symbol of Hungary for a millennium, ever since St István was crowned here on Christmas Day 1000. Hungary's largest cathedral, the present structure, dating from the 19th century, was built over a 47-year period from 1822 to 1869. It replaced the much smaller 12th-century St Adalbert's Cathedral, which was destroyed by the Turks as they retreated in the 18th century.

Treasury
Hungary's most valuable collection of liturgical and royal art, dating back to the early Árpád dynasty, is kept here, as well as a shrine with St István's skull.

★ Copy of Titian's Assumption of the Virgin (1853–4)
Behind the altar, this is the largest single-canvas painting in the world. The original (1516–18) hangs in Venice's Santa Maria Gloriosa dei Frari.

KEY

① Pillars supporting the Dome

② **The North Tower** is one of two identical basilica bell towers which rise to 71.5 m (235 ft), matching exactly the height of the main dome's interior. The unusual, octagonal form of their bases is thought to be unique in Hungary.

③ **Corinthian Columns** – 22 in total – give the basilica's entrance an unmistakable Neo-Classical appearance.

Tomb of Cardinal Mindszenty in the Crypt
Cardinal József Mindszenty was a pillar of resistance to both the Nazi and Communist regimes. He died in exile in 1975, and his body was laid to rest here in 1991.

★ Dome/Cupola
A steep flight of steps leads up to the dome's viewing platform, from where there are superb views over Esztergom and the Danube Bend – and Stúrovo in Slovakia on the northern bank.

VISITORS' CHECKLIST

Practical Information
Szent István tér 1. **Road Map** C3.
Tel (33) 40 23 54. **Open**
Cathedral: Mar–Oct: 8am–6pm daily; Nov & Dec: 8am–4pm daily.
Cupola & Bell Tower: Apr–Oct: 9:30am–5pm daily. Treasury: Mar–Oct: 9am–4:30pm daily; Nov–Dec: 11am–3:30pm Tue–Fri, 10am–3:30pm Sat & Sun.
Crypt: Mar–Oct: 9am–4:30pm; Nov & Dec: 10am–2:30pm daily.
🅿 🚻 ♿ ✉ Treasury, Crypt.
📷 🎦 Jun–Aug.

Transport
🚌 🚏 🚢

Basilica
Esztergom Basilica is distinguished by its outer simplicity and inner beauty. A grand but plain façade gives way to priceless treasures and superbly rich decoration.

★ Bakócz Chapel
The red-marble Bakócz chapel opens to the basilica's nave. Built in Florentine Renaissance style, it is named after Cardinal Tamás Bakócz (c.1442–1521), who is laid to rest here.

Primates of All Hungary
Former archbishops commemorated in statuary include the 15th-century Dénes Szécsi (*left*) and the 19th-century János Simor, whose vast private Christian art collection formed the basis of the Esztergom Christian Museum (*see pp146–7*).

③

Entrance

Main entrance

NORTHERN TRANSDANUBIA

For centuries, Northern Transdanubia was Hungary's golden triangle, the conduit in trade and commerce between the twin capitals of Vienna and Budapest; it was where the empire's greatest families built their mansions with profits made in the region's factories. Recently, tourism has surpassed industry as a main source of income, with Bük's thermal baths and Lake Fertő the main attractions.

Much of the western part of this region is classic frontier territory. The Őrség region, Kőszeg, Szentgotthárd and Sopron, Hungary's most westerly city, were for centuries bulwarks against invaders. Nowhere else in Hungary is it more apparent that Austria and Hungary were once parts of the same empire. Sopron, in fact, is closer to Vienna than to Budapest – its street signs are often in German and well-dressed Viennese throng its charming old town. Further south, in Szombathely, German as well as Hungarian can be heard, and, at the popular Lake Fertő, Hungarians are outnumbered by visitors in summer. Yet this is proudly Hungary.

Close to Győr, a city of legends that is as far from Vienna as it is from Budapest, is the astonishing abbey of Pannonhalma.

One of Hungary's most historic complexes, its Benedictine monks resisted all invasions and tests of their faith. The abbey at Zirc, further south, is no less important.

In recent times the west of the region has seen a determined search for oil. Although some oil has been found, many probes found little except hot water; indeed, the springs that serve the thermal resort of Bükfürdő were discovered this way.

The east of Transdanubia includes Székesfehérvár, where for 500 years Hungarian kings and queens were crowned, and Lake Velence, a quiet spot and a favourite with all nature-lovers. The real natural wonder of Northern Transdanubia, however, is the Bakony Forest, which offers some of the most spectacular driving routes in the country.

A verdant landscape in the rolling Northern Transdanubia hills

◀ The Firewatch Tower on the corner of the town hall, Sopron

Exploring Northern Transdanubia

The most varied region of Hungary, Northern Transdanubia is characterized by its gentle hills, green valleys, lush forests and beautiful imperial towns, including Székesfehérvár, one of the country's architectural gems. There is also the historic town of Kőszeg to see, the fortress-like Pannonhalma Monastery to explore, the thermal waters of Sárvár and Bük and Lake Fertő to relax in, as well as the vineyards around Pápa to visit.

The Trinity Column in Fő tér in Sopron, celebrating relief from the plague

Key

— Motorway

— Major road

— Secondary road

··· Minor road

—·— Main railway

— Minor railway

▬▬ International border

▬▬ Regional border

Getting Around

The M1 motorway between Budapest and Vienna provides quick access to Northern Transdanubia, and is ideal for exploring the places in this chapter, including Győr, Tata, Mosonmagyaróvár and Lake Fertő. High-speed trains run between Budapest and Vienna, many of which stop at Győr. Slower, local services serve other towns and cities in the region. From Győr, there are good roads – but poor rail and bus services – to the western cities of Zalaergerszeg and Szombathely.

Bas-relief on the Széchenyi Mansion in Nagycenk

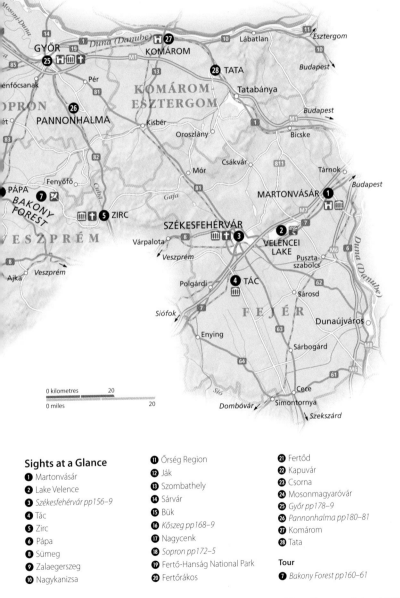

Sights at a Glance

For additional keys to symbols *see back flap*

Brunswick Mansion in Martonvásár, housing a small Beethoven Museum

❶ Martonvásár

30 km (19 miles) southwest of Budapest. **Road Map** C3. 🚊 5,500. 🚆 from Budapest. 🚌 from Budapest.

The village of Martonvásár has existed since medieval times, but its principal attraction is **Brunswick Mansion**. Towards the end of the 18th century, the entire village was bought by the German Brunswick family, and the original Baroque palace was built for Antal Brunswick. A century later, in 1875, it was totally rebuilt, this time in the Neo-Gothic style. While the house is closed to the public, the superb parklands can be enjoyed by visitors. The estate's church, built in 1775, is largely unaltered. Its interior is decorated with well-preserved frescoes.

Piano in the Beethoven Memorial Museum

Ludwig van Beethoven was a regular visitor to the original mansion and gave music lessons to the daughters. Some rooms adjoining the mansion now house a small **Beethoven Memorial Museum** (Beethoven Emlékmúzeum).

🏛 **Brunswick Mansion**
Brunszvick utca 2. **Open** (park only) 8am–5pm daily (to 4pm winter). 🚻 ♿

🏛 **Beethoven Memorial Museum**
Brunszvick utca 2. **Tel** (22) 56 95 00. **Open** 10am–noon, 2–4pm Tue–Fri, 10am–noon, 1–4pm Sat & Sun. 🚻 ♿

❷ Lake Velence

50 km (31 miles) southwest of Budapest. **Road Map** C4. 🚆 from Budapest to Velence or Gárdony. 🚌 from Budapest to Velence or Gárdony. 🛈 Tourinform, Szabadság út 24, Gárdony, (22) 57 00 77; Halász utca 37, Velence, (22) 47 03 02.

Velence means "Venice" in Hungarian, although there the similarities end. A shallow body of water with no islands, Lake Velence is popular with day-trippers from Budapest. It is less crowded than Lake Balaton, attracting mainly anglers and swimmers, the latter enjoying the warm water (up to 26° C/80° F in high summer). Three small beach resorts on the eastern shore, Velence, Gárdony and Agárd, more or less blend into each other. None has any great charm,

though all offer a variety of places to stay. Agárd is the most developed, and has an excellent thermal bath complex. Most non-Hungarian visitors to Velence head for the western shore. More than 30,000 birds spend the spring here, nesting in the marshes and reeds. Species to be spotted include spoonbills, herons and geese. Since 1958 the lake has been a protected bird reserve. The Tourinform office in Gárdony can put birdwatchers in touch with local tour groups and guides.

❸ Székesfehérvár

See pp156–9.

❹ Tác

11 km (7 miles) south of Székesfehérvár. **Road Map** C4. 🚊 1,500. 🚌 from Székesfehérvár. 🎭 Floralia Festival (late Apr–early May), Ludi Romani Festival (mid-Aug–mid-Sep).

On a vast site a 10-minute walk outside the tiny village of Tác are the impressive remains of the Roman city of Herculia. Uncovered during excavation work in 1934–9, Herculia began life in the 1st century AD as a military base called Gorsium, growing in size and importance to become the capital of the province of Valeria (Lower Pannonia) by the 3rd century.

Set up as the **Gorsium Open-Air Museum** (Gorsium Szabadtéri Múzeum in Régészeti Park) since 1962, the site is well cared for though lacking in

The mooring jetties on Lake Velence, popular with visitors from Budapest

major attractions. While it is possible with the naked eye to make out the shapes of houses, the theatre and the forum, the guidebook available from the ticket office is a must to understand how it all worked. Digs continue: unearthed treasure (including pottery, coins, masonry and weaponry) is displayed in a small museum by the entrance. There are Greek and Roman plays and other performances held as part of the ancient Floralia and Ludi Romani festivals. Details are available from the Tourinform office in Székesfehérvár.

🏛 Gorsium Open-Air Museum
Fő utca 6, Tác. **Tel** (22) 36 22 43. **Open** Apr–Oct: 10am–6pm daily; Nov–Mar: 10am–4pm daily. 🎫 ♿

Excavated Roman ruins, at the Gorsium Open-Air Museum in Tác

❺ Zirc

51 km (32 miles) northwest of Veszprém. **Road Map** B3. 🚆 7,500. 🚌 from Veszprém, Győr. 🚆 from Veszprém. 🛈 Tourinform, Rákóczi tér 1, (88) 83 00 08.

The small town of Zirc, on the northern fringes of the Bakony Forest *(see pp160–61)* is dominated by its **Cistercian Abbey** (Római katolikus cisztercita templom, Nagyboldogasszony). Standing on a hill above the town, at an altitude of 400 m (1,312 ft), the abbey was founded as early as 1182, although the current complex (including the twin-spired Baroque basilica) dates

Façade of the Zirc Cistercian Abbey, home to the Reguly Antal Library

from 1750. The altar paintings and frescoes inside are the work of Franz Anton Maulbertsch. The most visited part of the abbey, however, is its Reguly Antal Library, complete with 80,000 volumes kept on lush, cherrywood bookshelves. The abbey is also home to the Bakony Natural History Museum, with exhibitions on the flora and fauna of the Bakony hills and forest.

In the town of Zirc itself is an extensive arboretum, with more than 60 kinds of trees and shrubs, including an over 400-year-old oak tree. The Reguly Antal Museum, a small but interesting exhibition, is dedicated to the life of the early 20th-century pioneer in Finno-Ugric linguistics and explorer.

🏛 Zirc Cistercian Abbey
Rákóczi tér 1. **Tel** (88) 59 36 75. **Open** 9am–5pm Tue–Sun. 🎫 📷 **W** zircapatsag.hu

❻ Pápa

51 km (32 miles) northwest of Veszprém. **Road Map** B3. 🚆 34,000. 🚌 from Budapest, Tatabánya, Győr. 🚆 from Tatabánya, Veszprém. 🛈 Tourinform, Márton István utca 10, (89) 77 70 47. **W** papa.hu

An important fortified town first mentioned in 1051, Pápa was held by the Turks from 1594 to 1683. It fell into decline after being razed by fire in 1685. In the 18th century it was rebuilt and found new purpose in 24 watermills driven by the Tapolca river. The mills served the corn, textile and paper industries of the region. Pápa's two most important sights stem from this boom period.

The **Esterházy Palace** (Esterházy Kastély), on Fő tér, was constructed in 1783–4 by József Grossmann for Count Ferenc. Baroque in style, it was badly damaged in World War II and neglected under the Communists. Today, however, renovation is under way.

The giant **Great Church of St Stephen**, built in 1774–86 to designs by Jakab Fellner, dominates everything. After Fellner's death, József Grossmann completed the work. The statue above the gable and the frescoes inside feature St Stephen the Martyr.

🏛 Esterházy Palace
Fő tér 1. **Open** by appointment only during renovation; (70) 314 19 59. . **W** esterhazykastely.papa.hu

Statue of a lion outside the Esterházy Palace in Pápa

❸ Street-by-Street: Székesfehérvár

The cobbled, car-free streets of the old town in
Székesfehérvár are packed with historically and
religiously significant buildings. For 500 years
this was the location of Hungary's coronation
church; the sarcophagus of the country's first
Christian king, St István, is still here today. As
one of the last stands of the German Army
during World War II took place in these streets,
it is little short of a miracle that the medieval
and Baroque buildings surrounding Városház tér
survive. Around them everything was destroyed
– hence the bland feel of the rest of the city.

Town Hall
Székesfehérvár's
18th-century town
hall was originally
built as a palace for
the Zichy family.

Hetedhét Toy
Museum and
Hiemer-House

JÓKAI UTCA

JUHÁS

★ St Anne's Chapel
Dating from the
15th century, St Anne's
Chapel is the only part of
medieval Székesfehérvár
to have survived the
Turkish occupation.

**★ St István's
Cathedral**
The entrance to
the cathedral was
remodelled in the
1770s by Franz Anton
Hildebrandt. The
statues above the
door are of István,
László and Imre.

MEGYEHÁZ UTCA

ARANY J. UTCA

Clockwork

Budenz
House

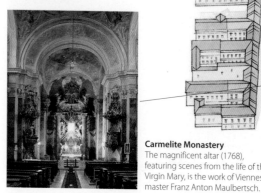

Carmelite Monastery
The magnificent altar (1768),
featuring scenes from the life of the
Virgin Mary, is the work of Viennese
master Franz Anton Maulbertsch.

| 0 metres | | 50 |
| 0 yards | | 50 |

Deák
Collection

Black Eagle Pharmacy Museum
Hundreds of old medicine
bottles and an amazing
frescoed ceiling adorn this
Baroque pharmacy, which
operated until 1971.

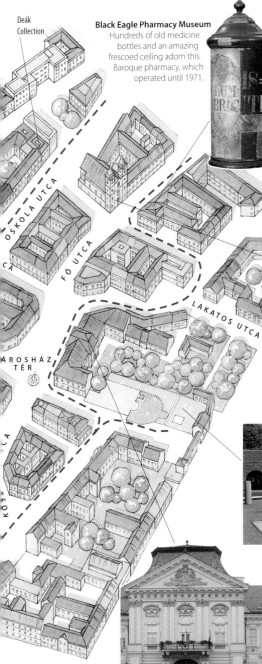

OSKOLA UTCA

FŐ UTCA

LAKATOS UTCA

VÁROSHÁZ
TÉR

KOSS

**Cistercian Church and
Monastery**
The Baroque 18th-century altar
fresco in this church was painted
by local artists under the
direction of the German-born
painter Caspar Franz Sambach.

Garden of Ruins
The vast size of the Royal
Basilica and burial chapel that
once stood here can be easily
imagined by tracing the
outline of the ruins.

★ Bishop's Palace
The Baroque palace, designed by Jakob
Rieder, was built in 1801 using stone taken
mainly from the ruins of the Royal Basilica.

Key
— Suggested route

Exploring Székesfehérvár

Around 897, the Magyar chieftain Árpád *(see p39)* created a permanent settlement, and with it the first Hungarian town, on the Székesfehérvár plain. Prince Géza, his great-grandson, built a castle here in 972, and St István, Géza's son, erected a vast basilica. The walled city that grew up around it was the site of Hungary's Diet, or Parliament, for 500 years, until the Turks occupied the city and the inhabitants fled in 1543. Székesfehérvár flourished in the 1800s and 1900s. In World War II much of the town was destroyed, but the historic centre *(see pp156–7)* was spared.

🏛 St István Király Museum
Szent István Király Múzeum
Fő utca 6. **Tel** (22) 31 55 83. **Open** May–Sep: 10am–4pm Tue–Sun; Mar, Apr, Oct–Dec: 10am–2pm Tue–Sun. 🎟 📷 German and Hungarian only. 🌐 **szikm.hu**

The friary of the Cistercian church *(see p157)* houses a collection of artifacts from the Fejér region. The earliest exhibits go back as far as the Neolithic Age, and there is also a significant collection of Roman treasure. The most recent finds include parts of the sarcophagus of St István, most of which is in the Garden of Ruins *(see p157)*. The friary itself was built at the same time as the church, and completed in 1751. It first housed Jesuit, then Franciscan, and finally Cistercian monks. The museum has temporary exhibitions at the Ceremonial Hall, Országzászló tér 3.

🏛 Black Eagle Pharmacy Museum
Fekete Sas Patikamúzeum
Fő utca 5. **Tel** (22) 31 55 83. **Open** 10am–6pm Tue–Sun. ♿

The city's pharmacy moved into this elegant two-storey Baroque house in 1774. It remained open for business until as late as 1971, when it was bought by the State and renovated and reopened as a museum two years later. The museum has a collection of old medicine bottles and medical implements, but much more interesting are the colourful frescoes on the arched ceiling, and the gorgeously intricate original wooden fixtures and fittings dating from 1758.

🏛 Deák Collection
Városi Képtár Deák-gyűjtemény
Oskola utca 10. **Tel** (22) 32 94 31. **Open** 10am–6pm Tue–Sun. 🎟 ♿

An overview of the history of modern Hungarian art, Dénes Deák's (1931–93) collection features early 20th-century artists Rippl-Rónai and Gulácsy, modern European School artists Imre Ámos and Margit Anna and Tihamér Gyarmathy's contemporary abstract art. Sculpture and graphic art are also represented.

🏛 St István's Cathedral
Szent István Székesegyház
Arany János utca 9. **Tel** (22) 31 51 14. **Open** Apr–mid-Oct: 9am–6pm Tue–Sun.

Béla IV founded this church, later renovated in Baroque style, in which parts of the original Hungarian coronation ceremony took place. After 1777 it became a cathedral and its prominent twin towers were added. The statues show István, László and Imre. The city's coat of arms sits above the main portal.

🏛 Hiemer-House
Hiemer-Ház
Oskola utca 2–4. **Tel** (22) 53 72 61. **Open** by arrangement only. ♿

The Hiemer House, with its Baroque-Rococo main façade, consists of three medieval buildings on Hungary's National Heritage list. One building, adjoining Jókai Street, once functioned as a parsonage; another, the Font house, was a school and store. The Caraffa building was a combination of school, flats and stores. One part of the complex houses the Hetedhét Toy Museum *(below)*.

Exhibits from the Hetedhét Toy Museum, displaying fascinating detail

🏛 Hetedhét Toy Museum
Hetedhét Játékmúzeum
Oskola utca 2-4. **Tel** (22) 20 26 01. **Open** 10am–6pm Tue–Sun. 🎟

The museum, located in part of the Hiemer-House *(above)*, holds Hungary's largest collection of dolls (mainly from the 18th-century), plus doll's houses, tin

Interior of St István's Cathedral, with ceiling frescoes by Johannes Cymbal

soldiers and castles and other toys, which have all been assembled by Éva Moskovszky, a retired librarian of the Hungarian National Museum. The detail and opulence of these toys are astonishing – the dolls wear genuine pearl necklaces and the tiny homes, copies of homes built between 1800 and 1930, are immaculately furnished with real Herend porcelain (*see p207*). Even the clocks on the doll's house walls are in full working order.

🏛 Carmelite Church
Karmelita templom
Petőfi utca. **Open** Apr–mid-Oct: 9am–6pm Tue–Sun. ♿

Not fully completed until 1769, the church was designed by an anonymous architect. The Carmelites were so desperate for a place to worship that they began holding their services in the unfinished (but consecrated) church in 1732, a year after construction began, when the building was little more than a shell. The exterior is Baroque, with a single, modest tower. The real glory of the church, however, are the colourful, dramatic ceiling frescoes inside, most of which are the work of Franz Anton Maulbertsch, a native of Vienna who worked on a number of churches in the area around Lake Balaton. He also painted the altar and the crucifix in the oratory. The ceiling frescoes were damaged during a minor earthquake in 1800, and suffered further during the Napoleonic wars when the church was transformed into a hospital. They were restored during the 1950s. Outside the church, set into the southern wall, is a statue of Louis the Great, the work of Hungarian sculptor Ödön Moiret.

⏰ Clockwork
Órajáték
Kossuth utca 9. ♿

The vivid and playful clock in the small pedestrian square behind No. 9 Kossuth Street chimes every 2 hours from spring to autumn, while small figures dressed as hussars march by. The clock is the

Detail on the clock at No. 9 Kossuth Street

focal point of a colourful Secessionist house that has become increasingly hemmed in by the less interesting buildings surrounding it. The interior of the building can be visited by prior arrangement.

🏛 Open-Air Ethnographical Museum
Palotavárosi Skanzen
Rác utca 11. **Tel** (22) 37 90 78. **Open** by arrangement. ♿ 📷 ♿

Unlike other village museums in Hungary, which are usually located outside towns, Palotavárosi is set close to the city centre, in the suburbs of Székesfehérvár. Visitors entering the cobbled streets of the museum (which for centuries was the Rácváros, or Serb area of the city) find themselves in a lost world. At No. 11 Rác utca, a

small museum tells the story of the area and of Székesfehérvár's Serb community, of its traders and craftsmen, with exhibitions on shoemakers, leather-workers and furriers. Also on Rác utca is the Ráctemplom, the single-nave Serb church, a Baroque 18th-century building with colourful, fully restored icons. Many of them had been hidden by soot for the best part of a century.

🏰 Bory Castle
Bory Vár
Máriavölgy utca 54. **Tel** (22) 30 55 70. **Open** Mar–Nov: 9am–5pm daily. 📷

The most-visited sight in Székesfehérvár is the whimsical Bory Castle, built over two decades by the sculptor and architect Jenő Bory (1879–1959). Construction first began in the mid-1920s, when Bory had a group of his students build him a small cottage and plant a vineyard. He then added various parts to it, the designs becoming gradually more colourful and daring, until, at the time of his death, the cottage had grown into a veritable fantasy land, part Roman forum, part Gothic castle, with touches of just about every other architectural style thrown in. Some of the castle's rooms exhibit Bory's sculptures, as well as paintings by his wife, Ilona Komócsin, also responsible for most of the exterior art.

The romantic Bory Castle, a blend of architectural styles

❼ A Tour Around the Bakony

The Bakony refers to the volcanic mountain range that rises behind the northern shore of Lake Balaton, as well as to the dense forests that cover the hills and valleys of the region, stretching from Balaton in the south as far as Pannonhalma Abbey in the north. Dotted with vineyards and old wine-press houses, it is one of the most scenic parts of Hungary. It was devastated during the Turkish withdrawal from Hungary in the 17th century, and resettled with Saxons from Germany in the 18th century. Many of the villages today have a distinctly Germanic feel.

⑤ Bakonykoppány
A centre of the Bakony wine-making industry, the area is famous for its full-bodied white wines. Visitors should look out for the wine-press houses, which are dotted amongst the vineyards.

⑥ Pápa
The Viennese artist Johann Ignaz Mildorfer is responsible for the beautiful ceiling fresco found at the Esterházy Palace Chapel. The town is also known for its rich, royal blue cloth, made here by the Kluge family since 1783, for seven generations until 1956.

⑦ Bakonyjákó
Set in a picture-postcard spot, this village was one of many in the Bakony that was popular with German settlers in the 18th century. Many of the houses are typically Saxon, set at a right angle to the main road.

⑧ Városlőd
At the meeting point of the Northern and Southern Bakony stand the ruins of the 11th-century Hölgykő Castle, destroyed by the Turks in the 16th century. Városlőd was repopulated by German settlers in the 18th century.

⑨ Ajka
Fine handmade glass, crystal and porcelain have been produced in Ajka since German settlers set up a factory here in 1878. Although the factory itself is not open to the public, there are two shops in the village selling wares made at the factory.

⑩ Úrkút
The route from Ajka to Herend, passing through Úrkút and the Szentgál Valley, is one of the most scenic in Hungary, offering up a wealth of gentle hills and wonderful views.

Map labels: Győr, 83, 83, ⑥ Pápa, Nagygyimót, Csót, Béb, Bakonyszücs ⑤, Borsosgyőr, Ugod, 83, Kéttornyúlak, Tapolcafő, Tapolca, Pápa-kovácsi, 83, Ganna, Döbrönte, Iharkút, ⑦, Németbánya, Farkasgyepü, 83, Magyarpolány, Csehbánya, Bakonygyepes, ⑧, 8, 8, Ajkarendek, Kislőd, Körmend, Torna, 9, Padragkút, 10

④ Kőris-hegy

An easy hiking trail takes walkers from Bakonybél at the foot of the hill up to the summit of Kőris-hegy; at 704 m (2,309 ft), the highest of the Bakony hills. The path leads back down to Zirc on the other side.

③ Bakonybél

The gently sloping, grassy hills above the pretty village of Bakonybél are accessible via a number of well-marked hiking trails, and make superb spots for picnic lunches.

Tips for Drivers

Tour length: 130 km (81 miles) All the roads on the tour are in good condition, though the minor routes from Zirc to Pápa and from Ajka to Herend get very narrow and twisty in places.

Stopping-off points: Zirc, with its museum, Cistercian Abbey and arboretum, is a good choice for a short stop, while the larger and busier town of Pápa, with its pretty historic centre, offers a wealth of choices for lunch.

② Zirc

Famous for its large Cistercian Abbey, Zirc is also home to the Bakony Natural History Museum.

① Veszprém

Hungary's best-preserved castle district rises above one of the country's most prosperous cities. With many fine restaurants, this is a good place to start and end the tour.

```
0 kilometres        5
0 miles             5
```

⑪ Herend

The hand-painted porcelain made here is famous the world over. Visitors may visit the museum and exhibitions, and also watch some of the 600 artists who work here in action.

Key

═══ Motorway
▬▬▬ Tour route
═══ Major road
··· Other road
━━ Main railway

For keys to symbols see back flap

❽ Sümeg

43 km (27 miles) north of Keszthely.
Road Map B4. 🚍 7,000. 🚉 from
Keszthely, Tapolca. 🚌 from Keszthely,
Zalaegerszeg. 🚏 Tourinform, Kossuth
Lajos utca 15, (20) 417 63 46.

This pretty town has been
inhabited since Roman times
and is dominated by its castle,
which sits atop the 270-m-
(885-ft-) high Castle Hill. **Sümeg
Castle** (Sümeg Vár), first built in
the 13th century though almost
completely reconstructed in
the 16th, is one of the best
preserved in Hungary. It houses
an exhibition on the town's
history, weapons, and coaches,
as well as a hair-raisingly realistic
torture chamber. During the
summer there are lively re-
enactments of historic battles,
jousting contests and medieval
dancing in the courtyard.
Tourinform will have details
of performances.

The town's main attraction,
however, is the **Roman Catholic
Church of the Ascension** (built
1756–7) on Bíró Márton utca.
Though unspectacular from
outside, inside it has a series of
frescoes by Austrian Franz
Anton Maulbertsch, a leading
figure in late Baroque art. The
frescoes, perhaps his greatest
work, were painted in 1757–8
and tell the story of the gospel,
from the Annunciation below
the organ gallery to the
Ascension in the dome.

🏯 Sümeg Castle

Tel (87) 35 27 37 or (30) 625 70 03.
Open daily, subject to weather. 📷

Courtyard of Sümeg Castle, now the site of re-enactments of medieval battles

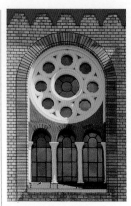
Decorative elements on the former
synagogue in Zalaegerszeg

❾ Zalaegerszeg

37 km (23 miles) east of Keszthely.
Road Map A4. 🚍 60,000. 🚉 from
Budapest. 🚌 from Keszthely.
🚏 Tourinform, Széchenyi tér 4–6,
(92) 31 61 60. 🛒 Piac tér, daily.
🌐 **zalaegerszeg.hu**

Zalaegerszeg, capital of the
Zala region and Hungary's
leading oil town, has two
attractions that make a stop
here worthwhile. The first is
the **Göcseji Village Museum**
(Göcseji Falumúzeum), the
oldest such in Hungary, located
on a tranquil backwater of the
River Zala. Set up in 1968, it
displays more than 40 buildings,
brought here from 22 nearby
villages. The museum also hosts
a Finno-Ugric exhibition, with
Finnish, Hanti and Manysi
homes. The Nodding Jennies
are part of Hungary's Oil
Industry Museum.

Zalaegerszeg's city centre is
brightened up by the former
synagogue, today a concert
and exhibition hall. Designed by
József Stern, its bright and lively
motifs betray its late Secession-
era construction (1904), though
the two domes add a little
religious dignity.

🏛 Göcseji Village Museum &
Finno-Ugric Ethnographical
Museum

Falumúzeum utca. **Tel** (92) 70 32 95.
Open Apr–Oct: 10am–6pm Tue–Sun;
Nov–Mar: 9am–5pm Mon–Sat. 📷 📷
Hungarian. ♿ 🌐 **zmmi.hu**

Statue of Sándor Petőfi and a soldier,
in Nagykanizsa

❿ Nagykanizsa

50 km (23 miles) south of Zalaegerszeg. **Road Map** A5. 🚍 53,000. 🚉
from Budapest. 🚌 from Keszthely,
Zalaegerszeg. 🚏 Tourinform,
Csengery utca 1–3, (93) 31 32 85.

Originally a castle town,
Nagykanizsa found wealth in
the late 17th century first as a
cattle-trading town, then in the
late 19th century as a hub for
food processing. The city centre
around Szabadság tér was built
over the site of the castle, used
as a mosque by the Turks and
destroyed by the Habsburgs in
1705. The fountain in the middle
of the square marks the former
castle entrance. The Baroque
Catholic church, on Zárda utca,
was built in 1702–14 using
remnants of the castle. The
city's Neo-Classical synagogue,
at Fő utca 6, built in 1807–10,
is being restored. In the
middle of Déak tér is a statue
of the Hungarian poet Sándor
Petőfi (1823–49).

Őriszentpéter, the largest of the villages in the Őrség region

⓫ Őrség Region

50 km (31 miles) west of Zalaegerszeg.
Road Map A4. 🚉 to Szentgotthárd
from Körmend. 🚌 to Őriszentpéter
Őrség from Szentgotthárd and
Körmend. 🛈 Tourinform Őrség, Siska-
szer 26A, Őriszentpéter, (94) 54 80 34.

Since the 10th century and the
first Magyar excursions into the
region, the Őrség has been a
frontier land, populated by
hardy warriors who swore to
defend Hungary's borders in
exchange for a lifetime's tax
exemption. Covered in lush
forests, the gently sloping
hills of the Őrség – today
designated a National Park –
were traditionally sprinkled with
small hilltop settlements, never
comprising more than 10
houses. Some 18 of these
settlements remain, almost all of
which are beautifully preserved,
many containing wooden
houses with characteristic
overhanging roofs, dating back
to the 13th century. The
settlements, called *szers*, all
follow the same pattern: the
houses are grouped around a
courtyard, in the middle of
which are stables.

The largest of the Őrség
villages is **Őriszentpéter**, which
in June hosts the Őrség Fair,
a weekend of folk music, craft
fairs and traditional dancing
competitions. Őriszentpéter
is, in fact, a collection of
timber and thatched *szers*
that came together to form
one community. The village

is rightly proud of its
13th-century Romanesque St
Peter Church, at Templomszer
15. It is almost entirely original,
containing fragments of
16th-century frescoes, which,
given the number of fires
that have plagued the village
over time, is little short
of miraculous.

Six km (4 miles) away, **Szalafő**
is the second-largest village in
the region, consisting of six
szers. The largest of these is
today the **Szalafő Open-Air
Ethnographical Museum**

(Őrségi Népi Műemlékegyüttes).
Here, visitors can see an Őrség
house as it would have looked
in the early 19th century,
complete with cooking utensils
and other domestic items.
Other settlements worth visiting
are **Velemér**, which has a
14th-century church with fine
frescoes, and **Hegyhátszent-
jakab**, where visitors can admire
a splendid medieval church.

Nearby, **Lake Vadása** is
popular with swimmers and
anglers. On the northern
borders of the Őrség are two
towns of note: **Szentgotthárd**
and **Körmend**. Both are good
access points for the Őrség, and
both have attractions of their
own: Körmend is home to the
Baroque **Batthány Mansion**
built for the family in the
17th century. A small part of
the building is open to visitors.
At Szentgotthárd the ceiling
frescoes of the Cistercian
Monastery Church, painted in
1785 by István Dorfmeister, are
outstanding.

🏛 Szalafő Open-Air
Ethnographical Museum
Pityerszer 12. **Tel** (94) 54 80 34. **Open**
Apr–Oct: 10am–5pm daily (to 6pm
Jun–Aug). 🎫 📷 Hungarian only. ♿

The grand façade of the 17th-century Batthány Mansion in Körmend

The library at Pannonhalma Abbey, a magnificent repository of Hungarian scholarship ▶

The impressive hilltop Benedictine abbey church in Ják

🕧 Ják

12 km (7 miles) south of Szombathely.
Road Map A4. 🏠 2,400. 🚌 from
Szombathely.

The Benedictine **St George's
Abbey Church** (Jáki Szent
György Bence's Apátsági
Templom) is the best-preserved
and most impressive example of
Romanesque architecture in
Hungary. Built in 1214–56, this
twin-towered masterpiece,
influenced by late Norman
architecture, sits imposingly on
a hilltop above the village. The
western façade is worthy of note
with its recessed doorway, a
richly decorated portal featuring
almost life-size carvings of Jesus
and the Apostles. This style,
called the Porta Speciosa
technique, was refined here
before becoming a model
for Romanesque
churches all over
Hungary. Inside the
church are original
14th-century
frescoes showing
the church's
founder, Jáki Nagy
Márton, and his
family. The church
was fully restored in 1890 by
Frigyes Schulek, who also
restored the Mátyás Church in
Budapest *(see pp66–7)*. The tiny
St Jakab Chapel opposite was
built in 1260 for the use of non-
monastic villagers.

Detail on the portal of the
Benedictine abbey in Ják

🏠 **St George's Abbey Church**
Fő tér. **Tel** (94) 35 60 14. **Open**
8am–6pm daily. ♿

🕧 Szombathely

101 km (60 miles) southwest of Győr.
Road Map A3. 🏠 115,000. 🚉 from
Sopron, Győr. 🚌 from Zalaergeszeg.
🛈 Tourinform, Király utca 1/A, (94) 31
72 69. 🎵 Bartók Classical Music
Festival (Jul); Savaria Carnival (Aug).

Founded by the Romans in
AD 43, and known as Savaria,
Szombathely was an important
trading and staging post on
the "Amber Road" from the
Baltic Sea to Italy. Every August
the Savaria Carnival recreates
those ancient days, and
hundreds of volunteers don
Roman costumes and engage
in battles, dancing and music.
The remains of the once-vast
Roman Forum (Savaria was the
capital of Roman Pannonia
Superior) are among
the city's leading
sights, with mosaic
floors and the
public baths clearly
visible. There is
more Roman
treasure on show
at the Savaria
Museum. Standing
next to the ruins is
the city's cathedral,
Hungary's largest Baroque
church, built in 1791–4. Its
interior suffered some damage
during World War II and is
undergoing continuous
restoration work. However, it is
open to the public. Next to it is
the Bishop's Palace, an attractive
Rococo building whose Sala
Terrena houses the Diocesan
Museum, which has a fine
collection of ecclesiastical art.
Another room contains a series
of frescoes by István
Dorfmeister based on life in
ancient Savaria.

A short walk from the
cathedral is Fő tér, today the
main centre of the city and a
shopper's paradise that is
popular with mothers and
children. There are further
Roman ruins at the Iseum Ruin
Garden on Batthány tér, featuring
a temple to the goddess Isis,
believed to be one of only three
ever found in Europe. Next door
is the Szombathely Gallery. In
May, when more than 50 kinds
of rhododendron are in full
bloom, the Kámoni Arboretum
north of the city centre is well
worth a visit.

Szombathely Cathedral, Hungary's largest
Baroque church

🕧 Sárvár

25 km (16 miles) east of Szombathely.
Road Map A3. 🏠 15,000. 🚉 from
Szombathely. 🚌 from Szombathely.
🛈 Tourinform, Várkerület 33, (95) 52
01 78).

The Magyars built an earth
castle (*sárvár* translates quite
literally as "mud castle") here in
the 10th century. Long before
that it appears the Romans had
some fortifications here, and
even the Celts found this
confluence of the Rába river a
sound defensive position. The
Sárvár Castle that now attracts
visitors is far from the mud of
yore, however, having been
built in the 16th century. Its
patrons were the Nádasdy

family, who bought the town in 1534. Patriarch Tamás Nádasdy brought in Italian architects to create a genuine Renaissance masterpiece, which, with various additions, survives more or less intact to the present day.

Much of the castle is given over to the **Ferenc Nádasdy Museum**, the highlight of which are two series of frescoes: 17th-century works showing the Hungarians in battle with the Turks and scenes from the Old Testament painted by István Dorfmeister in 1769. There are also exhibitions of the family's and town's histories, regional folk art and period furniture. The castle is reached via a long stone bridge over what was once a moat.

In 1961, during a search for oil *(see below)*, hot springs (44 °C/111 °F) were found in Sárvár, and the **Sárvár Spa and Wellness Centre** is now one of the largest bath complexes and, after its renovation and extension, the most modern in Hungary. It comprises indoor and outdoor pools, leisure and splash pools, a sauna and a treatment centre offering various therapies.

🏛 Ferenc Nádasdy Museum
Várkerület 1. **Tel** (95) 32 01 58.
Open Jul–Aug: 9am–9pm; Sep–Jun: 9am–5pm. 🅿 ◻

♨ Sárvár Spa and Wellness Centre
Vadkert utca 1. **Tel** (95) 52 36 00.
Open 8am–10pm daily. 🅿 ♿

One of the outdoor pools at the Bükfürdő Health and Adventure Centre

⓯ Bük

24km (15 miles) northeast of Szombathely. **Road Map** A3. 🔼 3,100. 🚆 from Szombathely, Sopron. 🚌 from Szombathely. 🛈 Tourinform, Eötvös utca 11, (94) 55 84 19.

Thermal springs were discovered at this village near the Austrian border in 1956 during a search for oil. Since then the **Bükfürdő Health and Adventure Centre** has grown to become one of Hungary's largest, and most attractive medicinal bath complexes. There are 32 indoor and outdoor pools of various sizes and temperatures, offering treatments for

a variety of different disorders, and the grounds are well laid out with grassy areas, children's playgrounds, snack bars and restaurants. A fair-sized resort has also grown up around the pool complex, and the Greenfield Hotel Golf and Spa *(see p293)*, a short walk from the thermal baths, is home to Hungary's finest golfing centre. It is the only 18-hole course in Hungary to have hosted a professional golf tournament.

♨ Bük Medicinal Baths
Termál kőrút 2. **Tel** (94) 55 80 80.
Open winter: 8:30am–6pm daily; summer: 8:30am–7pm daily. 🅿 ♿

Oil and Water

Many of the largest thermal bath complexes in Hungary, such as those at Bük and Sárvár, have only been in existence since the latter part of the 20th century, when the thermal springs that serve them were found during oil searches. Desperate to fuel its industrialization, Hungary's Communist government hoped that the discovery of the Nagylengyel oil field in the west of the country in 1951 would be the first of

Indoor thermal baths in Sárvár

many oil strikes in the region. Vast sums of money were spent foraging for oil, though all that was found was what became known as "white gold": thermal water. Some small deposits of crude oil were eventually located, but although Hungary does produce oil (Zalaegerszeg is the centre of the industry; *see p162*), domestic production accounts for less than 10 per cent of consumption.

The Knights Hall in Sárvár Castle, with superb battle frescoes

🔟 Kőszeg

Nestled in lowland hills just minutes from the Austrian border, modern-day Kőszeg is a small, quiet town, whose citizens are proud of its past. It is probably the only town in the world where the bells toll at 11am – in honour of Captain Miklós Jurisics, who led the Hungarians during a 25-day Turkish siege of Kőszeg Fortress in August 1532. The memory of Jurisics dominates the city, with its main square, castle and one of its museums carrying his name. Spared during World War II, Kőszeg is the most attractive town in the region.

Medieval wall painting in the southern nave, Church of St James

🏰 Jurisics Castle
Jurisics-vár
Rájnis József utca 9. **Tel** (94) 36 01 13. **Open** 10am–5pm Tue–Sun. 🈲 🚫 Hungarian only. ♿

It was here, in the carefully preserved Jurisics Castle, that Miklós Jurisics and 450 Hungarian soldiers held a 30,000-strong Turkish force at bay for 25 days in August 1532. The Hungarians eventually had to abandon their stand, only to return the following spring to retake the castle with Austrian help.

Crest above the gate to Jurisics Castle

A fire in 1777 destroyed part of the castle: the interior arcades were built after the blaze. The Castle Museum has displays on the town's history, including various depictions of the siege. It also has 18th- and 19th-century interiors and displays on the region's viticulture.

Heroes' Gate, a local landmark, in Miklós Jurisics Square

🏛 Miklós Jurisics Square
Jurisics Miklós tér

In the heart of Kőszeg's old town is this enclosed charming square, surrounded on all sides by churches, houses, museums and courtyards. The impressive entrance to the square, the Heroes' Gate, was erected to commemorate the 400th anniversary of the Turkish Siege. Though built in 1932 it recreates much older towers, and blends in impeccably with the surrounding – mainly Baroque – buildings. Of these, the Arcade House (Lábasház) next to the tower at No. 2 Jurisics tér is a highlight, complete with its courtyard colonnades. The Jurisics Museum on the other side of the tower, housed in the late Renaissance General's House (Tábornok), has a fine collection of memorabilia of the various guilds, artisans and tradesmen who inhabited the town. Next to the museum is the Town Hall, originally built in 1487, though the façade was remodelled in the Baroque style in the 18th century.

Today a pizzeria, the ornate Sgraffito House at No. 7 Jurisics tér dates from the 16th century. Sgraffito was an Italian method of creating lavish decorations by scratching through several layers of plaster. This is one of only few sgraffito houses in Hungary and, while time has not been kind to the façade, the effect is just still visible.

At the northern end of the square is the Baroque St Imre Church, completed in 1640 by Hungarian Lutherans who had been expelled from St James's Church (see below) by German Lutherans.

⛪ Church of St James
Szent Jakab templom
Rájnis utca 2. **Tel** (94) 56 33 97. **Open** 10am–6pm daily. 🈲 donation. ♿

Standing next to the more recent Church of St Imre, the Church of St James was completed in 1407, but much reconstructed in the 18th century. It remains clearly a Gothic building, however. The most important historic building in Kőszeg, the church has served Jesuit, Protestant and Roman Catholic congregations. The faded frescoes inside, by an unknown artist, depict the Magi, and are original, dating from 1403. Overpainted during the 17th century by the Lutherans, who disapproved of such ostentatious decoration, the frescoes were forgotten and only uncovered during interior restoration in the 1950s. The wooden statue of the Madonna is also an original from the Gothic era.

🕍 Synagogue
Zsinagoga
Várkör 38. **Tel** Anikó Béres (20) 934 87 30. **Open** by appointment.

Completed in 1859, this well-sized and imposing red-brick synagogue once served the considerable Jewish population in Kőszeg, which

Window detail on the front façade, Kőszeg Synagogue

was entirely wiped out during the Holocaust. Closed for some time, the synagogue is to undergo major restoration work, but parts of it can be visited by calling ahead to make an appointment. The synagogue's striking façade and Neo-Gothic towers can still be admired from the outside.

Golden Unicorn Pharmaceutical Museum
Arany Egyszarvú Patikamúzeum
Jurisics Miklós tér 11. **Tel** (94) 36 03 37.
Open by appointment.
Hungarians tend to be fascinated with old chemist

shops, but only rarely is one as deserving of interest as this particular example. As well as being set in a fine Baroque house on Jurisics tér, it contains a superb late 18th-century wooden apothecary counter, complete with old medicine bottles. It looks not unlike something from a film set. Upstairs the exhibition continues with a display showing how the medicines were cleaned, dried, stored and prepared. Most were remedies made from natural ingredients and plants grown in the pharmacy's own herb garden.

Jesus's Heart Church
Jézus Szíve templom
Fő tér. **Tel** (94) 56 33 97. **Open** 9am–6pm daily.
This fantastical Neo-Gothic wedding-cake church is famous for its colourful stained-glass altar windows depicting Saints István, Imre and Elizabeth. Built in 1892–4 to designs by the Austrian Otto Kott, its 60-m- (196-ft-) high tower is the tallest in the city. The

VISITORS' CHECKLIST

Practical Information
50km (31 miles) south of Sopron.
Road Map A3. 12,000.
Tourinform, Rájnis utca 7, (94) 56 31 20.

Transport
from Szombathely.
from Sopron.

interior, beautifully decorated, is filled with delicately patterned marble columns.

Interior of Jesus's Heart Church

Kőszeg City Centre

1. Jurisics Castle
2. Miklós Jurisics Square
3. Church of St James
4. Synagogue
5. Golden Unicorn Pharmaceutical Museum
6. Jesus's Heart Church

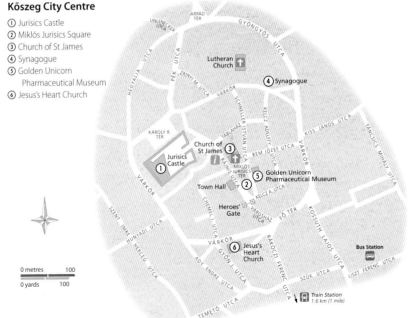

0 metres 100
0 yards 100

The façade of Széchenyi Mansion in Nagycenk

⑰ Nagycenk

15 km (9 miles) southeast of Sopron. **Road Map** A3. 🚗 1,900. 🚉 from Sopron. 🚌 from Sopron. 🎭 Nagycenk Art Days (Aug).

There are probably more public squares, streets, boulevards and avenues named after Count István Széchenyi (1791–1860), often called "the greatest Hungarian", than any other public figure, including St István himself. A philanthropic industrialist, his family home was the **Széchenyi Mansion** at Nagycenk, which is today a museum dedicated to his life and works. Stuffed with his personal effects, portraits, furniture and family history, the enormous Baroque mansion, built in the late 18th century for Széchenyi's grandfather, was all but destroyed in World War II, but was rebuilt as an exact replica of the original in the 1950s.

In 1815 the mansion was the first home in Hungary to benefit from gas lighting. Széchenyi made sure that the ordinary townsfolk of Nagycenk benefited from this technological wonder too, and they repaid his generosity by building him a mausoleum in the village cemetery. The Neo-Romanesque church, next to the cemetery, was designed by Miklós Ybl (see p93).

Nagycenk is also the starting point of the **Széchenyi Museum Railway**, a steam-powered train operation that runs along narrow-gauge tracks to Ferto-bőz. In the locomotive museum at the terminus, steam engines,

passenger coaches and freight and lumber wagons evoke the history of narrow-gauge railway lines.

🚉 **Széchenyi Mansion**
Kiscenki út 3. **Tel** (99) 36 00 23. **Open** Apr–Oct: 10am–6pm daily; Nov–Mar: 10am–5pm Tue–Sun. 🚗 📷 ♿

🚂 **Széchenyi Museum Railway**
Hársfasor. **Tel** (99) 51 72 44. **Open** Apr–Oct: Sat & Sun only. 🚗

⑱ Sopron

See pp172–5.

⑲ Fertő-Hanság National Park

16 km (10 miles) east of Sopron. **Road Map** A3. Rév-Kócsagvár, Sarród (Park Administration). **Tel** (99) 53 76 20. 📷 ♿ 🚉 from Sopron, Győr. 🚌 from Zalaergeszeg.

Based mainly on Lake Fertő, which for 40 years was one of the most heavily guarded parts of the Iron Curtain, Fertő-Hanság National Park (Fertő-Hanság Nemzeti Park) is now a protected nature reserve. As one of Europe's most significant water habitats, it became part of UNESCO's list of World Heritage Sites in 2001. With the eastern Alps as its dramatic backdrop, the lake is shallow, in most places less than 1 m (3 ft) deep, and is famous for its vast expanses of tall reeds. The lake's main sources of water are rainfall and two small streams. In fact, the lake has completely

dried up a number of times; the last, in 1867–71. There are numerous rare plant species – the park is famous for its "gallery" of snowdrops – and more than 200 species of birds nest here, including the Hungarian ibis, spoonbill and little egret. Many parts of the park can only be visited with special permits or on organized guided tours. Visitors can find out about both visits and tours at the park's administration office in Sarród.

The lake is circumnavigated by one of Europe's best cycle paths, which takes in spectacular landscapes in both Hungary and Austria. Favourable, frequent winds also make the lake a popular place to sail, while the shallow waters are inviting to swimmers. The main resort on the Hungarian side is Fertőrákos, where there are sailing boat launches, grassy beaches for sunbathing and many attractive nature walks.

⑳ Fertőrákos

8 km (5 miles) north of Sopron. **Road Map** A3. 🚗 2,300. 🚉 from Szombathely. 🚌 from Sopron. ℹ️ Tourinform, Joseph Haydn utca 2, Fertőd, (99) 53 71 40. 🌐 **fertorakos.hu**

The main resort on the coast of Lake Fertő, Fertőrákos is best known for its quarry, opened in 1628, which provided limestone for Vienna's St Stephen's Cathedral, among other buildings. The valuable Lajta rock was hewn

Cave theatre in the former limestone quarry at Fertőrákos

here from the time of the Antonines, though quarrying ended shortly after World War II. What remains is a surreal series of man-made, uneven caverns, colonnades and porticoes. In July the superb acoustics of the main cavern are put to perfect use as the setting for musical, dance and opera performances as part of the Sopron Festival Week.

A nature trail across the grasslands above the quarry offers magnificent, panoramic views of Lake Fertő and is also the site of the Pan-European Monument, a stark metal sculpture representing part of the Iron Curtain that commemorates the opening of the border in 1989.

㉑ Fertőd

25 km (16 miles) east of Sopron.
Road Map A3. 🚗 3,400. 🚌 from Szombathely. 🚍 from Sopron.
ℹ️ Tourinform, Joseph Haydn utca 3, (99) 37 05 44. 🎵 Haydn Festival (Jun–Sep).

The bedroom of the prince in the Esterhazy Palace in Fertőd

The small town of Fertőd was created in 1950 when two former estates belonging to the Esterházy family, called Süttör and Esterháza, were merged. It was for the Esterházy family *(see box)*, the wealthiest family in the region, that the town's masterpiece, the **Esterházy Palace** (Esterházy Palota), was built. First constructed as a two-storey hunting lodge in 1720, the grand palace is the result of vast extensions by the architect Melchior Hefel in the 1770s. The Neo-Baroque French gardens were laid out at the same time, though these were much remodelled along English ideas of garden design at the beginning of the 20th century.

The wrought-iron entrance gate, with its Rococo stone vase separating columns, is the perfect front to the palace, at which the visitor arrives along a yew-tree-lined path. The palace was badly damaged during World War II; however, a restoration project, parts of which have been completed, will transform it into a Central European cultural centre. The main ballrooms and drawing rooms have already been restored to their glorious best – priceless French furniture, Venetian mirrors and Flemish tapestries abound.

Joseph Haydn's presence at the palace from 1766 to 1790 is celebrated by the annual Haydn Festival with concerts of the composer's work. The focus is on his chamber music, performed by outstanding musicians in the Grand Gallery and the gardens.

🏛️ Esterházy Palace
Joseph Haydn utca 2. **Tel** (99) 53 76 40. **Open** Nov–mid-Mar: 10am–4pm Fri–Sun; mid-Mar–Oct: 10am–6pm Tue–Sun. 🅿️ 🎫 ♿

The Esterházy Family

For three centuries the Esterházy family was one of the richest and most powerful in Hungary. It flourished under the Habsburgs, whom family members served in a variety of political and military offices. The dynasty was founded by Count Nikolaus Esterházy (1582–1645) and his son, Prince Paul Esterházy, who sided with the Habsburgs during the Counter-Reformation *(see pp44–5)*. The family originated in – and derived its name from – the settlement Esterháza in modern-day Slovakia. The Esterházys moved to Eisenstadt, in Austria, in the 17th century, and set up home there. It was Paul Esterházy who decided to build the palace at Fertőd. After World War I, the family lost influence and was further weakened by internal feuds. Much Esterházy property is still bitterly fought over by various family branches.

Crest from the Esterházy Palace in Fertőd

⑱ Street-by-Street: Sopron Belváros

When visitors step through the Gate of Loyalty into Belváros – the Inner Town – they arrive in another world. Surrounded entirely by the modern city that has grown up around it, this historic part of Sopron is compact and easy to explore on foot. Belváros is centred around Fő tér and includes just four other streets, yet contains most of the city's main sights. There is a wealth of Secessionist architecture to see, as well as the Firewatch Tower, from where stunning views of Sopron unfold. A genuine city within a city, it is one of Hungary's treasures.

County Hall
Vencil Hild designed this elegant Classical building, constructed in 1829–34.

Museum of Mining
The museum, at Templom utca 2, is housed in the former town residence of the Esterházy princes.

The Lutheran Church (1782) was made possible by József II guaranteeing freedom of worship to his subjects.

Old Synagogue

★ **Benedictine Church**
Known as the Goat Church (see p174), this large Gothic church was built by Franciscan monks in 1280. It is the best remaining example of Gothic architecture in Hungary.

TEMPLOM UTCA

ÚJ UTCA

ORSOLYA TÉR

Ursuline Church
This former convent, founded by Ursuline nuns in 1747, is one of the most impressive buildings in the town. It holds an outstanding collection of ecclesiastical art.

★ **Storno House**
King Mátyás lived here in 1482–3. Originally a Renaissance building, it was remodelled in the Baroque style in 1720.

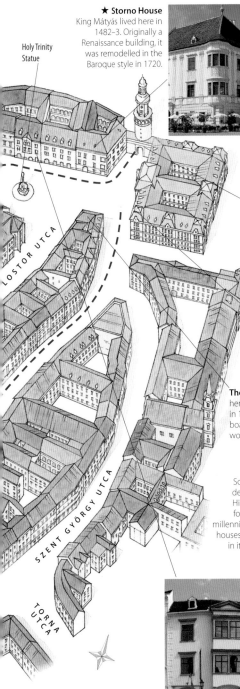

Holy Trinity Statue

LOSTOR UTCA

SZENT GYÖRGY UTCA

TORNA UTCA

0 metres   50
0 yards   50

VISITORS' CHECKLIST

Practical Information
Road Map A3. 🚆 56,000.
ℹ️ Tourinform, Liszt Ferenc utca 1, (99) 51 75 60. 🛒 daily, Csarnok utca. 🎭 Spring Days, including Liszt Festival (Mar); Sopron Festival Weeks (Jun–Jul); Volt Pop Festival (Jul); Christmas Market (Dec).

Transport
🚍 Mátyás Király utca; from Győr, Vienna, Wiener Neustadt.
🚌 Lakner Kristóf utca; from Győr.

★ **Firewatch Tower and Gate of Loyalty**
The symbol of the city, the tower rises to 61 m (200 ft), offering stunning views of Belváros.

The pharmacy
here was founded in 1642 and still boasts the original wooden counters.

Town Hall
Sopron's town hall, designed by Károly Hintrager and built for Hungary's 1896 millennium celebrations, houses a fine art gallery in its southern wing.

Fabricius House
Named after Sopron's mayor in the early 19th century, the Fabricius House was built over the ruins of a Roman bath.

Key
— Suggested route

Exploring Sopron

A border town of the Pannonia province, Austrian number plates and German-language shop and street signs are much in evidence in Sopron today, and it is easy to forget that this is still Hungary. In 1921, the people of Sopron voted to stay in Hungary, rather than join Austria, and the Gate of Loyalty is dedicated to the result of that plebiscite. One of Hungary's oldest cultural centres, Sopron has remains of Roman edifices and city walls as well as grand medieval buildings, including both churches and a synagogue. Among other sights are a Pharmacy Museum and an outstanding art collection.

🏛 Collection of Roman Catholic Church Art
Római Katolikus Egyházművészeti Gyűjtemény
Várkerület 25. **Tel** (99) 31 22 21.
Open May–Oct: 2–4pm Tue, 9–11am Thu. 🎫 📷

This fine collection of ecclesiastical art is owned and managed by Sopron's Catholic Convent. Most items are from the Baroque period, complemented by an early 19th-century collection. There are liturgical cups, crosses, christening bowls, historical altars and paintings. The finest painting, of St Dominic (1710), is by the Neapolitan Rococo master Martin Altamonte.

🏛 Museum of Mining
Központi Bányászati Múzeum
Templom utca 2 **Tel** (99) 31 26 67.
Open Apr–Sep: 10am–6pm Tue–Sun; Oct–Mar: 10am–4pm Tue–Sun. 🎫

This engaging museum presents the history and science of mining in Hungary over the course of a thousand years.

✡ Old Synagogue
Ó-Zsinagóga
Új utca 22. **Tel** (99) 31 13 27. **Open** Apr–Oct: 10am–6pm Tue–Sun. 🎫

Thought to have been built around 1300, the medieval synagogue of Sopron is one of the oldest in Europe. In line with anti-Semitic legislation of the day, the local Jewish community had to build their prayer hall set back from the main buildings on the street, which is why it stands behind two Baroque houses. Abandoned in 1526 when the Jews were expelled from Sopron, many of its original features remain intact, however, including the recess in the east wall holding a replica Ark of the Covenant.

Across the road, the New Synagogue was built in 1370 for the private use of a Jewish banker. It, too, fell into disuse in 1526, and though its exterior is in reasonable repair, it is closed to the public.

⛪ Benedictine Church
Kecske-templom
Templom utca 1, Fő tér. **Tel** (99) 33 42 31. **Open** summer: 9am–6pm daily; winter: 9am–4pm Tue–Sun. 🎫 ♿

Built by Franciscans in 1280, this great Gothic church was given to the Benedictines in 1787, when József II dissolved the Franciscan Order. It has remnants of medieval frescoes inside and an elegant Kapisztrán pulpit, unique in style. The church is known as Goat Church – a goatherd is said to have financed it from treasure found by his flock.

The Benedictine Church, originally belonging to the Franciscan Order

🏛 Fabricius House Museum and Apartments
Régészeti kőtár
Fő tér 6. **Tel** (99) 31 13 27. **Open** Apr–Sep: 10am–6pm Tue–Sun; Oct–Dec: by arrangement only. 🎫

The highlight of this museum's archaeological collection is the lapidarium, with headstones, sarcophagi and altars from all eras of Sopron's history. Another display features Sopron and the Amber Road. In a street-side wing are apartments furnished and decorated in the typical bourgeois styles of the 17th and 18th centuries.

🏛 Storno House & Exhibition of Regional History
Storno-gyűjtemény és Helytörténeti kiállítás
Fő tér 8. **Tel** (99) 31 13 27. **Open** Jan–Mar: 9am–5pm Tue–Sun; Apr–Dec: 10am–6pm Tue–Sun. 🎫

This grand 15th-century medieval house, the one-time home of King Mátyás, displays a fine collection of art, antiques and period furniture.

The Old Synagogue, its prayer hall set back from the street

Painting of St Dominic above the main altar of the Dominican Church

🔲 Firewatch Tower
Tűztorony

Fő tér. **Tel** (99) 31 13 27. **Open** Jan–Mar: 9am–5pm daily; Apr, Oct, Nov: 10am–6pm daily; May–Sep: 10am–8pm daily; Dec: 10am–6pm Tue–Sun. 🔲

The symbol of the city, the Firewatch Tower was built on the remains of the Roman wall in the 13th century. Balcony and spire are Baroque; they were added after the building burned down in 1676. The Gate of Loyalty, at the foot of the tower, was added in 1928 to designs by Rezső Hikisch.

🏛 Pharmacy Museum
Patika Múzeum

Fő tér 2. **Tel** (99) 31 13 27. **Open** Apr–Sep: 10am–2pm Tue–Sun; Oct–Dec: by arrangement only. 🔲 ♿

The former Angel Pharmacy (1601) opened as a pharmacy museum in 1966. It displays fascinating medical items, old manuals dating back to 1572 and beautiful Altwien china jars from Vienna.

🔲 Széchenyi tér and Dominican Church
Domonkos templom

Széchenyi tér.

Spacious and green, Széchenyi tér at the southern entrance to Belváros is surrounded by outstanding architecture on all sides. The Dominican Church on its southeastern corner – easily missed if approaching from the railway station – was designed by Lorenz Eysenkölbl and built in 1719–25, with the spires added in 1775. A local artist, Stephan Schaller, painted the picture of St Dominic above the altar. The adjoining two-storey building is the Baroque Dominican Priory, built in 1750. Across the road stands the Széchenyi Palace, built in 1851 for Ferenc Széchenyi. Today housing administrative offices and closed to the public, many of the first exhibits in Hungary's National Museum collection (see pp102–3) came from here. István Széchenyi is honoured with a huge bronze statue in the middle of the square. On the north side is the Ferenc Liszt Cultural Centre (Művelődési Ház), built in 1872. Liszt performed here regularly, and the centre hosts cultural events today.

🔲 Old City Walls
Várkerület

Having survived many attacks, Sopron's city walls – built by the Romans and once encircling the entire Belváros – were dismantled by locals at the end of the 19th century in order to improve access to the city. A walkway, the Castle Wall Promenade, takes in many of the remnants; some of the most impressive can be seen at the Várkerület, opposite Árpád utca, where there is an 8-m- (26-ft-) thick portion of wall and part of a fortified tower or barbican, the Great Round Bastion.

🏛 Zettl–Langer Collection

Balfi utca 11. **Tel** (99) 31 11 36. **Open** Apr–Oct:10am–noon Tue–Sun; Nov–Mar: 10am–noon Fri–Sun. 🔲

A century and a half ago, Gusztáv Zettl had to choose between his first love, art, or his father's business empire. He chose business, but never lost his love of art. Much of the money he made in business was invested in some of the finest art of the period.

His collection, which encompasses works from all genres, periods and fashions, has been exhibited in the Zettl family home since 1955 (Zettl himself died in 1951). The house itself has artisan windows, frescoed ceilings, Biedermeier furniture and paintings by Rembrandt, Paolo Veronese and István Dorfmeister.

A room in the Zettl family home, housing the Zettl-Langer Collection

🔲 Károly Lookout Tower
Károly-magaslati Kilátó

Lővérek. **Tel** (99) 31 30 80. **Open** daily; Mar: 9am–5pm; Apr–Oct: 9am–6pm (May–Aug: to 8pm; Sep: to 7pm); Nov–Feb: 9am–4pm. 🔲

The 23-m- (75-ft-) high tower, built in 1876, offers panoramic views of lush forests, Lake Fertő and the snow-covered Schneeberg range in Austria's Wienerwald, west of Vienna. A small exhibition outlines the unique natural features of the Sopron Nature Conservation Area.

St Anne's Church in Kapuvár, built in the Neo-Baroque style

㉒ Kapuvár

47 km (29 miles) west of Győr.
Road Map B3. 🏛 11,000.
🚌 🚐 from Győr, Sopron.

This small town's name translates as "Gate Fortress", and that is exactly what it was: a fortress protecting the gate that controlled access to the border area. Built in 1270, the fortress was dismantled in 1884 to prevent it being used by Austrian forces. It was replaced with a Neo-Baroque mansion. This today is the office of the mayor and home to the **Rábaközi Museum**, which has an exhibition on the history of the town, a collection of regional folk art, as well as work by the sculptor Pál Pátzay, who was born in Kapuvár in 1896. Rising above the mansion is **St Anne's Church**, built at the same time as the museum, also to a Neo-Baroque design, and replacing a wooden chapel.

Regional costume in the Rábaköz Museum in Kapuvár

㉓ Csorna

30 km (19 miles) west of Győr.
Road Map B3. 🏛 11,000. 🚌 from Győr. 🚐 from Győr.

Csorna is one of the oldest Christian towns in Hungary: a Premonstratensian Order settled here shortly after the Magyars, and in 1802 Csorna became one of the Hungarian

centres for the Premonstratensians. The site of their monastery is now occupied by the magnificent 19th-century Neo-Renaissance Premonstratensian Csorna Palace. The palace contains an exhibition of local folk art. Here, visitors can find out about local wood carvings and so-called "spider embroidery", as well as the blue-dyers of Csorna and the potters of Dör. Together with the church order, these were two groups that contributed significantly to the town's wealth and growth in the 18th and early 19th centuries.

Next to the palace is the complementary Premonstratensian St Helen's Church, built in 1938 after the original 19th-century church on this site had burned down.

㉔ Moson-magyaróvár

37 km (23 miles) northwest of Győr.
Road Map B3. 🏛 32,000. 🚌 from Győr. 🚐 from Győr. 🛈 Tourinform, Kápolna tér 16, (96) 20 63 04. 🎪 Voluta International Water Festival (Jun); Summer Festival (Aug).

The Romans built a fortress at Magyaróvár in the 3rd century AD. It was later extended by the Huns and then the Magyars, who constructed a large mud-brick fortress here. In 1271 Ottocar of Bohemia replaced this structure with the present stone **Magyaróvár Castle**. It has been extended and renovated many times since, and little of what remains is original apart from the two southern towers. Over the bridge from the castle (which is on an island) is Fő utca, on which stands at No. 19 the Gothic Cselley House (Cselley Ház). Inside is part of the Hanság Museum collection (the rest is at Szent István Király utca 1, further along Fő utca). Highlights include the Tibor Gyurkovich Collection, as well as a fine exhibition of Hungarian paintings, including works by Oszkár Glatz, Mihály Munkácsy and Gyula Rudnay. A short walk east on Szent Laszló tér is St Gotthard's Church. Its foundations were laid in 1668, although it was not completed until 1778, when the Baroque interiors were finished. The Habsburg prince Frederick and his wife Isabelle are buried in the crypt.

The town's long name, even by Hungarian standards, dates back to 1939, when the two separate towns of

The Magyaróvár Castle in Mosonmagyaróvár, on the site of a Roman fort

Aerial view of the largely hidden Monostor Fortress in Komárom

Moson and Magyaróvár became one and the two names simply joined together.

🏰 Magyaróvár Castle
Vár utca 2. **Tel** (96) 56 66 37.
Open 7:30am–6pm Mon–Fri.
🅿 🚻 to the grounds.

㉕ Győr
See pp178–9.

㉖ Pannonhalma Abbey
See pp180–81.

㉗ Komárom
38 km (24 miles) northeast of Győr.
Road Map C3. 🚗 20,000.
🚆 from Budapest, Győr. 🚌 from Győr. 🛈 Tourinform, Igmándi út 2, (34) 54 05 90.

A real border town, split in two by nature (the Danube) and politics (it straddles the Hungarian-Slovakian border), Komárom is the main crossing point between the two countries. Until 1920 this was one town, and on both sides of the river the two languages appear to be spoken interchangeably. The Hungarian part of the town is known for the colossal **Monostor Fortress** (Monostori Erőd), built by the Habsburgs 2 km (1 mile) upriver from the city centre after the 1848–9 uprising. Covering approximately 4 hectares (10 acres), it is the largest fortress

in the country, and one of the largest in Europe. Most of it is invisible from outside, as it is buried underground. It was sparsely used by the Habsburgs before becoming the property of the Hungarian army, who used it as a training camp. After World War II, the Soviet army held political prisoners here. The story of the fortress is told clearly in the museum that now occupies much of the main bastion. There is also a bread museum, where visitors may taste the "ration bread" given to the soldiers who had to man the place in the 19th century. The fortress hosts cultural events and battle recreations throughout the summer.

🏰 Monostor Fortress
Monostori Erőd, Dunapart 1. **Tel** (34) 54 05 82. **Open** 9am–6pm daily. 🅿 🚻 Tue–Sun; book tours in English a week in advance. 🖥 **fort-monostor.hu**

㉘ Tata
60 km (37 miles) east of Győr.
Road Map C3. 🚗 24,000. 🚆 from Budapest. 🚌 from Budapest. 🛈 Tourinform, Ady Endre utca 9, (34) 58 60 45.

Sitting on the banks of Lake Öreg, Tata is often referred to as the Hungarian Venice, mainly for the moated castle on the lake's north bank. Little except one tower and a wall remain of the 15th-century original: most of the current, nevertheless impressive, building dates from 1893.

The lake was once surrounded by water mills, but only a few remain; the Cifra Mill next to the castle is the oldest, dating from 1587. Another mill a short distance north houses the German Minorities Museum, with interesting artifacts from the region's once numerous German population.

On the other side of the castle, on central Hősök tér, is the eclectic Esterházy Mansion, built in 1777. Used as a mental hospital for years, it has now been largely restored.

Across the square is the **Greco-Roman Statue Museum**, a former synagogue containing full-size replicas of classical statuary, from David to Zeus.

On the shore of Tata's second lake, Lake Cseske, stands the folly of a ruined church.

🏛 Greco-Roman Statue Museum
Hősök tere 7. **Tel** (34) 38 12 51. **Open** Apr–Oct 10am–6pm Tue–Sun; Nov–Mar by appointment only. 🅿 🚻

Replicas of famous statues in the Greco-Roman Statue Museum in Tata

㉙ Győr

Located exactly halfway between Budapest and Vienna, where the rivers Danube, Rába and Rábca meet, Győr has long been the place where empires met, and often clashed. Celts founded the city, and called it Arrabona, before giving way to the Romans. The Magyars saw the value of the town's position and created a bishopric here, while during the Turkish wars it became the home of the most impenetrable fortress in Hungary at the time. Full of monuments and buildings that tell of its eventful past, Győr is also a modern, vibrant city. Outstanding communications make it an excellent base for exploring the Győr–Moson–Sopron region.

🏰 Bishop's Palace
Püspökvár
Káptalandomb 1. **Open** Museum 10am–4pm Tue–Sun. 🅿 ♿

The first castle on this imposing site was built during the reign of St István; nothing of it remains, however. The tower, known as the Runway Corridor, dates from the 14th (lower) and 18th century (upper part). The chapel was built from 1481 to 1486, and unusually extends over two levels. The fortifications were largely added during the 16th century by the Italian architect Pietro Ferrabosco, to keep out the Turks. He completed his work in 1575, but by 1594 the Turks had taken the castle and the city. During the 18th century, Bishop Ferenc Zichy renovated the castle in the Baroque style. In 1984 further renovation was carried out. A museum in the treasury is dedicated to Hungarian priest Vilmos Apor, shot by Soviet soldiers in 1945 while trying to prevent rape and pillage.

The stunning 18th-century Baroque interior of Győr Cathedral

🏛 Győr Cathedral
Székesegyház
Káptalandomb. **Tel** (96) 61 83 04. **Open** 8am–noon, 2–6pm daily. ♿

St István created the Győr Episcopate in the early 11th century, and the foundations of Győr Cathedral were laid then. Originally a three-aisled church with a raised sanctuary, it was destroyed by the Mongols in 1240, and rebuilt in Gothic style, with two imposing towers, in

1257–67. The 15th-century Gothic Chapel houses the Holy Herm, the remains of St László, one of Hungary's most sacred relics. A fire destroyed the towers around 1580, and the cathedral was remodelled by the Italian architect Giovanni Rava in the 17th century. The Baroque interior dates from the time after the Turkish period, when the altarpieces and superb frescoes by Franz Anton Maulbertsch were added. The painting of the Virgin Mary above the Baroque altar is one of Hungary's most significant sites of pilgrimage. It allegedly wept blood in March 1697.

🏛 Ark of the Covenant
Frigyláda emlékmű
Gutenberg tér. ♿

Built on the orders of Charles III in 1731, the Baroque Ark of the Covenant monument shows two angels holding the Ark in their hands. It was erected as an act of atonement for the violation of the Blessed Sacrament when Habsburg soldiers knocked the monstrance from the hands of the priest during the Corpus Christi procession in 1727. The soldiers were chasing a deserter and adulterer who had sought sanctuary in the procession.

🏛 Győr Diocesan Treasury and Library
Győri Egyházmegyei Kincstár és Könyvtár
Káptalandomb 26. **Tel** (96) 52 50 90. **Open** 10am–4pm Tue–Sat. 🅿 ♿

Hungary's finest collection of manuscripts is kept among this treasure trove of liturgical items. Alongside the Gothic chalices and Renaissance mitres is a codex from the 11th century, and the Korvina, an illuminated manuscript originating from the personal library of King Mátyás.

🏛 Margit Kovács Exhibition
Kovács Margit Állandó Kerámia Kiállítás
Apáca utca 1. **Tel** (96) 32 67 39. **Open** 10am–6pm Tue–Sun. 🅿 ♿

A vast collection of ceramics is on display in a monumental 16th-century mansion that underwent renovations in 1977. The exhibited works are by

The Bishop's Palace, built to defend the town from Turkish invaders

For hotels and restaurants see pp264–269 and pp276–285

Margit Kovács (1902–77), a local-born ceramic artist who is Hungary's leading 20th-century abstract sculptor. Items on display range from vases to religious pieces, with personal items and a model of her workshop.

Ceramics on the stairs at the Margit Kovács Exhibition

⊞ Széchenyi Square

Széchenyi tér 4. Imre Patkó Collection: **Tel** (96) 31 05 88. **Open** 10am–6pm Tue-Sun. Esterhazy Palace: **Tel** (96) 32 26 95. **Open** 10am–6pm Tue-Sun. 🏛 🛆

Once the city's marketplace, this cobbled square is ringed by splendid buildings. On the north side, in the so-called Iron Stump House, is the **Imre Patkó Collection** with ethnic pieces from Asia and Africa and 16th-century applied arts exhibits. Nearby, at Király utca 17, the Baroque **Esterházy Palace**, famed for its early example of a bay window, houses the Municipal Museum of Arts, which has several themed exhibitions. The south side of the square is dominated by the Baroque Ignatius Benedictine Church,

built by the Jesuits in 1627. The beautiful Baroque pulpit was added in 1757. After the Jesuit order was dissolved in 1802, the Benedictines added the two towers. Next to the church stands a working **Pharmacy Museum** boasting the beautifully carved ceiling. The Maria Column outside was built in 1686 to celebrate Buda's recapture from the Turks.

The Maria Column, in the centre of Széchenyi Square

⛪ Carmelite Church & Monastery
Karmelita templom
Aradi vértanúk utca 2. 🛆

The Carmelites settled in Győr in 1697. Their church, a wonderful mixture of the Baroque and the Italianate, was built in 1721–5 to the plans of Athanasius Wittwer, a member of their order. The monastery was completed in 1732. Neapolitan master Martin Altomonte painted the main altarpiece featuring saints István and Imre. In the church's chapel is a statue of Mary made in Rome and blessed in the Vatican's Loretto Chapel before being brought here in 1717.

Győr City Centre

① Bishop's Palace
② Győr Cathedral
③ Ark of the Covenant
④ Győr Diocesan Treasury and Library
⑤ Margit Kovács Exhibition
⑥ Széchenyi Square
⑦ Carmelite Church and Monastery

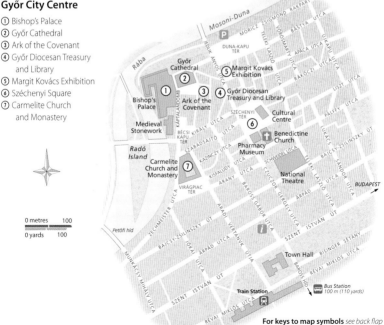

0 metres 100
0 yards 100

For keys to map symbols *see back flap*

㉖ Pannonhalma Abbey

The story of Pannonhalma Abbey is as old as Hungary itself. A UNESCO World Heritage Site since 1996, there has been an abbey here since 1002, the same year St István brought Christianity to the Magyars. The original abbey burned down and was replaced in 1137 with a Romanesque construction, itself superseded by the late Romanesque–early Gothic basilica still in existence today. The basilica's main portal of receding arches is one of the most important surviving examples of a *Porta Speciosa* extant in Hungary.

Basilica
The Basilica's stained-glass windows were added in around 1860. This one depicts St Ladislaus, or László I, a pious knight-king of the 11th century canonized a century after his death.

★ Arboretum
The arboretum on the eastern slope has been the site of more than 1,200 rare tree, shrub and herbaceous plant species since 1802. Most of the species have grown wild in the abbey's grounds.

★ Porta Speciosa
Though now hemmed in by extensions to the complex, the *Porta Speciosa* is an outstanding example of its kind – an ornamental portal held in red marble with rich wood carvings.

KEY

① **The Benedictine Grammar School** was founded in 1802 and is one of the finest in Hungary. The entrance exams are famously tough.

② **The Treasury** is home to a rich collection of ecclesiastical art and historical artifacts.

★ Library
The Neo-Classical library holds 400,000 volumes, including the Tihany Manuscript, the earliest example of written Hungarian.

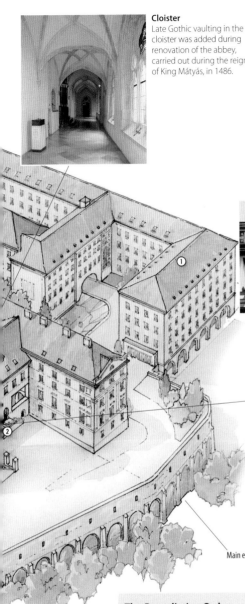

Cloister
Late Gothic vaulting in the cloister was added during renovation of the abbey, carried out during the reign of King Mátyás, in 1486.

Our Lady Chapel
On the far side of the abbey, Our Lady Chapel has three Baroque altars and a tiny organ. The abbey's monks are buried here.

Western Tower
Very much the abbey's calling card, and its most recognizable feature, the Western Tower, added in 1832, can be seen from far away.

Main entrance

The Benedictine Order

The Order of St Benedict, oldest of the religious orders, was founded by Benedict of Nursia, who set up the first monastery at Monte Cassino, Italy, in 529. Benedict wanted to re-establish a sense of community in the turmoil after the collapse of the Roman Empire, and ever since community and hospitality have been the hallmarks of the Benedictines. Benedictine monks are known for living by their labour; Pannonhalma is no exception. The 40 monks who still live at the abbey sell wine (vineyards surround the abbey), Benedictine liqueur, honey, tea and lavender products.

A wine produced at Pannonhalma

SOUTHERN TRANSDANUBIA

Shallow and warm, the waters of Lake Balaton have attracted visitors for centuries, and today the long, narrow lake is surrounded by holiday resorts. South of Balaton, the region is sparsely populated, with Pécs the only city of any size. Great wines are made in this, the sunniest region of the country; the Villány-Siklós wine route offers a chance to sample some of them in superb surroundings.

Lake Balaton has something for everyone, from brash beach resorts such as Siófok on the south bank to the serene tranquillity of the Tihany Peninsula that juts into the lake from the north. It is not difficult to see why so many Hungarians choose to spend their holidays here. Motorized water sports are forbidden, so swimmers, anglers and sailors have the lake pretty much to themselves. Though the main Balaton season is limited to high summer (the only time hot, sunny weather can be guaranteed), the nearby cities of Keszthely, Tapolca and Veszprém are year-round destinations for visitors.

To the west of the lake is Kis-Balaton, a nature reserve of world renown; in autumn, birdwatchers flock here like the migrating birds they come to watch.

There is more fauna, and flora, at the Duna–Dráva National Park, especially in the ancient Gemenc Forest, perhaps Hungary's lushest and most accessible nature reserve. To the south, human history takes centre-stage at the towns of Mohács and Szigetvár, both of which are known for the heroic battles that were fought and lost against the Turks here. In Pécs, the largest city in the region, the enormous former mosque is a permanent reminder that Sultans once held sway here.

Many of Hungary's best wines are made in Southern Transdanubia, both in the volcanic hills on the western shores of Balaton, and in the sun-kissed vineyards of the far south, in the Villány hills. Visitors will have ample opportunity to taste them all.

Vineyards near Badacsonytomaj with Mount Badacsony in the background, Lake Balaton

◀ The magnificent interior of St Peter's Cathedral, Pécs

Exploring Southern Transdanubia

Outside the capital, Southern Transdanubia is Hungary's most-visited region. Most holiday-makers are attracted by the vast Lake Balaton and the many activities it offers. One of the nicest resorts to visit here, and to enjoy the clean, warm waters of the lake, is the elegant town of Keszthely. The region has great topographical diversity, with the Gemenc forest, the Villány hills and the Dráva river all having an impact. The old town of Veszprém has narrow, cobbled streets and the picturesque Vár Castle, while Pécs is home to many fine galleries. Steeped in history, Southern Transdanubia witnessed a crucial battle: the Ottoman rout of the Habsburg rulers at Mohács in 1526.

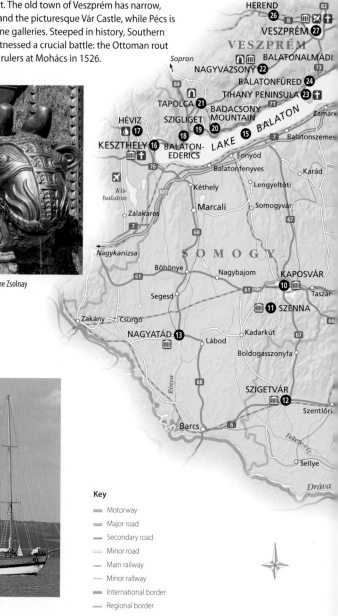

A glazed bull's head on the Zsolnay fountain in Pécs

Yachting on Lake Balaton

Key

▬ Motorway
▬ Major road
▬ Secondary road
···· Minor road
— Main railway
— Minor railway
▬ International border
▬ Regional border

For hotels and restaurants see pp264–269 and pp276–285

Interior of the Secession-style town hall, Kaposvár

Sights at a Glance
1. Dunaföldvár
2. Paks
3. Mohács
4. Duna–Dráva National Park
5. Villány
6. Siklós
7. Harkány
8. *Pécs pp190–93*
9. Dombóvár
10. Kaposvár
11. Szenna
12. Szigetvár
13. Nagyatád
14. Siófok
16. *Keszthely pp200–3*
17. Hévíz
18. Balatonederics
19. Szigliget
20. Badacsony Mountain
21. Tapolca
22. Nagyvázsony
23. Tihany Peninsula
24. Balatonfüred
25. Balatonalmádi
26. Herend
27. *Veszprém pp208–11*

Tour
15. *Lake Balaton pp198–9*

Getting Around
The M7 (E71) motorway serves Lake Balaton, though it literally creaks under the pressure of traffic during the summer, especially in July and August and at the weekends, and jams can be long. There are also trains from Budapest-Keleti to the southern Balaton resorts, departing every 15 minutes or so in summer. Pécs is served by route 6 from the capital, which is particularly pretty, as it follows the Danube for much of the way. Public transport connections in the far south of Transdanubia are poor, and a car is needed to explore the area around Pécs.

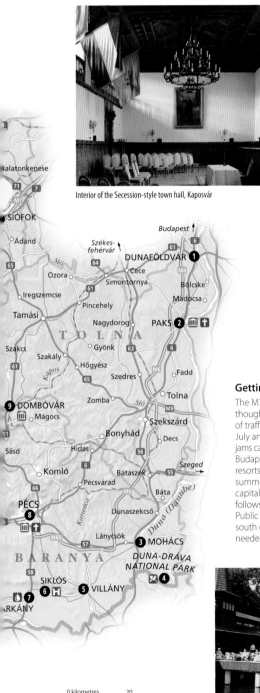

Bathing in the Thermal Lake in Hévíz

For keys to map symbols *see back flap*

❶ Dunaföldvár

69 km (43 miles) south of Budapest.
Road Map C4. 🏛 9,500. 🚉 from
Paks. 🚌 from Budapest. ℹ Tour-
inform, Rátkay köz 2, (75) 34 11 76.

With its elegant central square,
Béke tér, surrounded by well-
kept Baroque and Secession
buildings, especially the
spire-topped **town hall**,
Dunaföldvár is one of the
most attractive towns on the
southern stretch of the
Hungarian Danube.
Overlooking the town is
the Ruined Tower, all
that remains of a fort
which stood on the
site in the 16th
century. The tower,
on Rátkai utca,
affords superb views
of the city centre,
and of the Danube.
It is reached by way
of the ornate
wooden castle
gate, a 19th-
century replica of
the original. In the
same courtyard is the Fafaragó
Gallery, dedicated to the town's
woodcarvers.

Town hall clock tower
in Dunaföldvár

❷ Paks

21 km (13 miles) south of Dunaföldvár.
Road Map C4. 🏛 21,000. 🚉 from
Dunaföldvár. 🚌 from Budapest.

There would be little reason to
visit Paks were it not for the
town's strikingly modern
Catholic Church. Designed by
the controversial late Hungarian
architect Imre Makovecz, it was
completed in 1988 and is
constructed entirely of wood.
Resembling the wooden
churches of the Romanian
Maramures region, it has
three spires, which are
topped with a cross,
a sun and a crescent
The presence of the
crescent – a symbol
of Islam – caused
much furore when it
was unveiled.
The town, which is
the site of Hungary's
only nuclear power
station, is also home
to the **Paks Gallery**
(Paksi Képtár) of
contemporary art.
Inside the slightly worn but still
imposing Neo-Classical building
are four permanent exhibitions

dedicated to the works of local
experimental and fine artists,
dating from 1980 onwards.

🏛 **Paks Gallery**
Szent István tér 4. **Tel** (75) 83 02 84.
Open 10am–6pm Tue–Sun. ♿

Entrance arch to the Mohács
Memorial Park

❸ Mohács

46 km (29 miles) east of Pécs. **Road
Map** C5. 🏛 20,000. 🚉 from Villány.
🚌 from Budapest. 🚢 cross-Danube
car ferry. ℹ Tourinform, Széchenyi
tér 1, (69) 50 55 15. 🛒 daily,
Szabadság tér. 🎭 Busó Carnival
(Shrove Tue; Feb).

On 29 August 1526, in a field
7 km (4 miles) south of the
small town of Mohács, the Turks
comprehensively defeated
the Hungarians, clearing the
last obstacle on their march
to Buda *(see box opposite)*. To
commemorate the 400th
anniversary of the Battle of
Mohács, a Byzantine church
was erected in the main square,
Széchenyi tér, opposite the
Gothic town hall. The site of the
battle itself is marked by a
memorial to the soldiers who
fell, both in 1526 and in a lesser
battle in 1687. Their mass graves
are indicated by painted
wooden headstones. Five such
graves have been uncovered so
far, and work is ongoing in the
Memorial Park.
Mohács comes alive every
Shrove Tuesday, when it is the
scene of the Busó Carnival
(Busójárás). Today, a colourful
event is held to mark the passing of winter. The ritual of
dressing in rags and wearing

The organically shaped Catholic Church in Paks with its three spires

startling masks was originally devised to scare off the Turks – but it clearly didn't work.

❹ Duna–Dráva National Park

Road Map C5. 🚌 to Bárányfok from Szekszárd. 🚂 narrow-gauge railway from Bárányfok to Pörböly (regular service May–Sep only). Gemenc Excursion Centre, Bárányfok: (20) 566 80 76. Boat tours (summer): (74) 49 14 83.

This 500-sq-km (193-sq-mile) game reserve in the Gemenc Forest is Hungary's largest floodplain forest. A national park since 1996, it is covered with lakes and fens, and dotted with numerous islands. On many of these can be found old willow trees, high oaks and poplars, lilies of the valley on the forest floor, and wildlife including egrets, bald eagles, herons, black storks and stags. Hunting is restricted to certain areas.

Most of the park is protected, and there are four ways of visiting: on a nature trail from the park's main entrance, near Bárányfok; with a guide from the Gemenc Excursion Centre at Bárányfok; by narrow-gauge railway from Bárányfok to Pörböly; and by organized boat trip. The nature trails vary in length from 2.5 km (1.5 miles) to 40 km (25 miles). There is also a cycle trail, and bike hire, canoe hire, horse riding and carriage drives can be arranged.

One of the many wine cellars on Baross Gábor utca in Villány

❺ Villány

21 km (13 miles) southeast of Pécs. **Road Map** C6. 🔼 2,800. 🚂 from Pécs. 🚌 from Budapest. 🎪 Red Wine Festival (first week of Oct); European Wine Song Festival (late Sep).

A village of wine cellars, Villány is the starting point of the 14-km (9-mile) Villány–Siklós Wine Route, the first to be set up in Hungary in 1994. Wine has been made here since Roman times, and a small Wine Museum, housed in one of the village's traditional white-washed wine cellars, tells the story of local viticulture. Every year the village hosts a Red Wine Festival, dedicated to promoting Villány wines, including Kékoportó, Merlot, Blue Franc and Cabernet; red wines predominate around Villány; whites, around Siklós (see p188). Visitors can sample local wines at the wine cellars on Bem József utca or Baross Gábor utca. Four of the town's vintners have been awarded the title of "Wine Maker of the Year": Gere, Tiffán, Bock and Malatinszky.

The village of Villánykövesd, 4 km (2.5 miles) northeast on the road to Pécs (and not strictly on the Wine Route), is even more spectacular than Villány, as its many wine-cellar cottages are set on a split-level terrace. The village's Batthyány cellar, built by Italian artisans in 1754, is one of the venues for performances and events during the annual European Wine Song Festival, held in autumn.

An idyllic spot in the Duna–Dráva National Park

The Battle of Mohács

The Battle of Mohács is one of the most important battles in Hungarian – and European – history. On 29 August 1526, the Turks, having just achieved victory in the Battle of Belgrade, faced one final obstacle before reaching Buda: the Magyar garrison at Mohács. The Turks, however, outnumbered the Magyars three to one, and after a day-long battle they achieved victory by nightfall, killing at least two-thirds of the estimated 25,000 Hungarian soldiers at arms. The young Hungarian King, Lajos II, was killed during the battle. The Turks captured Buda soon after, and ruled Hungary for more than 150 years. To this day the battle is remembered as one of the greatest Hungarian tragedies.

The death of King Lajos II in battle

The impressive path to the drawbridge in Siklós Castle

➏ Siklós

15 km (9 miles) west of Villány. **Road Map** C6. 11,000. from Villány. from Pécs. Tourinform, Felszabadulás utca 3, (72) 57 90 90. daily, Dózsa György utca.

The star attraction in Siklós, the southernmost town in Hungary, close to the border with Serbia, is **Siklós Castle**, one of the best-preserved medieval forts in the country. The fort, which dates back to 1294, has enjoyed something of a charmed life. Uniquely among Hungarian fortresses, it was spared by the Turks as well as the Habsburgs (twice).

The fort's entrance is via an old drawbridge and through a gate decorated elaborately with the Batthyány family coat of arms. From the immaculately preserved ramparts spectacular views of the vineyards of the surrounding area can be enjoyed. Inside the fortress is a Gothic chapel, decorated with fading but impressive frescoes from the late 15th century.

The **Castle Museum**, in the fort's south wing, is equally impressive, containing a collection of medieval items and an exhibition on the lives of the various members of the Batthyány family who lived here as late as the 1940s.

Elsewhere in Siklós, the restored 16th-century Malkocs Bei Mosque, which is full of

memorabilia from the Turkish occupation, and the colourful 18th-century icons of the Serb Orthodox church are also worth seeing.

🏰 Siklós Castle
Vajda János tér 8. **Tel** (72) 57 94 27. **Open** Nov–Apr: 9:30am–4pm daily; May–Oct: 9:30am–6pm daily.

➐ Harkány

25 km (16 miles) southeast of Pécs. **Road Map** C6. 3,400. from Pécs. Tourinform, Kossuth utca 7, (72) 47 96 24. daily, Bajcsy-Zsilinszky utca. **W** harkanyturizmus.hu

According to local legend, the Devil ploughed the land around Harkány, and filled the furrows with sulphuric water. As it happens, such sulphuric water – said to be a cure for rheumatic and gynaecological disorders – is found nowhere else, and the Devil's work has become a boon for Harkány.

The town's thermal bath complex was opened in 1823, and is today one of the most visited in Hungary. As well as large indoor and outdoor pools (so large that they are never crowded), there is a special section for taking mud baths.

Other waters can be drunk to cure catarrh and stomach complaints. Solaria and a range of beauty treatments are also available.

💧 Harkány Spa and Open-Air Baths
Bajcsy-Zsilinszky utca 2. **Tel** (72) 58 08 80. **Open** 9am–6pm daily.

➑ Pécs

See pp190–93.

➒ Dombóvár

39 km (25 miles) north of Pécs. **Road Map** C5. 21,000.

Dombóvár and its surrounding area is one of the oldest inhabited regions of Hungary. The ruins of a 4th-century Roman fortress were found underneath nearby Alsóhetény and the Celts were here before that. Relics of even earlier unknown settlers from the Bronze Age have also been

Exercises in the outdoor pool, Harkány Spa and Open-Air Baths

found. These are on display at the **Dombóvár Region Historical Museum** (Dombóvári Helytörténeti Múzeum), which is also home to a possibly unique exhibition on the history of the artificial language Esperanto.

Among Dombóvár's other attractions are the Baroque Catholic Church, dating from 1757 and once a private chapel for the use of the Esterházy family *(see p171)*. Szigeterdő, a pretty park and nature reserve on Gyenis Antal utca, houses a reconstructed medieval building.

A short drive north is the tiny village of Gölle, the birthplace of István Fekete (1900–70), one of Hungary's most popular 20th-century writers, best known for his novel *Tüskevár*, a charming story of two boys from Budapest who spend their summers around Gölle and Lake Balaton. Fekete's childhood home in Gölle is now a small museum.

🏛 Dombóvár Region Historical Museum
Szabadság utca 16. **Tel** (74) 46 57 15, (mobile) (20) 910 80 66. **Open** 8am–4pm Mon–Fri, by appointment Sat & Sun. 📷 Hungarian only. ♿

Bust of the Hungarian writer István Fekete, born near Dombóvár

⑩ Kaposvár

43 km (27 miles) northwest of Pécs. **Road Map** B5. 🚗 66,000. 🚉 from Budapest, Pécs. 🚌 from Pécs. ℹ Tourinform, Fő utca 8, (82) 51 29 21. 🌐 **tourinformkaposvar.hu**

Boasting one of Hungary's largest pedestrian-only zones, Kaposvár is a superb city in which to stroll and enjoy an eclectic mix of architecture. The town is the birthplace of József

Stained-glass window, town hall in Kaposvár

Rippl-Rónai (1861–1927) and János Vaszary (1867–1939), two of Hungary's most important artists. It was also the birthplace of Imre Nagy (1896–1958), leader of the 1956 revolution *(see pp48–9)*.

The city's focal point is Kossuth tér. Most of the main sights are located around this street, including the **Vaszary Gallery**, which displays the paintings of János Vaszary, who was born in the building. There are more Vaszary works nearby in a Neo-Classical building, the former Somogy County Museum (now renamed the **Rippl-Rónai Museum**),

formerly the County Hall. The museum also presents an exhibition of local artifacts, including folk art that predates the Magyar invasion.

Kaposvár's **town hall** was built in 1904 in classic Secessionist style, though its slender spire carries a hint of the late Baroque. It is not officially open to the public but it is usually possible to go in and admire the interior. The frescoes above the lobby are by local artist Géza Udvary, and the fine stained-glass windows of the ceremonial hall are the work of the Miksa Róth workshop.

A short walk south is the **József Rippl-Rónai Memorial Museum**, the elegant Roma cottage where a number of Rippl-Rónai's works and personal items are on show.

🏛 Vaszary Gallery
Csokonai utca 1. **Tel** (82) 51 22 28. **Open** 10am–6pm Tue–Sat. 📷 Hungarian only. ♿

🏛 Rippl-Rónai Museum
Fő út 10. **Tel** (30) 869 60 56. **Open** Nov–Mar: 10am–3pm Tue–Sun; Apr–Oct: 10am–4pm Tue–Sun. 📷 ♿

🏛 József Rippl-Rónai Memorial Museum
Róma-hegy. **Tel** (82) 42 21 44. **Open** Nov–Mar: 10am–4pm Tue–Sun; Apr–Oct: 10am–6pm Tue–Sun. 📷 recorded tours. ♿

József Rippl-Rónai

József Rippl-Rónai (1861–1927) was one of the three most important artists of the Hungarian Secession movement. Born in Kaposvár he mastered a pastel-like style, seen best in his celebrated work *Mlle Dutile* (1892, József Rippl-Rónai Memorial Museum, Kaposvár). He moved to France when the Art Nouveau movement was at its peak. His masterpiece, *Woman in White-Spotted Dress* (1889, National Gallery, Budapest, *see pp62–3*), was painted during this period. It is regarded as the first Secessionist work by a Hungarian artist. On a visit to Italy, Rippl-Rónai became fascinated by decorative mosaics. His later works, including *The Manor House at Körtvélyes* (1907, National Gallery), reflect a move to bolder strokes and colour.

Rippl-Rónai's *Woman in White-Spotted Dress*

❽ Pécs

Cosmopolitan Pécs, 2010's European Capital of Culture, calls itself "Hungary's Mediterranean city". Given that the sun shines here for more than 200 days a year, and that the city's streets have a very Turkish, even Oriental, feel to them, this is not as strange as it may seem. Pécs was founded by the Romans, who called the place Sopianae, in the 3rd century AD. It served as the capital of Valeria Province and was an early centre of Roman Christianity – as evidenced by the 4th-century tombs on Apáca utca. It was the Turks, however, 1,000 years later, who left the deepest marks on the city's landscape. No other city centre in Hungary is quite so dominated by a former mosque as Pécs's Széchenyi tér (see pp192–3), yet no other city seems quite so at ease with the fact.

Entrance to the Zsolnay Museum, in the historic centre of Pécs

🏛 St Peter's Cathedral and Bishops' Palace
Szent Péter Székesegyház & Püspöki palota
Dóm tér. **Tel** (72) 51 30 57. **Open** Apr–Oct: 9am–5pm Mon–Sat, noon–5pm Sun. 🖼 ⬤ ♿

The historic centre of Pécs, Dóm tér, is dominated by St Peter's Cathedral, which was first built as a Neo-Romanesque church in 1009 when St István made Pécs a bishopric. The original church, burned down in 1064, was replaced by a Baroque cathedral built over nearly 200 years. Badly damaged by the Mongols, it was almost entirely rebuilt as a Gothic church in the 15th century. The current edifice, with its four severe corner towers, dates from 1891, and is the work of Viennese architect Friedrich Schmidt. The interior is impressive, especially the Károly Lotz frescoes in the chapels and the reliefs in

the crypt by György Zala. A bronze statue of Janos Pannonius, a leading humanist, stands in front of the cathedral.

Opposite is the attractive deep-red, 19th-century Neo-Renaissance Bishops' Palace. It has a statue of Ferenc (Franz) Liszt in a raincoat on the southern balcony. The palace is home to one of Hungary's largest libraries.

🏛 Zsolnay Museum
Zsolnay Múzeum
Káptalan utca 2. **Tel** (72) 51 40 45. **Open** May–Oct: 10am–6pm Tue–Sun; Nov–Apr: 10am–4pm Tue–Sun. 🖼 🖼 ♿ 🖼

Located in the oldest-known house of Pécs, this museum showcases the most significant pieces of the Zsolnay Ceramic Factory. Zsolnay tiles graced the palaces of the Austro-Hungarian monarchy and were famous for their unique metallic glaze. Also

on display are items of furniture and paintings produced by the family.

🏛 Csontváry Museum
Csontváry Múzeum
Janus Pannonius utca 11. **Tel** (72) 31 05 44. **Open** May–Oct: 10am–6pm Tue–Sun; Nov–Apr: 10am–4pm Tue–Sun. 🖼 🖼 ♿

Most of Tivadar Csontváry Kosztka's (1853–1919) master-pieces, including the startling *View of the Dead Sea from the Temple Square in Jerusalem*, have been on display in this Neo-Renaissance building since 1973. A tortured soul and former pharmacist, Csontváry Kosztka produced most of his work in 1903–9, after which he moved to Naples and went quietly mad.

🏛 Apáca Street and Early Christian Mausoleum
Apáca utca & Ókeresztény Mauzóleum
Apáca utca 8 & 14. **Tel** (72) 22 47 55. **Open** by appointment only. A World Heritage Ticket is required; enquire when phoning to arrange a visit.
🌐 **pecsorokseg.hu**

Four graves at Apáca utca 14, all from c.AD 390, mark one of the earliest Christian burial sites in Europe. The bodies are buried under the chapel, and not in sarcophagi. The mausoleum, below an excavated chapel, is even older, c.AD 275. It is decorated with biblical frescoes. These and two further burial chambers at Pécs (combined tickets are available) have UNESCO World Heritage status.

St Peter's Cathedral, with its distinctive corner towers

🏛 Archaeological Museum

Széchenyi tér 12. **Tel** (72) 31 27 19.
Open currently closed to the public:
phone ahead to enquire. ♿

The Archaeological Museum
features Goths, Huns, Tatars,
Visigoths and other invaders,
but perhaps the highlight is the
story of Roman Sopianae, a
popular posting for Roman
officers. A valuable treasure, a
bust of Marcus Aurelius has
a room to itself.

C Gazi Kasim Pasha Mosque/ Inner City Parish Church

**Gazi Kasim Pasha Dzámi/
Belvárosi templom**
Széchenyi tér. **Tel** (72) 32 19 76.
Open daily; phone ahead for times
as hours vary. ♿

Built on the site of a Gothic
Christian church in 1579 for
Pasha Gazi Kasim, this mosque
was the largest in Hungary,
and remains its most important
Turkish monument. Converted
into a Christian church in
the late 17th century, calligraphy at the entrance and
a prayer niche are reminders
of its origins.

🏙 Király Utca

Király utca.
Largely pedestrianized, Király
utca is an architectural showcase. Secessionist façades can
be seen at Nos. 5 (Palatinus
Hotel; superb lobby), 8, 10, 19
and the National Theatre; the
twin-towered St Pauline Church
at No. 44 is Baroque.

✡ Synagogue

Zsinagóga
Kossuth tér. **Tel** (72) 31 58 81.
Open May–Oct: 10am–5pm Sun–Fri,
or by appointment. ♿

This grand Neo-Renaissance
synagogue, built in the 1860s,
shows the high standing the
5,000 practising Jews had in
Pécs society until 1944,
when the Arrow Cross
government sent
all of them to
Auschwitz. Fewer
than 500 survived.
A memorial
commemorates
those who were
killed. Services
take place in the
smaller prayer hall
at the side.

Façade of Pécs Synagogue

C Jakovali Hassan Mosque

Jakovali Hassan Dzámi
Rákóczi út. 2. **Tel** (20) 400 93 03.
Open Apr–Oct: 10am–6pm Wed–Sun,
or by appointment. ♿

Even though the 16th-century
mosque was converted into a
Catholic church in 1714, its
23-m- (75-ft-) high minaret is
still intact (but closed).
A museum since
1975, it documents
the Turkish occu-
pation of Pécs. Many
of the exhibits were
donated by the
Turkish government as
a semi-official apology
in the early 1990s.

Pécs City Centre

① St Peter's Cathedral
  and Bishops' Palace
② Zsolnay Museum
③ Csontváry Museum
④ Apáca Street and Early
  Christian Mausoleum
⑤ Archaeological Museum
⑥ Gazi Kasim Pasha Mosque/
  Inner City Parish Church
⑦ Király Utca
⑧ Synagogue
⑨ Jakovali Hassan Mosque

Key

▨ Street-by-Street pp192–3

0 metres 100
0 yards 100

For keys to map symbols *see back flap*

Street-by-Street: Around Széchenyi tér

Once the bustling medieval heart of Pécs, comprising a marketplace, meeting point and general forum, today Széchenyi tér is a far more serene and reflective place. Sloping gently from north to south, the square is dominated – as is much of Pécs – by the former mosque of Gazi Kasim Pasha, the largest surviving original Islamic construction in Hungary. It is now a Catholic church and a museum.

Archaeological Museum
This large collection traces the history of human settlement in Pécs from the Early Stone Age to the present day.

★ **Gazi Kasim Mosque**
Correctly known as the Inner City Parish Church of St Mary, this was for two centuries the city's primary mosque. Its dome stands 28 m (92 ft) high.

Zsolnay Museum displays exquisite examples of Art Nouveau tiles.

Holy Trinity Monument
The column, restored by György Kiss in 1908, commemorates the victims of a plague outbreak in 1710.

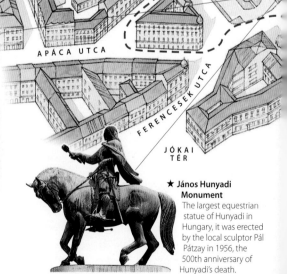

★ **János Hunyadi Monument**
The largest equestrian statue of Hunyadi in Hungary, it was erected by the local sculptor Pál Pátzay in 1956, the 500th anniversary of Hunyadi's death.

For hotels and restaurants see pp264–269 and pp276–285

National Theatre
This impressive theatre was built in 1893–5, in a mix of styles. It hosts first-class opera and ballet performances.

★ Király Utca
Traffic-free Király utca is lined with shops and cafés, making it ideal for a stroll. Its buildings boast Secessionist (Palatinus Hotel) and Baroque (St Pauline Church) façades.

MÁRIA UTCA

KIRÁLY UTCA

0 metres 20

0 yards 20

Town Hall
Pécs town hall was built in 1710, though its tall, slender tower was not added until 1907.

Key

— Suggested route

Zsolnay Fountain
This outstanding example of Secessionist design pays homage to Vilmos Zsolnay, who founded the Zsolnay tile factory nearby in 1853. It features the trademark Zsolnay blue glaze.

A typical 19th-century house in the open-air folk museum in Szenna

⑪ Szenna

Road Map B5. 🚷 750.
🚌 from Kaposvár.

The open-air **Szenna Ethno-graphic Museum** is unique in Hungary in that it has been established in a living village. Set around the village church, five thatched houses with wooden porches were brought here from surrounding villages in the 1970s. The houses date from the 1850s, and with their large kitchens are typical of post-revolutionary architecture in Hungary. All are decorated in the vernacular style. The whitewashed Calvinist church, erected in 1787 to a late Baroque design, is famous for its ceiling: the artist Tildy Zoltán painted it with 117 unique flowers, reflecting the rich flora of the Somogy region. Visitors can also admire the highly decorated wooden crown above the pulpit and the pews that are installed over two levels.

⑫ Szigetvár

33 km (21 miles) west of Pécs.
Road Map B5. 🚷 12,000.
🚆 from Pécs. 🚌 from Pécs.

At the siege of Szigetvár, in 1566, Captain Miklós Zrínyi and a small band of soldiers held the town's fortress against a Turkish attacking force of over 100,000 for 22 days. Only when the beleaguered Hungarians

were running desperately short of water did they leave the fortress, and even then they did not surrender, choosing instead to die heroic though futile deaths in close combat. Part of the fortress, restored in the 1960s, is the **Castle Museum**, dedicated to the heroes of the siege. There is also a monument to the fallen in the town's central square, Zrínyi tér. The fortress courtyard also houses a former mosque, which was built by the Turks after their victory.

Another former mosque, also on Zrínyi tér, is today a Catholic church. It was converted in 1789, when the frescoes by István Dorfmeister were painted. In the house at Bástya utca 3, the so-called **Turkish**

Exhibits in the former mosque inside the Szigetvár fortress

House (Török-Ház), is a small exhibition of life in the town during the Turkish occupation. On the field where Zrínyi led his forces into battle (5 km/3 miles north of the town) stands the Turkish-Hungarian Friendship Park, set up in 1996 by both governments. There is a replica of Sultan Süleyman's tomb, and oversized statues of the Sultan and of Zrínyi.

🏛 **Castle Museum**
Vár utca 19. **Open** check website for opening times. 🌐 **szigethvar.hu**

🏛 **Turkish House**
Bástya utca 3. **Tel** (73) 51 43 00.
📷 ♿

⑬ Nagyatád

28 km (18 miles) north of Barcs.
Road Map B5. 🚷 13,000. 🚌 from Kaposvár. 🛈 Tourinform, Széchenyi tér 1/A, Nagyatád (82) 35 15 06.

This city has a good thermal baths complex, with three covered and two large open-air pools as well as drinking cures, but Nagyatád is best known for its unique **Statue Park** featuring the works of a local wood-carvers' collective. The

A wooden wheel in the Statue Park in Nagyatád

park was set up in 1975, in an effort to preserve the wood carving skills of the region. There are 64 monumental statues (some more than 7 m/23 ft high) in all, laid out in a spacious and attractive park to the south of the city centre. Considered living art, there are no restrictions on touching or even climbing the statues, making this a great place to introduce children to sculpture. Another 24 wooden statues can be found in the city's public squares and buildings.

The surrounding countryside offers superb hiking routes in the Forest Park (Parkerdő) and the Rower Lake (Csónakázótó) nearby.

🏛 **Nagyatád Statue Park**
Göröndi út. **Tel** (82) 35 14 97.
Open daily. 🎧 Hungarian only. ♿

Hungary's Minorities

Some 90 per cent of Hungary's population are Magyars, but there are also significant minority groups of Serbs, Germans, Romanians and Jews. In all, 13 minority groups are recognized, although some (the Palóc, Armenians and Ruthenians, for example) number only a handful of people. The largest ethnic minority in Hungary is the Gypsies (Roma). The official figure is 400,000, yet many Gypsies see themselves as Hungarians, which means there could be as many as a million in the country. Until Hungary joined the EU in 2004, it had a less than fine record in its treatment of its ethnic minorities, especially of the Gypsies. Even since then, EU-funded programmes have been only marginally successful at integrating the Gypsy population.

The museum village of Hollókő, while primarily a tourist attraction, showcases Palóc traditions and culture. Its inhabitants wear traditional costume.

Few Roma still live the romantic life of a traveller. Most are on the fringes of society, with an unemployment rate of almost 70 per cent.

Szentendre was founded by Serbs and although they no longer make up the majority population group here, many Serbs still celebrate Easter according to the Orthodox Julian calendar.

People in Sopron in 1921 voted to stay in Hungary rather than join Austria. Over the next few decades most ethnic Germans moved away, but since 1990 many have returned, which has given the city a very international feel.

Fö tér
Hauptplatz

The popular image of Gypsy musicians is a *cigányzenekar*, which is a Gypsy band. It is one of the few ways Gypsies can earn a living in Hungary.

Budapest today is home to one of Europe's most dynamic Jewish communities. Budapest's synagogue is Europe's largest, and the city boasts many Jewish theatres, schools and kosher restaurants.

Many Orthodox Romanians are settled in and around the eastern town of Gyula. Although the two countries have had a strained relationship for centuries, more than 80,000 Romanians choose to live in Hungary.

Marina in Siófok, departure point for pleasure cruises and water sports

⑭ Siófok

88 km (54 miles) southwest of Budapest. **Road Map** C4. 🚗 23,000. 🚉 from Budapest. 🚌 from Budapest. ⛴ from Balatonfüred, Tihany. ℹ️ Tourinform, Fő tér 11, (84) 69 62 36. 🎭 Siófok Summer Evenings (Jun–Aug). 🌐 **siofokportal.com**

The largest and liveliest resort on Lake Balaton's southern coast, Siófok stretches along the shore for 17 km (11 miles). It is popular with weekenders from Budapest, many of whom have holiday homes in the town. The main attraction is the beach. It is split in two parts – Aranypart (Golden Shore) to the north and Ezüstpart (Silver Shore) to the south – by the Sió canal, which was originally built by the Romans in AD 276. Like all of Lake Balaton's resorts, however, Siófok offers mainly grass beaches. The resort's marina is at the head of the canal, from where pleasure cruisers and ferries depart for the Tihany Peninsula *(see p206)*. The port is a good place to find sailing boats for hire, and to organize a variety of other water sports *(see p291)*.

Visitors should note that during the summer nights Siófok comes alive with tens of thousands of young people looking for a good time in the resort's innumerable bars, discos and nightclubs, many of which are in the open air. If an early, quiet night is required, one of the smaller resorts along the coast would be a far better option.

⑮ Lake Balaton Tour

Lake Balaton is often referred to as Budapest-on-Sea, and during the summer months it may seem as if half the population of the capital has decamped here. Lake Balaton, however, at 596 sq km (230 sq miles) the largest lake in central Europe, is big enough to cope, and even in the high season the visitor is never far from a peaceful spot. Most of the southern side of the lake is very shallow, with an average depth of just 3.5 m (11 ft), and the waters are fairly warm, making this the most popular shore with bathers and families.

⑪ Kis-Balaton
The Kis-Balaton nature reserve at the mouth of the Zala river covers an area of 40 sq km (15 sq miles). It is inhabited by many rare plants and animals.

⑩ Balatonberény
One of the first genuine resorts on the lake to become popular, Balatonberény retains a late 19th-century charm, most apparent in its delightful lakeside cottages and rural houses.

Tapolca

Sopron

84

Badacsonytomaj

Zalaegerszeg • Keszthely 71

76 75 71

75

76 ⑩ ⑨ ⑧

M7

661

↓ *Barcs*

⑪

7

Nagykanizsa

• Zalakaros

⑧ Balatonfenyves
This small resort is very popular with families. A miniature railway runs to a nearby thermal bath.

⑨ Balatonmáriafürdő
This lively resort attracts water sports enthusiasts and those looking for a good range of bars and restaurants.

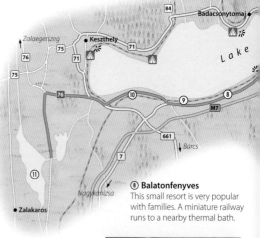

① Zamárdi

A world away from noisy Siófok, Zamárdi is home to some fine thatched cottages, including this arcaded house on Fő utca, now the village's museum.

② Balatonföldvár

Look out for the remains of the Iron Age fortifications (*földvár*) that gave this small town its name. The village's leafy promenade is generally considered the finest on the lake's south shore.

③ Kőröshegy

A short detour south of Balatonföldvár is Kőröshegy, where a well-preserved Gothic fortified church was built in 1460.

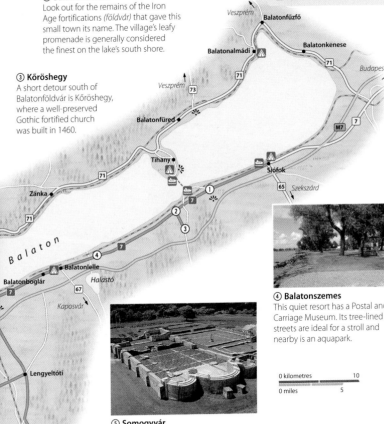

④ Balatonszemes

This quiet resort has a Postal and Carriage Museum. Its tree-lined streets are ideal for a stroll and nearby is an aquapark.

0 kilometres 10

0 miles 5

⑤ Somogyvár

Somogyvár is well worth the detour south from Buzsák – the impressive ruins of the Benedictine monastery here date back to the 11th century.

⑦ Fonyód

Unremarkable as a resort, Fonyód sits at the foot of the largest hill on the southern shore, Várhegy (233 m/764 ft), which is an extinct volcano.

⑥ Buzsák

The Living Museum of Arts and Crafts at Buzsák is the best place around Balaton to learn about the traditions of the lake and its people. Fine cloth, pottery and costumes are still made here.

Key

━━ Motorway
━━ Tour route
━━ Major road
┄┄ Other road
╍╍ Major railway
--- Ferry line

For keys to map symbols *see back flap*

⑯ Keszthely

Keszthely is the oldest of the towns that line the banks of Lake Balaton. Many of its elegant streets effortlessly preserve the small-town atmosphere of the 19th century, when the town was the sole property of the Festetics family, whose Baroque family seat, Festetics Palace *(see pp202–3)*, is one of Hungary's finest stately homes. The town possesses one of the few genuinely sandy beaches on the lake, and it is also the cultural hub of Balaton. Since the conversion in 2006 of a nearby former Soviet airfield into Hévíz-Balaton Airport, Keszthely is fast becoming one of the most-visited places in Hungary.

Church and former monastery buildings on Keszthely's main square

▦ Festetics Palace
See pp202–3.

▦ Fő tér and Town Hall
Polgármesteri Hivatal
Fő tér.
At the heart of Keszthely is the attractive, bustling Fő tér, dominated on its northern side by the late Baroque, pastel pink town hall. The town hall was built in 1769, although the façade was extensively remodelled in the 1850s. The square is one of the hubs of the town's charming Verkli Festival in September, when the air is filled by the fluting tones of dozens of fairground and barrel organs.

⚷ Fő tér Church
Fő téri templom
Fő tér 5. **Tel** (83) 31 24 59.
This grand building, towering over the southern side of the square, is the former church and monastery of the Franciscans, built in the 14th century. The tall Neo-Gothic tower with a 10-m

(33-ft) spire is an 18th-century addition. The crypt holds the tomb of György Festetics, the patriarch of the Festetics family and uncle of István Széchenyi. The church was originally built in Gothic style using stone taken from an old Roman settlement

Stained-glass window featuring the Virgin and Child in Fő tér Church

nearby. During restoration work in 1974, remains of 14th- and 15th-century frescoes were discovered. Lost during the Turkish occupation, when the church served as a fortress, these represent the largest collection of Gothic frescoes remaining in Hungary. The fine rose window above the eastern portal is also an original feature of the church.

▦ Doll and Waxwork Museum
Történelmi Panoptikum
Kossuth Lajos utca 10–11. **Tel** (83) 31 88 55. **Open** May–Sep: 9am–6pm; Oct–Apr: 10am–5pm. ▨
w babamuzeum-keszthely.hu
The highlight of this complex of museums is a collection of 700 porcelain dolls, each wearing the traditional costume of one particular Hungarian village, together with more than 200 scale models of village buildings, including houses, stables and churches.
    More esoteric collections include 500 life-size waxworks of eminent Hungarians, from Árpád to Imre Nagy; a museum of torture; and a display of Renaissance wax-modelled erotica. Don't miss the Snail Parliament, an astonishing 7-m- (23-ft-) long model of Hungary's Parliament that was made by Ilona Miskei from more than four million sea-snail shells.

▦ Georgikon Farm Museum
Georgikon Majormúzeum
Bercsényi Miklós utca 65–7. **Tel** (83) 31 15 63. **Open** Apr & Oct: 10am–5pm Mon–Fri; May–Sep: 10am–5pm Tue–Sun. ▨ ▨ Hungarian and German only. ♿ **w** elmenygazdasag.hu
Europe's first Academy of Agriculture was set up here by György Festetics, in 1797. This working museum traces the history of Hungarian agriculture from Celtic times to the present day. There are displays on wine production in the Balaton area, as well as antique agricultural equipment from Bronze Age tools to steam ploughs and an early motor tractor. Visitors can try their hand at traditional farming methods, and there are animals to meet and farm buildings to explore for children.

Promenading and people-watching on pedestrianized Kossuth Street

Kossuth Street
Kossuth utca.

Keszthely's main, pedestrianized thoroughfare is markedly the widest street in the older part of the town, lined with some fine houses, many of them protected buildings. The oldest, at No. 22, is the birthplace of the Hungarian-Jewish pianist Karl Goldmark. With its porticoes and covered upper-level loggia, the house is Mediterranean in feel. Just behind, in a leafy courtyard, is Keszthely's well-preserved Neo-Renaissance synagogue. Originally dating from 1780, it was entirely rebuilt in 1851–2 and assumed its current appearance in 1894.

Balaton Museum
Balatoni Múzeum

Múzeum utca 2. **Tel** (83) 31 23 51. **Open** May–Aug: daily; Sep–Apr: Tue–Sat.

The mustard-yellow Neo-Baroque Balaton Museum building, erected in the 1920s to a design by Dénes Györgyi, is well worth seeing in its own right. The exhibitions inside are equally interesting and include a fascinating look at life around Lake Balaton in pre-Roman times and displays showing the development of fishing on the lake. Children will love the models of sailing ships, steamers and paddleboats that once traversed the lake. A more sombre display explains the effects of pollution on life in the lake. Also shown is Roman stoneware from the region and an original milestone to Aquincum (*see p114*), 69 km (43 miles) away.

Excavated fishing equipment on display at the Balaton Museum

Keszthely City Centre

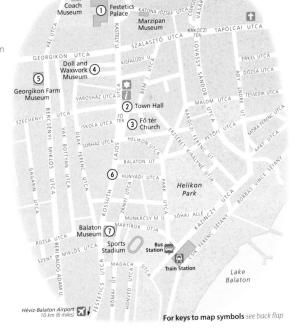

0 metres   300
0 yards   300

For keys to map symbols *see back flap*

Festetics Palace and Helikon Palace Museum

Originally the home of the Festetics family, the stately, Neo-Baroque Festetics Palace dates in its earliest parts to 1745; the final phase of building, by little-known architect Viktor Rumpelmayer, dates to 1883–7. The family was forced to flee in 1944, after which the palace was occupied by the German Army, then the Soviets; it was opened as a museum in 1974. About a quarter of the palace's 101 rooms are open to the public, and feature fine art, furniture and memorabilia from the Festetics family. Adjacent buildings house a superb model railway, an exhibition of weaponry and hunting trophies and a carriage museum. The palace is also famous for its extensive library and its magnificent English-style gardens.

★ Baroque Tower
The tower was inspired by the Zwinger in Dresden, Germany, while the northern wing (left of the tower here) was based on Vienna's Belvedere.

Main entrance

★ English Gardens
English – not French – stately homes were the inspiration for the palace gardens. They were laid out by the English landscape artist Henry Ernest Miller.

★ Palm House
The Palm House was built in 1880 using structural elements made in Paris by Gustave Eiffel. It was reopened only in 2012 and now exhibits rare and wonderful exotic flowers and plants from the Mediterranean and the tropics.

KEY

① **Rounded Belvedere-style Tower of Northern Wing**

② **Rooms** are each decorated in a different colour scheme and fully furnished.

Carriage Museum
In the palace's former stables, the Carriage Museum is home to a priceless collection of hunting and parade coaches, carriages and sleighs from the 18th and 19th centuries.

★ Mirror Room
The ornate Mirror Room, also known as the Main Hall, regularly hosts chamber music concerts and operettas.

VISITORS' CHECKLIST

Practical Information
Kastély utca 1, Keszthely. **Road Map** B4. **Tel** (83) 31 21 90.
🛈 Tourinform, Kossuth utca 30, (83) 31 41 44. **Open** May: 10am–5pm daily; Jun–Sep: 9am–6pm daily; Oct–Apr: 10am–5pm Tue–Sun. 🎨 🅿 ♿ 💻 📷 charge for photography and use of video cameras. 🌐 **keszthely.info.hu**

Transport
🚗 🚌 🚐

Chapel
The small, private Festetics Chapel was built in 1801, remaining unchanged by the enlargements of the 1880s.

Portrait Gallery
Portraits of almost every member of the Festetics family, Croatian in origin, as well as of related European nobility, line the walls of the palace.

★ Library
The panelled Helikon Library holds over 80,000 volumes on its oak shelves. Hungary's literary elite gathered here in György Festetics's time.

György Festetics

A polymath who combined a love of the land and the arts with the progressive ideals of the Enlightenment, György Festetics (1755–1819) was the grandson of Kristóf Festetics, who purchased the lands for the family estate here in 1739. György Festetics is best known for founding the Georgikon at Keszthely in 1797 *(see p200)*, Europe's first agricultural college. A generous patron of the arts, he organized cultural events including poetry and music festivals at the palace. He substantially expanded the palace's library, employing librarians and bookbinders to curate his literary treasures.

Statue of György Festetics

The Central Pavilion, dominating the relaxing warm waters of the thermal lake in Hévíz

⑰ Hévíz

6 km (4 miles) north of Keszthely.
Road Map B4. 🏔 5,000. 🚌 from
Keszthely. 🛈 Tourinform, Rákóczi
utca 2, (83) 54 01 31.

With its vast Central Pavilion in the middle of what is the world's largest thermal water lake, Hévíz is a spectacular sight. Covered with Indian water lilies, which flower in early September, **Lake Hévíz** has been used for bathing and treatments since 1795. Up to 30 m (98 ft) deep, the lake has a surface area of 47,500 sq m (56,800 sq yards) and a temperature of 36° C (96.8° F) in summer. It is replenished by a spring that produces 420 litres (92 gallons) of water per second. Even in winter the water temperature never drops below 28° C (82.4° F). The water is slightly radioactive and recommended for the treatment of rheumatism and arthritis. It also tastes surprisingly good, and is used to treat stomach disorders. The radioactive mud from the lake floor is also therapeutic.

Although most patrons prefer to bathe outside, even in winter, there is a small indoor pool. Hévíz also has the best range of hotels in the area.

Fountain in front of the entrance to Hévíz thermal baths

💧 Lake Hévíz

Dr Schulhof Vilmos sétány 1. **Tel** (83)
50 17 00. **Open** May–Oct: 8am–7pm
daily; Nov–Apr: 9am–6pm daily.
🔶 ♿ 🌐 spaheviz.hu

⑱ Balatonederics

14 km (9 miles) east of Keszthely.
Road Map B4. 🏔 1,200. 🚊 from
Tapolca, Keszthely. 🚌 from Tapolca,
Keszthely.

Balatonederics is one of the oldest settlements on Lake Balaton, its name first mentioned as long ago as 1262. The Roman Catholic church that stands in the village centre was built about the same time, originally as a Romanesque structure. It received its present Neo-Gothic look during renovation work in 1870–71. The Holy Trinity monument in front of the church dates from 1871.

An exclusive resort without hotels, Balatonederics nevertheless welcomes hundreds of thousands of day trippers a year, all visiting its **Africa Museum and Safari Park** (Afrika Múzeum és Állatkert). Founded in 1984 by a Hungarian big-game hunter, Dr Endre Nagy, the museum is home to Nagy's hunting trophies and ethnographical memorabilia that he collected in Tanzania. In the Safari Park, African animals including buffalo, zebra and camels – which can be ridden – roam freely, next to original Masai huts.

🦁 Africa Museum and Safari Park

Kültelek 11. **Tel** (87) 46 61 05.
Open Apr–Oct: 9am–4pm daily
(to 5:30pm Jun–Aug). 🔶 🎫 ♿
🌐 afrikamuzeum.hu

⑲ Szigliget

20 km (12 miles) east of Keszthely.
Road Map B4. 🏔 1,000. 🚊 from
Keszthely. 🚌 from Keszthely.
🚢 from Keszthely.

Underneath the ruins of the 13th-century **Szigetvár Island Castle** (often referred to as *Óvár*, Old Castle), the village of

A camel at the Africa Museum and Safari Park in Balatonederics

Szigliget stands on a small peninsula that – as the castle's name suggests – was once an island. The last waters receded about the time the castle was destroyed, in 1702, after an explosion in the gunpowder store. Some of the towers, part of the living quarters and the stables remain. The ruins are a steep, 30-minute walk uphill from the village, but the picturesque thatched cottages that line the route up and the stunning views from the top make the climb worthwhile.

The village itself is dominated by Esterházy Mansion, a Neo-Classical 19th-century building, now a hotel for the exclusive use of the Hungarian Writers' Union. The hotel's extensive gardens are open to the public. Szigliget also has a pleasantly quiet grass beach and an attractive harbour, always cheerful with its show of colourful sailing boats.

⓴ Badacsony Mountain

30 km (19 miles) east of Keszthely. **Road Map** B4. 2,400. from Tapolca. from Tapolca. from Keszthely, Fonyód. Tourinform, Park utca 14, Badacsony, (87) 43 10 46.

Beginning at the railway station in lovely Badacsony village is a well-marked and fairly gentle trail, signposted in yellow, which winds its way up to the Kisfaludy Lookout Tower at the top of Badacsony Mountain (437 m/1,434 ft). An extinct volcano, this offers the best hiking in the Balaton area, with spectacular views from the top across the lake.

On the way up, almost hidden among the vineyards that cover the volcanic soil, are two superb former wine-press houses. The first, 3 km (2 miles) from Badacsony, is the Róza Szegedy House, named after the wife of the 18th-century poet Sándor Kisfaludy. The couple met on the mountain and the house contains a small display dedicated to Kisfaludy's poetry, as well as a wine cellar where the locally produced

Badacsony Mountain, as seen from Szigetvár Island Castle

Grey Friar wine (Szürkebarát) can be sampled. The second wine-press house on the trail was once Kisfaludy's home, and today is also a wine cellar offering tastings. There are great views from its terrace. Passing Rose Rock, where the couple met, the trail continues to the top, from where longer, more strenuous hikes depart for two other hills, Gulács-hegy and Szent György-hegy.

㉑ Tapolca

26 km (16 miles) northeast of Keszthely. **Road Map** B4. 18,000. from Budapest, Keszthely. from Budapest. Tourinform, Fő tér 17, (87) 51 07 77.

Encircled by 14 cone-shaped hills of basalt rock, Tapolca has one of the most spectacular settings of any town on Lake Balaton. Equally picturesque is the thermal pond in the centre of the town, encircled by little squares and colourful 19th-century houses. Many have been converted into bars and restaurants, with terraces overlooking the lake.

An early 19th-century watermill in the middle of the mill pond is now the Hotel Gabriella. What most visitors really come to Tapolca for, however, is the **Cave Lake** (Tavas-barlang), a short walk from the town centre. The lake lies 18 m (59 ft) below the surface. It was discovered by accident when a well was being sunk in 1902, and is reached via a steep staircase. Part of the 300-m (328-yard) cave system can be seen from dry land, though much more can be explored in a rented boat.

🛈 Tapolca Cave Lake
Kisfaludy utca 3. **Tel** (87) 41 25 79. **Open** Jul & Aug: 9am–7pm daily; Sep–Jun: 10am–5pm daily.

Tapolca's unique attraction, the mysterious Cave Lake

Kinizsi Castle in Nagyvázsony, once a military fortress

㉒ Nagyvázsony

26 km (16 miles) southwest of
Veszprém. **Road Map** B4. 🗺 1,750.
🚌 from Balatonfüred.

Set in a valley between the
Balaton hills and Mount Kab,
Nagyvázsony boasts **Kinizsi
Castle**, a well-preserved
14th-century fortress. It was
given to local warrior Pál Kinizsi
in 1472 by King Mátyás in
recognition of his outstanding
military service. Families will
enjoy the games and entertainments of the period staged here
daily in July and August.
   From the top of the 29-m-
(95-ft-) high keep a superb
panorama of the surrounding
countryside unfolds. In the
dungeons is the **Pál Kinizsi
Castle Museum** (Kinizsi Pál
Vármúzeum), with a small wax-
work display of medieval
torture. Pál Kinizsi's sarcophagus lies in the chapel.
   Opposite the castle stands
St István Church, built for Kinizsi
in 1470 but rebuilt in Baroque
style in 1740. An **Ethnographic
Museum** (Néprajzi Múzeum)
with two cottages (a copper-
smith's and a weaver's) remain
as they were in the mid-1840s.

🏛 **Pál Kinizsi Castle Museum**
Vár utca 9. **Tel** (88) 26 40 11. **Open**
Mar, Apr & Oct: 10am–5pm; May, Sep:
9am–6pm, Jun–Aug: 9am–7pm, Nov–
Feb: 10am–4pm. 🎨

🏛 **Ethnographic Museum**
Bercsényi utca 21. **Open** May–Sep:
10am–6pm Tue–Sun. 🎨 ♿

㉓ Tihany Peninsula

15 km (9 miles) south of Veszprém.
Road Map B4. 🚃 to Balatonfüred.
🚌 from Balatonfüred to Tihany
village. ⛴ car ferry from Szántód.
🛈 Tourinform, Kossuth Lajos utca
20, Tihany, (87) 44 88 04.

Declared Hungary's first
conservation area in 1952, the
Tihany Peninsula is an outcrop
of volcanic rock extending for
5 km (3 miles) into Lake
Balaton. The symbol of the
peninsula, and visible from afar,
is the Baroque Abbey Church,
built in the 18th century on the
site of an earlier church, which
was consecrated in 1060 but
destroyed in 1702. Beneath
lies King András I, laid to rest
here in 1055. Károly Lotz's
superb frescoes of Faith,
Hope and Charity adorn the
church's ceiling.
   The western half of Tihany is
closed to motor traffic and
accessible only on foot, along
a number of well-marked trails,
most of which begin just
outside Tihany village. The
most intriguing route is the
Lajos Lóczy Nature Trail, which
takes visitors past the hermit
caves overlooking Tihany
village, and the peninsula's two
inland lakes: Belső-tó (Inner
Lake) and Külső-tó (Outer Lake).
Belső-tó is a volcanic crater and
an angler's dream, while Külső-
tó is a bird sanctuary and
nesting ground for tens of
thousands of birds.
   Tihany has good grass
beaches, although the most
popular, on the promenade at
Tihany village, get very busy
during high summer. The
passenger port, Tihany-rév at
the peninsula's southern tip, is
the prettiest on the lake. Car
ferries cross from here to
Szántód on Lake Balaton's
southern shore.

The High Altar in Tihany's ornate Baroque Abbey Church

A café near Lake Balaton in the elegant resort of Balatonfüred

㉔ Balatonfüred

23 km (14 miles) southeast of Veszprém. **Road Map** B4. 13,000. from Budapest. from Budapest. from Siófok. Tourinform, Blaha Lujza utca 5, (87) 58 04 80. Anna Ball (last Sat in Jul).

The site of the first medicinal retreat on Lake Balaton, Hungary's first sailing club and one of its oldest balls, Balatonfüred remains the grandest resort on the lake. Though its streets have a faded air, the villas, such as that of the romantic novelist Mór Jókai (1825–1904), still convey elegance; Jókai's home is today a museum dedicated to his works. Primarily a health spa, patients flock to the town's hospital to drink its mineral-laced water. The "miracle" water is available to all from the colonnaded drinking fountain in Gyógy tér.

Gyógy tér is also where the grand annual Anna Ball is held at the Árkád Hotel in July. The first ball in 1825 was a showcase event for the granddaughter of a local businessman. Traditionally, the debutantes all wear exactly the same gown, and the high point is the election of the belle of the ball.

Two great sandy beaches flank Balatonfüred's landing stage, from where the Lake Balaton ferry departs.

㉕ Balatonalmádi

13 km (8 miles) south of Veszprém. **Road Map** B4. 8,000. from Budapest. from Budapest. Tourinform, Városház tér 4, (88) 59 40 80. Hungaricum Festival (last week in Jul).

The second-largest resort on Balaton's northern shore, Balatonalmádi has welcomed bathers since the 1870s. It has a fine sandy beach, and is an excellent base for exploring the Balaton hinterland and hills on foot. From the railway station, a 6-km (4-mile) path (marked with blue crosses) leads up to the Wesselényi Viewing Tower at

A sailing boat on Lake Balaton

the top of Öreg-hegy (132 m/ 433 ft). A much tougher walk leads to the top of Felső-hegy (321 m/1,053 ft)

from the same starting point. The Hungaricum Festival held in summer features a huge folk art fair, folk dancing, sports events and evening concerts.

㉖ Herend

7 km (4 miles) northwest of Veszprém. **Road Map** B4. 3,400. from Veszprém. herend.com

The small village of Herend is famous mainly for its porcelain manufactory, which has been producing some of the finest porcelain in the world since 1826. The building itself is a masterpiece, and as such a listed building. A late Classicist edifice built in 1840, it has an amazing entrance, topped with an egg-shaped dome guarded by two giant angels.

The **Herend Porcelain Art Museum** (Herendi Porcelán-művészeti Múzeum Alapítvány), opened in 1964, has displays of the decorative Herend china and porcelain, from dinner plates to intricately painted figurines. There is also the opportunity to visit a workshop (porcelanium) to watch the production process. There are demonstrations by artists who meticulously hand-paint every detail. A vast factory shop sells some 12,000 porcelain items made here and painted in about 350 different patterns.

🏛 **Herend Porcelain Art Museum** Kossuth Lajos utca 140. **Tel** (88) 52 31 97. **Open** Apr–Oct: 9am–5:30pm daily; Nov–Mar: 9:30am–4pm daily (Nov–Dec: Tues–Sat).

The astonishing entrance of the Herend Porcelain Art Museum

㉗ Veszprém

The site of the nation's first bishopric, and for centuries the seat of the Queen of Hungary's household, Veszprém is one of Hungary's great historical towns. It was all but razed by the Turks as they fled Hungary in the 17th century. Spread over five hills, the most picturesque part of the city is the Vár (Castle District, *see pp210–11*), but the lower city offers some fine Baroque architecture, great museums and quaint streets. The twin towers of St Michael's Cathedral, visible from afar, are a symbol of Veszprém and of the Balaton and Bakony regions. Visitors need to be fit to explore this city, as many sights are at the top of long staircases or at the end of steep, cobbled streets.

The restored, grand interior of St Michael's Cathedral

⛪ St Michael's Cathedral
Szent Mihály Érseki Székesegyház
Vár utca 20. **Tel** (88) 32 80 38.
Open May–Oct: 10am–7pm (enter via side door). **Closed** Nov–Feb.

There was a church here as early as 1001, when St István created a bishopric, but the cathedral's present look is early 20th century. Remains of earlier styles include the Gothic undercroft (underground store) and the crypt's vaulting, both from 1380. Following sensitive restoration of many older features, the cathedral has returned to its former glory, crowned by two tall towers dating from 1723.

⛪ Gizella Chapel
Gizella Kápolna
Vár utca 18. **Tel** (88) 42 60 88.
Open May–Oct: 10am–5pm
Tue–Sun.

The tiny 13th-century Gothic Chapel commemorates the life of Gizella, wife of István and first Queen of Hungary. The chapel was lost and rediscovered only in the 1760s. Its faded Byzantine frescoes of the apostles on the walls are original.

🏛 Archbishop's Palace
Érseki Palota
Vár utca 16–18. **Tel** (88) 42 60 88.
Open May–Oct: 10am–5pm Tue–Sun.

This Baroque mansion (1764) was designed by Fellner and has his trademark rounded four-columned loggia. It houses the Archbishop's archive and only a few rooms are open to the public, with a fine collection of Baroque furniture and frescoes by Johann Cymbal.

🏛 Heroes' Gate
Hősök kapuja
Vár utca 2. **Tel** (88) 61 05 16/17.
Open 10am–6pm daily.

This restored city gate, which was built in 1938 to commemorate the Hungarian dead of World War I, houses a small exhibition on the history of the city and its original fortifications. The gate's tower affords fine views of the city from the top.

🏛 Óváros tér and Town Hall
Városháza
Óváros tér.

Óváros tér sits directly below the Castle District. Veszprém's former market square, it is surrounded by some fine little houses, many of which are today cafés. The Pósa House at No. 3 was built for a local merchant, Endre Pósa, in 1783. Its showy decoration, especially the two cherubs below the roof, was to offset the linearity of the building. The contours of the Secession-era house next door are gentler. Opposite is the Neo-Classical town hall, built in 1896 as church offices, but renovated and converted in 1990. Behind the town hall, up a flight of stairs, is Lenke Kiss's fountain *Girl with a Jug*, which is affectionately known as "Zsuzsi" by locals.

A late Secession-era stained-glass window in the Petőfi Theatre

🎭 Petőfi Theatre
Petőfi Szinház
Óvári Ferenc utca 2. **Tel** (88) 42 42 35.
Open during performances only.

The late Secession-era (1908) municipal theatre, set in well-kept gardens, is named after revolutionary playwright and poet Sándor Petőfi (*see p46*). The theatre was designed by István Medgyaszay, who studied in Vienna under Otto Wagner. It has intricate folk motifs on the façade, typical of later Secessionist buildings.

Façade of the Neo-Classical town hall, built in 1896

🏛 Laczkó Dezső Museum

Laczkó Dezső Múzeum
Erzsébet sétány 1. **Tel** (88) 78 81 91.
Open 10am–6pm Tue–Sun.

The County Museum, designed by the local architect István Medgyaszay, was opened in 1922. Its collection consists of local artifacts, including folk costumes dating back to Celtic times. Most of the collection was donated by local Piarist monks, for whose leader, Laczkó Dezső, the museum was named. It also housed Hungary's first public library, still a leading research facility.

🏛 Bakony Regional Folk House

Bakonyi Ház
Erzsébet sétány 3. **Tel** (88) 56 43 10.
Open Apr–Oct: 10am–6pm Tue–Sun.

Hungary's first ethnographic museum, the Bakony House (1935) was modelled on the 19th-century houses of Öcs, south of Veszprém. The house is built on high foundations and has a full-length covered terrace. A small staircase leads to a single door. Inside, items on show date back to 1700.

St István Viaduct, designed by the Hungarian architect Róbert Folly

🎫 St István Viaduct

Szent István völgyhíd
Szent István völgyhíd.
Stretching over the Fejes Valley, from Dózsa György utca to the St László Church, the St István Viaduct was built in 1938, a major engineering achievement at the time. Designed by a Hungarian, Róbert Folly, it rises 50 m (164 ft) above the River Séd at its highest point. It affords magnificent views of the castle, the Betekints Valley and the Bakony Mountains to the north.

🦒 Veszprém Zoo

Kittenberger Kálmán Növény és Vadaspark
Kittenberger Kálmán utca 15–17.
Tel (88) 56 61 40. **Open** May–Sep: 9am–6pm daily; Oct–Apr: from 9am daily, closing times vary with season.
🌐 **veszpzoo.hu**

Hungary's best zoo, named after Africa explorer Kálmán Kittenberger (1881–1958), is spread over 130,000 sq m (155,500 sq yards) in the lovely Fejes Valley. It is home to 120 species, including Sumatran tigers and Kamchatka bears, giraffes and elephants, seals, penguins and fine exotic birds.

A giraffe in Veszprém Zoo

Veszprém City Centre

① St Michael's Cathedral
② Gizella Chapel
③ Archbishop's Palace
④ Heroes' Gate
⑤ Óváros tér and Town Hall
⑥ Petőfi Theatre
⑦ Laczkó Dezső Museum
⑧ Bakony Regional Folk House
⑨ St István Viaduct
⑩ Veszprém Zoo

0 metres 200
0 yards 200

Key

 Street-by-Street pp210–11

Street-by-Street: Veszprém Vár

With the exception of Buda, Veszprém contains Hungary's best-preserved and most accessible Castle District *(Vár)*. Built on an outcrop of dolomite rock, it consists basically of one street, which is narrow in parts and delightful with its mixture of medieval and Baroque architecture. From here, the views over the modern city from the Szent István and Gizella Monument are stunning, and make the walk up worthwhile.

PATAK TÉR

Gizella Chapel
Lost for hundreds of years, the 13th-century Gizella Chapel was rediscovered in the 1760s during construction of the Archbishop's Palace.

Szent István and Gizella Monument
Huge statues featuring Hungary's greatest king and his wife were raised in 1936, on the 900th anniversary of István's death.

★ St Michael's Cathedral
Standing on the site of an 11th-century church founded by King István, St Michael's Cathedral was extensively rebuilt in Neo-Romanesque style in 1908.

Dubniczay House
Built in 1751, the Dubniczay House incorporates part of the old castle wall.

Key

 Suggested route

Franciscan Church
After the original 18th-century church burned down in 1909, it was rebuilt to mirror the Neo-Romanesque façade of the cathedral opposite.

Holy Trinity Statue
Commissioned by the then Bishop of Veszprém, Márton Padányi-Bíró, this statue was raised in 1750. The Bishop also commissioned the Bíró-Giczey House opposite.

★ **Archbishop's Palace**
Veszprém's finest building is an outstanding example of Baroque design, the work of Jakab Fellner, who also designed the dormitory for ecclesiastical staff next door. Seven of the mansion's rooms, including the frescoed dining room, are open to the public.

St Emeric Piarist and Garrison Church
On the walls of this early 19th-century church are engraved the letters MMT: a Greek acronym for Mary, Mother of God.

Fire Lookout Tower
Open from April to October, the views of modern Veszprém from the top of this elegant, Baroque 48-m- (157-ft-) high tower are superb.

VÁR UTCA

★ **Heroes' Gate**
Veszprém's history, and the history of the gate itself, is explored in an exhibition within the restored castle gate and tower.

0 metres   30
0 yards   30

Route down to Óváros tér
Visitors should note that the Vár remains open to motor traffic, and beware of cars.

THE NORTHERN HIGHLANDS

Among the gems hidden in the mountains and forests of the Northern Highlands are grand palaces and castles, mysterious caves and grottoes, healing baths and thermal springs. The Hungarian uplands are remote, lying beyond mountain passes and deep forests, and their plantlife and wildlife are well protected in the national parks. This region also produces Hungary's best wine – Tokaji.

From Hollókő in the west to the Zemplén Hills on Hungary's eastern border with Ukraine, the Northern Highlands feel remote and other-worldly. Home to a number of peoples who are not of Magyar descent (the Palóc of Hollókő, for example), this is the least homogenous region of the country. Yet the people of the mountains are proudly Hungarian, and proud that at Eger Castle the most heroic rearguard action in the nation's history was fought and won – and the myth of Bull's Blood born.

The region has much for sports enthusiasts: skiing, hiking, caving and horse riding are pursued in the resorts of the Mátra Mountains. Bathers and those seeking hydrotherapy can take the waters at Parádfürdő or at Miskolctapolca, the

most spectacular of all Hungary's thermal baths. Nature-lovers will head for the Bükk National Park, where over 22,000 species of animal and plant live in a protected environment.

Tokaji is Hungary's finest wine: the golden wine of Aszú is made in the far east of the country, a place where Calvinism, not Catholicism, is the predominant religion. Many of the towns and villages east of the Tokaj hills are remote – to journey to gorgeous Baroque towns such as Sárospatak and Sátoraljaújhely really is to step off the beaten track.

This area is not short of good places to stay, however. Converted palaces such as the Sasvár Kastély in Parádfürdő, or the Palota in Lillafüred, offer accommodation fit for royals.

Pedestrianized Széchenyi Street, leading to the Bishop's Palace and Lyceum, Eger

◀ The castle at Hollókő, a UNESCO-recognized centre for the indigenous Palóc culture

Exploring the Northern Highlands

While the Mátra and Bükk Mountains, boasting Hungary's highest peaks, define the Northern Highlands, this is, in fact, the most geographically diverse region. Some of the country's most evocative sights are found here. Castles, such as the legendary fortress at Eger, bear witness to troubled times, while many thermal baths have drawn bathers since imperial times. This is also wine country, with Tokaj and Eger the foremost towns of international acclaim, and the home of the Palóc people, who fiercely guard their traditions.

The traditional Palóc settlement of Hollókő, preserved as a World Heritage Site

Eger, with Cannon Hill and the famous castle in the background

For hotels and restaurants see pp264–269 and pp276–285

Key

━━ Motorway

━━ Secondary road

═══ Minor road

⌁⌁ Main railway

── Minor railway

▬▬ International border

▬▬ Regional border

Getting Around

The region is reasonably well served by railway, although the geography may force visitors to travel back on themselves in order to reach a new destination by train. There are trains from Budapest to Gyöngyös, Eger and Miskolc, with regional onward services from there. To get the most out of a visit to the region, however, it is best to hire a car. Roads are good and allow much quicker access to some of the more remote sights.

Bacchus, in the wine town of Tokaj

Vineyard in Felsőtárkány, between Eger and the Bükk National Park

Sights at a Glance

1. Balassagyarmat
2. Ipolytarnóc
3. *Hollókő pp218–19*
4. Gyöngyös
5. Mátra Mountains
6. Parád & Parádfürdő
7. *Eger pp220–23*
8. *Bükk National Park pp224–5*
9. Szilvásvárad
10. Aggteleki National Park
11. *Miskolc pp230–31*
12. Miskolctapolca
13. Szerencs
14. Tokaj
15. Zemplén Hills
16. Sárospatak
17. Sátoraljaújhely

For keys to map symbols *see back flap*

The Palóc Museum in Balassagyarmat, keeping up folk traditions

❶ Balassagyarmat

80 km (50 miles) north of Budapest. **Road Map** D2. 🚍 18,000. 🚉 from Vác. 🚌 from Budapest. 🛈 Tourinform, Köztársaság tér 6, (35) 50 06 40.

Capital of the Palóc region, Balassagyarmat stands on the southern bank of the Ipoly river, which marks the border between Hungary and Slovakia. The origin of the Palóc people, famous for retaining their own cultural traditions, remains something of a mystery. The nearby village of Hollókő *(see pp218–19)* is the best-known and best-kept Palóc settlement in Hungary.

The townsfolk of Balassagyarmat no longer wear Palóc costume, but many examples of their colourful, elaborate dress are on display at the city's **Palóc Museum** (Palóc Múzeum). Here, visitors can also admire the rich artistic skills of the Palóc in the handicrafts on show. There are superb embroideries, intricate woodcarvings and colourful ceramics as well as a mock-up of a classroom and a wedding. Unfortunately, there is less on display than there once was, because as much as 90 per cent of the collection was looted by the German army during World War II.

🏛 **Palóc Museum**
Palóc liget 1. **Tel** (35) 30 01 68. **Open** 9am–4pm Tue–Sat.
🎫 🚻

❷ Ipolytarnóc

43 km (27 miles) northeast of Balassagyarmat. **Road Map** D2. 🚍 550. 🚉 from Szécsény, Balassagyarmat. 🚌 from Szécsény.

Around 22 million years ago, a volcanic eruption buried the area around what is today the village of Ipolytarnóc in hot ash. Hundreds of animals were caught at their drinking place and their fossilized remains can be seen today as part of a Geological Study Path that is unique in Europe. It departs from the visitors' centre of the **Ipolytarnóc Fossils Nature Protected Area** (Ipolytarnóci Ősmaradványok Természet-védelmi Terület) on the village's outskirts. Before setting off, watch the short film telling the story of the eruption and explaining the natural history of the area. A guide is needed for the Geological Study Tour, but the Biology and Rock Park Tours can be taken unaccompanied.

Fossilized rhino footprints in Ipolytarnóc

In the visitors' centre, the teeth of 24 species of sharks, crocodiles and dolphins, fossilized trees, the imprints of more than 5,000 subtropical exotic leaves and the footprints of 2,000 animals can be admired. A 4-D cinema and adventure park make the visit even more enjoyable for families.

🏕 **Ipolytarnóc Fossils Nature Protected Area**
Ipolytarnóc külterület. **Tel** (32) 45 41 13. **Open** Apr–Oct: 9am–4pm Tue–Sun. 🎫 🚻

❸ Hollókő

See pp218–19.

❹ Gyöngyös

77 km (48 miles) east of Budapest. **Road Map** D3. 🚍 33,000. 🚉 from Vámosgyörk. 🚌 from Budapest, Eger. 🛈 Fő tér 10, (37) 51 03 10. 🛒 daily (until noon), Köztársaság tér.

At the foot of the Mátra hills, Gyöngyös is the home of some of Hungary's best white wines. Visitors can sample many of these at the Mátra House of Wines, a shop and cellar that stocks over 200 local vintages. It is located on Fő tér, Gyöngyös's elegant pedestrianized central square. The centrepiece of the square, however, is the yellow Baroque **St Bertalan Parish Church**, originally built in 1301, then remodelled in the 18th century. The high-ceilinged – but plain – main hall is the largest surviving Gothic church building in Hungary. Opposite the church is the House of the Holy Crown, so called because the Hungarian royal crown was brought here for safekeeping early in the 19th century. Today, the **St Bertalan Treasury Museum** (Szent Bertalan Templom Kincstára) accommodates a large treasury of ecclesiastical art.

Gyöngyös's other star sight is the **Mátra Museum**, housed in

Interior of St Bertalan Parish Church in Gyöngyös

the former Orczy Mansion, close to the narrow-gauge railway station. The late 18th-century mansion is a mixture of Neo-Baroque and Neo-Classical styles.

Heves county is known for its sports, and the Mátra Museum's best exhibition is devoted to hunting, complete with various trophies. In the beautiful park around the mansion, there is a three-storey pavilion with exhibitions on natural history. The pride of the collection is a 40,000–50,000-year-old mammoth skeleton found nearby. The Palm House is also home to living animals, reptiles, fishes and birds.

St Bertalan Treasury Museum
Szent Bertalan utca 3. **Tel** (37) 30 00 72. **Open** 10am–5pm Tue–Sat; Sun by appointment only.

Mátra Museum and Microarium
Kossuth Lajos utca 40. **Tel** (37) 50 55 30. **Open** 9am–5pm Tue–Sun.

❺ Mátra Mountains

85 km (52 miles) northeast of Budapest. **Road Map** D3/E3. from Mátrafüred. from Mátrafüred. Tourinform Gyöngyös, Fő tér 10, (37) 51 03 10.

The most spectacular way to traverse the steep Mátra Mountains is by narrow-gauge railway from Gyöngyös to **Mátrafüred**, the largest village in the region. In summer, Mátra-füred is pure heaven for lovers of challenging mountain hikes. There are trails of various

lengths, all well marked, but note that all contain at least one relatively difficult section. Mátrafüred is also great for mountain biking, and many pensions hire out good-quality bikes. Non-hikers can pass the time at the **Palóc Ethnographical Museum** (Palóc Néprajzi Magángyűjtemény és Baba-kiállítás), where a large and colourful collection of dolls shows the traditional costumes of the Palóc people.

About 8 km (5 miles) further into the mountains is the smaller resort of **Mátraháza**, with more hiking trails, and slightly further north is **Mátraszentistván**, Hungary's leading ski resort and also a base for summer hiking. **Kékestető**, at 1,015 m (3,330 ft) the highest peak in Hungary, lies east of Mátraháza. It is served by bus or takes

Footpath marker in the Mátra Mountains

45 minutes to hike up. The mountain is topped by a 90-m- (295-ft-) high TV tower, which offers spectacular views from the viewing platform at the top.

For more relaxing pursuits, there is good fishing at the picturesque **Lake Sástó**, which, at an altitude of 500 m (1,640 ft), is one of the highest in Hungary. It is found between Mátrafüred and Mátraháza.

Palóc Ethnographical Museum
Pálosvörösmarti utca 2, Mátrafüred. **Tel** (30) 913 49 87. **Open** May–Oct: 9am–5pm daily; Nov–Mar: 10am–3pm daily. Hungarian only.

❻ Parád and Parádfürdő

30 km (19 miles) north of Gyöngyös. **Road Map** E3. 2,400. from Budapest. from Budapest.

The waters at Parádfürdő have been taken as a cure for digestive disorders and bathed in as a cure for gynaecological ailments since the 17th century. The real treasure of the twin villages, however, is the so called Fancy Stable (Cifra Istálló). Commissioned by Count György Károlyi it was designed by Miklós Ybl (who also designed the State Opera House in Budapest (see pp93–3). Completed in 1880, much of the stable's elaborate decoration is of red marble. Few horses have finer homes, and the famous Lipizzaner horses are still bred here. The rest of the building is the **Parád Coach Museum** (Parádi Kocsi-múzeum), which has a wide selection of elaborate horse-drawn coaches, some of which were once used by the Hungarian royal family. There are also interesting displays on carriage building, traditional Palóc music, dance, folk costumes and tools.

Parád Coach Museum
Kossuth Lajos utca 217. **Tel** (36) 36 40 83. **Open** Apr–Sep: 10am–5pm daily; Oct–Mar: 10am–4pm Tue–Sun.

A typical thatched Palóc cottage in the village of Parád

❸ Street-by-Street: Hollókő

Set in a narrow valley in the Cserhát hills, Hollókő is one of the few entire villages in the world to have been placed on UNESCO's World Heritage List. The Palóc have lived here since the 13th century, when the castle on Szárhegy was built. They use colourful dialect and costume. Yet, in Hollókő all is not what it appears: the 58 houses, churches and workshops protected by UNESCO are little more than a century old. Once entirely made of wood and thatch, the village has burned down many times, and was almost completely rebuilt in 1909 with brick walls and tiled roofs.

★ **Palóc Village Museum**
The vibrant costumes and lifestyles of the Palóc people, with three generations living under one roof, are vividly represented at the museum.

★ **Hollókő Castle**
A short walk from the village centre are the ruins of a 13th-century fortress, destroyed during the Turkish retreat. It was partly rebuilt in the 1990s.

Ruins of the Castle

Doll Museum
These wonderfully detailed china dolls are dressed in miniature versions of Palóc dress. The Doll Museum has more than 200 dolls in its collection.

Local Dress

The Palóc are Slovak in origin, and their traditional dress, worn by many of the village's residents, is distinctly Slavic, with intricately embroidered motifs, often of bright flowers. Married women wear headscarves; while, unmarried girls don lace bonnets. Palóc men wear black hats with embroidered ribbons. The finest costumes can be seen on Sundays, when locals dress up for the morning church service.

Hungarian women in traditional Palóc dress

★ The Village Church

This elegant whitewashed church with wooden belfry, built in 1889, is at the very centre of the village and is the focal point of Hollókő.

The Potter's House

A showcase of simple but elegant Palóc pottery, the Potter's House hosts pottery-making demonstrations and sells local wares.

Village House

This 19th-century wooden house with a thatched roof is one of the few to have survived the many fires that ravaged the village over the centuries.

Main entrance

0 metres	50
0 yards	50

Post Museum

Two rooms in a small cottage display telegraph and communications equipment, as well as documents relating to the history of the postal service in Nógrád County.

Key

— Suggested route

For keys to map symbols *see back flap*

❼ Eger

Situated off the main road from Budapest to the east of Hungary, Eger is a sleepy, provincial town known today for its Bull's Blood wine *(see p223)* and for its university. The castle *(see pp222–3)* and the legend of the great siege of 1552 dominate but it is, in fact, the Church that has twice saved the city from doom. After destruction by the Mongols in 1241, it was rebuilt with money from the Minorite and Franciscan orders. And after the withdrawal of the Turks in 1687, the local bishopric revived the city by commissioning many of the Baroque masterpieces that remain today, including the Cathedral, the Lyceum and the Bishop's Palace.

🏛 Eger Cathedral
Főszékesegyház – Szent János apostol és evangélista Szent Mihály főangyal
Pyrker tér 1. **Tel** (36) 51 57 25.
Open 8am–6pm daily. ♿

Although its garish yellow colour and architectural mixture of Neo-Classical and Neo-Romanesque styles may not be to everyone's taste, there is no doubt that Eger Cathedral – the second-largest church in Hungary – is the most astonishing sight in the city. It was built from 1831 to 1837 to a design by the architect József Hild, who would later design the even larger and more stunning basilica at Esztergom *(see pp148–9)*. The cathedral at Eger is unique in Hungary, having a cupola – at 40 m (131 ft) – that is shorter than the two western towers, measuring 44 m (144 ft). At the other end of the building, three gargantuan statues loom over the colonnaded Neo-Classical façade. They represent Faith, Hope and Charity

and were the work of the Italian sculptor Marco Casagrande.

Inside, the cupola is decorated with frescoes of the *Kingdom of Heaven* by Viennese artist Johann Kracker. The cathedral also has Hungary's largest organ; from April to October there are performances on Monday to Saturday at 11:30am and on Sunday at 12:45pm.

🏛 Bishop's Palace
Római katolikus érseki palota
Széchenyi utca 9. **Tel** (36) 51 75 89.
Open call ahead for opening times. 🗝

The second element of central Eger's ecclesiastical architectural triumvirate is the former Bishop's Palace on Széchenyi utca. Like the Lyceum, it was built in Baroque style to the designs of Jakab Kellner, and completed in 1766. Inside, the palace houses the Ecclesiastical Collection of the Eger Bishopric, which includes the coronation cloak of Habsburg Empress Maria Theresa (r. 1740–80) and other priceless objects.

The sombre interior of Eger Cathedral, brightened by ceiling frescoes

🏛 Lyceum
Líceum, Eszterházy Károly Főiskola
Eszterházy Károly tér 1. **Tel** 32 52 11.
Open Library: call ahead for details. Tower: Feb–mid-Mar & Nov–mid-Dec: 9:30am–1pm Sat & Sun; mid–Mar–Oct: 9:30am–3pm Tue–Sun (to 4:30pm May–Aug). 🗝 🅿 ♿

The Lyceum was founded in 1765 as a Catholic university, but imperial authorities opposed the idea of a church university and relegated it to the rank of lyceum. The ceiling of the library boasts Johann Kracker's fresco depicting the meeting of the Council of Trent (1545–63). The library itself holds over 150,000 volumes, including the first book ever printed in Hungary, in 1473. In the 53-m (174-ft) "Magic Tower" is Hungary's leading centre of astronomy, with a museum, a planetarium and a 19th-century camera obscura.

Main façade of the Lyceum, built as a Catholic university

🏛 Kossuth Street
Kossuth utca.

Kossuth utca, a wide boulevard, has long been Eger's best address. For centuries it was where the richest and holiest men in the city lived. At No. 4 is the Vice-Provost's Palace, a pastel-shaded Rococo mansion with a façade of hewn stone dating from 1758, which today is closed to the public.

On the same side of the street, at No. 14, is the Franciscan Church and Monastery, a single-nave church built in 1738 on the ruins of a former mosque. Opposite (at No. 9) is the Baroque County Hall, completed in 1758. It is famed for its two grand wrought-iron gates, crafted by the blacksmith Henrik Fazola (1730–79), who moved to Eger from Würzburg to

Kossuth Street, Eger's smartest address, seen from the air

take the city's waters. He is also responsible for most of the ironwork that typifies many of the buildings on Kossuth Street, as well as the Hungarian National Gallery in Budapest (see pp62–3) and Festetics Castle in Keszthely (see pp202–3).

Minorite Church
Szent Antonius Minorita templom
Dobó István tér

Set against the background of the open spaces of Dobó István tér, the ornate exterior of the former Minorite Church is far more pleasing on the eye than that of Eger Cathedral. The

rounded, tiered façade and twin towers are the work of Bohemian architect Johann Ignaz Dientzenhofer, who completed the church in 1773. Dedicated to St Anthony of Padova, scenes of the saint's life feature in the ceiling frescoes painted by Márton Reindl. He is also depicted alongside the Virgin Mary on the altar, in a painting by the Austrian Johann Kracker.

Main façade of the former Minorite Church, built in the 18th century

VISITORS' CHECKLIST

Practical Information
Road Map E3. 56,000.
Tourinform, Bajcsy-Zsilinszky utca 9, (36) 51 77 15. Dobó István tér; daily.

Transport
Vasút utca; from Budapest. Pyrker János tér; from Budapest.

Minaret
Knézich Károly utca 4. **Tel** (70) 202 43 53. **Open** Apr–Oct: 10am–6pm daily.

The most northerly Ottoman relic in Europe, Eger's minaret is a classic of its genre. Sleek and perfectly symmetrical, the 14-sided sandstone tower rises on an incline to its needle-like point 40 m (131 ft) above the street. It is topped with a crescent moon and a cross. Closed for 150 years after the mosque next to it was demolished in 1841, the 17th-century minaret is now open to visitors, who are rewarded for climbing the 97 steps up to the balcony with fine views of the city.

Castle
See pp222–3.

Eger City Centre

① Eger Cathedral
② Bishop's Palace
③ Lyceum
④ Kossuth Street
⑤ Minorite Church
⑥ Minaret
⑦ Castle pp222–3

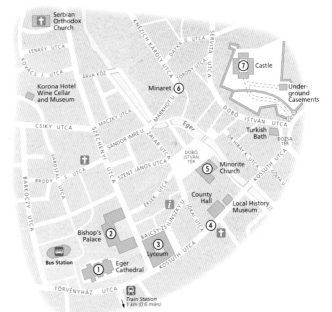

0 metres 100
0 yards 100

Serbian Orthodox Church
Korona Hotel Wine Cellar and Museum
Minaret ⑥
Castle ⑦
Underground Casemates
Turkish Bath
Minorite Church ⑤
County Hall
Local History Museum
Bishop's Palace ②
Lyceum ③
Bus Station
Eger Cathedral ①
Train Station 1 km (0.6 miles)

For keys to map symbols see back flap

Eger Castle

Entering Eger Castle through its tiny gate set into walls 3 m (10 ft) thick, with the walls of the upper fortress menacing in the background, it is not difficult to understand how its defenders held out for so long against the invading Turks. For it was here at Eger, in 1552, that the greatest rearguard action in Hungarian military history was carried out. The castle, defended by a garrison of just 2,000 soldiers ably assisted by the women of the town, held out against a Turkish force five times that size for six weeks. The Turks retreated, but took the castle 44 years later, only for much of it to be destroyed in 1702 by the Habsburgs.

★ Bishop's Palace
The names of all those who defended the castle in 1552 are engraved on a marble tablet in the main hall.

Waxworks in Fold Bastion
A great collection of lifelike figures, displayed over three levels of the bastion, recreates scenes from the siege.

Art Gallery
The Art Gallery hosts an unrivalled collection of Baroque Hungarian paintings and sculptures, including this bas-relief above the entrance.

KEY

① Round Tower
② Ticket office
③ Three Crosses Hill
④ Tomb of Gárdonyi
⑤ Cannon Hill

Dobó Bastion
The bastions and walls were built or fortified from the mid-1500s under István Dobó, who led the defenders at the Siege of Eger.

★ **Ruins of Romanesque Cathedral**
The ruins of a 10th-century Baptistry in the inner court-yard feature the grave of Eger's first Bishop, Buldus.

★ **Underground Corridors**
Castle Hill is a warren of underground chambers and paths, dug by the Turks in order to attack the castle from below. Some 200 m (656 ft) are open to the public.

Main entrance

Bull's Blood Wine

Bull's Blood of Eger is Hungary's most celebrated wine. Comparable to Bordeaux reds, Bull's Blood is robust and fruity, made of a mix of Cabernet Sauvignon, Merlot and Cabernet Franc grapes.

During the Siege of Eger in 1552, copious amounts of the wine were drunk by the soldiers who defended the castle against the Turks, and word was put about that their bravery was based on the blood of bulls that had been added to the wine. The stories were almost certainly false, but they impressed the superstitious Turks, and played a minor role in their defeat and retreat.

Egri Bikavér, Hungary's Bull's Blood wine

Ippolito Gate and Bornemissza Bastion
The castle gate is named after an Italian cardinal, Ippolito d'Este, who became Archbishop of Esztergom.

❽ Bükk National Park

The Bükk Mountain region, most of which has been classified as a National Park since 1977, extends from Eger to Miskolc, not far from Hungary's northern border with Slovakia. An area of outstanding natural beauty, it is renowned for its more than 1,000 caves, steep cliffs and lush beech forests (*bükk* means "beech"). There is some skiing in winter at Bánkút, but the main activities in the park are hiking, mountain-biking, horse riding and caving. Routes of all grades and lengths crisscross the park, forming a broadly triangular area between the main towns of Miskolc, Eger and Szilvásvárad.

Lipizzaners in Szilvásvárad Horse Museum
The famous white horses were first brought here from Lipica, in Slovenia, in the 16th century.

Fátyol Waterfall
Staggered limestone steps make this 17-m-(56-ft-) long waterfall one of the most attractive in Hungary. The steps enlarge a little every year as the water deposits more lime.

Romanesque **Bélapátfalva Abbey**, erected by Cistercian monks in the 1200s, is the best preserved in Hungary.

The **Szalajka Narrow-Gauge Railway** runs along the entire length of the Szalajka Valley in the summer.

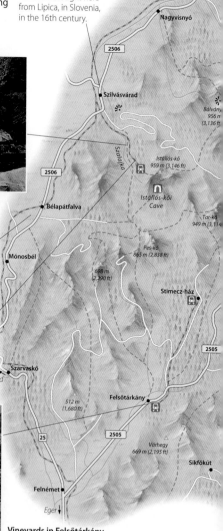

Nagyvisnyó

2506

Szilvásvárad

Bálvány
956 m
(3,136 ft)

Szalajka

Istállós-kő
959 m (3,146 ft)

2506

Istállós-kői
Cave

Bélapátfalva

Tar-kő
949 m (3,114

Pes-kő
865 m (2,838 ft)

Mónosbél

698 m
(2,290 ft)

Stimecz-ház

2505

Szarvaskő

Ózd

Felsőtárkány

512 m
(1,680 ft)

2505

25

Várhegy
669 m (2,195 ft)

Sikfőkút

Felnémet

Eger

Vineyards in Felsőtárkány
The leafy town of Felsőtárkány, surrounded by vineyards and parks, is one of the best entrance points for Bükk National Park.

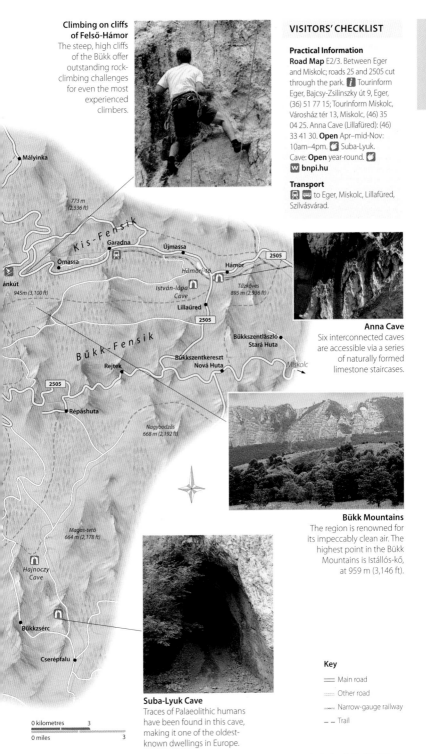

Climbing on cliffs of Felső-Hámor
The steep, high cliffs of the Bükk offer outstanding rock-climbing challenges for even the most experienced climbers.

VISITORS' CHECKLIST

Practical Information
Road Map E2/3. Between Eger and Miskolc; roads 25 and 2505 cut through the park. [i] Tourinform Eger, Bajcsy-Zsilinszky út 9, Eger, (36) 51 77 15; Tourinform Miskolc, Városház tér 13, Miskolc, (46) 35 04 25. Anna Cave (Lillafüred): (46) 33 41 30. **Open** Apr–mid-Nov: 10am–4pm. [⊘] Suba-Lyuk. Cave: **Open** year-round. [⊘] [W] bnpi.hu

Transport
[R] [🚌] to Eger, Miskolc, Lillafüred, Szilvásvárad.

Anna Cave
Six interconnected caves are accessible via a series of naturally formed limestone staircases.

Bükk Mountains
The region is renowned for its impeccably clean air. The highest point in the Bükk Mountains is Istállós-kő, at 959 m (3,146 ft).

Suba-Lyuk Cave
Traces of Palaeolithic humans have been found in this cave, making it one of the oldest-known dwellings in Europe.

Key
═══ Main road
⋯⋯ Other road
〰〰 Narrow-gauge railway
– – Trail

Grapevines growing in the fertile soil of the Tokaj hills ▶

The Fátyol Step-Waterfall in Szilvásvárad

❾ Szilvásvárad

30 km (19 miles) north of Eger. **Road Map** E2. 🔼 1,700. 🚃 from Eger. 🚌 from Budapest, Eger. 🏇 Bükk Carriage Driving Trophy (last weekend in Jul).

Szilvásvárad is a leading centre of Hungarian equestrianism, and white Lipizzaner horses – the same breed as those used at the famous Spanish Riding School in Vienna – are bred at the **Szilvásvárad Stud Farm** (Állami Ménesgazdaság Szilvásvárad). The farm is open for visitors, who can also book riding and even carriage-driving courses here. In July an international carriage-driving race takes place here.

The village itself has more information on the famous horses in its fascinating **Lipizzaner Horse-Breeding Exhibition** (Lipicai Lótenyésztés Történeti Kiállítás). Also on display here are a number of coaches and a complete working smithy.

But there is more to Szilvásvárad than horses – it is also the gateway to the beautiful Szalajka Valley. A narrow-gauge steam railway runs the 5 km (3 miles) from the village to Szalajka-Fátyol-vizesés, site of the gentle but wide Fátyol Step-Waterfall, as well as the **Open-Air Forestry Museum** (Szabadtéri Erdészeti Múzeum). The exhibits of early people's tiny huts, furnaces and elementary hunting tools are fascinating. At the head of the valley is the Istállóskő Cave, which burrows under Mount

Istállóskő – at 959 m (3,146 ft) the highest peak in the Bükk Mountain Range. The cave is known to have provided shelter for prehistoric people as early as 7,000 years ago.

🐎 Szilvásvárad Stud Farm
Egri út 16. **Tel** (36) 56 44 00. **Open** 8am–7pm daily. 🐾 ♿

🏛 Lipizzaner Horse-Breeding Exhibition
Park utca 8. **Tel** (36) 56 44 00. **Open** 9am–noon, 1–5pm Tue–Sun. 🐾 ♿

🏛 Open-Air Forestry Museum
Szalajka-völgy. **Tel** (36) 35 55 05. **Open** Apr–Oct: 9am–4pm daily (Oct: to 3pm); Nov–Mar: 9am–2pm daily. ♿

❿ Aggteleki National Park
Aggteleki Nemzeti Park

Tengerszem oldal 1, Jósvafő. **Road Map** E2. **Tel** (48) 50 60 00. 🚃 from Miskolc. 🚌 from Budapest. 🛈 Baradla oldal 1, Aggtelek (048) 50 30 00. 🌐 **anp.hu**

First established in 1985, the Aggteleki National Park is one of Hungary's World Heritage Sites. It straddles the Slovak border, and officially also includes a vast area of the Slovak Karst National Park. Large parts of the park are covered with deciduous forest, with clearings scattered liberally throughout the area. These rocky outcrops provide a perfect habitat for rare plants and insects, including giant swallowtail butterflies, as well as 220 species of birds. Imperial eagles and woodpeckers are a common sight. There are marked nature trails, including a 7-km (4-mile) trail from Aggtelek to Jósvafő.

The park also has some 200 caves to explore, of which the longest system – both in the park and in Hungary – is the **Baradla Cave** (Baradla Barlang). At 25 km (16 miles), it extends into Slovakia. While archaeological evidence suggests the cave was used by early humans

Spectacular rock formations in the Baradla Cave in Aggteleki National Park

The Cave Baths in Miskolctapolca, unique in Europe

thousands of years ago, all knowledge of it was lost, and its entrance was rediscovered only in 1569. The cave was fully mapped in 1839, and has been open to the public ever since. There are entrances in both Aggtelek and Jósvafő. Many caverns have been spectacularly lit. Parts of the cave are open to all-comers, but the best way to view it is on a tour. There are several to choose from, all beginning at the Aggtelek entrance; one tour of 7 hours takes in a part of the cave known as Domica under Slovakian territory. Occasionally the cave, which boasts splendid acoustics, hosts classical and other music concerts.

Baradla Cave
Baradla oldal 1, Aggtelek. **Tel** (48) 50 30 00. **Open** (guided tours only) Apr–Sep: 8am–5pm daily; Oct–Mar: 8am–3pm daily; Oct: 8am–5pm Sat.

⓫ Miskolc

See pp230–31.

⓬ Miskolctapolca

Pazár sétány, Miskolctapolca.
Road Map E2. **Tel** (46) 56 00 30. ⬛ from Búza tér, Miskolc. **Open** May–Aug: 9am–7pm daily; Sep–Dec, Feb–Apr: 9am–6pm daily.
barlangfurdo.hu

The cave baths of Miskolctapolca, set amid the backdrop of the Bükk Hills, are the most spectacular in Hungary. A vast resort has grown around the caves, which, discovered in the 16th century, have been attracting bathers ever since. Carved out

over centuries, the caves contain water that is high in calcium and magnesium, and is particularly suited for treating joint and back problems. The water is a warm 30° C (86° F) all year round. The cave baths are surrounded by a large park with a rowing lake, and there is also a cave chapel nearby. While the 150-m- (492-ft-) long cave baths are the primary attraction, the resort also offers all the attractions of a conventional thermal bath complex, complete with sauna, massage and other treatments, near-freezing-cold plunge pools and, on the recreational side, water slides and children's pools.

⓭ Szerencs

32 km (20 miles) east of Miskolc. **Road Map** F2. 🚶 11,000. 🚃 from Miskolc, Budapest. 🚌 from Budapest.

The little town of Szerencs is dominated by its historical links with the Rákóczi family, who owned the town and much of the surrounding area for

centuries. It was the Rákóczis who built **Szerencs Castle** at the beginning of the 16th century, today the most-visited attraction in the town.

Converted to domestic use after defeat against the Turks, the castle houses the **Zempléni Museum**, which tells the story of Rákóczi Zsigmond and the castle's military history, as well as boasting the largest postcard collection in the world (over 900,000). Exhibits also include period furniture, arms and the artistic works of goldsmiths.

Szerencs's main source of wealth and employment was, until its closure some years ago, a huge sugar factory – the third largest in Europe. In the town's **Sugar Museum** one can see fascinating details about the history and technology of sugar beet cultivation and sugar production, and displays some 800 sugar packages from around the world.

The Gothic Reformed church on Kossuth tér dates from 1480, and hosted the Hungarian parliament in 1605. Three generations of the Rákóczi family are buried in the crypt. Szerencs also has an elaborate though badly weathered Baroque Greek Orthodox church, built in 1799, on Ondi utca in the north of the town.

Zempléni Museum
Rákóczi-vár. **Tel** (47) 77 77 70.
Open 10am–4pm Tue–Sun.

Sugar Museum
Gyár út 1. **Tel** (47) 77 77 72.
Open 8am–4pm daily.

Szerencs Castle, housing the Zempléni Museum

⓫ Miskolc

Home of Hungary's largest university, Miskolc is the fourth-largest city in the country. An industrial town first and foremost, much of the outskirts, and even parts of the city centre, are less than attractive, having been built in the aftermath of heavy bombing during World War II. Amid the concrete, however, a wealth of historical buildings can be explored, including Hungary's oldest theatre, wooden churches of every Christian denomination, fine public squares and a fascinating museum. Miskolc is also the site of Diósgyőr Castle, renovated and restored to its full medieval glory.

Façade of the National Theatre, which hosts an opera festival in summer

🎭 National Theatre
Miskolci Nemzeti Színház
Déryné utca 1. **Tel** (46) 51 67 35.
🅿️ ♿

Hungary's oldest permanent, Hungarian-language theatre stood here between 1823 and 1843. Its Neo-Classical replacement was opened in 1857, with a play by Mihály Vörösmarty, and despite much renovation over the years it is that structure which mostly survives today. With its protruding three-arched loggia over the entrance it resembles Hungary's State Opera House in Budapest (see pp92–3). The tower, added in 1880, was originally used as a fire lookout point.

The restored Baroque interior has intricate statuary decorating the two rows of private boxes. The theatre is the main venue of the Miskolc Opera Festival, which takes place here every June, and features the work of the Hungarian composer Béla Bartók and others.

🏛 Theatre Museum
Színháztörténeti és Színészmúzeum
Déryné utca 3. **Tel** (70) 943 29 17.
Open 9am–5pm Tue–Sun. 🅿️ 🅲 ♿

In this museum, visitors can discover the secrets behind the fire that destroyed the original Miskolc Theatre in 1843, as well as the fact that an earlier theatre in Kolozsvár (today the town of Cluj-Napoca in Romania) in fact has a previous claim on the title of first Hungarian theatre. There are also countless costumes, bill posters and theatrical memorabilia on display, as well as a photographic exhibition about the theatre's role in the city's development. A sketch shows the late 18th-century wooden theatre that once stood on the site.

🔼 Greek Orthodox Church and Museum
Görögkeleti, Ortodox templom; Magyar Ortodox Egyházi Múzeum
Deák Ferenc tér 7. **Tel** (46) 41 54 41.
Open May–Sep: 10am–6pm Tue–Sun; Oct–Apr: 10am–4pm Tue–Sun.
🅿️ ♿

Icon from the Greek Orthodox Church

At 16 m (52 ft) in height, and boasting 88 images of the life of Jesus, the iconostasis in the Greek Orthodox Church is the most important sight in Miskolc. Dating from 1793, it was carved in the workshop of Miklós Jankovits of Eger; the pictures were painted by Anton Kuchelmeister. To its left is a painting of the Black Mary of Kazan, a gift from Empress Catherine II of Russia. The church itself was completed in 1806, and was originally intended to be topped with a classic Orthodox onion dome, but local Protestant authorities forbade this. Next door in the **museum** is the richest Orthodox liturgical collection in Hungary, opened in a former school in 1988. Its permanent exhibition includes ceremonial robes, sepulchres and more than 200 icons.

Entrances to the many wine cellars on the slopes of Avas Hill

🍷 Avas Hill and Ottó Herman Museum
Avas hegy.

More than 800 cinder caves have been dug out here and used as wine cellars since the 16th century; some are open during the summer for tastings. The cellars line cobbled streets that wind their way up to the Lookout Tower on Avas Hill, from where splendid views of the city are to be had.

At the foot of the hill is the **Ottó Herman Museum**, named after Ottó Herman (1835–1914), a local archaeologist. The museum is housed in a charming 19th-century house, with wooden, external balconies. It contains good collections of archaeological finds, stones and minerals, as well as displays on industrial history and coins. The fine art collection comprises masterworks by all famous Hungarian painters. The museum's library (on Görgey Artúr utca) holds more than 200,000 volumes and is renowned throughout the world for its collection of scientific works.

🏛 Ottó Herman Museum
Görgey Artúr utca 28. **Tel** (46) 56 01 70. **Open** 10am–4pm Tue–Sun. 🅿️ ♿

🏛 Calvinist Church
Avasi református templom
Papszer utca 14. **Tel** (46) 35 86 77.

The Calvinist Church below the Avas Hill, with its steep, detached belfry, is the oldest building in Miskolc. Originally Romanesque in style, the 13th-century building was destroyed by Turks in 1544. It was rebuilt – with the tower – in 1557. The clock on the belfry is one of the symbols of the city, and can be heard chiming every 15 minutes. The large and immaculately kept cemetery that surrounds the church is the resting place of a number of local dignitaries, including the poet Mihály Tompa, author of the romantic collection *Virágregék* (Legends of Flowers).

🏛 Diósgyőr Castle
Diósgyőri vár
Miskolc-Diósgyőr, Vár utca 24. **Tel** (46) 53 33 55. **Open** Apr–Oct: 9am–6pm daily; Nov–Mar: 10am–6pm daily. 🎫 ♿

Diósgyőr's medieval castle is located 8 km (5 miles) from the centre of Miskolc. The first

Diósgyőr Castle, rebuilt in the 13th century

castle here was probably built in the 12th century, and is thought to have been an earthwork castle. It guarded the route from Venice to KraKow for a long time and was destroyed during the Mongol invasion of 1241–2. The castle that stands here today was built during the reign of Béla IV, who, after the Mongols left the country, decreed that a castle be built "on every hilltop". The castle was subsequently used as a residence by several monarchs, although it lost its military status after the withdrawal of the Turks in 1687, and fell into neglect. Completely restored over two

VISITORS' CHECKLIST

Practical Information
Road Map E2. 🗺 161,000.
Deák Ferenc tér. 🛈 Tourinform, Széchenyi utca 16, (46) 35 04 25. 🎭 Jelly Festival (Feb); Miskolc Opera Festival (Jun); Castle Theatre evenings (Jul–Aug); Cinefest Film Festival (Sep).

Transport
🚉 Kandó Kálmán tér; from Budapest, Debrecen. 🚌 Búza tér; from Budapest, Debrecen.

decades from 1953 to 1971, the castle today hosts an exhibition of its history (in the northeastern tower), alongside a display of medieval weaponry. Life-size waxworks recreate the signing of the Treaty of Turin in 1381, while others, in the outer battlements, feature scenes of everyday life in medieval Diósgyőr. Twice a year, in May and August, plays and a medieval fair are held in the castle grounds, with jousting, archery and dance.

Miskolc City Centre

① National Theatre
② Theatre Museum
③ Greek Orthodox Church and Museum
④ Avas Hill and Ottó Herman Museum
⑤ Calvinist Church
⑥ Diósgyőr Castle

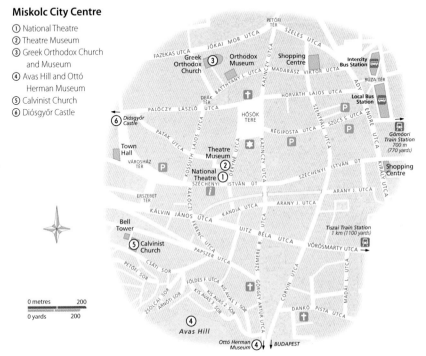

0 metres 200
0 yards 200

For keys to map symbols *see back flap*

⑭ Tokaj

40 km (25 miles) northwest of Nyíregyháza. **Road Map** F2. 🚐 4,600. 🚉 from Miskolc. 🚌 from Debrecen, Budapest. 🛈 Tourinform, Serház utca 1, (47) 55 20 70 or (47) 35 22 59.

At the confluence of the rivers Bodrog and Tisza, rich, fertile soil facilitates the cultivation of Hungary's best grapevines. These produce the country's finest wines. Smooth and delicately sweet, Tokaji dessert wine is made exclusively in and around Tokaj. In 2002 UNESCO placed the region on its World Heritage List.

The best place to learn about Tokaji wine is in one of the many cellars. The most famous are the 16th-century **Rákóczi Cellars**. Here, visitors can taste Aszú, which is matured on the premises.

The wine industry dominates the town, but the **Tokaj Museum** (Tokaji Múzeum) is mainly devoted to revealing life on the Bodrog and Tisza rivers long before wine was made in these parts. There is also a large collection of ecclesiastical art on display.

🍷 **Rákóczi Cellars**
Kossuth Lajos tér 15. **Tel** (47) 35 24 08. **Open** 10am–8pm daily. 🏛 📷 ♿

🏛 **Tokaj Museum**
Bethlen Gábor út 7. **Tel** (47) 35 26 36. **Open** 10am–4pm Tue–Sun. 🏛 📷 ♿

The Louis XI-style Lajos Kossuth Memorial Museum in Monok

⑮ Zemplén Hills

50 km (31 miles) north of Nyíregyháza. **Road Map** F2. 🚉 to Sátoraljaújhely. 🚌 to Sátoraljaújhely, Pálháza, Füzér. 🛈 Tourinform Sátoraljaújhely, Kossuth Lajos tér 5, (47) 32 14 58.

More than 2,000 km (1,243 miles) of marked hiking trails cover both the eastern and western flanks of the Zemplén range. Volcanic in origin, the highest of the hills is the 896-m- (2,940-ft-) high Nagy-Milic, which marks Hungary's border with Slovakia.

The village of **Pálháza**, 19 km (12 miles) north of Sátoraljaújhely, is a good base to explore the Zemplén. It is also the starting point of a narrow-gauge railway that runs up to **Rostalló**, from where the vast majority of the Zempléns' hiking trails depart. Wildlife to look out for include snakes,

birds of prey, woodpeckers, Ural owls, spoonbill ducks and a large number of butterflies, many of which, such as the twin-spotted fritillary, are thought to be unique to the Zemplén mountain range.

Further north, in the tiny village of **Füzér**, is the Füzér Village Museum, consisting of just one painted house, furnished as it would have been in the 1870s. High above the village on a crag sit the ruins of Füzér Castle (1310).

Monok, 10 km (6 miles) northwest of Szerencs, is the birthplace of the Hungarian lawyer and politician Lajos Kossuth, who was elected Regent of Hungary during the revolution of 1848–9. The **Lajos Kossuth Memorial Museum**, in the family's 18th-century home, exhibits portraits and memorabilia from flags to documents. The museum opened on 15 March 1948, the 100th anniversary of the revolution.

🏛 **Lajos Kossuth Memorial Museum**
Kossuth Lajos utca 18, Monok. **Tel** (47) 35 60 39. **Open** Mar–Oct: 10am–5pm Tue–Sun. 🏛 ♿

⑯ Sárospatak

70 km (43 miles) northeast of Miskolc. **Road Map** F2. 🚐 15,000. 🚉 from Budapest, Miskolc. 🚌 from Debrecen, Miskolc. 🛈 Tourinform, Eötvös utca 6, (47) 31 53 16.

Try as it might to promote its other sights, it is the castle that is the first port of call for all visitors to the leafy, riverside town of Sárospatak. The reason is the inner keep, which bears an uncanny resemblance to the Palazzo Vecchio in Florence. It was the first part of the castle to be built, in the 1530s when the keeper of the Hungarian crown, Peter Perényi, was awarded the estate after the Battle of Mohács (see p187).

The castle was extended in the 17th century by Prince György I (Rákóczi), who added four wings, all built in extravagant Neo-Renaissance style. The balconies,

---

Tokaj's Golden Wine

Tokaji, also known as Aszú, is one of the world's great dessert wines. It was once thought to actually contain gold dust. Famous as far back as the time of Mátyás I, a chronicler wrote in 1458 that "the men of Tokaj are obtaining gold from their volcanic land. Even the vines bear golden fruit." A century later the Swiss philosopher Paracelsus tested the local grapes for traces of gold. He found none but

Wine maturing in barrels in the Rákóczi Cellars, Tokaj

concluded that "in the grapes of Tokaj the natural and the mineral combine". The secret of the wine's flavour and golden appearance is less exotic: the grapes for Aszú are harvested late (in early November), after they have begun to rot and a mould has formed. This "noble rot" naturally increases sugar content by up to 70 per cent.

The Neo-Renaissance Castle in Sárospatak, home to the Rákóczi Museum

loggias and entrances are all fabulously expressive. Much of this part of the castle is today given over to the **Rákóczi Museum**, which has exhibitions on the building of the castle and the history of the Rákóczi family, as well as Renaissance-era food and winemaking.

At the opposite end of the town centre is the Calvinist **Sárospatak Reformed College**, founded in 1531 but dating in its present form from 1806–22. There are guided tours of the library in the south wing, a masterpiece of Neo-Classical architecture that was designed by Mihály Pollack. Its enormous roof is supported by 16 marble columns. In the extensive gardens are statues of former pupils, including the Czech humanist Johann Amos Comenius.

The modernist shopping centre and apartment buildings in the centre of the city, the work of local architect Imre Makovecz, are also worth seeing. Built in 1972, the four-storey buildings form a series of interlinking white towers, all leaning slightly forwards and topped with steep brown roofs – a modern interpretation of Árpád tents.

🏛 **Rákóczi Museum**
Szent Erzsébet utca 19. **Tel** (47) 31 10 83. **Open** 10am–6pm Tue–Sun. 🔲 📷 ♿

🏫 **Sárospatak Reformed College**
Rákóczi út 1. **Tel** (47) 31 10 57. Library: **Open** Mar–Oct: 9am–5pm Mon–Sat, 9am–1pm Sun; Nov–Feb: by appointment only. 📷 📷 ♿

⓻ Sátoraljaújhely

13 km (8 miles) northeast of Sáros-patak. **Road Map** F2. 🔢 18,000. 🚆 from Miskolc. 🚌 from Sárospatak. 🛈 Tourinform, Kossuth Lajos tér 5, (47) 32 14 58.

At the foot of the Zemplén Hills, Sátoraljaújhely, the most northerly town in Hungary, is known for its atmospheric Baroque centre. Most of the town's sights are based on Kossuth Lajos tér, and of all the squares named for that revolutionary in Hungary, this is perhaps the most deserving. In 1830, Lajos allegedly made his first political speech from the balcony of the Baroque town hall (built in 1762–8) that stands at No. 5. The building itself is a unique example of experimental architecture with its short, squat ground floor topped by an oversized upper level. An imposing statue of

Lajos Kossuth stands in the middle of the square that is named after him.

Just north of the town hall stands a Neo-Classical building that houses the **Ferenc Kazinczy Museum**, named after the language reformer Ferenc Kazinczy, a tireless campaigner for replacing German with Hungarian as the nation's official language and a reformer of the Hungarian language itself. The museum contains exhibits about Kazinczy's work, as well as regional history.

Kazinczy died in a cholera epidemic in 1831 and is buried in the elaborate **Kazinczy Mausoleum** (and memorial museum) at Széphalom, 3 km (2 miles) north of the town centre. Visited by tens of thousands of literary pilgrims each year, the Neo-Classical mausoleum was designed by Miklós Ybl (see p93) and built on the site of the Kazinczy mansion.

Near Kazinczy Ferenc utca, a derelict synagogue and its cemetery are sad reminders of the Jewish community that once lived here. Only a handful of the town's Jews survived the Holocaust.

🏛 **Ferenc Kazinczy Museum**
Dózsa György út 11. **Tel** (47) 32 23 51. **Open** 9am–5pm Tue–Sun. 📷 📷 Hungarian only. ♿

🏛 **Kazinczy Mausoleum**
Kazinczy park, Széphalom. **Tel** (47) 52 12 36. **Open** Apr–Oct: 9am–5pm Tue–Sun; Nov–Mar: 8am–4pm Tue–Sun. 📷 📷 ♿

Original furniture at the Ferenc Kazinczy Museum in Sátoraljaújhely

THE GREAT PLAIN

If Budapest is Hungary's heart, then her soul is the Great Plain, where her character has been forged over the centuries, and preserved ever since in the work of the nation's writers, poets and musicians. Nomadic horsemen and their cattle, shepherds and their unique sheep, fields of ripening paprika and fish soup in huge kettles over open fires are evocative images that every visitor should see.

Mainly barren and dry, the Great Plain is a vast area, covering more than half of the country (about 56 per cent). Here, long, hot summers give way to bleak, freezing winters, with little in between. However, there is a wide variety of terrain on the Great Plain, as well as some outstanding cities and a diverse flora and fauna.

As recently as medieval times, the Great Plain was, in fact, not a steppe, but forested and lush, rich in agriculture and dotted with thousands of farmsteads that were set up by the Magyars as they populated these fertile lands on both banks of the Tisza. And this is where the legends begin: the Turks invaded Hungary, and almost two centuries of constant war, from 1526 to 1699, devastated the region. In many parts they chopped down the forests and burned vegetation and

livestock. The population fled to the cities of Debrecen, Nyíregyháza, Szeged, Kecskemét and even Budapest for protection, food and livelihoods, and the term Puszta was coined to describe the emptiness left in the Ottoman wake.

A few hearty souls stayed on. The csikósok horsemen (see p239) thrived, as severe flooding in the 19th century allowed the grass to regrow, making the Plain prime grazing territory. Fortunes were made by cattle owners, and romantic poets wrote of the heroes and villains.

The csikósok survive, but today their traditions only entertain visitors. At the Hortobágy National Park and in other protected areas of the Plain, these historic grasslands are sheltered from the advances of industrial agriculture.

Zsolnay ceramic tiles on Kiskunfélegyháza's Secession-era Town Hall

◀ A flock of characteristic longhaired sheep, or *racka*, grazing on lush grass

Exploring the Great Plain

Covering almost half the country, the Great Plain defines Hungary and the Hungarians more than any other region. It was here that great battles were fought and that many of the country's traditions were preserved during foreign domination. Sparsely populated, there are few cities and only a couple of large towns, but there is much to see and do – whether watching the stunning displays of the Puszta horsemen or luxuriating in one of the thermal spas, exploring Hortobágy National Park or admiring Secessionist architecture in Szeged and ambling around Debrecen.

The artificial Mediterranean beach at the Hajdúszoboszló spa

The breathtaking "Puszta Fiver", at Bugac

Getting Around

The Great Plain is not easily accessible by public transport, and to get the best out of this region visitors are advised to travel by car. The major cities are, of course, well served by train from Budapest, especially Debrecen (the journey takes around 2 hours). Debrecen also makes an excellent base for exploring much of the northern part of the plain, including Hortobágy National Park and Tisza Lake.

Key

═══ Motorway

═══ Major road

── Secondary road

┄┄┄ Minor road

┅┅┅ Main railway

── Minor railway

▬▬▬ International border

═══ Regional border

0 kilometres   30
0 miles   30

Kisvárda

CSARODA 21

22 **SZATMÁRCSEKE**

Tokaj 38

SZABOLCS
SZATMÁR-BEREG

41 *Tisza*

491

Tiszavasvári 36 18 **NYÍREGYHÁZA** Mátészalka Túristvándi

Miskolc 35 M3 M3 **MÁRIAPÓCS** 19 49 *Szamos*

Hajdúnánás 20 **NYÍRBÁTOR**

471

Hajdúböszörmény

TISZA LAKE 14 13 **DEBRECEN** 48

rud **TISZAFÜRED** 33 17 15

köre **HORTOBÁGY**

Abadszalók 34 **HORTOBÁGY NATIONAL PARK** 16 **HAJDÚSZOBOSZLÓ**

AGYKUN ZOLNOK **HAJDÚ-BIHAR**

Püspökladány 47

4 Kisújszállás

Túrkeve Berettyóújfalu

42

ezótúr Szeghalom 47 *Berettyó*

46

Gyomaendrőd

BÉKÉS

Szarvas 443

44 Békés Sarkad

Békéscsaba **GYULA** 10

Orosháza

17

Makó 43

The dome in the New Synagogue in Szeged, a stunning Secessionist building

Sights at a Glance

① Baja
② Hajós
③ Kalocsa
④ Kiskunsági National Park
⑤ *Kecskemét pp240–43*
⑥ Kiskunfélegyháza
⑦ *Szeged pp246–7*
⑧ Ópusztaszer National Historical
   Memorial Park
⑨ Hódmezővásárhely
⑩ Gyula
⑪ Szolnok
⑫ Jászberény
⑬ Tiszafüred
⑮ *Debrecen pp254–5*
⑯ Hajdúszoboszló
⑰ Hortobágy & Hortobágy
   National Park
⑱ *Nyíregyháza pp258–9*
⑲ Máriapócs
⑳ Nyírbátor
㉑ Csaroda
㉒ Szatmárcseke

Tour

⑭ *Lake Tisza pp252–3*

For keys to map symbols *see back flap*

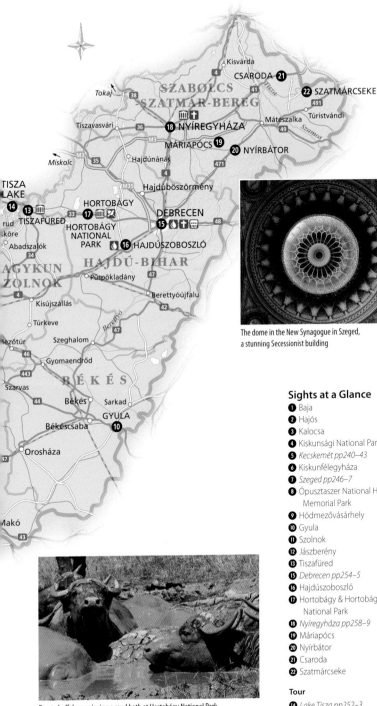

Puszta buffaloes enjoying a mud bath at Hortobágy National Park

The Fish Soup Festival in Baja, a record-breaking soup-cooking contest

❶ Baja

100 km (62 miles) west of Szeged.
Road Map C5. 🚉 36,000. 🚌 from
Budapest. 🚆 from Budapest, Kalocsa.
ℹ️ Tourinform, Szentháromság tér 5,
(79) 42 07 92. 🏪 fish market Tue–Sun.
🎭 Fish Soup Festival (Bajai Halfőző
Fesztivál, 2nd weekend in Jul).

This wealthy town, long
populated by a large Serb
minority, is dominated by its
large public square, Szentháromság tér, one side of which
opens onto the Danube.
Baroque 18th-century town
houses, one of which is now
the town hall, line the other
three sides. The square plays
host every July to the unique
Baja Fish Soup Festival, when
hundreds of cauldrons are set
up to cook the local fish stew,
consisting of freshwater fish
and a very hot paprika.

The **Türr István Museum** just
north of the square contains a
lively collection of exhibits
celebrating the role of the
Danube in Baja's history. Just
opposite stands a magnificent
Baroque Franciscan church,
complete with a superb bell
tower, built in 1756.

North of the city centre is the
late 19th-century Neo-Classical
Synagogue. Now a public
library, the Hebrew script above
the portico is one of few clues
to its past. On Miklós utca stands
the Serb Orthodox church,
built at the end of the 18th
century and housing probably
Hungary's finest Orthodox
iconostasis. Some 10 m (33 ft)
tall, it depicts countless saints.

The beaches on Petőfisziget,
the island in the middle of the
Danube, serve as Baja's summer
playground, offering sailing,
water-skiing, fishing and other
leisure activities. The island is
reached via a footbridge from
Szentháromság tér.

🏛️ **Türr István Museum**
Deák Ferenc utca 1. **Tel** (79) 32 41
73. **Open** 10am–4pm Tue–Sat. 🎫
🅿️ ♿

❷ Hajós

21 km (13 miles) southeast of Kalocsa.
Road Map D5. 🚉 3,600. 🚆 from
Kalocsa. 🏪 craft market during the
St Orbán Wine Festival. 🎭 St Orbán
Wine Festival (last weekend in May).

In the small village of Hajós,
1,200 tiny 18th-century houses,
almost identical in size and
design, sit above 1,200 identical
wine cellars dug into the soft
clay below. Built by Swabians,
a Germanic people who settled
here in the Middle Ages in order
to make use of the fertile soil,

almost all the houses remain
occupied today. However, many
are used only as summer or holiday homes. Others offer wine
tasting and accommodation.

The St Orbán Wine Festival
in May, celebrated to honour
the guardian saint of grape
growers and winemakers, is the
village's annual highlight. As
many as 20,000 visitors attend
the wine tastings, horse shows,
craft markets and folk dancing
displays.

❸ Kalocsa

120 km (74 miles) south of Budapest.
Road Map C5. 🚉 19,000. 🚌 from
Kiskőrös. 🚆 from Budapest, Kiskőrös.
🚢 Danube cruisers. 🚢 daily.
🎭 Kalocsa Paprika Festival (mid-Sep).

A popular stop for Danube
cruise ships, Kalocsa is at the
centre of Hungary's paprika-
growing region. There is a
paprika harvest festival here
every September and what is
perhaps the world's only **Paprika
Museum** (Fűszerpaprika
Múzeum). On display are jars of
the spice, in an astonishing
number of different varieties.

One of the most important
buildings in Kalocsa is the
cathedral, a twin-towered
Baroque construction from
1772, restored slightly after a
small fire in 1816. Ferenc (Franz)
Liszt adored the cathedral's
organ and often played here.
The town owes its existence to
St István, who created an arch-
bishopric here in 1006. The
Archbishop's Palace (built in
1776 on the site of a medieval
castle) today houses an amazing
collection of 100,000

The many small houses with wine cellars in Hajós

manuscripts, codices and books, the earliest dating from 1040.

At the **House of Folk Arts** (Népművészeti Tájház), the local craft society displays and sells its colourful wares in a traditional Puszta cottage.

🏛 Paprika Museum
Hunyadi utca 2. **Tel** (78) 46 18 60. **Open** Apr–Oct: 9am–5pm Tue–Sun. 🚫 📷 Hungarian only. ♿

🏛 House of Folk Arts
Tompa Mihály utca 5–7. **Tel** (78) 46 15 60. **Open** mid-Apr–mid-Oct: 10am–5pm Tue–Sun. 🚫 📷 Hungarian only. ♿

Early machinery at the Paprika Museum in Kalocsa

❹ Kiskunság National Park
Kiskunsági Nemzeti Park

25 km (16 miles) west of Kecskemét. **Road Map** D4. National Park Head-quarters, House of Nature, Liszt Ferenc utca 19, Kecskemét, (76) 48 226 11. **Open** 10am–4pm Tue–Sat. 🚌 from Kiskunfélegyháza to Bugac-felső; from Kecskemét to Izsák for Lake Kolon. 🚍 from Kiskunfélegyháza to Bugac park entrance; from Kecskemét to Fülöpháza. 🛈 Tourinform Kecskemét, Kossuth tér 1, Kecskemét, (76) 48 10 65. 🚫 ♿ ✏ 🖥 📷 🌐 knp.hu

Kiskunság is Hungary's second-largest national park after Hortobágy *(see 256)*. Spread over 759 sq km (293 sq miles), the park is divided into a number of unique natural habitats, which are not all interlinked. A visit to the park's administration office, in the Kecskemét *(see pp240–43)* House of Nature enables visitors to get their bearings. A popular

way into the park is via Nagybugac. This village is a worthy attraction in itself, with its fascinating horse-riding displays. The **Bugac Stud Farm** (Bugaci Ménes) just outside the village puts on daily shows. These may, however, be cancelled if there are too few spectators; it is best to book an organized tour (www.bugacpuszta.hu). Not to be missed are the performances of the legendary Puszta Fiver, where one man – usually with a moustache as long as his whip – rides five horses simultaneously *(see box below)*. Visitors can ride one of the many thoroughbreds at the stables themselves, and join a day-long horseback-tour of the surrounding area.

Nagybugac's tiny **Herdsmen's Museum** (Bugaci Pásztor-múzeum) exhibits a small collection of folk art, costumes and tools but most visitors to Nagybugac are merely passing through on their way to the park. The village is the gateway to the largest area of the park, the Bugac – a vast 100-sq-km (39-sq-mile) expanse of grass-land, marshes, freshwater lakes and reeds. A number of well-marked nature trails start at the park entrance.

Birdwatchers should head for Lake Kolon, northwest of the Bugac and accessible via the village of Izsák, where great

One of many birdwatching towers in Kiskunság National Park

bustards, herons and spoonbills can be seen. The unparalleled flora and fauna in the reeds and marshes around the lake include rare species of orchid, as well as otters, weasels, water snakes, turtles and lizards.

The Fülöpháza with its shifting sand dunes is a unique environment in the park and is the habitat of hoopoes, golden orioles and bee-eaters. Trails around the dunes begin at the village of Fülöpháza, 30 km (19 miles) west of Kecskemét.

🔘 Bugac Stud Farm
Nagybugac Ménes. **Tel** (76) 57 50 28. **Open** daily. 🚫 ♿ for horse shows, it is advisable to book in advance with Herdsmen's Museum.

🏛 Herdsmen's Museum
Nagybugac, **Tel** (76) 57 51 12. **Open** May–Oct: 10am–6pm daily. 🚫

Csikós Horse Shows
The equine skill of the Hungarian cowboys (or csikósok; also csikós meaning "wrangler"), goes back as far as the first Magyar migrations and was originally military in nature. The Hungarian mounted soldier typically carried light weapons and rode light horses without a saddle. Today's csikós shows contain much pseudo-military posturing, usually beginning with a horse parade and salute, followed by displays of equestrian skill, control and dressage. What is unusual is the way the csikósok can make their horses walk at almost a crawl: a legacy of fighting battles in the open plains. The highlight of these horse shows is the Puszta Fiver *(pusztaötös)*: one man riding five horses simultaneously. The Fiver's origins are unknown – perhaps the rider was bringing back the horses of his dead comrades after a battle.

A horseman practising for the impressive Puszta Fiver

❺ Kecskemét

The town of Kecskemét dates back to 1368, though little of that era remains today. Kecskemét benefited from self-government during Turkish rule, and the Habsburgs encouraged the development of agriculture in the region, often termed the "Garden of Hungary". One local product is the apricot, which is the source of a delicious brandy. An earthquake in June 1911 shook the city, but the outstanding Baroque and Secessionist city centre was mercifully spared. Home to some great museums, Kecskemét is a superb place to explore.

🏛 Piarist Church & School
Piarista Templom & Rendház
Jókai utca 1. **Tel** (76) 48 16 03. **Open** Church: by appointment.

The Piarists are a relatively progressive, scientific Catholic order founded in Rome in 1617 by St Joseph Calasanctius. They arrived in Kecskemét in 1715 and founded the school on Jókai utca, which still operates to this present day. (The present, bland school building, however, was built in the late 1940s.) The Baroque church opposite was erected between 1729 and 1765, to designs by Andreas Mayerhoffer. St Joseph Calasanctius is represented by one of four statues on the front of the building, alongside the Virgin Mary and Saints István and László.

🏛 Cifra Palace
Cifrapalota
Rákóczi út 1. **Tel** (76) 48 07 76. **Open** 10am–5pm Tue–Sun. 🐾 🚻

This Secessionist masterpiece, completed in 1902, is the work of architect Géza Márkus. The green and orange tiled roof is

The Secessionist Cifra Palace

outstanding. An art gallery since World War II, the palace holds over 10,000 works, and exhibitions on the Secessionist architects Tóth and Glücks.

🏛 Hungarian Photography Museum
Magyar Fotográfiai Múzeum
Katona József tér 12. **Tel** (76) 48 32 21. **Open** noon–5pm Tue–Sat. **Closed** public holidays. 🐾 🚻 🌐 fotomuzeum.hu

This outstanding museum, housed in a splendid 18th-century mansion, formerly the horse-changing station of the Pest–Szeged mail-coach route and a synagogue, displays the work of every great Hungarian photographer, including André Kertész and László Moholy-Nagy. There are regular exhibitions by international artists, and the attached photography bookshop is one of the best.

🏛 József Katona Theatre and Holy Trinity Monument
Katona József tér 5.
Tel (76) 50 11 70. **Open** for performances only. 🚻 ✉

This Neo-Baroque theatre was the creation of Austrian architects Ferdinand Fellner and Hermann Helmer. Completed in 1896, it was named after Kecskemét's playwright son, József Katona. It is as impressive inside as out; the ceiling in particular is worth attending a performance for. The Holy Trinity Monument in front of the theatre was erected to offer thanks after the passing of the most recent outbreak of plague, in 1742.

🏛 Old Catholic Church
Nagytemplom
Kossuth tér 2. **Tel** (76) 48 75 01. **Open** noon–7pm Mon, 6am–7pm Tue–Sun. 🐾 🚻

The Old Catholic Church was built in 1774–99. Its spire rises to 73 m (240 ft); its clockface is the largest in Hungary, and the clock's works among the oldest. The Baroque exterior features statues and reliefs of figures from Hungarian history. Inside, grand steps lead up to the pulpit.

Room in the Museum of Medicinal and Pharmaceutical History

🏛 Museum of Medicinal and Pharmaceutical History
Orvos- és Gyógyszertörténeti Gyűjtemény
Kölcsey utca 3. **Tel** (76) 32 99 64. **Open** May–Oct: 10am–2pm Tue–Sun; Nov–Apr: by appointment. 🐾 🚻

Although this museum has a small collection, consisting mainly of some colourful medicine bottles, old surgical instruments and various reference works, it is housed inside a superb building, itself once a pharmacy, and seeing that alone is well worth the small entrance fee.

🏛 Museum of Hungarian Naïve Art
Magyar Naiv Művészek Múzeuma
Gáspár András utca 11. **Tel** (76) 32 47 67. **Open** Mar–Oct: 10am–5pm Tue–Sun. **Closed** Nov–Feb. 🐾 📷

This charming museum is devoted to contemporary and earlier local Naïve artists who produced some stunning work. Unique in Hungary, the museum provides a thorough survey of the genre: there are more than 2,500 exhibits on display, with the collection of small animal sculptures a special highlight.

Display of mechanical toys in the Toy Museum and Workshop

🏛 Szórakaténusz Toy Museum and Workshop
Szórakaténusz Játékmúzeum és Műhely

Gáspár András utca 11. **Tel** (76) 48 14 69. **Open** Mar–Oct: 10am–12:30pm, 1–5pm Tue–Sat; Nov–Feb: 10am–4pm Tue–Sat. 🈲 🈲

Next to the Museum of Hungarian Naïve Art is this children's paradise, housed in a specially built wooden building. There are displays of Hungarian toys from the 18th century to the present, with dolls and wooden toys taking pride of place. Older children will enjoy the often clumsy mechanical toys that were considered state

of the art in the 1950s. There are also interactive toy workshops for children during the summer.

🏛 Zwack Fruit Brandy Distillery and Exhibition
Matkói utca 2. **Tel** (76) 48 77 11. **Open** 10am–6pm Mon–Fri, by appointment only. 🈲 🈲 compulsory.

The Hungarian market leader in fruit brandy, the factory of the Zwack Unicum Company offers a fascinating insight into the world of alcohol distillation. Visitors can see how the brandy is made – before tasting it – as well as learning about the life of the Zwack family. The plant is open only for groups; Tourinform will provide information on where and when to join one.

🏛 Collection of Applied Folk Art
Népi Iparművészeti Múzeum

Serfőző utca 19. **Tel** (76) 32 72 03. **Open** Mar–Oct: 10am–5pm Tue–Sat; Nov–Feb: 10am–4pm Tue–Sat; Dec & Jan: by appointment only. 🈲 🈲 Hungarian only. ♿

This vast and enchanting building and garden was formerly a brewery for nearly

200 years. Opened to the public in 1984 as the Museum of Popular Folk Art, the permanent collection expanded rapidly and now covers woodcarving, pottery, embroidery and weaving. There are workshops on site where visitors can watch and then try embroidering a waistcoat or tablecloth themselves, before tasting local specialities fresh from the traditional ovens. The workshops and kitchen are open only on selected days in the summer.

Kecskemét City Centre

1. Piarist Church and School
2. Cifra Palace
3. Hungarian Photography Museum
4. József Katona Theatre and Holy Trinity Monument
5. Old Catholic Church
6. Museum of Medicinal and Pharmaceutical History
7. Museum of Hungarian Naïve Art
8. Szórakaténusz Toy Museum and Workshop
9. Zwack Fruit Brandy Distillery and Exhibition
10. Collection of Applied Folk Art

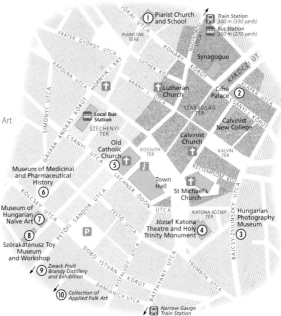

0 metres 100
0 yards 100

Key

▨ Street by Street pp242–3

Street-by-Street: Around Kossuth tér

At the heart of Kecskemét there are edifices of different eras, designs, religions and cultures. Few public squares in Europe are surrounded by all of these: Roman Catholic, Franciscan, Calvinist and Jewish places of worship; fewer still are those with Art Nouveau masterpieces on all sides. Even the modern Aranyhomok Hotel – which would be little more than a dreary box in most city squares – adds something to the eclectic Kecskemét mix. Large enough to take the summer visitor crowds with ease, the twin Kossuth and Szabadság squares bustle with life from morning until late.

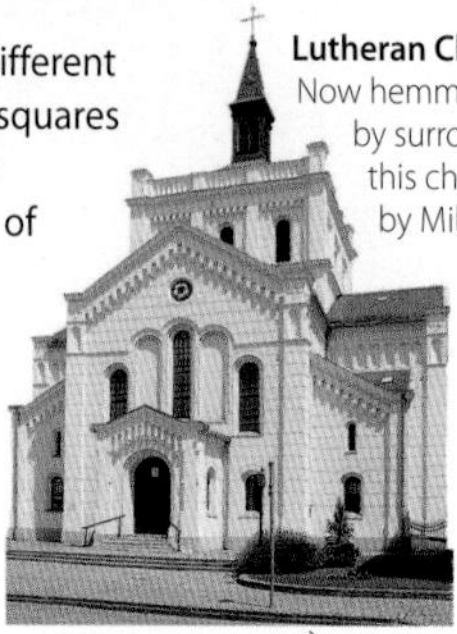

Lutheran Church
Now hemmed in on three sides by surrounding buildings, this church was designed by Miklós Ybl *(see p93)*, but built to a simplified plan in 1862–3. Inside stands a Romantic altar by József Gaál.

Mátyás Pharmacy

Great Catholic Church
Kecskemét's pride, the Neo-Baroque tower – topped with a small golden dome – can be climbed for superb views of the city.

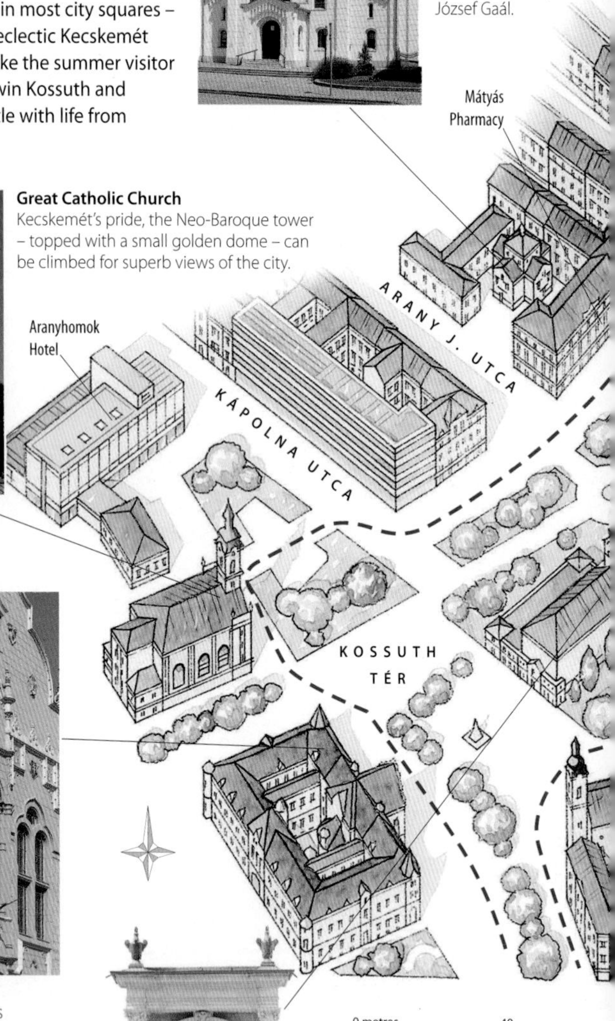

Aranyhomok Hotel

ARANY J. UTCA

KAPOLNA UTCA

KOSSUTH TÉR

★ Town Hall
Bold in pink and yellow, this masterpiece was erected in 1891, when the Secessionist movement was in full swing.

0 metres 40
0 yards 40

Calvinist Church
The Turks allowed this stone church to be built in 1684, after a Catholic mob had burned down a wooden church during the Counter-Reformation in 1678.

Key

— Suggested route

★ Synagogue
Abandoned in 1945 when Kecskemét's remaining Jews were forced to flee the city, this glorious Baroque building is today known as the House of Science and Technology. It has been converted into a conference centre exhibiting replicas of Michelangelo sculptures.

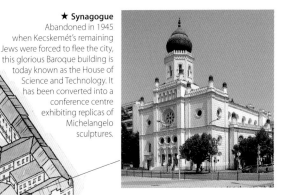

★ Ornamental Palace
Built as a private home in 1902, and covered in brightly coloured arabesques, the Cifra Palota hosts exhibitions of the City Art Gallery.

Calvinist New College
This imposing building from 1912 is still a college today, but a part is given over to an exhibition of Calvinist ecclesiastical art and history.

Zoltán Kodály Institute of Music Education

Franciscan Church
While this is the oldest church in the city, dating from the 14th century, the Baroque tower and interior frescoes date from the 1790s.

Decorative detail of the Town Hall roof in Kiskunfélegyháza

❻ Kiskunfélegyháza

28 km (18 miles) south of Kecskemét.
Road Map D4. 🗺 30,000. 🚊 from Kecskemét, Budapest. 🚌 from Kecskemét, Budapest.

Kiskunfélegyháza has a Roman Catholic church and a regional museum, but the Secessionist **Town Hall** is really the only sight worth seeing in this southern town. It is truly outstanding. Completed in 1912, it is something of a high-water mark for Secessionist architecture. Designed by József Vass and Nándor Morbitzer, its façade is a riot of colour, floral patterns and interwoven motifs. Many of the patterns are, in fact, copied from the folk art of the Kiskun region: they can also be seen on traditional lace tablecloths. The roof is covered entirely in tiles made at the Zsolnay factory in Pécs (see pp190–93). On a gable, the city crest can be seen, surrounded by tulip motifs.
   Although the town hall is an official building and still used for administrative purposes today, nobody seems to mind visitors wandering in every day to admire the main hall, which is as richly decorated as the exterior.

🏛 **Town Hall**
Kossuth Lajos utca 1.
Tel (76) 46 12 55. **Open** 7:30am–4pm Mon–Fri. ♿

❼ Szeged

See pp246–7.

❽ Ópusztaszer National Historical Memorial Park

Ópusztaszeri Nemzeti Történeti Emlékpark

31 km (19 miles) north of Szeged. **Road Map** E5. 🚊 to Kistelek, then coach. 🚌 from Kistelek, local bus from Ópusztaszer. 🛈 Tourinform, Szoborkert 68, Ópusztaszer, (62) 27 51 33. **Open** Apr–Jun: 10am–6pm daily; Jul–Oct: 10am–6pm Tue–Sun; Nov–Mar: 10am–4pm Tue–Sun. Feszty Panorama: **Tel** (62) 27 52 57. 🅿 ♿ 💻 📷 🌐 opusztaszer.hu

According to legend it was on this site in 896 that the Magyar clan chiefs made their blood pact and chose Árpád as their single leader. The enormous Neo-Classical **Árpád Memorial**, erected in 1896 for Hungary's Millennium Celebrations (see p108), commemorates the event. Before that, a monastery stood here, from perhaps the 12th century (its ruins can still be seen), and it may have been a pagan burial ground earlier still. In 1945, this historic site was chosen by the Communists to announce their agricultural collectivization policy. North of the memorial stands a well-presented **Ethnographic Museum** comprising some 19th-century houses, windmills, farmhouses and workshops from the local area. In summer the workshops demonstrate various folk crafts, and much of what is produced is sold. To the left of the museum stand tents known as yurts.
   The **Feszty Panorama**, an astonishingly detailed depiction of the Magyar migration onto the Great Plain, can be seen here. The 120-m- (394-ft-) long painting, created by 24 artists in 1892–4, was badly damaged in World War II but has been restored and can be viewed by appointment.

❾ Hódmezővásárhely

25 km (15 miles) northeast of Szeged. **Road Map** E5. 🗺 45,000. 🚊 from Szeged. 🚌 from Szeged. Andrassy út, Kossuth tér. 🛈 Tourinform, Szőnyi utca 1, (62) 24 93 50. 🎭 Agricultural Festival (end Apr); St István's Day (20 Aug).

One of the oldest settlements in Hungary, the small city of Hódmezővásárhely is famous for its Agricultural Festival. Much

The Neo-Classical Árpád Memorial at the Ópusztaszer Memorial Park

Gyula Castle, almost intact after many years of Turkish rule

of the event is based on Kossuth tér, a large pedestrianized square. Here stands the large Secessionist **Town Hall**, whose tower can be climbed. The building next door (formerly a school) now houses the **Alföld Gallery**, which exhibits the work of Great Plain artists, for example, József Koszta, Gyula Rudnay and Vilmos Aba-Novák.

The enormous New Calvinist church is impressive but a fair walk east along Andrássy utca. Opposite is a superb Secessionist synagogue (1903), with an exhibition dedicated to those killed in the Holocaust. It often hosts official commemorative events on Holocaust Day.

⓾ Gyula

15 km (9 miles) east of Békéscsaba.
Road Map F4. 🏛 31,000. 🚉 from Békéscsaba, Budapest. 🚌 from Békéscsaba. 🛈 Tourinform, Kossuth Lajos utca 7, (66) 56 16 80. 🎭 Gyula Castle Open-Air Theatre Festival (Jul, Aug).

At one time Scythians, Huns and Avars all passed through the area around the present town of Gyula, but a settlement called Gyulamonostora was first mentioned in 1313. The impressive **castle**, which miraculously survives almost intact, was built in the 14th–15th centuries. Taken by the Turks in 1566, it stayed under their control for 130 years.

The castle is the city's leading sight, and it dominates the sprawling park that makes central Gyula so pleasant a place. Visitors can clamber over its walls and climb the lookout tower, or in summer enjoy a concert in the courtyard. Also in the park is the beautifully restored 18th-century **Almásy Mansion**, which has one

of Hungary's best thermal bath complexes. The mansion also features an exhibition on everyday life – and life as a servant – in a Hungarian mansion.

Another attraction is the charming **Százéves**, Hungary's second-oldest café, which opened in 1840. Ferenc Erkel, who composed grand operas and the Hungarian national anthem, was born in the house at Apor Vilmos tér 7. It now has a small museum dedicated to his life and work.

⓫ Szolnok

100 km (59 miles) east of Budapest.
Road Map E4. 🏛 73,000. 🚉 🚌 🛈 Tourinform, Hild J. tér 1, (56) 42 07 04.

Located where the river Zagyva flows into the Tisza, Szolnok has long been the last obstacle for invaders on the road to

Budapest. The city's substantial **castle** was built by St István in 1075 but sacked first by the Mongols, then by the Turks, so that nothing remains of it today.

The most important historical monument in the city now, a short walk west of the centre, is the Baroque **Franciscan church**, built in 1727–54. On the way is the former synagogue at Templom utca 2, a Secessionist building, restored in the 1950s. Also worth a visit is the **János Damjanich Museum**, north of the centre. Named after the general who led the Hungarians to victory over the Habsburgs in the Battle of Szolnok in 1849, it exhibits folk art, archaeological items, and work by the Szolnok Artists Colony.

The Baroque Franciscan Church, the oldest building in Szolnok

Hungarian Calvinism

Calvinism flourished in eastern Hungary and in Transylvania from the second half of the 16th century to around 1700. Preaching to a public that considered Catholicism the religion of the Habsburgs, and therefore foreign, a great number of reformers were active in Hungary before the Reformation movements of Martin Luther and John Calvin. The Turks actively encouraged the Reformation as a bulwark against Catholicism, and the Hungarian Reformed Church quickly became the largest in central Europe. Calvinism rejected consubstantiation, and had a theocratic view of the state, popular with Hungarians under Turkish rule. When the Turks were finally expelled in 1699, the Habsburgs confiscated Calvinist property. This Counter-Reformation bred resentment, and was a major factor in the creation in the 18th century of a national independence movement, both in eastern Hungary and in Transylvania.

The Calvinist College in Debrecen, founded in 1538

❼ Szeged

The fourth-largest city in the country, Szeged straddles the River Tisza less than 20 km (12 miles) from the point where Hungary, Serbia and Romania meet. Almost completely destroyed by spring floods in 1879, Szeged was entirely remodelled before being rebuilt, and its wide avenues, numerous public squares and vast array of architectural styles, from the Neo-Romanesque cathedral to the Secessionist Reök Palace, are testimony to enlightened town planning. Famous for its free-thinking university, which was at the vanguard of the 1956 uprising, the city is today the most important on the southern Great Plain, and a centre of the salami and paprika trade.

The brown-brick twin-towered Neo-Romanesque Votive Church

🏛 Votive Church
Szegedi Dóm
Dóm tér. **Tel** (62) 42 01 57. **Open** 8am–5pm Mon, Wed, Fri & Sat, noon–5pm Tue, 1–5pm Sun. 🅿 ♿

Neo-Romanesque in design, the Votive Church was constructed in 1913–30. Everything about it is grand in scale. Designed by Frigyes Schulek and Ernő Foerk, it is dominated by two towers that reach just short of 100 m (328 ft). The eastern tower can be climbed in summer. Above the 10-m- (33-ft-) tall entrance is an enormous Madonna with Child, while inside the church several frescoes by Schulek can be found, as well as the third-largest organ in Europe.

🏛 Demetrius Tower and Dóm tér
Dóm tér. ♿
The oldest structure in Szeged is the 12th- and 13th-century Demetrius Tower (Dömötör-torony) in Dóm tér. Part of a once much larger church, and the traditional centre of town, the tower was only rediscovered

in 1925, when a damaged former Baroque cathedral was cleared to make way for the Votive Church. It was fully restored and converted into a baptistry by Béla Rerrich.

On the south side of the square, a pantheon celebrates famous Hungarians. The Ecclesiastical Museum and Treasury on the square's western side holds a collection of Catholic memorabilia. Behind Dóm tér is Aradi Vértanuk tere, with a monument to the Martyrs of Arad, and the Gate of Heroes (1937) honouring the heroes of World War I, the 12,000 fallen soldiers who came from Szeged.

🏛 Serb Orthodox Church
Görögkeleti Szerb Templom
Révai utca. **Tel** (62) 42 42 46.
This single-towered church, founded by Serb immigrants in the 18th century, was remodelled in the Neo-Classical style in 1830. Its beautiful original iconostasis by Jovan Popovic contains 80 icons engraved in pear wood.

The superbly intricate iconostasis of the Serb Orthodox Church

🏛 Reök Palace
Reök palota
Tisza Lajos körút 56.
Built for István Reök, a wealthy local merchant, in 1907, this extraordinary, fairy-tale building is a Secessionist masterpiece. Designed by Ede Magyar Oszadszki, it looks like a giant cake topped with striped marzipan. The rotund balcony on the corner, as well as the intricate ironwork – including the blue flowers that surround the building like a cummerbund – are the work of Fekete Pál, working to designs by Magyar Oszadszki. Today the building is used by a Hungarian bank.

Secessionist elements on the façade of Reök Palace

🏛 Széchenyi tér and Town Hall
Városháza
Széchenyi tér. ♿
The pond in this large square commemorates the devastating flood. In front of it stands a statue of Count Széchenyi (see p46). The balcony and colourful ceramic tiles of the Neo-Baroque Town Hall, built in 1883 by Ödön Lechner, pre-empt the Secession (which Lechner founded). A "Bridge of Sighs" replica links the town hall to the building next door. The Neo-Classical house (1844) at No. 9 survived the flood.

🏛 Ferenc Móra Museum
Közművelődési Palota
Roosevelt tér 1–3. **Tel** (62) 54 90 40. **Open** Jun–Aug: 11am–6pm daily; Sep–May: 10am–5pm Tue–Sun. 🅿 ♿

Looking very much like a Neo-Classical mansion built for

a wealthy merchant, the Palace of Popular Culture (Közművelődési Palota) has in fact been a museum since its completion in 1899. There are excellent exhibitions on archaeology, ethnography and the history of the Csongrád region. One of the highlights is the enormous painting by Pál Vágó showing Szeged after the flood of 1879. The art gallery displays works by Hungarian master József Rippl-Rónai, though the main attraction is Mihály Munkácsy's *Hungarian Conquest*.

🏛 Castle Museum
Vármúzeum – Kőtár

Stefánia sétány 2. **Tel** (62) 54 90 40. **Open** 10am–5pm Tue–Sun. 🖼

The castle was built when Béla IV fortified Szeged in 1247 and extended by János in 1547. The scene of one of the Turks' last stands in Hungary, in 1688, it was all but destroyed in the floods of 1879. All that remains today is a tiny part of a bastion. The small museum tells the castle's history (open only in midsummer).

Detail on main entrance to the Castle Museum

🎭 National Theatre
Nemzeti Színház

Déak Ferenc utca 12. **Tel** (62) 47 92 79. Opened in 1883, the theatre burned down two years later. It was restored to its original Neo-Baroque design by the Austrian architects Fellner and Helmer. The lush interior, with three levels of boxes and an intricately decorated ceiling, can be seen during performances of the philharmonic orchestra, opera or ballet.

✡ Jewish Quarter
Zsidó Negyed

South of Nagy Jenő utca. New Synagogue: Jósika utca 10, (62) 42 38 49. **Open** Apr–Sep: 10am–noon, 1–5pm Mon–Fri & Sun; Oct–Mar: 9am–2pm Mon–Fri & Sun.

The enormous **New Synagogue** was built in 1900–3 in Secessionist style, with a grand 48-m (157-ft) dome. Its marble tabernacle is covered with gold leaf, while the dome, representing the night sky, is topped by deep blue glass and dotted with stars. At Hajnóczy utca 12,

the **Old Synagogue** has a high-water mark on its outer wall showing the level of the floods in 1879.

New Synagogue, built and decorated in Secessionist style

Szeged City Centre

1 Votive Church
2 Demetrius Tower and Dóm tér
3 Serb Orthodox Church
4 Reök Palace
5 Széchenyi tér and Town Hall
6 Ferenc Móra Museum
7 Castle Museum
8 National Theatre
9 Jewish Quarter

0 metres 200
0 yards 200

BUDAPEST
RÁKÓCZI TÉR
Bus Station 100 m (110 yards)
KOSSUTH SGT
KÁLVIN TÉR
TISZA LAJOS KÖRÚT
KAZINCZY UTCA
THERMAL BATHS
Thermal Baths
9 Great Synagogue
5 Town Hall
8 National Theatre
JEWISH QUARTER
Old Synagogue
SZÉCHENYI TÉR
7 Castle Museum
6 Ferenc Móra Museum
Open-Air Thermal Baths
KLAUZÁL TÉR
Reök Palace 4
ROOSEVELT TÉR
Open-Air Pools
Belvárosi bridge
DUGONICS TÉR
Szeged University
3 Serb Orthodox Church
HONVÉD TÉR
Demetrius Tower and Dóm Tér 2
1 Votive Church
DÓM TÉR
Tisza
ARADI VÉRTANUK TERE
Heroes' Gate
Train Station 300 m (330 yards) 🚉

For keys to map symbols *see back flap*

Freshwater fishing in the Hortobágy National Park ▶

⑫ Jászberény

50 km (31 miles) east of Budapest.
Road Map D3. 🚇 27,000. 🚉 from
Szolnok, Budapest. 🚌 from
Kecskemét. 🅸 Tourinform, Lehel
vezér tér 33, (57) 40 64 39. 🎭 Csángó
Folklore Festival (early Aug).

Jászberény is named for the
Jász, an allegedly Iranian people
who settled in the area around
1200. A number of other towns
and villages in the region bear
the *Jász-* prefix, yet there is
nothing to set apart the Jász
today. Their Persian language
has long been assimilated, and
their heritage is preserved only
in the **Jász Museum**, the main
sight in Jászberény. Here visitors
will find the legendary Lehel
Horn *(see box)*, as well as background on the life of the Jász
people. There is a poignant
exhibit commemorating Jász
children, some as young as 14,
who fought and defeated the
Habsburgs in the Battle of
Tápióbicske in 1849.

In August, the town plays
host to the Csángó Folklore
Festival, a celebration of the
traditions of the Csángós, a
Hungarian-speaking people
who fled eastern Hungary for
Moldavia during the Mongol
invasion. As many as 70,000
Csángós still live in Moldavia
(eastern Romania) today.

🏛 **Jász Museum**
Táncsics Mihály utca 5. **Tel** (57) 50
26 10. **Open** Apr–Oct: 9am–5pm
Tue–Sun; Nov–Mar: 9am–4pm Tue–Fri,
9am–1pm Sat & Sun. 🎭 ♿

Sunset over the man-made Lake Tisza, which incorporates a nature reserve

⑬ Tiszafüred

63 km (39 miles) west of Debrecen.
Road Map E3. 🚇 11,500. 🚉 from
Debrecen. 🚌 from Debrecen, Budapest. 🅸 Tourinform, Fürdő utca 21,
(59) 51 11 23.

The largest resort of Lake Tisza
(see pp252–3) is a bustling town
and probably the best place for
a long stay on the Tisza. Though
there are no luxury hotels, there
are plenty of good, well-priced
pensions and many good
traditional restaurants. The main
attraction of the town is, of
course, the lake itself, and the
tourist information office can
help with arranging boating,
fishing and cycle hire. The only
real tourist site in the town is
the **Pál Kiss Museum**, based in
a Neo-Classical villa in the city
centre. One of Hungary's oldest
regional museums, founded in
1877, its displays include
wooden panels, painted
furniture and pottery, as well as
an excellent archaeology exhibition, with Roman coins and
mosaics. The museum is named
after Pál Kiss, one of the
generals of the revolution of
1848–9. It also showcases
leather goods made at the
Leather Production House, on
Ady Endre utca.

🏛 **Pál Kiss Museum**
Tariczky sétány 6. **Tel** (59) 35 21 06.
Open 9am–noon, 1–5pm Tue–Sat.
🎭 Hungarian only. ♿

Costumes of the Jász people, at the Jász
Museum in Jászberény

The Lehel Horn

Legend has it that in AD 955, the Hungarians – who spent much
of the period pillaging throughout central Europe – came up
against fierce resistance at Augsburg in Germany. Two Hungarian
warriors, Lehel and Bulcsú, were captured and brought before
the German commander, who intended to reward their bravery
by allowing them to choose the manner of their death. Lehel
asked the Germans to bring him his horn, to help him meditate
upon his answer. Once he had the horn in his hands he struck
the German commander with it, killing him instantly. Lehel and
Bulcsú were brutally executed soon after, but having dispatched
the enemy first meant that he would have to serve Lehel in the
afterlife. The horn – miraculously – made its way back to
Jászberény. Sadly for
romantics and lovers of
legends, the horn on
display at the Jász
Museum dates from
the 10th or 11th century,
and is of Byzantine origin.

The Lehel horn, one of Hungary's most
important treasures

The Horsemen of the Great Plain

Since AD 900, when Magyar horsemen struck fear into the hearts of all who crossed their paths as they rode through the Carpathians into Western Europe, Hungarians have been renowned for their excellence in horsemanship. For more than 1,000 years, Hungarian military and economic power relied in many respects on the skill of its horsemen, and on the sturdiness of the short-necked horses they rode, since much of the country's history took place on horseback. While the romantic nomads of yore have long since disappeared, the Hungarian traditions of horsemanship are preserved in the many equestrian centres on the Great Plain, which offers an ideal climate for riding tours and hunting. Horsemen put on shows with great feats of horsemanship (such as the Puszta Fiver, *see p239*), and the enterprise of breeding thoroughbreds has enjoyed a renaissance.

The *patrac* is a unique saddle without a girth to tie it around the horse, used only on ceremonial occasions: Puszta horsemen ordinarily eschew saddles.

The classic view of the Puszta: man, horse and an improvised well. It is not without reason that this part of Hungary is considered a land only for the hardy.

Modern Puszta shows are strictly for the benefit of visitors, yet these performances allow the Puszta horsemen, known as Csikós, to preserve and demonstrate their prowess in – and out – of the saddle.

Bogrács, the traditional method of Puszta cooking, involves a large beef or pork stew being cooked very slowly in a kettle over an open fire.

The Horse Lay was a necessary method of protection, as the terrain offered little cover for the advancing cavalry. The Puszta horsemen trained their horses to lie down and to "crawl" in the grass.

The horses of the Puszta are mainly of the Hortobágy Nonius breed, known for their discipline. They are increasingly popular – especially in the US, where they are trained as dressage and equestrian competition horses.

⑭ A Tour Around Lake Tisza

Although it is today considered one of the natural wonders of Hungary, Lake Tisza is, in fact, an artificial lake, created in the early 1970s when the River Tisza was dammed for the irrigation of the Great Plain. Covering 127 sq km (49 sq miles), it is second in size only to Lake Balaton, and is increasingly challenging its more famous neighbour as a popular summer holiday destination. Most of the northern part of the lake is a protected nature reserve, much loved by birdwatchers, and accessible only with a guide.

⑧ Négyes
Peregrine falcons are just one of many bird species which enjoy the microclimate generated by the lake waters. Of the 380 species found in Hungary, up to 200 can be seen at the Lake Tisza Nature Reserve.

⑦ Poroszló
Rowing boats are available for hire to those who wish to explore the lake, and there is a popular nature trail that snakes its way around this village and the surrounding countryside.

⑥ Sarud
Sarud is a superb little village, famous for its many attractive 18th- and 19th-century thatched cottages, and it also boasts a great shallow beach that is perfect for children.

⑤ Kisköre
This delightful family-oriented resort is home to Lake Tisza's best beaches, which even in high summer rarely get crowded.

Dózsatelep

Borsodi-
vánka

Tiszavalk

Pusztarábóly

Tisza

33

34 → Debrecen

Puszta
domaháza

Kunmadaras

Tisza

Tiszaszőlős

③ Tiszaderzs

A quiet town
set slightly back
from the shores
of the lake,
Tiszaderzs has
two fine churches,
both on Fő utca: a
Romanesque church,
originally from the 13th
century but rebuilt in the
1600s, and a fine 18th-century
Baroque Reformed church.

Tips for Drivers

Tour length: 71 km (44 miles)
Stopping-off points:
Outside Tiszafüred the best
places to eat are the small
pensions and restaurants of
Abádszalók, while Kisköre has a
good choice of pensions offering
fine local food. Though not part
of this tour, note that the area of
the lake north of motorway 33 is
part of Hortobágy National Park
and accessible only with a guide.

① Tiszafüred
The main resort on the lake, Tiszafüred has
many grass beaches, boat launches and a
couple of good museums *(see p250)*. It is
also a major birdwatching centre.

② Patkós Csárda
A traditional Puszta restaurant just
outside Tiszafüred on motorway 33,
the Patkós (Horse Shoe) is a popular
stopping-off point for motorists. The
inn serves huge portions of local dishes,
including a wide range of game.

| 0 kilometres | 3 |
| 0 miles | 3 |

Key

Tour route
Major road
Other road
Main railway

④ Abádszalók
The large water park at Abádszalók is one of the most
popular attractions around the lake. The resort itself is
an excellent base from where to try water sports.

⑮ Debrecen

This charming town of 200,000 people barely counts as a metropolis, yet it is Hungary's second-largest town. Famous for its Calvinist Reformed College (1583) and Calvinist Church (1821), there has been a settlement here since Roman times, and Debrecen has always been an important market town. During the revolution of 1848 it served as Hungary's capital and its parliament met here. Today celebrated for its grand bath complex and excellent university, Debrecen is one of the most pleasant towns in Hungary. Almost all its sights are situated around a pedestrian-only public square, while its thermal baths are in a lovely wooded spot just north of the centre.

Interior of the Small Reformed Church, bastion of Protestantism

🏛 Piac Street and Town Hall
Piac utca; Városháza
Piac utca. &

Piac utca translates as "Market Street", and derives from the important cattle markets held here in the 16th and 17th centuries. Debrecen's main street, it leads from the rather bleak area around the railway station to its central square, tér. Apart from its magnificent church *(see below)*, one of the most eye-catching buildings of the square is Hotel Aranybika, a Secessionist masterpiece designed by Alfréd Hajós, Hungary's first Olympic champion, and opened in 1915. The square is also used to host concerts and festivals, including the Flower Carnival in August and seasonal food festivals. The Neo-Classical building on the corner of Piac utca and Kossuth utca is Debrecen **Town Hall**, built in 1842–3 to a design by local architect Ferenc Povolny.

🏛 Great Reformed Church
Református Nagytemplom
Piac utca 4–6. **Tel** (52) 41 26 94. **Open** Mar–Oct: 9am–4pm Mon–Fri, 9am–1pm Sat; Nov–Feb: 9am–1pm Mon–Fri.. **Closed** during services. 🏛 &

Debrecen's defining landmark towers above much of the city. Originally called St Andrew's Church and dating from 1291, it was destroyed by fire in 1802. The present church was built in 1819–23, to designs by Mihály Péchy. Its enormous organ was added in 1838, and recitals featuring organists form part of the church's concert schedule. Hungary's parliament met at

this quietly dignified church from 1848–9, and inside the chair from which Lajos Kossuth declared Hungary's independence is preserved for posterity. From the top of the towers there are great views of the city.

The Great Reformed Church and fountain at Kossuth Square

🏛 MODEM Center of Modern and Contemporary Art
MODEM Modern és Kortárs Művészeti Központ
Baltazár Dezső tér 1–3. **Tel** (52) 52 50 10.**Open** 10am–6pm Tue, Wed, Fri–Sun, noon–8pm Thu. **Closed** Mon. 🎨 free for children under 7, students, disabled plus one attendant. 🎫 & 🚻 📷
🌐 **modemart.hu**

A magnificent arts centre built in 2006, MODEM stages some 10–15 exhibitions a year of, often, world-class 20th-century and contemporary art: paintings, sculpture, photography, video installations and multimedia art from Hungary and elsewhere in Europe. Performance spaces are also used for theatre, film, dance, workshops, lectures and other teaching events. Talks and literary evenings are often held in the museum's Artists' Coffee House.

🏛 Small Reformed Church
Református Kistemplom
Révész tér 2. **Tel** (52) 34 28 72. **Open** 9am–noon Mon–Fri, or by appointment. &

The tower of this charming church was originally topped by an Orthodox-style onion dome, but high winds blew the dome off in 1907, and a replacement suffered a similar fate a few years later. The tower was then finished with crenellations and took on the rather truncated look it has today, earning it its nickname of "stumpy church". A bastion of Protestantism, it was here in 1860 that Péter Balogh, Bishop of Debrecen, declared the Hungarian Protestant churches to be independent of the Habsburg emperors.

🏛 St Anna's Church
Római katolikus templom Szent Anna
Szent Anna utca 15. **Tel** (52) 53 66 52. **Open** 6:30am–7pm daily. & 📷

Debrecen's largest Catholic church was built in 1726–46 to appease the Habsburg emperor, who would not have one of his Royal Free Towns without a Catholic church. Quite who worshipped here is not known;

Detail from the exterior of St Anna's Church

when asked by the emperor in 1748, Bishop Csáky, the founder of the church, had converted none of the Calvinists. The key sight inside the church is its altarpiece, depicting St Anna teaching Mary. The work of an Austrian painter, Karl Rahl, it was added during reconstruction of the church in the 19th century.

Calvinist Reformed College
Református kollégium

Kálvin tér 16. **Tel** (52) 41 47 44. **Open** 10am–4pm Mon–Fri, 10am–1pm Sat. for museum. **W** reformatuskollegium.ttre.hu

The college was founded by Dominican monks, anxious to create a seat of learning in the area, in 1538. Teachers were trained here (in Latin) before being sent to one of 140 free schools the college operated in the region. Rebuilt in 1675 and in 1816, the present building was designed by Mihály Péchy, who was also commissioned to design the Great Reformed Church. Designated as a national monument in 2013, the college has a museum dedicated to the school's history, student life, and the religious art of the Reformed Church in the region.

Déri Museum and Square
Déri Múzeum

Déri tér 1. **Tel** (52) 32 22 07. **Open** 10am–6pm Tue–Sun. **W** derimuzeum.hu

An outstanding example of its kind, the Déri Museum showcases not only exhibits of local cultural interest, but also the huge collection of art and antiquities amassed by Viennese silk manufacturer Frigyes Déri. The Egyptian collection is especially fine; another star attraction is the *Jesus Trilogy* by Mihály Munkácsy. The group of four statues by Ferenc Medgyessy in the restful **square** in front of the main building was awarded the Grand Prize at the 1937 Paris Exposition.

The grand main entrance to the Neo-Baroque Déri Museum

Aquaticum Health and Spa Centre
Aquaticum Gyógy- és Fürdőközpont

Nagyerdei 1. **Tel** (52) 51 41 00. Thermal Baths: **Open** 7am–9pm daily. Pleasure Baths: **Open** 11am–9pm Mon–Thu, 10am–9pm Fri–Sun. **W** aquaticum.hu

Debrecen's famous, extensive thermal bath complex comprises several large indoor pools and baths, an outdoor pool and a vast water-therapy treatment centre. The modern, indoor pleasure baths cater to families and young people, with water slides, children's pools and Thai massage.

Debrecen City Centre

① Piac Street and Town Hall
② Great Reformed Church
③ MODEM Center of Modern and Contemporary Art
④ Small Reformed Church
⑤ St Anna's Church
⑥ Calvinist Reformed College
⑦ Déri Museum and Square
⑧ Aquaticum Health and Spa Centre

For keys to map symbols *see back flap*

The Mediterranean beach at the spa complex in Hajdúszoboszló

⓰ Hajdúszoboszló

20 km (12 miles) west of Debrecen. **Road Map** F3. 24,000. from Debrecen, Budapest. from Debrecen, Budapest. Tourinform, Szent István park 1–3, (52) 55 89 28. **W** hajduszoboszlo.hu

The most popular spa resort on the Great Plain and the largest thermal bath complex in Hungary, the waters here have been attracting visitors since the 1920s. The extensive **Hajdúszoboszló Medicinal Spa** (Hajdúszoboszló Gyógyfürdő) has been modernized, with giant water slides, wave pools, an artificial Mediterranean beach and children's play areas complementing the traditional spa waters. The latter are brown, very salty and contain iodine and bromine. Sufferers of rheumatism swear by their curative effect, and they are also said to help cure gynaecological disorders. Non-water-related activities include restaurants, cafés and the István Bocskai Museum, which has an exhibition of the town's history, including the story of how the waters were discovered during the search for oil (see p167).

🖽 **Hajdúszoboszló Medicinal Spa**
Szent István Park 1–3. **Tel** (52) 55 85 58. Thermal baths: **Open** 7am–7pm daily. Aqua Park: **Open** Jun–Aug: 10am–6pm daily (to 7pm 5 Jul– 10 Aug); open at weekends off-season when weather permits.

⓱ Hortobágy & Hortobágy National Park
Hortobágyi Nemzeti Park

Road Map F3. National Park: (52) 58 91 70. 🖽 Tourinform, Pásztor-múzeum, Petőfi tér 1, Hortobágy, (052) 58 93 21. **Open** National Park: 8am–4pm daily. 🖽 **W** hnp.hu

This enormous national park was the first to be created in Hungary, in 1973, and remains the largest, stretching over 820 sq km (317 sq miles) from Lake Tisza to Debrecen. It was added to UNESCO's World Heritage List in 1999. The vast plain, known locally as the Puszta (meaning "emptiness"), is the nesting site of as many as 152 species of bird, including great bustards, herons, storks and spoonbills, while up to 342 different bird species have been spotted here in migration, including tens of thousands of screeching cranes, which can be seen in late September.

A stork in the Hortobágy National Park

Cattle, horses, buffalo, the Hungarian *racka* (a long-haired sheep) and *parlagi* (a goat) continue to be herded by semi-nomadic farmers here, as they have for almost 1,000 years.

The **Hortobágy Máta Stud Farm** riding centre located inside the park is an 18th-century stud and Hungary's best. It organizes Csikós riding performances (see box, p239), as well as providing riding lessons for visitors throughout summer.

While much of Hortobágy National Park is open to visitors all year round, some parts have limited access. The park's administration and visitors' centre is in the tiny but charming village of Hortobágy itself.

The village has three small hotels and the 17th-century Hortobágy Csárda restaurant, which serves Hungary's national dish, goulash (*gulyás-leves*), which originated in the Puszta. There is also a small **Shepherds' Museum** (Pásztormúzeum) with fascinating facts about the life of the Puszta shepherd. The unique Nine-Arch Bridge (Kilenclyukú híd), built in 1827–33 to designs by Ferenc Povolny, crosses the River Hortobágy and once formed part of the main road from Budapest to Debrecen.

🖽 **Hortobágy Máta Stud Farm**
Czinege J. Utca 1, Hortobágy. **Tel** (52) 58 93 69. **Open** 8am–6pm daily. 🖽 riding lessons, other activities by appointment.

🖽 **Shepherds' Museum**
Petőfi tér 1, Hortobágy. **Tel** (30) 565 74 73. **Open** May & Jun: 9am– 5pm daily; Jul & Aug: 9am–6pm daily; Sep: 9am–5pm daily. **Closed** Oct–Apr.

⓲ Nyíregyháza
See pp258–9.

The 19th-century Nine-Arch Bridge in Hortobágy

The miraculous icon of the Virgin Mary in the Greek Catholic church in Máriapócs

⑲ Máriapócs

31 km (19 miles) from Nyíregyháza. **Road Map** F3. ⚑ 2,300. ▥ from Nyíregyháza. ▥ from Nyíregyháza, Nyírbátor. ☑ 15 Aug (Assumption Day).

In 1696 an icon of the Virgin Mary in the twin-domed **Greek Catholic church** in Máriapócs was seen weeping. The icon was immediately taken to Vienna (to St Stephen's Cathedral) and replaced with a replica. When the replica wept again in 1715 and in 1905, the fate of Máriapócs as a place of pilgrimage was sealed. Today, as many as one million Catholics make the trip every year, many on or around Assumption Day (15 August), when the village is literally besieged by the faithful.

🏛 Greek Catholic church
Kossuth tér 25. **Tel** (42) 38 51 42. **Open** 7:30am–7pm. ♿

⑳ Nyírbátor

36 km (22 miles) from Nyíregyháza. **Road Map** G3. ⚑ 12,500. ▤ from Nyíregyháza, Debrecen. ▥ from Nyíregyháza, Debrecen.

This small town is inextricably linked to the notoriously bloody Báthory family, who owned it in the Middle Ages. Besides bloodlust and murder, however, the Báthorys left two magnificent churches to Nyírbátor's citizens. One of these, a **Roman Catholic**

church, was built around 1480. Partially destroyed during raids by Vlachs (Romanians) in 1587, it was left to rot until 1720, when it was restored in the Baroque style by the Minorite Order. The **István Báthory Museum** next door holds a number of artifacts from around the region, including a vast section on Count István Báthory, Prince of Transylvania, from 1488 to 1511, and the Báthory family. The other historic church of the town is the **Calvinist church** on Egyház utca, a late Gothic building built by István Báthory. This church, built as the Báthory Mausoleum, is a masterpiece of medieval architecture. The nave consists of one single large hall, with a small tower in its southwestern corner and the two-storey sacristy at the northeastern side. Two István Báthorys rest here: the Lord Chief Justice of Hungary and author of psalms in a stone tomb and, next to him, under red marble, the earlier Count István Báthory.

🏛 István Báthory Museum
Károlyi Mihály utca 21. **Tel** (42) 51 02 18. **Open** Apr–Sep: 10am–6pm Tue–Sun; Oct–Mar: 8am–4pm Mon–Fri, weekends by appointment. ☑ Hungarian (in German by prior arrangement). ♿

㉑ Csaroda

15 km (9 miles) east of Vásárosnamény. **Road Map** G2. ⚑ 560. ▥ from Vásárosnamény, Tákos, Fehérgyarmat.

Standing on a hill surrounded by Csaroda Creek, the Calvinist Church at Csaroda was built in late Romanesque style in the 13th century. In 1640, its walls were whitewashed and decorated with flowers. Restoration of the church revealed the original medieval frescoes depicting Saints Peter and Paul, among others.

Fresco from the Calvinist church in Csaroda

㉒ Szatmárcseke

27 km (17 miles) southeast of Vásárosnamény. **Road Map** G2. ⚑ 1,600. ▥ from Vásárosnamény, Fehérgyarmat.

At Szatmárcseke, the Protestant cemetery is a unique sight worth visiting. Almost all the grave markers are 2-m- (6.5-ft-) high boats, preserving, it is thought, the ancient Finno-Ugric custom of burying the dead in boats. The tomb of poet Ferenc Kölcsey (1790–1838) is on a hill in the centre of the cemetery, surrounded by white Neo-Classical columns. The poet lived in the village in the early 19th century and wrote many of his famous poems here, including the words of the Hungarian National Anthem, written in 1823. An exhibition in the Cultural Centre commemorates the time Kölcsey spent in Szatmárcseke.

Some 10 km (6 miles) south, on the banks of the River Túr, is the tiny village of Túristvándi, known for its 18th-century wooden water mill. Although it is no longer used as a mill, visitors may see the wheels and the millstones at work.

Boat-shaped grave markers in the cemetery in Szatmárcseke

⑱ Nyíregyháza

A vibrant university town, Nyíregyháza is a charming place and its trio of churches and synagogue make it a great destination for lovers of ecclesiastical architecture. Centred on a large, leafy and bustling pedestrianized square, the city, with its large population of college students, is particularly lively during term time. Only a short way north of Nyíregyháza is the spa resort of Sóstógyógyfürdő, home to one of the country's best village museums.

🏛 Kossuth Square and Town Hall
Városháza
Kossuth tér 1. Town Hall: (42) 52 45 01. ♿

The heart of Nyíregyháza is a very pleasant public square. It was completely rejuvenated by much redevelopment at the end of the 1990s and is now pedestrianized. There are statues and play areas, terraces and cafés, and even an old tramcar for children to climb aboard. It is surrounded on three sides by colourful buildings, the most impressive of which is the very yellow, Neo-Classical **Town Hall**, dating from 1842 and originally designed by Károly Benkó. The low balcony that is its outstanding feature today was added 30 years later, during a face-lift carried out in 1871. On the other side of the square is the forget-me-not blue, early Secessionist Corona Hotel, designed by Ignác Alpár and opened in 1895. The building does, however, look far better from the outside than from within.

View of the main altar and transept in the Great Catholic Church

🏛 Great Catholic Church
Római katolikus templom
Kossuth tér 4. **Tel** (42) 40 96 91. **Open** 6am–6:30pm daily (to 6pm Oct–Apr). ♿

This red-brick Catholic church was built in 1902–4. Designed by local architect Virgil Nagy, its twin bell towers reflect the steep wooden bell towers common on older churches in the northern part of the Great Plain. The plain interior of the church is lit by the stained-glass windows. The most beautiful part, however, is the impressive transept, with the figures of the four Evangelists in the bays of the arches.

🏛 Lutheran Church
Evangélikus templom
Luther utca 1. **Tel** (42) 50 87 70. **Open** 9am–5pm Mon-Fri. 🅿 donation. Key at vicarage next door if locked.

The largest church in the city, on its highest point, is the Lutheran Church, reflecting the importance of the Reformation in this part of Hungary (see p44). Designed by the Italian Giuseppe Aprilis, it was built in the Neo-Baroque style in 1784–6. The church entrance has four Neo-Classical marble columns. Inside, the walls are adorned with paintings and the main altar, from the Greek Catholic church in Máriapócs (see p257), is richly carved.

🏛 András Jósa Museum
Jósa András Múzeum
Benczúr tér 21. **Tel** (42) 31 57 22. **Open** Apr–Oct: 9am–5pm Tue–Sun; Nov–Mar: 8am–4pm Tue–Sun. 🅿 Hungarian only.

Local painter Gyula Benczúr and writer Gyula Krúdy star at this fascinating museum, named after András Jósa, a wealthy local scientist who owned the building. Born in Nyíregyháza in 1844, Benczúr spent little of his life here, although the museum honours him with a permanent exhibition devoted to his life and work (note that most of his paintings are in The Hungarian National Gallery in Budapest, see pp62–3). Krúdy, famous the world over for his novel The Adventures of Sinbad (1918), was a chronicler of Budapest. The museum displays all his first editions, newspaper articles and other memorabilia.

🏛 Greek Catholic Church & Bishop's Palace
Görög Katolikus templom és Egyházművészeti Gyűjtemény
Bethlen Gábor utca 5. **Tel** (42) 50 00 06. **Open** 8am–4pm Mon–Fri (get key from Sacristy next door). 🅿 museum.

This eclectic Greek Catholic church was designed and built by Vojtovits and Baczó, and completed in 1897. Combining

Kossuth Square, and the yellow Neo-Classical town hall

The plain façade of the Synagogue, in early Minimalist style

Byzantine and Baroque, it was hit by a Soviet bomb at the end of World War II, and had to be extensively rebuilt. Miraculously, the highly ornamented iconostasis featuring St Nicholas survived intact. The nearby **Bishop's Palace** holds a priceless collection of Greek Catholic religious artifacts.

✠ Synagogue
Zsinagóga
Mártírok tere 6. **Tel** (42) 41 79 39.
Open by appointment only, Tue–Thu.
🅿️ 🚻 ♿

Nyíregyháza's synagogue is a beautifully simple building whose outside walls are devoid of any real decoration. Built in 1924–32 to the plans of Lipót Baumhorn, its straight lines and

unfussy façade bear witness to the birth of Minimalism. The murals on the walls inside depicting the night sky and biblical scenes were painted by Pál Szalay, a local artist and teacher. On an outside wall a long plaque commemorates the Nyíregyháza Jews killed in the Holocaust.

Environs
Opened in 1979 the **Open-Air Village Museum** at Sóstó-gyógyfürdő, a spa town 7 km (4 miles) north of Nyíregyháza, is famous for its beautiful rural architecture. More than 50 buildings (houses, a school, a shop, a pub, a fire station) represent the regional styles. In summer, a wide range of

activities are organized: craft fairs, dancing and concerts. The **Aquanus Spa** and the **Sóstó Zoo** are also worth a visit.

Inside a house at the Open-Air Village Museum at Sóstógyógyfürdő

Nyíregyháza City Centre

① Kossuth Square and Town Hall
② Great Catholic Church
③ Lutheran Church
④ András Jósa Museum
⑤ Greek Catholic Church and Bishop's Palace
⑥ Synagogue

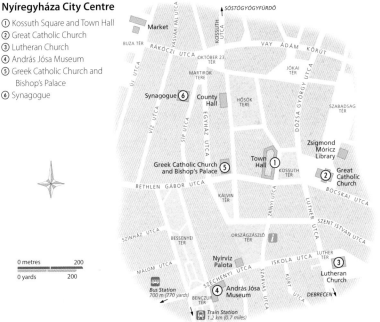

0 metres 200
0 yards 200

TRAVELLERS' NEEDS

WHERE TO STAY

Hungary offers accommodation to cater for all tastes and pockets, from the smallest, family-run pension to the largest and most luxurious five-star hotels, with all the international chains represented. Many hotels have their own spa centres, providing on-site beauty, hydrotherapy and massage treatments for guests. In addition there are hundreds of campsites and youth hostels throughout the country with facilities for the budget-conscious; private accommodation is big business in Hungary too. Choice is, of course, greatest in the capital, Budapest, where there has also been an explosion in the number of design, or boutique, hotels, which are often far more competitively priced than their luxury counterparts. Outside the capital there is less choice, although most towns have one or two large, imperial-era hotels and a number of pensions. The exception is Lake Balaton, where the popular resorts boast hotels to rival Budapest.

Hotels

Budapest's stock of accommodation is now as exciting and varied as in any other European capital, with luxury and design hotels leading the way – such as the magnificent Gresham Palace – closely followed by the grand spa hotels, like the Gellért. Also in the capital, and elsewhere throughout the country, you'll find plenty of hotels occupying formerly grand buildings, such as the Brody House in Budapest or the La Contessa Kastélyhotel in Szilvásvárad. Most hotels have official star-ratings, but note that Hungary's stars roughly equate to one star less in Western Europe; at the luxury end, all rooms have a bathroom, telephone, TV, refrigerator, air-conditioning and Wi-Fi, along with requisite services – 24-hour service, fitness facilities and the like. Three-star hotels usually have at least one restaurant and one bar, and staff are expected to speak at least one foreign language. Roughly two-thirds of rooms in the two-star category have their own bath or shower, while rooms in one-star hotels simply have washbasins with hot and cold running water.

Rates and Reservations

Accommodation in Hungary generally represents decent value for money. Inevitably, prices are highest in Budapest, closely followed by Lake Balaton, though many hotels offer greatly reduced rates for booking in advance, or for staying at the weekend or in low season. Rates peak from around mid-June to September, except in Budapest, where rates are consistent – that said, prices are ramped up significantly for the Hungarian Grand Prix in July/August, marginally less so for the Spring Festival in March.

Booking a room in advance is highly recommended, and is essential in Budapest and at Lake Balaton throughout the high season. Both VAT and

Creatively decorated accommodation at Baltazár *(see p264)*, in Budapest

resort tax are included in the price of a room, although a 30 per cent surcharge is usually levied for stays of less than three days in some resorts and in private accommodation. Breakfast is usually, but not always, included in the price.

Invariably, you'll find the lowest prices on a hotel's own website, but you could always try a central online agency like **Hotel Online Hungary** (*see Directory*). Almost all the hotels and pensions listed in the *Where to Stay* section take major credit cards (Visa and Master-Card), but American Express and Diners Club are less frequently accepted.

Camping

Camping is enormously popular in Hungary, and there are more than 200 well-equipped campsites (*kemping*) all over

Entrance to the art'otel Hotel *(see p265)*, in Budapest

◀ The famous Széchenyi themal bath complex in Budapest

the country, though there's a particularly large cluster around Lake Balaton; these range from large, local authority-run sites to smaller sites, often in someone's garden (especially around Balaton in high season) – better sites typically have a restaurant, shop, sports facilities and a play area. Campsites do not usually hire out tents, though some have small and basic bungalows for rent. The Hungarian National Tourist Office has full details of the country's campsites, with information on what services they provide. Note that camping is only permitted in designated areas.

A room in the Cotton House Hotel *(see p264)* in Budapest

Youth Hostels

Hungary has over 100 registered youth hostels (*ifjúsági szálló*), though these are mostly confined to the larger towns and cities, in particular Budapest, which is bursting with them. In most places, dormitory accommodation is complemented by twin- or double-bedded en-suite rooms, while most hostels would have, at the very least, a kitchen and common area. A dorm bed typically costs around 3,000–4,500 forints (€10–15) outside the capital, slightly more in Budapest itself. Bookings are best made online via **Hostels.com** or **Hostelworld.com**. Most hostels offer small discounts for members of the **Hostelling International** (HI) association.

In many towns, you can also stay in college dormitories (*kollégium*) during July and August, and sometimes at weekends during the rest of the year – check with the local Tourinform office for details.

Pensions and Private Accommodation

Hungary's network of pensions (*panzió*) is large and legendary, and there's at least one in every town and village in the country. These family-run establishments

Sign for Leo Panzio pension
(see p265) in Central Pest

offer bed and breakfast (and often an evening meal) in comfortable surrounds and at low prices. In Budapest, many are, in fact, large houses in the suburbs, often with gardens – a good choice for families travelling on a fixed budget. Another popular budget option is private accommodation – either a room or an apartment – which can be booked on the Hungarian Tourist Office's website *(see p297)* or through agencies such as **IBUSZ Private Accommodation Service** and **Balatontourist**, both of which have extensive listings. Otherwise, you'll see plenty of signs (*szoba kiadó* and *Zimmer frei*) on the streets, particularly around Balaton.

Recommended Hotels

The accommodation listed in this guide is a varied selection of the best types of places to stay in Hungary. There are six themes in all, the first of which is luxury, top-of-the-range places that incorporate all the facilities and comfort you'd expect of a four- or five-star hotel. Historic hotels are those that occupy distinguished buildings, of which Hungary has many – a Baroque manor or castle, perhaps – while design hotels are typically smaller, more intimate places manifesting a cool, contemporary aesthetic.

Another theme is spa hotels, entirely appropriate given that Hungary is blessed with so many thermal springs. On the outskirts of Budapest, and prevalent throughout the rest of the country, are pensions, which provide a cheaper, more restful option. The last theme is hostels, the biggest and best concentration which is, inevitably, in Budapest. Where somewhere has an exceptional feature, or perhaps an outstanding view or impeccable service, it has been designated a DK Choice.

DIRECTORY

Central Booking

Hotels Online Hungary
W hotelonlinehungary.com

Youth Hostels

Hostelling International
W hihostels.com

Hostels.com
W hostels.com

Hostelworld.com
W hostelworld.com

Pensions and Private Accommodation

Balatontourist
Tel (88) 544 400.
W balatontourist.hu

IBUSZ Private Accommodation Service
Tel (1) 485 27 67.
W ibusz.hu

Where to Stay

Budapest

Castle District

Baltazár
Design   Map 1 A4
Országház utca 31
Tel *(1) 300 70 51*
W baltazarbudapest.com
Decadent, arty rooms inspired by
the likes of Warhol and Westwood,
with clever extras: the music
systems link into your smartphone.

Hotel Castle Garden
Design   Map 1 A5
Lovas út 41
Tel *(1) 224 74 20*
W castlegarden.hu
Lovely property with clean and
cosy rooms, well regarded for its
excellent level of service.

DK Choice

**Buda Castle
Fashion Hotel**
Historic   Map 1 A4
Úri utca 39
Tel *(1) 224 79 00*
W budacastlehotelbudapest.com
This sublime 15th-century
merchant's house has been
converted into one of the city's
leading hotels, presenting a mix
of smartly furnished, spacious
rooms and luxurious mini-
suites; the highlight, though, is
breakfast in the impeccably
manicured garden courtyard.

Hilton Hotel
Luxury   Map 1 B4
Hess András tér 1–3
Tel *(1) 889 66 00*
W placeshilton.com
Boasting characterful features
and modern comforts, this hotel
is set high above the Danube.

Lánchíd 19
Design   Map 3 C1
Lánchíd utca 19
Tel *(1) 419 19 00*
W lanchid19hotel.hu
Superb waterside location, with
glass walkways and colourful,
individually themed rooms. Even
the staff wear designer clothes.

**St George's Residence
Hotel**
Historic   Map 1 A4
Fortuna utca 4
Tel *(1) 393 57 00*
W stgeorgehotel.hu
A former medieval inn, now a
stunning selection of suites
furnished in Grand Empire style.

Gellért Hill & Tabán

Ábel Panzió
Pension
Ábel Jenő utca 9
Tel *(1) 209 25 37*
W abelpanzio.hu
Early 1900s villa boasting ten
rooms of considerable charm,
as well as a drawing room and
garden terrace.

Danubius Hotel Gellért
Spa   Map 4 D3
Szent Gellért tér 1
Tel *(1) 889 55 00*
W danubiushotels.com
Legendary spa hotel with indoor
and outdoor pools and an array
of treatments, though the rooms
have seen grander days.

Around Parliament

Aventura Boutique Hostel
Hostel   Map 2 D3
Visegrádi utca 12
Tel *(1) 239 07 82*
W aventurahostelbudapest.com
Four fantastic loft rooms at this
agreeable, family-run hostel, each
decorated to reflect a different
country or culture.

Cotton House
Design   Map 2 E3
Jókai utca 26
Tel *(1) 354 26 00*
W cottonhouse.hu
Some of the best and most
thoughtfully decorated rooms
anywhere in the capital, themed
around America's Jazz Age.

Home Made Hostel
Hostel   Map 2 E4
Teréz körút 22
Tel *(1) 302 21 03*
W homemadehostel.com
Superbly conceived, rustically
styled hostel with bags of charm
and first-rate facilities including
a fabulous kitchen.

Price Guide

Prices are based on one night's stay in
high season for a standard double room,
inclusive of service charges and taxes.

(HUF)	up to 25,000 HUF
(HUF)(HUF)	25,000 to 50,000 HUF
(HUF)(HUF)(HUF)	over 50,000 HUF

Radisson Blu Béke
Historic   Map 2 E3
Teréz körút 43
Tel *(1) 889 30 00*
W radissonblu.com
Magnificently restored hotel with
well-equipped rooms armed
with all the latest facilities.

DK Choice

**Four Seasons
Gresham Palace**
Luxury   Map 1 C5
Széchenyi István tér 5-6
Tel *(1) 268 60 00*
W fourseasons.com
This splendidly refurbished,
magnificent building is now
one of the finest hotels in
central Europe. The rooms are
luxurious, the staff impeccable
and the whole place a real treat.

K&K Hotel Opera
Luxury   Map 2 E5
Révay utca 24
Tel *(1) 269 02 22*
W kkhotels.com
Behind the splendid façade the
rooms are modern, immaculately
turned out and incredibly spacious.

Central Pest

Danubius Astoria Hotel
Historic   Map 4 E1
Kossuth Lajos utca 19–21
Tel *(1) 889 60 00*
W danubiushotels.com
Grand, Secessionist-style hotel
with fine rooms and a stunning
Neo-Baroque breakfast room.

Budget accommodation with style: the Aventura Boutique Hostel

Lavender Circus
Hostel **Map** 4 E1
Múzeum körút 37
Tel *(1) 417 77 63*
🌐 lavendercircus.com
Imaginatively conceived hostel/
hotel decorated with vintage furn-
iture, artwork and goldfish tanks.

Leo Panzió
Pension **Map** 4 E1
Kossuth Lajos utca 2/a
Tel *(1) 266 90 41*
🌐 leopanzio.hu
Modest yet comfortable rooms
in an impressive location. Great
views of the lively streets below.

Nemzeti
Historic **Map** 2 F5
József körút 4
Tel *(1) 477 45 00*
🌐 hotel-nemzeti-budapest.hu
Concealed behind the powder-
blue façade lies a grand staircase
leading to sumptuous rooms.

Bohem Art Hotel
Design **Map** 4 D2
Molnár utca 35
Tel *(1) 327 90 20*
🌐 bohemarthotel.hu
Former factory, now a high-class
boutique hotel offering compact,
creatively designed rooms.

Brody House
Design **Map** 4 E1
Bródy Sándor utca 10
Tel *(1) 266 12 11*
🌐 brodyhouse.com
Fashioned into a super-cool retreat
with wonderfully idiosyncratic,
artistically themed rooms.

Casati Budapest Hotel
Historic **Map** 2 E5
Paulay Ede utca 31
Tel *(1) 343 11 98*
🌐 casatibudapesthotel.com
An 18th-century apartment block
featuring comfortable rooms
with stripped-back walls
overlooking a pretty courtyard.

Hotel Palazzo Zichy
Historic **Map** 4 F2
Lőrinc pap tér 2
Tel *(1) 235 40 00*
🌐 hotel-palazzo-zichy.hu
Flamboyant, fantastically run
hotel in the one-time residence
of the eponymous Count.

Zara Boutique
Design **Map** 4 E2
Só utca 6
Tel *(1) 776 66 01*
🌐 boutiquehotelbudapest.com
Modestly sized but impressively
turned out rooms at this
understatedly cool and
conveniently central hotel.

Buddha Bar Klotild Palace
Historic **Map** 4 D1
Váci utca 34
Tel *(1) 799 73 00*
🌐 buddhabarhotelbudapest.com
Occupying the magnificent
former palace, this place is almost
overwhelming in its opulence.

Continental Hotel Zara
Spa **Map** 2 F5
Dohány utca 42
Tel *(1) 815 10 00*
🌐 continentalhotelbudapest.com
Art Deco-inspired hotel with
great amenities, not least a
rooftop garden with pool.

Corinthia Grand Hotel
Luxury **Map** 2 F5
Erzsébet körút 43
Tel *(1) 479 40 00*
🌐 corinthia.com
From the glittering lobby to
the mahogany-furnished rooms,
the Corinthia oozes class.

Soho
Design **Map** 2 F5
Dohány utca 64
Tel *(1) 872 82 92*
🌐 sohoboutiquehotel.com
A spectacular Pop Art lobby leads
to funkily designed rooms with
Swedish hardwood floors.

Further Afield

Beatrix Panzió
Pension
Széher út 3
Tel *(1) 275 05 50*
🌐 beatrixhotel.hu
Guests at this inviting pension
inevitably find themselves at the
regular grill and goulash parties
held in the pretty garden.

Buda Villa Panzió
Pension
Kiss Áron utca 6
Tel *(1) 275 00 91*
🌐 budapansio.hu
Ten tidy rooms complement the
enjoyable lounge bar, but the
best aspect is the lush garden.

Dominik Panzió
Pension
Cházár András utca 3
Tel *(1) 460 94 28*
🌐 dominikpanzio.hu
The private, dormitory-style
rooms here are clean and simple.
Bathrooms are shared.

Pál Vendégház
Pension
Pálvölgyi köz 15
Tel *(30) 312 93 51*
Just four double rooms in this cosy
guesthouse, located in the leafy
hills near popular tourist sites.

More than a touch of Italianate glamour
at the Boscolo Budapest

Aquincum Hotel
Spa
Árpád fejedelem útja 94
Tel *(1) 436 41 00*
🌐 aquincumhotel.com
Massive hotel with a host of great
facilities, including pools, fitness
studio and steam baths.

art'otel
Design
Vizíváros, Bem rkp. 16–19
Tel *(1) 487 94 87*
🌐 artotels.com/budapest
Rooms are individually decorated
using a host of artworks and
designs by artist Donald Sultan.

Mamaison Hotel Andrássy
Luxury
Andrássy út 111
Tel *(1) 462 21 00*
🌐 mamaison.com
Elegance and charm abound at
this tasteful hotel, which exudes
a certain French chic style.

Mirage Fashion Hotel
Design
Dózsa György út 88
Tel *(1) 462 70 70*
🌐 miragehotelbudapest.com
A 19th-century villa tastefully
converted into a beautiful hotel
overlooking Heroes' Square.

DK Choice

Boscolo Budapest
Historic **Map** 2 F5
Erzsébet körút 9–11
Tel *(1) 886 61 11*
🌐 budapest.boscolohotels.com
Built in 1894 and magnificently
restored by the Italian Boscolo
group, the rooms here are the
height of luxury, while the main
hall is something to marvel at.
Once a hub of literary life, the
gilded domes of the Coffee
House make a perfect spot to
while away the time.

For more information on types of hotels *see pp262–3*

Warm, natural tones characterize the decor at the Centrum Panzió, Szentendre

Around Budapest

ESZTERGOM:
Alabárdos Panzió ⓗ
Pension   Road Map C3
Bajcsy-Zsilinszky út 49
Tel *(33) 31 26 40*
ⓦ alabardospanzio.hu
Attractive, Mediterranean-style
villa with eclectically styled
rooms in two adjacent buildings.

ESZTERGOM: Bazilika Panzió ⓗ
Pension   Road Map C3
Batthyány utca 7
Tel *(33) 52 06 85*
ⓦ bazilika.eu
Gorgeous rooms painted in
soothing cream and beige tones
offset with splashes of burgundy.
Sauna and Jacuzzi too.

ESZTERGOM: Ria Panzió ⓗ
Pension   Road Map C3
Batthyány utca 11–13
Tel *(33) 31 31 15*
ⓦ riapanzio.com
Welcoming pension with rooms
in two buildings, one of which is
wheelchair accessible.

ESZTERGOM:
Szent Anna Panzió ⓗ
Pension   Road Map C3
Erzsébet Királyné útja 2
Tel *(20) 391 44 07*
ⓦ szentannapanzio.hu
A former watermill, with cosy
rooms set around a pretty,
flower-filled inner courtyard.

SZENTENDRE: Centrum Panzió ⓗ
Pension   Road Map D3
Dunakorzó
Tel *(26) 30 25 00*
ⓦ hotelcentrum.hu
One of the few really decent
options in town, a welcoming
place with peach-coloured rooms,
some overlooking the Danube.

SZENTENDRE:
Mathias Rex Panzió ⓗ
Pension   Road Map D3
Kossuth utca 16
Tel *(26) 50 55 70*
ⓦ mathiasrexhotel.hu
Classy, modern pension with
large, fashionable rooms fea-
turing big beds and gleaming
bathrooms. Good restaurant too.

VISEGRÁD: Hotel Vár ⓗ
Historic   Road Map C3
Fő utca 9
Tel *(26) 39 75 22*
ⓦ varhotel.hu
Erstwhile hunting lodge turned
handsome riverfront hotel, with
nice touches such as floor rugs
and wood-framed prints.

Northern Transdanubia

BÜK: Danubius Health Spa
Resort ⓗⓗ
Spa   Road Map A3
Európa út 1
Tel *(94) 88 94 00*
ⓦ danubiushotels.com
Top-end spa resort with beautiful
rooms and a choice of both
indoor and outdoor pools.

BÜK: Greenfield Hotel
Spa and Golf ⓗⓗⓗ
Spa   Road Map A3
Bükfürdő, Golf út 4
Tel *(94) 80 16 00*
ⓦ greenfieldhotel.net
Superb four-star hotel with
exemplary service and high-class
pampering – and, of course, golf.

GYŐR: Fehér Hajó Panzió ⓗ
Pension   Road Map B3
Kiss Ernő utca 4
Tel *(96) 31 76 08*
ⓦ feherhajerpanzio.hu
Cheery, with big, bright rooms
and a fabulous buffet breakfast.

GYŐR: Golden Ball ⓗ
Spa   Road Map B3
Szent István út 4
Tel *(96) 61 81 00*
ⓦ goldenball.hu
Vast gym and health spa offering
great-value accommodation,
particularly the split-level rooms
with raised sleeping areas.

GYŐR: Hotel Fonte ⓗ
Historic   Road Map B3
Kisfaludy utca 38
Tel *(96) 51 38 10*
ⓦ hotelfonte.hu
Named after a well discovered
during construction, this
gorgeous Baroque building has
fantastically comfortable rooms.

GYŐR: Hotel Klastrom ⓗⓗ
Historic   Road Map B3
Zechmeister utca 1
Tel *(96) 51 69 10*
ⓦ klastrom.hu
In an 18th-century priory; the
monks' cells are now elegant, if
somewhat spartan, rooms.

GYŐR: Hotel Schweizerhof ⓗⓗ
Luxury   Road Map B3
Sarkantyú köz 11
Tel *(96) 51 23 58*
ⓦ schweizerhof.hu
A fine hotel with a lobby on each
floor and individually styled,
designer-furnished rooms.

KŐSZEG: Arany Strucc ⓗ
Historic   Road Map A3
Várkör utca 124
Tel *(94) 36 03 23*
ⓦ aranystrucc.hu
Thought to date from the 1590s,
the "Golden Ostrich" has simple
rooms but oodles of character.

KŐSZEG: Portré Panzió ⓗ
Pension   Road Map A3
Fő tér 7
Tel *(94) 36 31 70*
ⓦ portre.com
Stylish pension with vivid red
rooms, subtly furnished in wood
with smart rugs.

MOSONMAGYARÓVÁR:
Thermal Hotel ⓗⓗ
Spa   Road Map B3
Kolbai utca 10
Tel *(96) 20 68 71*
ⓦ thermal-movar.hu
This well-regarded hotel has good
sized rooms, most with garden
views, and lots of treatments.

SÁRVÁR: Danubius Health
Spa Resort ⓗⓗ
Spa   Road Map A3
Rákóczi utca 1
Tel *(95) 88 84 00*
ⓦ danubius.com
Supremely comfortable, with
in-door and outdoor pools, sauna,
gym and a host of wellness options.

SOPRON: Jégverem Fogadó ⓗ
Pension   Road Map A3
Jégverem utca 1
Tel *(99) 51 01 13*
ⓦ jegverem.hu
Converted 18th-century inn
named after the old ice pit in the
middle of its warming restaurant.

SOPRON: Hotel Lővér ⓗⓗ
Spa   Road Map A3
Várisi utca 4
Tel *(99) 88 84 00*
ⓦ hotellover.hu
Peaceful and secluded, with
well-appointed rooms, a pool
and tennis courts.

DK Choice

SOPRON: Hotel Wollner
Luxury   **Road Map** A3
Templom utca 20
Tel *(99) 52 44 00*
🆆 wollner.hu
A superb 18th-century building in the heart of the Belvaros, this hotel oozes class; rooms have handsome beds, oak bureaus and splashes of artwork. It also boasts a beautiful inner garden courtyard where you can kick back with a glass of wine.

SZÉKESFEHÉRVÁR: Budai Panzió
Pension   **Road Map** C4
Budai ut 286
Tel *(22) 78 95 69*
🆆 budaivendeghaz.eu
Restful, just out of the centre, with homely rooms and a welcoming ambience; the breakfast is terrific.

SZÉKESFEHÉRVÁR: Hotel Szárcsa
Luxury   **Road Map** C4
Szárcsa utca 1
Tel *(22) 32 57 00*
🆆 szarcsa.hu
Classy hotel whose beautifully conceived rooms come with wood-carved antiques and period furnishings.

SZOMBATHELY: Hotel Wagner
Luxury   **Road Map** A3
Kossuth Lajos utca 15
Tel *(94) 32 22 08*
🆆 hotelwagner.hu
This small, compact hotel offers beautifully styled rooms with lush green carpets and oak desks.

TATA: Hotel Kiss
Luxury   **Road Map** C3
Bacsó Béla utca 54
Tel *(34) 58 68 88*
🆆 hotel-kiss.hu
Dull location but magnificently appointed rooms, as well as a stunning indoor pool and a host of other amenities.

Southern Transdanubia

BALATONALMÁDI: Ramada Resort
Luxury   **Road Map** B4
Bajcsy-Zsilinszky utca 14
Tel *(88) 62 06 20*
🆆 ramadabalaton.hu
Impeccably turned-out rooms with big windows from which to soak up the stunnng lake views.

BALATONFÜRED: Blaha Lujza Hotel
Historic   **Road Map** B4
Blaha utca 4
Tel *(87) 58 12 10*
🆆 hotelblaha.hu
Former summer home of the erstwhile singer, this handsome Neo-Classical villa offers smart, if rather boxy, rooms.

BALATONFÜRED: Anna Grand Hotel
Luxury   **Road Map** B4
Gyógy tér 1
Tel *(87) 58 12 00*
🆆 annagrandhotel.hu
This is the lake's most opulent hotel, from the cool marble lobby to the immaculate airy rooms.

BALATONLELLE: Viktoria
Pension   **Road Map** B4
Szent István út 13
Tel *(85) 55 42 33*
A few paces from the railway halt, the polished, well-furnished rooms in this tidy pension are top value.

FONYÓD: Boros Castle
Historic   **Road Map** B4
Csisztai út 10
Tel *(85) 36 04 58*
🆆 boroskastely.hu
This wonderful folly of a palace offers apartments in delightful garden surrounds, plus a small pool that's ideal for families.

HÉVÍZ: Astoria Panzió
Pension   **Road Map** B4
Rákóczi utca 11
Tel *(83) 34 03 93*
🆆 astoriapanzio.hu
Homely pension near the baths with an appealing mix of small and large air-conditioned rooms.

HÉVÍZ: Danubius Health Spa Resort Aqua
Spa   **Road Map** B4
Kossuth Lajos utca 13–15
Tel *(83) 88 95 00*
🆆 danubiushotels.com
Luxurious rooms with gigantic beds, superb swimming pools and an endless range of curative treatments.

HÉVÍZ: Park Hotel
Spa   **Road Map** B4
Petőfi utca 26
Tel *(83) 34 11 90*
🆆 parkhotelheviz.hu
Elegant hotel housed in two villas linked by a walkway, with comprehensive facilities including sauna and Jacuzzi.

KESZTHELY: Barbara Panzió
Pension   **Road Map** B4
Zámor utca 2
Tel *(83) 31 98 65*
🆆 barbara-pension.hu
In an enviable location just a stone's throw from the lake, this jolly place has an enticing pool and garden.

KESZTHELY: Tokajer Panzió
Pension   **Road Map** B4
Apát utca 21
Tel *(83) 31 98 75*
🆆 pensiontokajer.hu
Charmingly old-fashioned rooms – each with a terrace or balcony – are spread across three adjoining buildings.

PÉCS: Palatinus Hotel
Historic   **Road Map** C5
Király utca 5
Tel *(72) 88 94 00*
🆆 danubiushotels.com
Renovated Secession pile with a magnificent lobby, sumptuous rooms and a sparkling basement spa and sauna.

SIÓFOK: Rózsa Panzió
Pension   **Road Map** C4
Karinthy Frigyes utca 5
Tel *(84) 31 07 22*
🆆 renegadehotel.hu
Large, peaceful pension situated midway between the station and the beach, with basic rooms and apartments on offer.

The grand main staircase of the Palatinus Hotel in Pécs

For more information on types of hotels *see pp262–3*

A suite decorated in a romantic theme at the Janus Atrium, Siófok

SIÓFOK: Azúr Hotel 🅦🅛🅗🅛
Luxury   Road Map C4
Vitorlás utca 11
Tel *(84) 50 14 00*
🆆 hotelazur.hu
The resort's premier hotel;
faultless rooms and a superbly
equipped wellness centre.

SIÓFOK: Janus Atrium 🅗🅛🅗🅛
Design   Road Map C4
Fő utca 93–95
Tel *(84) 31 25 46*
🆆 janushotel.hu
Room themes range from Gothic
to Gustav Klimt in this super-cool
boutique hotel.

TIHANY:
Hotel Holiday Tihany 🅗🅛🅗🅛
Design   Road Map B4
Batthyány utca 2–6
Tel *(70) 675 00 13*
🆆 holidayhoteltihany.hu
Delightful hotel offering colourful
rooms plus a neat terrace garden.

TIHANY: Tihany Atrium 🅗🅛🅗🅛
Luxury   Road Map B4
Kenderföld utca 19
Tel *(87) 53 81 00*
🆆 hoteltihany.com
Elegance and style come very well
priced at this wonderfully located
four-star hotel on the lakeshore.

VESZPRÉM: Gizella Hotel 🅗🅛
Historic   Road Map B4
Jókai Mór utca 48
Tel *(88) 57 94 90*
🆆 hotelgizella.hu
Request an attic room – white
walls, sloping roofs and beams –
in this 18th-century building.

VESZPRÉM: Péter Pál Panzió 🅗🅛
Pension   Road Map B4
Dózsa György út 3
Tel *(88) 32 80 91*
🆆 peterpal.hu
Engaging little pension with a
mix of rooms, some of which have
their original bare-brick walls.

DK Choice

VESZPRÉM: Oliva Hotel 🅗🅛🅗🅛
Design   Road Map B4
Buhim utca 14–16
Tel *(88) 40 38 75*
🆆 oliva.hu
In the old centre, this marvellous,
Mediterranean-accented hotel
sports 11 dark-wood-furnished
rooms, nine deluxe suites, a
terrific restaurant and all sorts of
wellness facilities.

VESZPRÉM: Villa Medici 🅗🅛🅗🅛🅗🅛
Luxury   Road Map B4
Kittenberger utca 11
Tel *(88) 59 00 70*
🆆 villamedici.hu
The attention to detail here is
marvellous; check out the vividly
tiled Turkish baths too.

Northern Highlands

EGER: Kulacs Panzió 🅗🅛
Pension   Road Map E3
Szépasszonyvölgy
Tel *(36) 31 13 75*
🆆 kulacscsarda.hu
A handful of pine-furnished, cosy
rooms with dinky balconies.

EGER: Imola Hotel Platan 🅗🅛🅗🅛
Design   Road Map E3
Csákány utca
Tel *(36) 51 38 88*
🆆 imolaplatan.hu
Child-free; the lime-green and
chocolate-brown rooms feature
fabulous walk-in showers.

EGER: Senator-ház 🅗🅛🅗🅛
Historic   Road Map E3
Dobó tér 11
Tel *(36) 411 711*
🆆 senatorhaz.hu
From the happily cluttered lobby
to the character-laden rooms,
this 18th-century inn is delightful.

LILLAFÜRED:
Hunguest Palota 🅗🅛🅗🅛🅗🅛
Historic   Road Map E2
Erzsébet sétány 1
Tel *(46) 33 14 11*
🆆 hunguesthotels.hu
Nostalgic, medieval-styled castle
– built in the 1920s – with fine,
elegant rooms.

MISKOLC: Talizmán Panzió 🅗🅛
Pension   Road Map E3
Vár utca 14
Tel *(46) 37 86 27*
🆆 talizmanpanzio.hu
Impeccably kept en-suite rooms,
and a lovely, verdant little garden.

MISKOLC: Bástya Hotel 🅗🅛🅗🅛
Spa   Road Map E2
Miskolctapolcai utca 2
Tel *(46) 56 15 90*
🆆 bastyawellnesshotel.hu
Smart hotel with an array of
wellness facilities, including
indoor and outdoor pools.

PARÁDFÜRDŐ:
Erzsébet Park 🅗🅛🅗🅛
Historic   Road Map E3
Kossuth út 372
Tel *(36) 44 40 44*
🆆 erzsebetparkhotel.hu
Ybl-designed building offering
a full range of wellness amenities.

PARÁDSASVÁR:
Hubertus Panzió 🅗🅛
Pension   Road Map D3
Rákóczi út 2
Tel *(36) 44 44 44*
🆆 khs.hu
Opposite the Kastélyhotel *(below)*
and, obviously, much cheaper,
but lovely in its own right.

PARÁDSASVÁR: Kastélyhotel
Sasvár Resort 🅗🅛🅗🅛🅗🅛
Luxury   Road Map D3
Kossuth utca 1
Tel *(36) 44 44 44*
🆆 khs.hu
Magnificent, opulent Neo-
Classical pile in its own parkland.

SÁROSPATAK:
Vár Vendéglő Panzió 🅗🅛
Pension   Road Map F2
Árpád út 35
Tel *(47) 31 13 70*
🆆 varvendeglo.hu
Six serene and immaculately
turned-out rooms, some with
superb views across to the castle.

SÁTORALJAÚJHELY:
Hunor Hotel 🅗🅛🅗🅛
Luxury   Road Map F2
Torzsás utca 25
Tel *(47) 52 15 21*
🆆 hotelhunor.hu
Plush place with fabulously
bright and tidy rooms.

DK Choice

SZILVÁSVÁRAD: La Contessa Kastélyhotel
Luxury Road Map E2
Park utca 6
Tel *(36) 56 40 64*
W lacontessa.hu
Unbridled palatial pomp in this imperious castle hotel, from the gleaming marble-floored lobby to the dazzling white corridors that lead to rooms of distinction.

TOKAJ: Torkolat Panzió
Pension Road Map F2
Vasvári utca 26
Tel *(20) 942 34 32*
W torkolatpanzio.hu
The individual touch is everywhere in this charming guesthouse; free use of canoes and bikes too.

TOKAJ: Grof Degenfeld Castle Hotel
Historic Road Map F2
Terézia kert 9
Tel *(47) 58 04 00*
W hotelgrofdegenfeld.hu
Family-run; rooms are every bit as classy as the winery for which this place is really renowned.

The Great Plain

BAJA: Kaiser Panzió
Pension Road Map C5
Tóth Kálmán utca 12
Tel *(79) 52 04 50*
W panziokaiser.hu
Terrific-value pension whose smooth, largely red-coloured rooms come with leather sofas.

DEBRECEN: Centrum Panzió
Pension Road Map F3
Péterfia utca 37A
Tel *(52) 41 61 93*
W panziocentrum.hu

Modern designer decor and a first-rate spa at the Art Hotel, Szeged

---

Homely, family-run; the comfy rooms have a little sink and micro-wave as well as a small terrace.

DEBRECEN: Grand Hotel Aranybika
Historic Road Map F3
Piac utca 11–15
Tel *(20) 363 61 21*
W hotelaranybika.com
Reputedly Hungary's oldest hotel; the rooms in the older wing are a touch classier than those in the newer, modern part.

DEBRECEN: Aquaticum Thermal Hotel
Spa Road Map F3
Nagyerdei park 1
Tel *(52) 51 41 11*
W aquaticum.hu
Plush four-star hotel offering sparkling, glassy rooms with sofas and large plasma screen TVs.

HAJDÚSZOBOSZLÓ: Hotel Silver
Spa Road Map F3
Mátyás Király utca 25
Tel *(52) 36 38 11*
W hotelsilver.hu
This spa hotel has a wide range of rooms and apartments, but the pools are the real draw.

KECSKEMÉT: Fábián Panzió
Pension Road Map D4
Kápolna utca 14
Tel *(76) 47 76 77*
W panziofabian.hu
Sweet, family-run pension with lilac-coloured rooms overlooking a lush, flower-laden garden.

KECSKEMÉT: Aranyhomok Hotel
Spa Road Map D4
Kossuth tér 3
Tel *(76) 50 37 30*
W hotelaranyhomok.hu
This quite ugly-looking building conceals very agreeable rooms, some facing the attractive park.

NYÍRBÁTOR: Hotel Hódi
Historic Road Map G3
Báthory utca 11
Tel *(42) 28 10 12*
W hotelhodi.com
This beautiful Baroque old town house was the home of the renowned Báthory family.

NYÍREGYHÁZA: Fürdőház Panzió
Spa Road Map F3
Sóstógyógyfürdő, Szódaház utca 18
Tel *(42) 50 01 06*
W furdohaz.hu
The "Bath House" has warm, comfortable and reasonably priced modern rooms, plus free use of the thermal baths.

NYÍREGYHÁZA: Hotel Pagony
Spa Road Map F3
Újmajori út 14–18
Tel *(42) 50 12 10*
W hotelpagony.hu
Top-notch spa hotel north of town; the rooms are gorgeously furnished and thoughtfully lit.

NYÍREGYHÁZA: Svájci Lak Panzió
Pension Road Map F3
Sóstógyógyfürdő, Sóstói út 75
Tel *(42) 41 14 44*
W svajcilak.com
This lovely green and white "Swiss Chalet" is a charismatic pension with attractive rooms.

SZEGED: Art Hotel
Design Road Map E5
Somogyi utca 16
Tel *(62) 59 28 88*
W arthotelszeged.hu
Artistically conceived hotel, from the neon-lit lobby to the vividly coloured rooms. First-rate spa and restaurant too.

SZEGED: Dóm Hotel
Luxury Road Map E5
Bajza utca 6
Tel *(62) 42 37 50*
W domhotelszeged.info
A gem of a place on a closed-off street, with businesslike rooms, sauna and Jacuzzi.

DK Choice

SZEGED: Hotel Tiszavirág
Design Road Map E5
Hajnóczy utca 1/b
Tel *(62) 55 48 88*
W tiszaviragszeged.hu
There are few places in Hungary like this romantic, mid-19th-century house, fronted by a wonderful volute balcony; inside, the all-white rooms mix oakwood, glass and marble to wonderful effect. Stunning spa complex and restaurant.

TISZAFÜRED: Nádas Panzió
Pension Road Map E3
Kismuhi utca 2
Tel *(59) 51 14 01*
W nadaspanzio.hu
Delightful thatched-roof pension that also boasts a kidney-shaped pool and a fine wine cellar.

TISZAFÜRED: Tisza Balneum
Spa Road Map E3
Húszöles út 27
Tel *(59) 88 62 00*
W balneum.hu
Outstanding rooms furnished with local craftsmanship; the hotel's pools are unrivalled.

For more information on types of hotels *see pp262–3*

WHERE TO EAT AND DRINK

Hungary has a long tradition of hospitality and culinary excellence. Budapest especially is full of exquisite, luxurious restaurants fit for the emperors of old – the city is, in fact, home to some of central Europe's most historic restaurants. These, though, are slowly being usurped by a new wave of smart, contemporary establishments with younger, more dynamic chefs committed to creating dazzling, modern interpretations of classic Magyar cooking. Eating out, however, remains a relatively low-cost experience because an ever-increasing number of restaurants make a special effort to ensure that visitors to any Hungarian city will be able to enjoy local delicacies. These are usually served in enormous portions at low prices, offering excellent value for money. Hungary's coffeehouses, meanwhile, are legendary, and there's no greater pleasure than sitting and chatting over coffee and cake in one of Budapest's great *kávéház*.

The outdoor terrace of the Pest-Buda Vendéglő *(see p276)*

Types of Restaurants and Cafés

As a general rule, Hungarian restaurants carry a name tag that indicates what kind of eatery it will be. *Étterem* simply means restaurant, and any type of cuisine may be served. A *csárda* comes in various forms: most are folksy restaurants offering interesting variations on local dishes, while a fisherman's *csárda*, known as a *halázscsárda*, will offer mainly fish dishes and soups. There are two types of inn: a *vendéglő*, which has an informal ambience, and a *kisvendéglő* (literally "small inn"), which is similar to a bistro.

Besides restaurants, a great place to eat a light snack in Hungary is in a wine bar (*borozó*). Typically, such snacks consist of a slice of bread and dripping with raw onion, sprinkled with paprika, or *pogácsa* (a scone with crackling, cheese, caraway seeds or paprika). Beer houses, called *söröző*, serve an even wider range of moderately priced snacks and hot dishes.

Hungary has one of the oldest coffee-drinking traditions in Europe. Introduced to Hungary by the Turks during their occupation, the coffee culture blossomed, and towards the end of the Habsburg era, there were almost 600 *kávéház* in Budapest alone; aside from coffee, these institutions invariably serve pastries, cream cakes and ice cream.

Opening Hours

Most restaurants open around 11am and close around 10 or 11pm. It is unusual for them to close during the afternoon, though many, especially outside Budapest, close on Sundays and/or Mondays. Some restaurants in the Balaton area are open only during the season from May to September. Cafés and patisseries generally open at 8am, running through to around 6pm, though those that serve alcohol generally close much later.

Vegetarian Food

Although vegetarian cuisine is hardly found in abundance in Hungary, there are a growing number of places – particularly high-end restaurants – that offer more adventurous dishes. Meat-free dishes can be found on most menus: *főzelék*, a vegetable dish that normally accompanies steak, sausage or a hamburger, can be ordered on its own or with egg, while *lecsó* is a tomato and pepper casserole that makes a substantial meal by itself. Other meat-free specialities include *túrós csusza*, a pasta dish with cottage cheese and sour cream. There are also many sweet and savoury *palacsinta* (pancakes).

A list of restaurants and shops can be found on the website of the Hungarian branch of the International Vegetarian Union, www.vegetarian.hu.

Peaceful courtyard for al fresco dinning at Kéhli Vendéglő (see page 279), in Budapest

Centrál Kávéház café *(see p277)*, one of Budapest's historic coffeehouses

Reservations

A prior reservation is really only necessary in the best restaurants, especially in Budapest. In Hungary, it is customary to join other guests at a table, especially during the busy lunchtime. To secure a private table in advance, it is advisable to reserve it.

Children

Children are welcomed in all restaurants almost without exception. Most places can provide a highchair for toddlers, while there will often be a children's (or a light) portion on the menu; if not, then the chef will prepare a suitable dish usually at a slightly cheaper price. The only exception might be dessert, but the desserts in Hungarian restaurants are so delicious (and sweet) that most children will happily eat a whole portion.

Menus

By law, all Hungarian restaurants must display a menu with prices, and while many will have English translation, this is less common outside the capital: a staff member or fellow diner may be able to help out. The name of the dish is usually followed by a brief description. Remember that for many Hungarians lunch is the main meal of the day. Many restaurants and cafés therefore offer a two- or three- course set menu, consisting of a soup, a main course and often a dessert. This can be a good opportunity to sample local food and mingle with locals.

Prices, Tipping and Payment

Like most countries, the cost of a meal in Hungary varies according to the location and type of establishment. Notwithstanding the fact that Budapest now has some incredibly upmarket restaurants, the cost of eating out here is, anyway, higher than elsewhere in the country, while you may also find prices slightly higher around Lake Balaton.

The prices should also be displayed, but if they are not, go elsewhere. The introduction of printed and itemized bills has made it increasingly difficult for hidden extras to be added to the final bill, as in days of yore, but remain wary and always check the bill assiduously. In some restaurants, a service charge is included in the final bill, but this is not common practice; if such a charge has not been levied, it is customary to leave your waiter a tip of around 10 per cent, while loose change is perfectly acceptable in cafés. Credit cards are accepted in the majority of restaurants, though you'd do well to check in more rural establishments before ordering your meal.

Recommended Restaurants

The restaurants listed here cover a range of cuisine styles and are the best of their kind in Hungary. Traditional Hungarian cooking remains the dominant theme throughout the country, particularly in the countryside, where the archetypal goulash and paprika-based dishes still form the mainstay of most restaurant menus. That said, many newer establishments are now offering a fresh, modern take on age-old recipes, and we've listed a number of restaurants that reflect the changing, and more innovative, trends in Magyar cooking. Although a fairly loose term, international cuisine is increasingly popular in many restaurants – especially in Budapest – and here you'll find a number of outstanding places each offering a menu of diverse dishes inspired by national cuisines from across the globe. Ethnic eateries are almost exclusively confined to the capital, where there are some first-class Italian, French and Asian restaurants, in particular. The specially recommended restaurants, marked as DK choice, have been chosen because they offer a unique experience – typically a combination of superb cuisine and a truly special atmosphere.

The refined dinning room at Tigris *(see p283)*, Budapest

The Flavours of Hungary

The fusion of Magyar, Turkish, Balkan and even French influences has made Hungarian cuisine one of the most interesting and flavourful in central Europe. Hungary is a country where cooking know-how has always been a key aspect of the national culture. The improvised stews of nomadic Asiatic settlers survive as a delicacy to this day. Although noted for its game, foie gras and rich meaty preparations, such as goulash and the legendary Debreceni sausages, it is also a good place to enjoy fresh-water fish and an array of delicious cakes and pastries.

Hungarian peppers

Sausages and meats on sale at the Central Market Hall, Budapest

Meat

Beef is Hungary's favourite meat and, as a consequence, is produced in large quantities, usually to a very high standard. A variety of cuts of beef are a regular feature on Hungarian tables and menus, especially in Budapest, and veal is also becoming increasingly popular. Steak is widely dished up with a rich sauce, as in *Belszín Budapest módra* (chicken livers, mushrooms and peas). Beef is also used to make the many types of goulash, although pork is another key ingredient in this dish, especially in *gulyásleves* (goulash soup). Pork is found in a wide range of other stews and sausages, and is eaten as bacon.

Poultry and Game

Gosse plays a large part in the culinary tradition of Hungary, which is the world's second biggest producer of foie gras (after France). Foie gras is almost the national dish, usually cooked in its own fat and served warm. It is also found in pâtés and confits. Goose skin is widely enjoyed too, fried in its own fat

Chestnut slice
Chocolate marzipan cake
Chocolate wafer cake
"Domino" cake
Apple slice
Cheesecake
Poppy seed slice

Selection of typical Hungarian cakes and pastries

Local Dishes and Specialities

Despite strong foreign influences, the classic dishes of Hungary dominate menus in the country's restaurants and cafés. Many show their roots in one of Hungary's three historical regions. Goulash and its many variants, for example, is a dish of the Great Plain, the traditional method of cooking it in a kettle reflecting the nomadic past of the Plain's inhabitants. Foie gras may have been introduced into the country by the Austrian Habsburgs, but has become so popular that it is key to the cuisine of the Northern Highlands, where most geese are now bred. Transdanubia and the area around Budapest have always had the sweetest tooth and nearly all the nation's favourite cakes and desserts originate from here.

White asparagus

Lángos Crisp and golden, deep-fried potato flour doughnuts make a popular, filling snack, served with soured cream.

Market stall laden with root vegetables and strings of dried peppers

and served with pickles. Duck is another regular on Hungarian menus, frequently roasted with chestnuts or berries and served with red cabbage. Partridge may also be on offer, roasted with bacon and herbs. Rabbit, hare and venison are common as well, usually dished up in spicy, goulash-style sauces.

Fish

Trout is probably the most widely eaten fish, although carp, perch, roach, zander and even eels can be found on most menus. A popular soup is *halászlé*, made with trout and carp and seasoned with a generous dash of paprika. Another favourite is *csuka tejfölös tormával* (pike in horseradish sauce). Many Budapest restaurants offer a variety of imported fish, but these are usually expensive.

Vegetables

Potatoes, parsnips and cabbage are usually the main vegetables. But from May to July, fine white asparagus appears on market stalls, with many restaurants serving *spárgaleves*, a rich creamy soup made from asparagus and veal stock.

Roasting chestnuts, a common sight on Budapest's winter streets

Paprika peppers are a culinary staple. They are either cooked as part of a dish – *töltött paprika* (peppers stuffed with meat and rice) are served up everywhere – or dried and ground up to be used as a spice. There are hundreds of different types of ground paprika, which vary in flavour and strength, but they all fit into seven broad categories: "special" (sweet and very mild); "mild" (faintly spicy); "delicatesse" (slightly hot); "sweet" (mild but fairly aromatic); "semi-sweet" (medium hot); "rose" (hot); and "hot" (fiery).

BEST LOCAL SNACKS

Sausages Street vendors everywhere offer the lightly smoked Debreceni sausage, made from beef, pork, paprika and garlic. It is generally eaten with bread and mustard.

Chestnuts In winter, Budapest is crammed with stalls selling freshly roasted chestnuts.

Pancakes, fritters and doughnuts Snack bars all over the country serve tasty fried doughy snacks all day long. Try *alma pongyolában* (apple fritters).

Gingerbread Shops devoted to selling gingerbread are everywhere. At Christmas it is often highly decorated and given as a present.

Belszín Budapest Módra Slices of fine sirloin steak are served with a rich mushroom, pea and chicken liver sauce.

Gulyásleves A type of goulash, this pork, beef and vegetable soup is flavoured with onion, caraway and paprika.

Dobos Torta Fine slices of sponge cake are layered with chocolate cream and topped with chocolate icing.

What to Drink in Hungary

Hungary is famous for its excellent wines and, although it is not a big country, it has over 20 wine regions *(see pp32–3)*. These regions produce all the characteristic wine styles, from *pezsgő* (sparkling wine) and light whites that come from Mátra, near Lake Balaton, to dry reds from Villány or Eger, as well as Tokaji, a distinctive sweet dessert wine from Tokaj. Many wines from different vineyards are matured in the maze of underground cellars in Budafok. They are all widely available in Budapest's restaurants, wine bars and wine shops. As well as being a prominent wine producer, Hungary also makes beer, *pálinka* (a drink distilled from different orchard fruits), several types of brandy and a bitter herb liqueur called Unicum.

Light Hungarian beers

Pálinka

Kecskemét is the largest region that produces the alcoholic drink *pálinka,* which is distilled from fruit grown in the orchards situated on the Great Hungarian Plain, some 100 km (60 miles) southeast of Budapest. *Pálinka* is a spirit native to Hungary and comes in a variety of flavours including *barack* (apricot) and *cseresznye* (cherry). The best of them, however, is *szilva* (plum), which comes from the Szatmár district and is much favoured by the Hungarians.

Pálinka is not the only spirit indigenous to Hungary. Other examples include Törköly, a spirit distilled from rape, which possesses a very delicate flavour, and Vilmos, a brandy made from Williams pears.

Barack pálinka

Pezsgő and Hungaria by Törley

Today, Hungary has several other vineyards producing *pezsgő*, mainly concentrated around Budapest, in the Pannónia and Balatonboglár regions. As well as Törley, Hungaria is another good label to look out for.

Hungarian Beers

Hungarians have been turning increasingly to beer as their chosen drink, as it goes exceptionally well with many traditional, paprika-flavoured Hungarian dishes, goulash among them. There are three remaining authentic Hungarian breweries. These are Arany Ászok, Kőbányai (which was established in the Kőbánya district of Budapest in 1854) and the excellent Dreher brewery. Unfortunately, many other formerly Hungarian breweries have now been taken over by large foreign corporations. However, many of these brands are also well-known and all are widely available in Budapest.

Hungarian Wines

The choice of good wine available in Hungary has increased dramatically over the past few years. This is thanks to the ever-improving wines being matured in private cellars. The styles currently favoured by the producers include dry white Chardonnay and Riesling, medium-dry

Sparkling Wines

Sparkling wine, called *pezsgő* (the Hungarian word for "sparkling"), enjoys a good reputation in Hungary. The classic method of producing these wines was introduced to Hungary from France by József Törley, in 1881. It was Törley who built the first production plant in Budafok, which continues to produce excellent sparkling wines.

One of Budafok's cellars, where wines are aged in barrels

Egri Bikavér, "Bull's Blood", a full-bodied red wine

A dry white wine from the Badacsony vineyards

Zőldszilváni, Hárslevelű and Szürkebarát, medium-sweet Tramini and the aromatic Muskotály, which is produced in Badacsony, Balatonboglár, Csopak and Somló.

Among red wines, the dry Kékfrankos, Burgundi, Oportó, Cabernet and Pinot Noir are popular, as is the medium-dry Merlot, which is produced in Siklós, Sopron, Szekszárd, Tihany and Villány.

Another vine-growing district is Eger, which is famous for its aromatic, robust red Egri Leányka and the dry red Egri Bikavér, or "Bull's Blood", which is produced from a combination of three grape varieties. Other Hungarian wines take their names from their place of origin or the variety of grape from which they are produced.

Tokaji

The dessert wine Tokaji has a very different style. Its bouquet and flavour come from a mould that grows only in the fork of the Bodrog and Tisza rivers and the volcanic soil in which the vines grow (see p232). Tokaji ranges from sweet to dry and is full-bodied and rich. Worth sampling is Aszú, which is made with the addition of overripe grapes harvested after the first frost. The proportion of these grapes added to the must (grape juice) determines the body and sweetness. The more grapes used, the richer and sweeter the Aszú.

Although cheap varieties of Tokaji do exist, they lack the quality of the genuine article.

Unicum

Invented in 1790 to subdue indigestion, Unicum is made from a blend of 40 Hungarian herbs. The herbs, which are gathered in three separate areas, are combined to produce this bitter liqueur.

Unicum can be drunk either as an apéritif before a meal or afterwards as a digestif with coffee.

The recipe has been held by the Zwack family, and remained a secret, since the reign of Austrian Emperor Joseph II. Originally, Unicum was prescribed as a remedy for the king

Unicum herb liqueur

by the court physician, who was himself a member of the Zwack family.

Sweet Tokaji Szamorodni

Dry Tokaji Szamorodni

Tokaji Aszú, a renowned golden dessert wine

Pear-flavoured Vilmos liqueur

Sisi, an apricot liqueur

Where to Eat and Drink

Budapest

Castle District

Ruszwurm Cukrászda
Café   Map 1 B5
Szentháromság utca 7
Tel *(1) 375 52 84*
Budapest's oldest patisserie is perhaps its finest too, with plenty of calorific strudel and *rétes* (filo pastries filled with curd cheese), and some delicious coffees.

DK Choice

21 – Magyar Vendéglő
Modern Hungarian   Map 1 B4
Fortuna utca 21
Tel *(1) 202 21 13*
A super-stylish restaurant that strives to create traditional Magyar cuisine in a thoroughly contemporary setting. Brick walls, wooden floors and subdued lighting create the perfect atmosphere in which to enjoy first rate foie gras and other classic dishes, such as chicken paprika with buttered dumplings. The wine list is particularly inspired.

Café Pierrot
International   Map 1 B4
Fortuna utca 14
Tel *(1) 375 69 71*
The original, elegant Socialist-era interior contributes to the 1980s retro feel; the food is a classy international take on quality Hungarian produce. Check out the photo wall of celebrity diners.

Fekete Holló Vendéglő
Hungarian   Map 1 A4
Országház utca 10
Tel *(1) 356 23 67*

A little gem where the kitsch medieval decor does little to detract from the excellent food, though it's perhaps a bit too touristy for some.

Pest-Buda Bistro
Hungarian   Map 1 B4
Fortuna utca 3
Tel *(1) 225 03 77*
Elegant restaurant with arched walls and ceiling that form part of an underground cave system. The food, meanwhile, is interesting and excellently prepared.

Rivalda Café & Restaurant
International   Map 1 B5
Színház utca 5–9
Tel *(1) 489 02 36*
Contemporary international cuisine with a changing menu reflecting the seasons, using mostly local ingredients. Great evenings of jazz too.

Vár a Speiz Étterem
International   Map 1 B4
Hess András tér 6
Tel *(1) 488 74 16*
Sophisticated restaurant offering the likes of foie gras with Tokaj wines. In the adjoining Ham and Wine Bar, you can sample a superb range of cured meats from all over Europe.

Alabárdos
Modern Hungarian   Map 1 A4
Országház utca 2
Tel *(1) 356 08 51*   **Closed** *Sun, lunch Mon–Fri*
Truly exclusive place in an outstanding Gothic building. The menu features Hungarian specialities from pre-paprika times made to please today's taste buds.

The graceful architectural design in the dining room at Alabárdos

Price Guide
Prices are based on a three-course meal for one with half a bottle of wine and including service:
up to 5,500 HUF
5,500 to 8,500 HUF
over 8,500 HUF

Gellert Hill & Taban

Café Déryné
Hungarian and French   Map 1 B5
Krisztina tér 3
Tel *(1) 225 14 07*
Evoking the atmosphere of a grand-scale dining room, the classic brasserie menu here features simple local and French favourites.

Aranyszarvas Vendéglő
International   Map 3 C1
Szarvas tér 1
Tel *(1) 375 64 51*
At the handsome "Golden Deer" you can choose from an eclectic menu, from tenderloin of wild boar with white bean purée to duck breast with orange, carrot and pak choi.

Búsuló Juhász
Étterem
Hungarian   Map 3 C3
Kelenhegyi út 58
Tel *(1) 209 16 49*
Sited on the slopes of Gellert Hill, Búsuló is worth visiting as much for the views as the food, which is beautifully prepared but expensive.

Around Parliament

Európa Kávéház
Café   Map 2 D3
Szent István Körüt 7–9
Tel *(1) 312 23 62*
Large and bustling café that's invariably packed to the gills with locals filling up on coffee and generously portioned slices of cake.

Govinda Étterem
Vegetarian   Map 2 D5
Vigyázó Ferenc utca 4
Tel *(1) 473 13 10*   **Closed** *Sun*
Fast-food style joint serving individual dishes as well as set meals, in addition to their all-you-can-eat menu.

Gresham Kávéház
Café   Map 2 D5
Széchenyi István tér 5–6
Tel *(1) 268 60 00*
Perfect place for a light lunch or early evening meal, or you could just opt for one of the wickedly enticing cakes any time.

DK Choice

Café Bouchon
Hungarian and French **Map** 2 E4
Zichy Jenő utca 33
Tel *(1) 353 40 94*   **Closed** *Sun*
Outstanding combinations of French and Hungarian flavours mark out this welcoming little neighbourhood restaurant popular with theatre-goers; it's also well stocked with some of the country's finest wines. The nicely spaced out tables, lovely Art Deco furnishings and impeccable service round things off beautifully.

Café Kör
Modern Hungarian   **Map** 2 D5
Sas utca 17
Tel *(1) 311 00 53*
Popular, modestly sized bistro-style place serving enticing bowls of salad and grilled meat dishes. Fine wines too.

Kispiac Bisztró
Modern Hungarian   **Map** 2 D4
Hold utca 13
Tel *(1) 269 43 21*   **Closed** *Sun*
A sweet little local with barely a handful of tables, it offers some sumptuous dishes, but the roasted duck beats the lot.

Krízia
Italian   **Map** 2 E4
Mozsár utca 12
Tel *(1) 331 87 11*   **Closed** *Sun*
This pretty restaurant showcases some fabulous Italian cuisine; the home-made pastas and noodles are quite something, and there's a truffle menu too. It closes for the afternoon from 3pm to 6:30pm.

Authentic Italian cuisine at Krízia, a few minutes' walk from the State Opera House

Folk-inspired decor at the Italian-style Pomo D'Oro

Marquis de Salade
International   **Map** 2 E4
Hajós utca 43
Tel *(1) 302 40 86*
Dishes from Azerbaijan and Georgia feature strongly in this wittily (but harmlessly) titled and beautifully decorated establishment – check out the Persian rugs downstairs.

Művész Étterem
Hungarian   **Map** 2 E2
Vígszínház utca 5
Tel *(1) 784 44 83*   **Closed** *Sat lunch*
Intimate restaurant with antique furniture and walls displaying photos of theatre personalities; the cooking is uncomplicated yet extremely tasty.

Pomo D'Oro
Italian   **Map** 2 D4
Arany János utca 9
Tel *(1) 302 64 73*
A labyrinthine trattoria with large wood-burning ovens firing up thin-crust pizzas; the charcoal-grilled meats are worth trying too.

Sir Lancelot Lovagi Étterem
International   **Map** 2 E3
Podmaniczky utca 14
Tel *(1) 302 44 56*
If you relish a themed eating experience, this is for you: hefty portions of Renaissance-inspired dishes served by waiters in period costume, accompanied by Renaissance music.

Borkonyha
International   **Map** 2 D5
Sas utca 3
Tel *(1) 266 08 35*   **Closed** *Sun*
Elegant venue where the wine is as important as the food, which is exceptional; expect dishes like rabbit millefeuille and suckling pig carpaccio.

Tigris
Modern Hungarian   **Map** 2 D5
Mérleg utca 10
Tel *(1) 317 37 15*   **Closed** *Sun*
Hungarian cuisine is rendered with flair and ingenuity here, from the smoked meats prepared in-house to a special foie gras menu.

Central Pest

Centrál Kávéház
Café   **Map** 4 E1
Károlyi Mihály utca 9
Tel *(1) 266 21 10*
This was one of Budapest's foremost literary cafés in the early 20th century. It remains a grand affair, and the pastries are truly spectacular.

Gerbeaud
Café   **Map** 2 D5
Vörösmarty tér 7
Tel *(1) 429 90 00*
A period gem, exquisitely furnished and decorated *(see p98),* that's been serving some of the best, and most expensive, coffees and cakes in the country for well over 100 years.

Művész Kávéház
Café   **Map** 2 E4
Andrássy út 29
Tel *(1) 343 35 44*
Eternally popular coffeehouse that, like Gerbeaud, is as notable for its extravagant Baroque decor as for its coffee and cakes.

Vapiano
Italian   **Map** 4 D1
Bécsi utca 5
Tel *(1) 411 08 64*
Collect a card, place your order (pizza or pasta), then watch it being prepared before your very eyes. Great fun.

For more information on types of restaurants *see pp270–71*

Araz, offering a repertoire of both French and Hungarian dishes

DK Choice

Borbíróság
Modern Hungarian   **Map** 4 E2
Csarnok tér 5
Tel *(1) 219 09 02*   **Closed** *Sun*
Across from the Great Market Hall, this fantastic-looking restaurant has a split-level interior and small terrace. The highlights of a limited but exceptional menu are the duck carpaccio and duck steak, though there are many more options, like tuna and veal with foie gras. The choice and quality of wine is second to none.

Cyrano
International   **Map** 4 D1
Kristóf tér 7
Tel *(1) 266 47 47*
Toasted goat's cheese with lavender and honey is the signature dish here, which gives you some idea as to the inventiveness on offer.

Fülemüle Étterem
Jewish   **Map** 4 F1
Kőfaragó utca 5
Tel *(70) 305 30 00*
Homely, old-style, family-run restaurant serving typical Jewish meals like *solet*, goose stew, and goose soup with dumplings.

Gerlóczy Kávéház
Modern Hungarian   **Map** 4 E1
Gerlóczy utca 1
Tel *(1) 501 40 00*
Not only does this atmospheric street corner cafe offer delicious Hungarian fare, but it's also a great place for breakfast.

Kárpátia Étterem
Hungarian   **Map** 4 E1
Ferenciek tere 7–8
Tel *(1) 317 35 96*   **Closed** *lunch*
Open since 1877, standards in this beautifully ornamented establishment remain impeccably high; the food is usually spot on.

Két Szerecsen
Spanish   **Map** 2 E4
Nagymező utca 14
Tel *(1) 343 19 84*
Bright, buzzy place with a varied tapas menu complementing a strong selection of mains, such as salmon steamed in white wine.

Kőleves Vendéglő
Hungarian   **Map** 2 E5
Kazinczy utca 37–41
Tel *(1) 213 59 99*
Jerusalem artichoke cream soup with roast walnuts is a typical dish in this quaint, rather idiosyncratic restaurant.

DK Choice

Menza
Modern Hungarian   **Map** 2 E4
Liszt Ferenc tér 2
Tel *(1) 413 14 82*
By far the most appealing, and popular, place on this busy square, Menza offers sublime retro-inspired food amidst uber-cool 1970s decor, and there's a fabulous terrace too. The two-course lunch menu is a steal.

Soul Café
Hungarian and French   **Map** 4 E2
Ráday utca 11–13
Tel *(1) 217 69 86*
Lightly North African-themed, offering beautifully prepared French and Moroccan food.

Araz
French   **Map** 2 F5
Dohány utca 42–44
Tel *(1) 815 11 00*
Comforting French dishes, such as chicken breast with creamy kale, and Hungarian classics; the Sunday brunch is a good bet too.

Carmel Étterem
Jewish   **Map** 2 E5
Kazinczy utca 31
Tel *(1) 342 45 85*   **Closed** *Fri eve*
Legendary kosher restaurant invariably crowded with locals here to enjoy its famed *solet* (*cholent*), a slow-cooked stew with smoked goose.

Costes
International   **Map** 4 E2
Ráday utca 4
Tel *(1) 219 06 96*   **Closed** *Mon & Tue; lunch Wed–Sun*
One of only three Michelin-starred restaurants in Budapest; here, if your pocket can stretch to it, you'll be treated to an unforgettable array of colour, flavour and texture combinations.

Fausto's
Italian   **Map** 2 F5
Dohány utca 3
Tel *(1) 589 18 13*   **Closed** *Sun*
Gorgeously understated restaurant that remains the best Italian option in Budapest; on Wednesdays and Thursdays there's an oyster menu.

Klassz
International   **Map** 2 E4
Andrássy utca 41
As much wine bar as restaurant, this small but striking place offers an accomplished menu. They don't take bookings, therefore do not list a telephone number.

Fillet steak with sweet roasted garlic and wild mushrooms at Menza

Snacking at pavement tables at the Eco Cafe

Rézkakas Bisztró
Hungarian   Map 2 D5
Sas utca 8
Tel *(1) 318 00 38*
The "Golden Cockerel" is a smart-looking establishment offering beautifully crafted classic Hungarian dishes, and the live music is recommended.

Further Afield

Briós kávézó
Café   Map 2 D2
Pozsonyi út 16
Tel *(1) 789 61 10*
Family-friendly neighbourhood café serving super breakfasts including American pancakes and filled croissants.

Eco Cafe
Café   Map 2 F3
Andrássy út 68
Cheery bio café and bakery serving up a selection of fresh sandwiches, cakes and salads in a vaguely countrified interior.

Rétes Büfé
Café
Normafa, Eötvös utca 50
A hut at the top of the Buda Hills where you can choose from a delectable range of pastries to munch on alongside your coffee.

Bagolyvár Étterem
Hungarian
Gundel Károly út 4
Tel *(1) 468 31 10*
The little sister of the famous Gundel restaurant *(see right)*, the enchanting "Owl Castle" offers homely Hungarian cooking at more affordable prices.

Kéhli Vendéglő
Hungarian
Mókus utca 22
Tel *(1) 368 06 13*

Standards at this delightful inn have not dropped since the great Hungarian food writer Gyula Krudy ate here over a century ago.

Kerék Vendéglő
Hungarian
Bécsi út 103
Tel *(1) 250 42 61*
Another landmark restaurant up in Obuda: the pretty garden is a lovely place to dine on the likes of venison stew.

New York Kávéház
Café   Map 2 F5
Erzsébet körút 9–11
Tel *(1) 886 61 11*
Another of Budapest's great literary cafes of yesteryear, though these days it's even more exclusive, and very pricey.

DK Choice

Bock Bisztró
Modern Hungarian   Map 2 F5
Erzsébet körút 43–49
Tel *(1) 321 03 40*
Named after the eponymous Hungarian vintner, Bock is one classy establishment, from the elegant cork-filled glass tables to the beautifully crafted food; well-thought-out tapas dishes complement exciting renditions of rich Hungarian fare like veal paprika. The wine list is one of the finest in Budapest.

Csalogány utca 26
Modern Hungarian   Map 1 B3
Csalogány utca 26
Tel *(1) 201 78 92*   **Closed** *Tue & Sat*
Distinguished restaurant/café with a modern, bright and breezy interior. Excellent poultry, fish and meat dishes grilled on lava stones for a real burst of flavour. Closes from 3pm to 7pm.

Gundel Étterem
Hungarian
Állatkerti körút 4
Tel *(1) 468 40 40*
Budapest's most famous restaurant offers innovative Hungarian and international cuisine in posh surrounds, and people flock here for their Sunday brunch.

La Perle Noire
International
Andrássy út 111
Tel *(1) 462 21 89*
Inventive, French-inspired gourmet restaurant located inside the smart Mamaison Andrássy Hotel. It offers an unsurpassable wine list.

Robinson
International
Városligeti Tó
Tel *(1) 663 68 71*
In an unbeatable location on the lake: the outdoor terrace is a wonderful spot to indulge in some exotic seafood dishes.

DK Choice

Rosenstein
Hungarian
Mosonyi utca 3
Tel *(1) 333 34 92*
In an area near Keleti station not known for fine dining, this is a true standout; an inviting, family-run establishment offering its guests a sophisticated menu, with plates such as wild boar ragout with forest mushrooms, as well as some Jewish favourites. The wine list is similarly of the highest order.

Zeller Bistro
Modern Hungarian
Izabella utca 38
Tel *(1) 651 08 80*   **Closed** *Sun & Mon*
Small but utterly charming restaurant serving outstanding nouvelle cuisine, and you won't find better service anywhere in the city. It closes between 3pm and 6pm.

Around Budapest

ESZTERGOM: Csülök Csárda
Hungarian   Road Map C3
Batthyány utca 9
Tel *(33) 412 420*
The cosy "Knuckle Inn" serves, unsurprisingly, a range of pork knuckle dishes, as well as other traditional and hearty fare such as smoked ox tongue.

For more information on types of restaurants *see pp270–71*

Fine Hungarian wines strikingly showcased at La Mareda

ESZTERGOM:
Központi Kávéház 🕸
Café   Road Map C3
Vörösmarty utca 2
Tel *(33) 52 05 70*
Glitzy Art Nouveau patisserie-cum-chocolatier with an irresistible array of coffees and cakes; sit down or take away.

ESZTERGOM: Primás Pince 🕸🕸
Hungarian   Road Map C3
Szent István tér 4
Tel *(33) 54 19 65*   **Closed** *Sun eve*
Live music and classic Hungarian cuisine in the castle cellars: no wonder visitors love this place.

GÖDÖLLŐ: Galeria 🕸
International   Road Map D3
Szabadság tér 8
Tel *(28) 41 86 91*
A slight lack of elegance is compensated for by terrific value for money and bags of charm in this unfussy pension restaurant.

RÁCKEVE: Savoyai 🕸🕸
Hungarian   Road Map C4
Kossuth utca 95
Tel *(24) 42 41 89*
Gorgeous vaulted cellar restaurant in the sumptuous Savoy Castle, where the wine is as well regarded as the food.

SZENTENDRE: Palapa 🕸
Mexican   Road Map D3
Dumsta Jenő utca 14a
Tel *(26) 30 24 18*
Vibrant, colourful restaurant/bar with pile-it-high Tex-Mex grub, fancy cocktails and live music.

SZENTENDRE:
Aranysárkány 🕸🕸🕸
Modern Hungarian Road Map D3
Alkotmány utca 1a
Tel *(26) 30 14 79*

The long-established "Golden Dragon" is a smart, upscale establishment offering good game dishes as well as other traditional meats: look for goose, venison and pigeon on its accomplished menu.

DK Choice

SZENTENDRE: Mjam 🕸🕸
International   Road Map D3
Városház tér 2
Tel *(70) 440 37 00*   **Closed** *Mon*
The Danube Bend's standout restaurant offers an innovative fusion menu of South American, Asian and Caribbean cuisine, resulting in mouthwatering dishes like Curaçao burger, fish sausage and tempura; all dishes are matched to one of the excellent wines which have been carefully sourced from both Hungary and abroad. A coffee and croissant breakfast is another enticing possibility.

VÁC: Remete Pince 🕸
Hungarian   Road Map D3
Fürdő lépcső utca 16
Tel *(27) 30 21 99*
Intimate brick-vaulted cellar with candle-topped tables and wrought-iron chairs, which makes this a lovely, relaxing spot to spend a long evening.

VISEGRÁD: Don Vito 🕸
Pizzeria   Road Map C3
Fő utca 83
Tel *(20) 373 69 41*
The Godfather would surely have approved of this enjoyable joint, whose stone-baked pizzas are superb. It's a decent spot for a refreshing pint, too.

VISEGRÁD: Renaissance 🕸🕸
Hungarian   Road Map C3
Fő utca 11
Tel *(26) 39 80 81*
Medieval-themed, meat-heavy restaurant hammed up for tourists; you can even wear a cardboard crown if you wish.

Northern Transdanubia

BÜK: Bajor 🕸
Bavarian   Road Map A3
Gyurácz utca 6A
Tel *(94) 35 83 24*
A fine mix of Hungarian and German cuisine in this fabulous pension; a plate of gut-busting home-made sausages and a cool, crisp Bavarian beer will hit the spot.

GYŐR: Belgian Beer Café 🕸🕸
Belgian   Road Map B3
Árpád utca 34
Tel *(96) 88 94 60*
Settle down at one of the long wooden tables in this perennially popular restaurant and feast on *moules frites* (mussels and chips) with some delicious Belgian beer.

GYŐR: Komédiás 🕸🕸
Modern Hungarian Road Map B3
Czuczor Gergely utca 30
Tel *(96) 52 72 17*
Understatedly cool cellar restaurant serving an appealing menu of game, grilled meats and stews, plus better-than-average vegetarian options.

GYŐR: La Maréda 🕸🕸
Modern Hungarian Road Map B3
Apáca utca 4
Tel *(96) 51 09 80*
Great-looking restaurant dating from the early 17th century decorated with stucco reliefs; the food doesn't disappoint either.

GYŐR: Fonte 🕸🕸🕸
Modern Hungarian Road Map B3
Kisfaludy utca 38
Tel *(96) 51 38 10*   **Closed** *Sat & Sun*
As classy as the hotel in which it is housed, Fonte offers some enticing pork- and goose-based dishes, as well as a marvellous wine list.

GYŐR: Schweizerhof 🕸🕸🕸
Modern Hungarian Road Map B3
Sarkantyú köz 11–13
Tel *(96) 51 23 58*
Along with Fonte, this is the pick of Győr's restaurants; restrained but refined decor, and wonderfully accomplished food.

The Renaissance restaurant in Visegrád, ready for round-table revelries

KŐSZEG: Portré Panzió
Café   Road Map A3
Fő tér 7
Tel *(94) 36 31 70*
Bar, bistro and café all in one, this is a super little place to stop off for a light bite or some liquid refreshment.

KŐSZEG: Taverna Flórián
Italian   Road Map A3
Várkör utca 59
Tel *(94) 56 30 72*   **Closed** *Mon*
Splendid, bright-red house accommodating a ground-floor restaurant, dining and wine cellars and street café – take your pick.

LAKE VELENCE: Nádas Étterem
Hungarian   Road Map C4
Agárd, Balatoni út 60
Tel *(22) 37 00 06*
It may be the quintessential tourist restaurant, but that doesn't make it any less enjoyable, and the food is surprisingly good.

LAKE VELENCE: Ponty
Seafood   Road Map C4
Gárdony, Szabadság utca 9
Tel *(22) 35 54 54*
Dedicated fish restaurant with heaps of the stuff from the lake, the best of which is the delicious *fogas* (pike-perch), typically rolled in paprika and fried.

SOPRON: Fórum Pizzeria
Pizzeria   Road Map A3
Szent György utca 3
Tel *(99) 34 02 31*
Waiters scuttle around furiously delivering thin-crust pizzas, spaghetti and lasagne in this most enjoyable restaurant.

DK Choice

SOPRON: Erhardt
Hungarian   Road Map A3
Balfi utca 10
Tel *(99) 50 67 11*
A beautiful Baroque interior sets the scene for food and wine of distinction, and Erhardt certainly rates as one of the finest restaurants in northern Hungary. The food combinations – typically with a French or Italian influence – are wonderful, like rabbit leg wrapped in prosciutto with pea risotto, and mangalica pork with garlicky French beans. Serious wine lovers should make a beeline for the cellar.

SOPRON: Vadászkürt Vendéglő
International   Road Map A3
Udvarnoki utca 6
Tel *(99) 31 43 85*
From the polished parquet floors and convivial garden terrace to dishes such as pheasant and quail egg soup, everything about this place exudes class.

SOPRON: Wollner
International   Road Map A3
Templom utca 20
Tel *(99) 52 44 00*   **Closed** *Sun & Mon*
The accent is on refined international cuisine at this glittering cellar restaurant; hence dishes such as roast duck with sour beetroot sauce and polenta.

SÜMEG: Várcsárda
Hungarian   Road Map B4
Kisfaludy kert
Tel *(87) 35 09 24*

Despite catering mainly to the busloads of visitors that arrive here to nose around the castle, the wooden-beamed Castle Inn offers an extensive menu at attractive prices.

SZÉKESFEHÉRVAR: Kiskulacs Vendéglő
Hungarian   Road Map C4
Budai út 26
Tel *(22) 50 29 20*
If steak is your thing, look no further than this local favourite, which is a great place to enjoy a long, lingering Hungarian meal.

SZOMBATHELY: Öreg Sam Sörkert
Hungarian   Road Map A3
Gagarin út 14   **Closed** *Sun*
Large, frequently rammed beerhall, where the food and drink has a strong German slant; the pretty garden terrace is great for supping in too.

SZOMBATHELY: Hotel Wagner
Modern Hungarian   Road Map A3
Kossuth Lajos utca 15
Tel *(94) 32 22 08*
Although renowned for its extensive collection of wines, the food at the sophisticated Wagner hotel lives right up to the same standards.

TATA: La Casa
Seafood   Road Map C3
Országgyűlés tér 3
Tel *(70) 252 28 84*
It's unusual to find a decent fish restaurant in this part of the country, but this is certainly one; expect the likes of barbecued crabs and grilled swordfish.

Traditional inn-style signage and gateway at Erhardt in Sopron

For more information on types of restaurants *see pp270–71*

Southern Transdanubia

BADACSONY: Borbarátok 🅗🅛🅟
Hungarian   Road Map B4
Római út 88
Tel *(87) 47 10 00*
Opt to dine in the attractive restaurant, cellar, gallery or garden of this superb winery; the menu is skewed towards fish, with nicely thought-out dishes like pike-perch with crab penne.

BADACSONY: Kisfaludy Ház 🅛🅟
Hungarian   Road Map B4
Kisfaludy Sándor utca 28
Tel *(87) 43 10 16*
Beautifully situated amid lush vineyards in hills high above the lake, this lovely wooden house has some fine game dishes to complement a stellar wine list.

BALATONFÜRED: Arany Csillag 🅛
Pizzeria   Road Map B4
Zsigmond utca 1
Tel *(87) 48 21 16*
Warm and buzzy pizzeria that can conjure up some two dozen types of pizza, including stuffed ones, as well as fresh pasta and crisp salads.

BALATONFÜRED: Karolina Kávéház 🅛
Café   Road Map B4
Zákonyi sétány 4
Tel *(87) 58 30 98*
Effortlessly cool café and cocktail bar with soft lighting, fabulous furniture and cracking cakes and coffee.

BALATONFÜRED: Blaha Lujza 🅛🅟
Hungarian   Road Map B4
Blaha Lujza utca 4
Tel *(87) 58 12 10*
In the hotel of the same name, this quietly refined spot is the most appealing option in town; well-crafted Hungarian standards and impeccable service.

BALATONFÜRED: Borcsa 🅛🅟
Seafood   Road Map B4
Tagore sétány
Tel *(87) 58 00 70*
Large and convivial lakeside terrace serving up substantial plates of grilled meat and fish dishes to a packed house.

HÉVÍZ: Magyar Csárda 🅛
Hungarian   Road Map B4
Tavirózsa utca 2
Tel *(83) 34 32 71*
Archetypal Hungarian *csárda*, with solid, meat-heavy dishes and a regular band of Gypsy musicians to keep things lively.

HÉVÍZ: Tavirózsa 🅛
Hungarian   Road Map B4
Tavirózsa út 4
A few paces along from Magyar Csárda *(above)*, this is possibly a little more polished and with superior vegetarian offerings.

KESZTHELY: Bacchus 🅛🅟
Modern Hungarian   Road Map B4
Erzsébet királyné utca 18
Tel *(83) 51 04 50*
Lake fish takes pride of place on the menu at Bacchus, whose handsome interior features dark wooden beams and tables and chairs crafted from old wine presses.

KESZTHELY: Lakoma 🅛🅟
International   Road Map B4
Balaton utca 9
Tel *(83) 31 31 29*
If the stew of cock's testicles doesn't appeal, then there's plenty more on the menu to satisfy in this charmingly staffed restaurant.

KESZTHELY: Tompos 🅛🅟
Modern Hungarian   Road Map B4
Pázmány utca 56
Tel *(30) 902 83 45*
A refreshingly colourful and contemporary restaurant with a menu as long as your arm; a typical standout dish could be grilled goose liver with sour cherry ragout.

PÉCS: Az Elefántos 🅛
Café   Road Map C5
Jókai tér 6
Tel *(72) 21 60 55*
Part pizzeria, part café, "At the Elephant" is a fun place to stop off for a quick coffee, or to perhaps linger a while longer over something more substantial.

PÉCS: Jókai Bisztró 🅛🅟
Modern Hungarian   Road Map C5
Jókai tér 6
Tel *(20) 360 73 37*
Bright, colourful and crisp-looking restaurant offering highly appealing dishes like roasted red pepper risotto with mangalica pork, and melon salad with prawns and raspberry vinaigrette.

PÉCS: Tüke Borház 🅛🅟
International   Road Map C5
Böckh János utca 39
Tel *(20) 317 81 78*   **Closed** *Mon–Wed, Sun eve*
It's worth the steep uphill walk for both the views and the utterly delicious food, such as oven-roasted pork knuckle, red tuna steak and Argentine sirloin.

PÉCS: Zsolnay 🅛🅟
Modern Hungarian   Road Map C5
Zsolnay Vilmos utca 37
Tel *(72) 22 24 86*   **Closed** *Mon, Sun eve*
Another restaurant that's done much to raise the standard of cuisine in Pécs, Zsolnay offers a highly creditable menu of inventive modern Hungarian food.

SIÓFOK: Amigó Étterem 🅛
Pizzeria   Road Map C4
Fő utca 99
Tel *(84) 31 09 23*
If you like your food hot, then check out the "sharpfood" menu at this modern eatery whose menu extends beyond the two dozen or so pizzas on offer.

Art Nouveau prints soften the modern styling at Karolina Kávéház, Balatonfüred

A nod to the baronial banqueting hall at traditional Piroska Csárda, Siófok

SIÓFOK: Fogas
Seafood   Road Map C4
Fő utca 184
Tel *(84) 31 14 05*
Housed in the town's former post office, the "Perch" does exactly what it says on the tin; fabulously tasty pike-perch plucked straight from the lake.

SIÓFOK:
Magyar Halászcsárda
Seafood   Road Map C4
Petőfi sétány 3
Tel *(84) 50 67 86*
The most agreeable of the many lakeside restaurants, a large, two-floored establishment serving heaps of fishy treats.

SIÓFOK: Piroska Csárda
Hungarian   Road Map C4
Zamárdi út 37
Tel *(84) 35 06 83*
Treat yourself to a steaming bowl of goulash in this cheery old-style csárda with tables set around a vast open hearth and folk art adorning the walls.

TIHANY: Echo Étterem
Modern Hungarian   Road Map B4
Viszhang domb 23
Tel *(30) 896 62 96*
Soak up magnificent lake views from the terrace of this funky café-cum-restaurant; clever interpretations of Hungarian standards, such as goose liver on sweet milk loaf with caramelized apples, are to the fore here.

TIHANY: Ferenc Pince
Hungarian   Road Map B4
Cser-hegy 9
Tel *(87) 44 85 75*   **Closed** *Tue*
Pleasantly secluded restaurant and winery 1 km (half a mile) south of the village, well worth the trek for its grilled and roast meat dishes, and wine of course.

TIHANY: Pál Csárda
Hungarian   Road Map B4
Viszhang utca 19
Tel *(87) 44 86 05*
A pretty vine-shaded terrace, a warm buzz and some great-value daily set menus make this one of the more enticing possibilities in the village.

DK Choice

VESZPRÉM: Oliva
International   Road Map B4
Buhim utca 14
Tel *(88) 40 38 75*
It's unusual to find a restaurant outside Budapest where the food combinations are so varied, but the chef at Oliva consistently manages to come up with some ingeniously thought-out dishes like crispy breaded crab tails with chilli jam. The best part about Oliva, however, is the grill garden where, in summer, there are regular barbecues accompanied by live jazz.

VESZPRÉM: Villa Medici
International   Road Map B4
Kittenberger Kálmán utca 11
Tel *(88) 59 00 70*
Posh and fantastically pricey restaurant, but worth every penny; guinea fowl consommé with porcini-stuffed pasta is typical of the fine dining menu.

VILLÁNY: Oportó Panzió
Modern Hungarian   Road Map C6
Baross Gábor utca 33
Tel *(72) 49 25 82*
A foodie and wine-lover's treat; beautifully presented food created to complement the outstanding wine from the cellar. The imperial-style decor, meanwhile, is stunning.

Northern Highlands

EGER: Görög kávézó
Café   Road Map E3
Dobó utca 22
Tel *(36) 41 55 35*   **Closed** *evenings*
It's not easy finding good espresso in Hungary, but you can here. Whilst you're at it, try one of the calorific cakes too.

EGER: Il Padrino Pizza Club
Pizzeria   Road Map E3
Fazola Henrik utca 1
Tel *(36) 78 60 40*
Italian visitors love this place, that's how good it is; the smoked meat pizzas are particularly worth devouring.

EGER:
Fehérszarvas Vadásztanya
Hungarian   Road Map E3
Klapka György utca 8
Tel *(36) 41 11 29*
As the rows of stuffed (animal) heads would suggest, game is very much the theme here at the "White Deer Hunter's Farm" restaurant. Folklore shows, too.

DK Choice

EGER: Macok Bisztró
International   Road Map E3
Tinódi Sebestyén tér 4
Tel *(36) 51 61 80*   **Closed** *Sun eve*
The striking bistro in the Imola hotel bears all the hallmarks of a top-class restaurant – neatly arranged tables with crisp white tablecloths beckon. Foie gras brûlée, smoked trout mousse and carp tempura give you some idea of what to expect; the four- or six-course tasting menus are flavour sensations. The adjoining St Andrea wine bar is also worth a visit.

For more information on types of restaurants see pp270–71

EGER: Szantofer Vendéglő 🅗🅛🅕🅗🅛🅕
Modern Hungarian   Road Map E3
Bródy Sándor utca 3
Tel *(36) 51 72 98*
Classic Hungarian cuisine – pork knuckle, paprika, veal stew and the like – but jazzed up for modern tastes.

GYÖNGYÖS:
Kékes Étterem 🅗🅛🅕🅗🅛🅕
International   Road Map D3
Fő tér 7
Tel *(37) 50 01 25*
Superb Secessionist house with beautifully arranged tables upon which diners can feast on dishes such as braised veal with roasted peaches and almond potatoes.

HOLLÓKŐ:
Muskátli Vendéglő 🅗🅛🅕
Hungarian   Road Map D2
Kossuth út 61
Tel *(32) 37 92 62*   **Closed** *Mon & Tue*
A cutesy little coffee shop in one of the village's UNESCO-protected houses that also rustles up simple, peasant-style dishes. Closed in the evenings.

LILLAFÜRED:
Mátyás Étterem 🅗🅛🅕🅗🅛🅕
Hungarian   Road Map E2
Erzsébet sétány 1
Tel *(46) 33 14 11*
You can actually take your pick from several good restaurants inside the Palota Hotel, though the Renaissance-inspired Mátyás just about wins out.

MISKOLC: Zip's Brewhouse 🅗🅛🅕
International   Road Map E2
Arany János tér 1
Tel *(46) 95 21 92*
There's more to this ace micro-brewery than beer; salivate over foie gras terrine with mango, or duck breast gnocchi in a wild mushroom sauce. Closed 3–6pm.

MISKOLC: Café du Boucher 🅗🅛🅕🅗🅛🅕
Belgian   Road Map E2
Görgey Artúr utca 42
Tel *(46) 43 23 20*
A little pricey but good, offering generously portioned, Belgian-accented food that complements the enticing line-up of draught beers to perfection.

PARÁDFÜRDŐ:
Erzsébet Park Hotel 🅗🅛🅕🅗🅛🅕
Modern Hungarian   Road Map E3
Kossuth út 372
Tel *(36) 44 40 44*
Formal without being overly stuffy, the high-class restaurant in the Park is worth making a stop for, as much for the ambience and parkland vistas as the food itself.

SÁROSPATAK:
V. András Étterem 🅗🅛🅕🅗🅛🅕
Hungarian   Road Map F2
Béla király tér 3
Tel *(47) 31 24 15*
Mellow place with model aeroplanes and airships dangling from the ceiling – not that any distractions are needed from the exquisite menu, featuring the likes of creamy veal stew with mushrooms.

SÁROSPATAK:
Vár Vendéglő 🅗🅛🅕🅗🅛🅕
Modern Hungarian   Road Map F2
Árpád utca 35
Tel *(47) 31 13 70*
The restaurant of the pension of the same name, this is a serene little spot with a fantastic wooden-roofed terrace and some delicious interpretations of classic Hungarian dishes.

TOKAJ: Gróf Degenfeld 🅗🅛🅕🅗🅛🅕
Modern Hungarian   Road Map F2
Tarcal, Terézia kert 9
Tel *(47) 58 04 00*

Goulash, gingham and red geraniums at the quintessentially rustic Hortobágyi Csárda

The short but superb menu in the posh Degenfeld castle hotel offers mouthwatering dishes like breaded goose liver with spring onion mash and fried apples.

The Great Plain

BAJA: Sobri Halászcsárda 🅗🅛🅕🅗🅛🅕
Seafood   Road Map C5
Petőfi-sziget, Március 15, sétány 10
Tel *(79) 42 06 54*
Founded by champion Danube *halászé* (fisherman) Jószef "Sobri" Farkas, this striking white villa is the place to head to in town for all things fishy.

BAJA: Véndió Étterem 🅗🅛🅕🅗🅛🅕
Seafood   Road Map C5
Petőfi-sziget, Március 15, sétány 1
Tel *(79) 42 47 09*
Not quite in the same league as Sobri (above), but very accomplished all the same, and with a sunny, summery terrace overlooking the water.

BUGAC: Karikás Csárda 🅗🅛🅕
Hungarian   Road Map D4
Nagybugac 135
Tel *(76) 57 51 12*
People flock to this converted stables at the entrance to the park for Puszta specialities like *bogrács gulyás*, a stew cooked slowly over an open fire.

DEBRECEN: Flaska Vendéglő 🅗🅛🅕
Hungarian   Road Map F3
Miklós utca 4
Tel *(52) 41 45 82*
The countrified, peasant-style decor sets the scene for regional speciality dishes, notably Palóc soup and Hortobágy pancakes.

Dine in grandeur at Gróf Degenfeld, located in Degenfeld castle, Tokaj

DEBRECEN:
Bohem Belgian Beer Café 🏷️🏷️
Belgian   Road Map F3
Piac utca 29
Tel *(52) 53 63 73*
Pub-style place where you can tuck into Belgian standards like mussels and boudin sausages, all washed down with Leffe ale.

DEBRECEN:
Csokonai Étterem 🏷️🏷️
Modern Hungarian   Road Map F3
Kossuth utca 21
Tel *(52) 41 08 02*
Sweet cellar restaurant with wall lamps and candle-topped tables that's perfect for a romantic dalliance; trout fillet with Cognac sauce is a typical offering.

DEBRECEN: IKON 🏷️🏷️
Modern Hungarian   Road Map F3
Piac utca 23
Tel *(30) 555 77 66*   **Closed** *Mon, Sun eve*
One of the new breed of modern Hungarian ventures, IKON specializes in imaginative gastronomic fare like rabbit *paprikás* and duck breast with cabbage ravioli.

GYULA: Kisködmön 🏷️
Hungarian   Road Map F4
Városház utca 15
Tel *(66) 46 39 34*
The wall-to-wall folksy interior is a little over the top, as are the peasant-attired waitresses, but there's no denying the quality of the food and the welcome here.

HAJDÚSZOBOSZLÓ:
Kemencés Csárda 🏷️
Modern Hungarian   Road Map F3
Daru zug 1
Tel *(52) 36 22 21*
Generous portions of smoked pork knuckle, creamed veg stews and the like are to be found at this rustically styled inn where you're almost certainly guaranteed some live music, too.

HORTOBÁGY: Hortobágyi Csárda 🏷️
Hungarian   Road Map F3
Petőfi tér
Tel *(76) 57 51 12*
Tourist trappings aside, this venerable establishment is worth heading to for local treats like guinea-fowl soup and kettle-cooked goulash.

KECSKEMÉT: Géniusz 🏷️🏷️
French   Road Map D4
Kisfaludy utca 5
Tel *(76) 49 76 68*
The food here manifests a discernible French twist (stuffed chicken breast with Camembert),

Modern elegance warmed by soft lighting at Tiszavirág in Szeged

while the restaurant itself looks fabulous, particularly the mosaic-tiled flooring.

KECSKEMÉT:
Kecskeméti Csárda 🏷️🏷️
Hungarian   Road Map D4
Kölcsey utca 7
Tel *(76) 48 86 86*   **Closed** *Sun eve*
A classic Hungarian *csárda*, with blue-dyed tablecloths, painted ceramics and strings of paprika lining the walls; the house speciality, knuckle of mangalica pork, is not to be missed.

KISKUNFÉLEGYHÁZA:
Kulacs Vendéglő 🏷️
Seafood   Road Map D4
Széchenyi István utca 39
Tel *(76) 43 13 86*
Very reasonably priced menu of largely steak and fish, with a dinky terrace for warm weather. There's often live music.

NYÍRBÁTOR: Hódi 🏷️🏷️
International   Road Map G3
Báthori István utca 11
Tel *(42) 28 10 12*
Housed in a stunning Baroque hotel, the food here is high-end modern European, though there's also plenty of choice if you prefer a local dish.

NYÍREGYHÁZA: Svájci Lak 🏷️🏷️
Modern Hungarian   Road Map F3
Sóstógyógyfürdő, Sóstói út 75
Tel *(42) 41 44 44*
Writer Gyula Krudy and actress Lujza Blaha would have once dined here at the "Swiss Cottage", and very classy it is, too; the lake fish is exceptional.

SZEGED: Alabárdos 🏷️🏷️
International   Road Map E5
Oskola utca 13
Tel *(62) 42 09 14*

Alabárdos incorporates both a smart formal section where you can dine on garlic goose liver, and an adjoining lounge-like area for pizzas and suchlike.

SZEGED:
Kiskörössy Halászcsárda 🏷️🏷️
Seafood   Road Map E5
Felső Tisza-part 336
Tel *(62) 55 58 86*
On the banks of the Tisza, this was a favoured haunt of England's Prince of Wales (the future King Edward VII) in the 1890s. It's still going strong, and you'll not find a better fish menu for miles around.

DK Choice

SZEGED: Tiszavirág 🏷️🏷️
International   Road Map E5
Hajnóczy utca 1/b
Tel *(62) 55 48 88*   **Closed** *Sun, Mon lunch*
Szeged's finest hotel has an equally high-class restaurant, which looks fantastic and is made all the more enjoyable by the open kitchen. To keep things fresh, the menu changes weekly, but expect wonderfully concocted dishes like rack of lamb with fried buckwheat and yam purée. There's also a bar and café.

TISZAFÜRED:
Molnár Vendéglő 🏷️🏷️
Seafood   Road Map E3
Húszöles út 31
Tel *(59) 35 27 05*
Located by the Tisza, it's entirely appropriate that Molnár serves up a welter of fish dishes, from catfish and carp to pike-perch; try the *halpaprikás* (fish in paprika sauce).

SHOPPING IN HUNGARY

Some people complain that the explosion of shopping malls has taken much of the charm out of shopping in Hungary, yet visitors with a little patience and the right inside knowledge can still find some of the most wonderful, unique shops in Europe. The city centres bustle with small, family-owned shops selling inimitable trinkets, crafts and luxuries – foie gras is one of the nation's biggest exports. Then there are the flea markets, packed with the bizarre and the beautiful, the useful and the quirky. Souvenir hunters are spoiled for choice too. Those looking for something typically Hungarian could buy Zsolnay porcelain, handmade textiles from the Folkart shops, vintage Tokaji wine, paprika or spicy Debreceni sausages. Horse-lovers will find the craft shops in the towns of the Great Plain a delight, where saddles, riding boots, crops and hats are of the highest standard and great value.

Opening Times

Most small shops usually open at 9am and close at 7pm; some stay open later, until 9pm or 10pm, especially in modern, purpose-built shopping centres. Most shops open all day on Saturday, and an increasing number of outlets also open their doors on Sundays. Markets are set up seven days a week. Large supermarkets also open seven days a week, until at least 8pm. Some, usually smaller shops, open on public holidays, with the exception of Christmas Day and New Year's Day. Many small kiosks selling bus tickets, alcohol, groceries and household essentials are open 24 hours a day.

Dried paprika and handmade wicker baskets in the market in Tihany

Payment

Most shops now accept credit and debit cards, though producing one from your wallet may elicit groans from the vendor. If you are using a debit card, you may be asked for further means of identification, so carry your passport with you while shopping.

Visitors are advised to have a fair amount of cash on them at all times, however, as some smaller shops will simply refuse to take payment with a card.

VAT and Tax-Free Shopping

The price of all goods in Hungary includes a Value Added Tax (ÁFA) of 27 per cent. With the exception of works of art and antiques, it is possible for non-EU residents to claim back the ÁFA on any purchase costing more than 45,000 forints (€175) when leaving the country.

If you wish to reclaim the tax, you must make sure when purchasing the item that the shop will be able to give you a special ÁFA refund receipt. Only those shops geared to selling to foreign tourists tend to keep the necessary forms to hand. You then have to present the paperwork and the goods, together with your passport, at a customs post within 90 days of purchase in order to receive customs certification for your claim form. To apply for the refund, your sales receipt and currency exchange or credit card receipt are also required. The money can then be claimed within 183 days of returning home. Payment is usually made direct to a bank account, minus a small service charge.

Department Stores and Shopping Malls

There are a number of department stores in Hungary, many of which are housed in spectacular old buildings. Besides the enormous shopping centres in Budapest, Debrecen, Pécs and Szeged all have large shopping centres,

Westend City Center shopping mall in Budapest

Typical goods for sale at the Central Market Hall in Budapest

called *plazas*, within walking distance of the city centre. Open until late, and with a vast variety of food outlets, as well as multi-screen cinemas, these all-purpose malls are very popular. In all, there are more than 110 plazas in towns around the country. There are also 115 popular Tesco hypermarkets, selling a wide range of food and non-food items. With a few exceptions, however, they are on the outskirts of cities, and difficult to reach without a car.

Markets

Markets of all sorts are an essential part of everyday life all over Hungary. Apart from good, fresh produce, they offer a delightfully traditional shopping experience to visitors. Many cities also organize open-air craft and folk art markets. The best is in Hollókő and, though some of the wares are kitsch by most standards, prices are good and souvenir ideas limitless. Debrecen city council also organizes an excellent craft fair during August in Kossuth tér.

Traditional folk crafts in a Szentendre market

Handicrafts and Folk art

Hungary has a long tradition of producing high-quality porcelain and pottery, with the Herend and Zsolnay names carrying a worldwide reputation. Herend porcelain is famous for its decorative and highly colourful designs, and the factory shop in the small town of Herend *(see p207)*, north of Lake Balaton, stocks a small selection of recent productions. The Zsolnay porcelain factory in Pécs *(see p190)* also has a shop. Bright colours are also characteristic of Ajka crystal, which has been recognized as Hungary's finest for more than 150 years. It is made in the small town of Ajka, close to Veszprém. There are two stores selling Ajka crystal in the village itself, and many more throughout Hungary.

For best examples of the finest Hungarian embroidery (found on dresses, tablecloths, place mats and cushion covers), the village museum of Hollókő is a great outlet. Prices are high, but the quality is outstanding. Lower-priced examples can be found in the many stalls and small shops that line the busy pedestrian streets of

Szentendre. Other local goods worth looking out for include carpets (especially rugs with plain, naive designs), and wooden toys (especially toy soldiers in Habsburg-era uniforms). Hungary is also renowned for its wonderful, handmade teddy bears, which although expensive make superb presents.

Delicacies

Hungary exports more foie gras than any other country in the world with the exception of France. It is available from delicatessens all over the country, and prices are far lower than abroad. Look out for the distinctive black and gold labels and packaging of the Rex Ciborum brand: a guarantee of quality.

Paprika – as a condiment – can be bought in all colours, shapes, varieties and degrees of heat in Hungary. Alternatively there are many products containing paprika as an ingredient, from paprika pastes to spicy Hungarian salamis or sausages (try *gyulai kolbász* or Debreceni, for example). Most cheeses are mild; the pungent Pálpusztai is a glorious exception, if something of a liability in one's luggage. Markets all over the country will also sell their own regional specialities.

Paste made from Hungarian paprika

Equestrian Goods

Given the pedigree of its horsemen, such as the famous Puszta Fivers *(see p239)*, it comes as no surprise to discover that Hungary is a great place to purchase tack. Finely crafted saddles made from the best leather, boots, bridles, crops and even polo mallets are made to the highest specifications at a great number of workshops throughout the country. The best are those from the Great Plain – Hungary's pre-eminent equestrian region – and there is no shortage of excellent sporting goods shops in Debrecen, Hortobágy and Szeged.

ENTERTAINMENT IN HUNGARY

The range of cultural events and entertainment in Hungary is wide and richly varied. It is a vibrant country where people have always known how to have a good time, and both mainstream and more eclectic forms of entertainment have always been encouraged. Music festivals – from opera in Miskolc, Baroque music in Sopron and jazz in Debrecen – feature regularly on the international arts calendar. Yet even the smallest Hungarian town usually has its own orchestra, dance company and theatre, while during the summer central squares and plazas are abuzz with outdoor concerts, plays and other artistic happenings. For entertainment in Budapest see pp120–21.

Music, Opera, Dance and Cinema

While Budapest is home to one of Europe's finest opera houses, it does not hold a monopoly on Hungarian opera and music. In **Miskolc**, for example, the sublime **Grand National Theatre** often hosts excellent operatic performances. During the **Miskolc Opera Festival**, held over two weeks in June, some of the world's best performers can be seen here.

Pécs also has a rich cultural heritage. The city has both opera and ballet companies of world renown, performing at the **National Theatre**, usually accompanied by the Pannon Philharmonic Orchestra. Some of the finest choirs in Hungary gather here to celebrate the grape harvest in autumn with ten days of wine and song. Veszprém, likewise, is known as a musical city, and small-scale chamber concerts in the Castle District courtyard are a highlight of all summer visits here. For details

of music festivals throughout Hungary, including the annual **Jazz Days** in Debrecen, and the **Baroque and Early Music Days** of **S**opron, see pp34–7.

Most major Hungarian cities have a multiplex cinema, usually housed within the city's shopping centre. They show a wide range of films, some in the original language. Most foreign films in Hungary are both dubbed and subtitled into Hungarian, leaving cinema-goers free to choose which version they prefer. Non-Hungarian speakers should opt for the *angol nyelvű* (English soundtrack) version. Films may even be shown in English with no subtitles at all – these are advertised as *angol nyelvű, felirat nélkül* (English language, no subtitles). The cinemas also show Hungarian films, both the latest releases and repertory films from a time of cinematic glory, when Miklós Jancsó and István Szabó received international awards as directors.

Palace Disco, a lively nightspot outside Siófok

Nightlife

While for nightlife nowhere in Hungary compares to Budapest, there are plenty of nightspots in the regions to keep disco dancers and night owls happy. The university cities of Szeged, Miskolc and Győr are among the liveliest, with a wide range of pubs, clubs and nightclubs. Győr's **Vigadó Pince Pub** has live bands most nights. Veszprém, too, gets lively in the evenings, with the **Expresszó Club** living up to its name as buzziest venue. The **Mythos Music Club** has either live acts or top international DJs at weekends. During the summer almost all of Lake Balaton's resorts thump to the universal beat of Europop. Siófok especially can be loud and really quite boisterous of an evening. The **Palace Disco Club** is one of the country's largest, though it is a 15-minute walk out of the town centre. A little more sophisticated is the north Balaton resort of Balatonfüred, where **SunCity**, a cultural and party venue in Greek-style buildings, and **Cocomo Café** on the beach attract the crowds.

A performance at the Miskolc Opera Festival, held each year in June

Casinos were once ubiquitous in Hungary, but gaming laws enacted in 2012 forced virtually all of them to close; the government intends to award only 11 new licences for the whole of the country. The same laws removed the slot machines once found in almost every Hungarian café and bar. While the dress code at the casinos still in business has largely been relaxed, visitors must purchase a token "membership" in order to enter, so take some photo ID.

Information

The best listings magazines in Hungary are published by *Pesti Est*, the famous Budapest weekly. Though published almost entirely in Hungarian, the colourful ads should be decipherable to most people. As it is published weekly in 22 Hungarian cities visitors can find local editions of *Est* distributed for free in many bars, restaurants, hotels and shops. Hotel reception desks and TourInform offices will also usually be happy to help visitors with information about concerts and nightlife.

Veszprémi Est magazine

Children

Hungarians of all ages love puppets, and most cities in the country have excellent puppet theatres. The best are those at Szeged and Kecskemét, which also has a toy museum and workshop that is very popular with children. Kids of all ages enjoy narrow-gauge and steam railways such as those at Bugac, Balaton, Nyíregyháza and Kecskemét. Horse riding is another great way of entertaining children, and you are never far from an equestrian centre in Hungary (*see p292*). Swimming pools, too, are found across the country, although children often prefer modern

Pony riding in Budapest, one of many activities for children

aquaparks such as those in Debrecen and Zalaegerszeg (*see p290*).

Spectator Sports

Football (soccer) is the most popular spectator sport in Hungary. The domestic league is highly competitive, and crowds can be large. The country's best sides include Újpest, Honvéd and Ferencváros of Budapest; Videoton Székesfehérvár; Zalaegerszeg; and Debrecen. The season runs August–December and March–June. Tickets can be purchased from stadium ticket offices on the day. Handball is also popular, and both the male and female teams are world-class. Water polo, rowing, basketball, gymnastics tournaments and international swimming competitions also attract crowds. For details of the Hungarian Formula 1 Grand Prix, see p35.

Flatwater Rowing Championship in Szeged

(*see p290*).

DIRECTORY

Theatres & Opera Houses

Miskolc Grand National Theatre (Miskolci Nemzeti Színház)
Déryné utca 1, Miskolc.
Tel (46) 51 67 35. **W** mnsz.eu

Pécs National Theatre (Pécsi Nemzeti Színház)
Színház tér 1, Pécs.
Tel (72) 51 26 60. **W** pnsz.hu

Festivals

Debrecen Jazz Days
W iranydebrecen.hu

Miskolc Opera Festival
W operafesztival.hu

Sopron Early Music Days
W filharmonia.hu

Pubs, Clubs & Discos

Cocomo Café
Zákonyi Ferenc sétány 4 (Silver Court), Balatonfüred.
Tel (70) 330 33 78.

Expresszó Club
Brusznyai Árpád utca 2, Veszprém.
Tel (20) 938 04 11.

Mythos Music Club
Szabadsag tér 1, Veszprém.

Palace Dance Club
Deák Ferenc sétány 2, Siófok.
Tel (84) 35 06 98. **W** palace.hu

SunCity
Fürdő utca 35, Balatonfüred.
Tel (70) 361 93 78.
W suncity-balaton.hu

Vigadó Pince Pub
W vigadogyor.hu

Casinos

Casino Sopron
Lackner K. utca 33/A, Sopron.
Tel (99) 51 23 50.

Las Vegas Casino
Széchenyi István tér 2, Budapest.
Tel (1) 317 60 22.

Children

Aquaticum Debrecen
Nagyerdei park 1, Debrecen.
Tel (52) 51 41 00.

AquaCity Zalaegerszeg
Fürdő sétány 2, Zalaegerszeg.
Tel (92) 59 91 01.

SPORTS AND ACTIVITIES IN HUNGARY

Hungarians adore the great outdoors, and spend a great deal of their leisure time finding new ways of enjoying nature, both in winter and summer. Most Hungarians, at some stage, partake in the national ritual that is bathing, and since virtually all towns and cities feature at least one thermal baths visitors should take the opportunity to join in. On the Great Plain, horses remain an important part of everyday life, and there are a number of equestrian centres in and around the region's larger towns. They offer riding courses at all levels, as well as putting on displays of Hungarian horsemanship.

Turista információ - Tourist information
Tourist Information Office sign

General Information

Tourinform offices are an excellent source of information on sports and outdoor activities in Hungary. Most stock special publications outlining activities in the surrounding area, and will provide addresses, telephone numbers and directions to nearby thermal bath complexes, swimming pools and equestrian centres. Two helpful brochures in a number of languages, "Spas and Wellness Packages" and "On Horseback", can be downloaded for free from Tourinform's excellent website (www.tourinform.hu).

Swimming Pools and Thermal Baths

Most Hungarians view public bathing as a birthright, and with more than 300 operating thermal bath complexes in the country, most of which have larger swimming pools attached, it is not difficult to see why. Hungarians need no excuse at all to strip off and head for a steam bath, even in the outdoors in the middle of winter. Old men playing chess in the outdoor pool at Budapest's Széchenyi baths, steam rising from the water and snow on all sides, is one of Hungary's defining sights. With the exception of the football team of the 1950s, all of Hungary's most successful and best-known athletes have been swimmers, including Alfréd Hajós, who won the first ever Olympic swimming gold medal in 1896, and after whom a swimming pool on Margaret Island, Budapest, has since been named.

It is no great surprise, then, that Hungary has made an industry out of its thermal baths. Visitors have for centuries flocked to this country from all over Europe to take to the waters, and to swim in its outdoor pools. The modern aquaparks, including the super Aquaticum complex at Debrecen, which has slides, water jets, Jacuzzis and artificial waves, make sure that children catch the swimming bug early. In summer, Lake Balaton is a popular swimming venue, and while most Balaton resorts do not restrict water access to swimmers, some parts of the lake are reserved for water sports. The water quality in Hungary is usually good. People even occasionally swim in the Danube, especially around the Danube Bend towns of Esztergom and Szentendre.

For more information on Hungary's thermal bath complexes see pp26–7.

Slides at the Aquaticum thermal baths complex in Debrecen

Boats in the marina at Balatonföldvár, Lake Balaton

Water Sports

Lake Balaton is a major water sports centre. Among the activities available here are water-skiing, windsurfing, rowing, canoeing and water polo, the last being a popular spectator sport. Ever since the Siófok Balaton Company opened its doors to paying customers in 1893, however, Hungary's favourite water sport has been sailing. In fair weather Lake Balaton can look like a floating forest of sailing boats.

Siófok is the main sailing resort, although there are also yachting centres at Szigliget, Balatonföldvár, Badacsony and Balatonlelle. All offer sailing lessons to novices, and will hire out boats of various sizes to the more experienced. Visitors wishing to lease a boat require an International Sailing Licence, or need to be able to explain (in best pidgin Hungarian) that they know what they are doing. Usually, a driving licence, passport or credit card need to be deposited with the boatyard. For information contact the **Balaton Regional Tourist Office**.

To learn how to water-ski, visitors are advised to head for Siófok or Balatonfüred or contact the **Hungarian Water Ski Federation**.

Hiking

In summer trains heading for the hills are packed with hikers. The northeast of the country is home to some superb, challenging hiking trails, and there are easier, flat trails on the Great Plain and along parts of the Danube. In all, Hungary has over 11,000 km (6,835 miles) of trails, marked with a coloured stripe according to the length of the trail (blue for a long-distance trail, yellow for a short, local trail). All the National Parks have well signposted trails.

One of the best trails for good amateur walkers is the Balaton-felvidék trail in the southern Bakony Hills. The 94-km (58-mile) blue trail starts at Pétfürdő station in Várpalota, and goes through the most spectacular part of the Balaton-felvidék before ending at the railway station in Badacsony.

Tourinform have an excellent free brochure on hiking in Hungary, giving details of routes and accommodation.

Road sign aimed at walkers

Cycling

Cycling became popular in Hungary post-Communist times as in that era roads were never really good enough to make cycling attractive. Today, however, pedal power is one of the best ways to explore the Hungarian countryside. In Budapest, the city council has invested heavily in creating a city-wide cycle path network. It extends to over 200 km (124 miles). Nationwide there are more than 2,000 km (1,243 miles) of cycle paths, though not all of these are paved. Two EuroVelo routes traverse Hungary, one following the eastern bank of the Danube, one hugging the eastern bank of the River Tisza. In Northern Transdanubia, some of Europe's best cycle routes are around Lake Fertő. There are superb routes in the Northern Highlands.

Visitors can hire bikes from a number of rental centres in Siófok and most of the resorts on Lake Balaton – where the sport is especially popular – as well as at Bikebase in the capital. Cyclists may take their bikes on trains within Hungary for a fee (around 25 per cent of the ticket price), but only on specially designated trains identified by the bicycle icon on the timetable.

Cyclists pausing in front of the Millennium Monument, Városliget, Budapest

Steeplechase, a popular equestrian pursuit

Horse Riding

Hungary and the Hungarians are invariably linked to horses and horsemanship, and riding is still a popular activity with people of all backgrounds. Basically, if an activity or sport involves horses, you will almost certainly be able to find it somewhere in Hungary. From simple pony-trekking rides to carriage driving and show-jumping, it is all on offer here. Even polo has made a comeback. The sport was popular here before World War II – Hungary had 76 polo clubs competing in 19 leagues in 1936 – but the Communists condemned the activity as bourgeois. There are now two polo clubs in Hungary, and the Hungarian Open Championship held each May at the La Estancia Polo Club at Etyek, outside Budapest, attracts professional players from as far away as Brazil and Argentina.

There are more than 1,000 riding centres in the country, and just as there seems to be a thermal spa in every town in Hungary, riding centres also abound. The **Hungarian Equestrian Tourism Association** (MLTKSZ) rates all equine centres using a five-horseshoe system, similar to the star ratings awarded to hotels. As a rule, the wider the range of activities that are on offer at an equestrian centre, the more horse-shoes it will have in its rating. Many riding centres also offer over-night accommodation. All offer gentle pony-trekking trails for children or beginners, as well as riding lessons for all abilities. Some riding centres offer special children's riding camps in summer.

The MLTKSZ is helpful and provides information about all the equestrian centres it rates. It also has details of shows, races, riding holidays and travelling with Gypsy caravans, as well as riding facilities for the disabled. Local tourist centres also have brochures of riding centres in their area.

Fishing

Almost half a million Hungarians fish at one time or another during the year; indeed, after swimming, fishing is the nation's favourite participation sport. Lakes Tisza, Balaton and Velence are superb and popular fishing grounds, while a stretch of the Danube near Ráckeve is also renowned for the richness of species and quality of fish. Anglers are able to land carp, pike, pike-perch, bream, razor fish and even eels in Hungarian waters. Anglers can fish in just about any stretch of water in the country, more or less at any time of year, but they do require a Hungarian National Fishing Licence to do so; this is available from angling shops or from the **National Federation of Hungarian Anglers** (MOHOSZ). The licence, valid for up to a year, costs around 2,000 forints (€6) and also requires the angler to pass a test. Fishing enthusiasts may also need to buy a local licence, depending on the stretch of water where they plan to fish. Local licences can usually be bought at the entrances to major fishing areas. Local tourist offices will have a list of sales points.

Waiting for river fish to bite in the Danube, near Esztergom

Hunting

Hungary is a nation of hunters but hunting is now strictly controlled. After years of free-for-all shooting, great emphasis is now placed on conservation and sustainability. Depending on the time of year, the hunter can shoot stags, fallow deer, roebuck, wild boar, fox, rabbit and pheasant. The biggest prize is a stag, but the season is short – September and October – and interested visitors will need to join an organized shoot.

Anyone wishing to join a hunt in Hungary must hold a valid hunting licence, and there are strict regulations on the import of firearms for hunting purposes. Trophy fees are charged for almost all game; these are calculated according to the size of the bagged catch. There are a number of companies who organize hunting holidays and tours, and who will take care of all the paperwork. OMVK, the

Fishing in Lake Balaton, a well-liked sport among locals and visitors

Skating at the ice rink in Varosliget, Budapest

Hungarian National Chamber of Hunters, offers advice on all hunting matters.

Winter Sports

Hungarians love skiing, but they are more likely to ski in Austrian or Slovakian resorts, many of which are no more than a couple of hours' drive away. Hungary does have one small downhill ski resort of its own, however, the **Mátraszentistván Sípark** in the Mátra Mountains. It offers pleasant but rather tame skiing. In all there are five ski lifts giving access to seven short ski runs, none of which is more than 1 km (0.5 mile) in length. There is, however, a good ski school, and children and beginners especially will love the quiet, gentle slopes here. Floodlit skiing is possible at night.

Mátraszentistván is 96 km (60 miles) away from Budapest, and can be reached by a daily bus service departing from Stadion Buszpályaudvar at 8:15am and arriving at the resort at 10:35am. The return bus leaves at 3pm,

arriving in Budapest at 5:30pm. Drivers should take the M3 motorway from Budapest to Gyöngyös, then the H24 passing through Mátrafüred, Mátraháza, Galyatető and Mátraszentlászló. Although the highest point of the resort is just 834 m (2,736 ft), there is usually enough snow for skiing from November to April.

Ice-skating is also popular, and the best place to do this is at the superb outdoor skating rink in Városliget in Budapest *(see pp110–11)*.

Golf

A sport gaining in popularity in the country, Hungary has seven full 18-hole golf courses, virtually all located in or around the capital. Golfing remains an expensive and exclusive sport in Hungary, however, and green fees at most courses are high: around 17,500 forints (€55) at weekends, slightly less during the week. The best course in the country is at the **Greenfield Hotel Golf and Spa**, close to Bükfürdő, about 50 km (31 miles) from Budapest. It is

the only course in Hungary to have hosted an international golf tour event.

Visitors can find out more about golfing in Hungary at the excellent website www.golfhungary.hu.

DIRECTORY

Water Sports

Balaton Regional Tourist Office
Blaha Lujza utca 2, Balatonfüred.
Tel (87) 34 28 01.

Hungarian Water Ski Federation
1033 Hajógyári Sziget 108, Budapest.
Tel (1) 487 20 41.

Horse Riding

Hungarian Equestrian Tourism Association (MLTKSZ)
Aranyhal utca 4, Budapest.
Tel (1) 215 35 60.

Fishing and Hunting

Hungarian National Chamber of Hunters (OMVK)
Medve utca 34–40, Budapest.
Tel (1) 355 61 80.
W omvk.hu

National Federation of Hungarian Anglers (MOHOSZ)
Korompai utca 17, Budapest.
Tel (1) 248 25 90.
W mohosz.hu

Winter Sports

Hungarian Ski Federation (MSSZ)
Dózsa György út 1–3, Budapest.
Tel (1) 460 68 93.

Mátraszentistván Sípark
Tel (37) 37 66 85.

Golf

Greenfield Hotel Golf and Spa
Golf utca 4, Bükfürdő.
Tel (94) 80 16 00.
W greenfieldhotel.net

Hungarian Golf Federation (MGSZ)
Istvánmezei út 1–3, Budapest.
Tel (1) 460 68 59.
W hungolf.hu

Teeing off at the Greenfield Hotel Golf and Spa, Bükfürdő

SURVIVAL GUIDE

PRACTICAL INFORMATION

Hungary is not a large country, but it is highly centralized, and almost all roads and railways lead to Budapest. Any visit beyond the capital is well worth organizing in advance. Most visitors also find the Hungarian language hard to learn, remember and pronounce, and there is little or no English spoken outside the cities. Fortunately, Tourinform, the Hungarian National Tourist Office, is one of the best and most efficient information services in Europe. Most Hungarian towns have modern facilities for the traveller, including good banking services and emergency medical care, and public telephone and transport systems are good. Customs and border controls now apply mainly to travellers from countries outside the EU. For EU and EEA citizens the entry procedure is a formality.

One of many tourist information offices, run by Tourinform

Tourist Information

Hungary operates tourist offices abroad in some 20 countries, all run by **Tourinform**. Their websites *(see Directory)*, also have a wide variety of useful information, brochures and maps, all of which can be downloaded for free in various formats. Holiday brochures can also be sent by post, free of charge. Once in Hungary, travellers can make use of the services of more than 150 Tourinform offices nationwide. In most of these offices young, friendly and multi-lingual staff will do everything to make visitors feel welcome in their country.

Passports and Customs

Citizens of the European Union (EU), the European Economic Area (EEA), countries that are signatories of the Schengen agreement, the USA, Canada, Australia and New Zealand, as well as and a few other countries, are free to enter Hungary as tourists without requiring a visa. Almost everybody else – including South Africans – needs a visa, which must be obtained from a Hungarian Consulate outside Hungary before travel. Visitors should keep their passports (or at least a copy) on them at all times. A valid passport needs to be shown when registering at a hotel.

Visitors returning to EU countries may export unlimited quantities of alcohol and tobacco, provided these are for personal use. However, while Hungarian customs officers will not bother you, note that some EU countries have imposed their own limits on imports from countries such as Hungary where cigarettes and alcohol are cheap. Though these unilateral limits are illegal under EU law, they are strictly enforced. The UK, for example, limits cigarette imports from Hungary to just 800. Check before leaving home.

Opening Hours

Museums and galleries are open all year round, though there are some exceptions. Opening times for specific venues are given under their individual entries. Typically, museums open from 10am to 6pm from April until October, and a couple of hours less in winter, from November to March. Most museums are closed on Mondays. Almost all charge an entrance fee, but many offer discounts.

Most small shops open from 9am to 7pm; some stay open until 9pm or 10pm, especially in modern shopping centres. Shops usually open all day on Saturdays, and an increasing number open their doors on Sundays too. Markets operate seven days a week from early morning to around 3pm. Large supermarkets also open seven days a week, until at least 8pm. Small shops may open on public holidays. Many of the small kiosks selling bus tickets, food and alcohol

Signs indicating local amenities and attractions

are open 24 hours a day. Restaurants usually open at 11:30am and rarely close in the afternoon; Hungarians like to lunch early, and at leisure.

Etiquette

Bans on smoking in public places are increasingly common. All bars, cafés and restaurants are non-smoking, and all museums, public transport, stations, airports and other public buildings are also entirely non-smoking. Smokers should note that tobacco goods can only be purchased at shops signposted "Nemzeti Dohánybolt",

Staircase especially adapted for disabled use

with their opaque windows. Entrance is restricted to people aged over 18.

Hungarians are usually very friendly towards visitors. They queue patiently, except when getting on and off any form of public transport. The only stumbling block is the language barrier – many older Hungarians speak no Western languages.

Casual clothing is acceptable everywhere, even in the restaurants of Budapest's most expensive hotels. At business meetings, too, suits and ties are much less common than elsewhere in Europe. But at the theatre or classical music concerts you are expected to dress up, black tie if possible.

If invited to the home of a Hungarian, ensure you bring something: flowers or a bottle of good whisky are favourites.

In hospitals, it is common practice to tip doctors, nurses and domestic staff to make things happen just that little bit faster. The same is true of any Hungarian public official, a legacy of Communist-era bureaucracy.

Disabled Travellers

Hungary has made giant strides towards improving life for its disabled citizens and visitors, a major plus point of the country's entry into the EU in 2004. That said, it can be tough for all but the very fittest to get on and off some forms of public transport: trains and trams are especially troublesome. On the Budapest Metro, the M4 line is fully accessible by lifts, while the older lines are only wheelchair-accessible at certain stations.

Most hotels can accommodate disabled visitors, often in specially adapted rooms. As a rule of thumb, the better the hotel, the more likely disabled visitors are to find rooms suitable for them.

For advice and help, contact the **National Federation of Disabled Persons' Associations**. Their excellent website lists accessible hotels, restaurants, museums and other public buildings, as well as transport links.

Public Toilets

Unfortunately, when it comes to the provision of decent public toilets, Hungary remains in the dark ages. Public conveniences are rare, and those that one does come across can be very unappealing. Most are free; the modern, cubicle-style toilets now common in parks and public squares are sometimes coin-operated. Cafés and restaurants usually allow toilet access only to customers; at service stations and fast-food outlets, there may be a charge if you do not order anything from the menu. Most railway stations have toilets, but they can be unhygienic.

Apart from the generally understood picture symbols, the toilets are signed in Hungarian: *Hölgyek* (ladies) and *Urak* (gentlemen) or *Nők* (women) and *Férfiak* (men).

Electrical and Gas Appliances

The Hungarian electricity supply is 230 V; the plugs are the standard continental Europe type, with two round pins. Sockets are generally earthed, and the plugs are most commonly of the flat type. Adaptors are widely available.

Gas cookers have a bimetallic safety device – after lighting, the knob should be held down until the burner warms up.

Street sign for Váci utca, not to be confused with Váci út

Hungarian Time

Hungary adheres to Central European Time in keeping with most of mainland Europe – it is 2 hours ahead of Greenwich Mean Time (GMT) in summer and 1 hour ahead in winter.

If it is noon in Budapest it is 11am in London, 6am in New York, 5am in Dallas, 3am in Los Angeles, 1pm in Bucharest, 2pm in Moscow, 7pm in Perth, 8pm in Tokyo, 9pm in Sydney and 11pm in Auckland.

Hungarian Addresses and Street Names

Most famous Hungarians have squares *(tér)*, streets *(utca)* and avenues *(út)* named after them in every large city and town, which it is easy to confuse. Many first-time visitors to Budapest thus confuse Váci utca (the pedestrian street in the city centre) with Váci út (the wide avenue north of the city centre).

Hungarian addresses are written with the postcode first, followed by the street name and building number. In Budapest the district code is usually added to the city name, using Roman numerals. The floors of tall buildings are numbered from the floor above the ground floor, exactly as in the UK.

Safety and Health

Hungary has a relatively low crime rate, although pick-pocketing can be a problem on public transport and in crowded sightseeing areas. The healthcare system is well-funded, efficient and most emergency treatment is free for visitors. Visitors are still advised, however, to take out a good health insurance policy before they depart. Most towns have modern facilities for the traveller, including good emergency medical care. The Hungarian National Tourist Office can help with language problems.

Hungarian police officers, on foot patrol in the streets

Personal Security

Although Hungary is a relatively safe place, it is wise to take care. Popular outdoor events attract bag-snatchers and pickpockets. In Budapest and in crowded public areas, visitors should be particularly careful to keep an eye on their property, especially handbags and cameras. Public transport in Budapest (especially the buses) is notorious for the gangs of pickpockets that operate there.

Visitors should make sure they lock valuables and personal documents in a hotel safe. It is equally important not to leave valuables in a car. Ideally, a hotel's car parking facilities should be used (parking space may be available at a small supplement – it is worth it). There is no need to carry large amounts of cash around, because most credit and debit cards are widely accepted, and cash machines (ATMs) are also widely found, even in the countryside.

Personal Safety

The Hungarian word for "police" is *rendőrség*. Hungarian police officers are frequently seen patrolling the streets on motorbikes, on foot or in cars. They may also be seen on horseback. Even the smallest village has its own police station. In the event of any loss or theft of property, a report should be made immediately to the police, as a number will be required for any insurance claim. This, however, is easier said than done, as some police stations may not have anyone around who speaks the relevant language. In this

Fire department sign

case your embassy or consulate *(see Directory)* may be able to help out. (Australian visitors should note that Australia no longer has an embassy in Budapest; the nearest is in Vienna.) Visitors who are arrested, for whatever reason, should try to contact their embassy and consular representative immediately.

Random ID checks are rare, but visitors and locals alike are required to have some form of identification with them at all times.

CCTV is now common in Hungary's cities and towns, and has been installed on the Budapest Metro, on some buses, in department stores and in shopping centres.

Hungary also has one of the most modern speed-camera systems in Europe, and speeding, along with other traffic offences that these cameras can record, attracts heavy fines, even imprisonment in extreme cases *(see also Travelling by Car, pp308–9)*. Drink-driving is strictly forbidden in Hungary – there is absolutely no permissible blood alcohol level. Even a first drink-driving offence can lead to imprisonment.

The possession of all drugs is illegal. Prostitution is illegal, though tolerated in most big cities if practised discreetly. In any case, contact with street

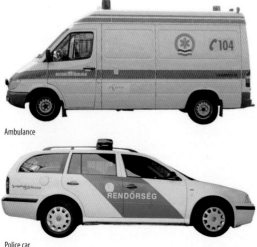

Ambulance

Police car

prostitutes (of which there are many in and around railway stations at night) should be avoided, as they are often run by criminals. In general, all of Hungary's railway stations can be rather unsafe places at night, as they are popular places for drunks and petty criminals to hang out.

All visitors must take care not to overstay their welcome – most tourists are permitted to stay in the country for up to 90 days without a temporary residence permit. Visitors who extend their stay beyond the 90 days and then attempt to leave the country may be hit with a large fine, or prevented from leaving.

Emergencies

The emergency telephone number for police, fire or ambulance is 112, and all operators speak English, French and German. There is also an English-language Tourist Information Service, run by Tourinform, which can provide information on English-speaking police stations, and give general advice if visitors are lost or need other kinds of assistance. The telephone number is (1) 438 80 80; it operates around the clock. Visitors who believe they have been overcharged by a restaurant, or a taxi driver, should report the incident to the police. Officers can be approached in the street or at any police station.

Healthcare

Even during Communist times Hungary was a world leader in medical research and development. Hungarian doctors are superb, though underpaid, and standards in hospitals and even local clinics in small towns and villages are generally high. Emergency treatment is in theory free for all, although visitors should take out a good health insurance policy before travelling abroad. Any treatment (and all medicines) need to be paid

Ornately decorated interior of a pharmacy, Budapest

for, as do hospital stays. The actual cost incurred by a visitor will depend on Hungary's reciprocal agreement with the relevant country. EU citizens are entitled to free treatment and hospital stays, although they will usually be asked to pay for medicines. Keep any receipts for treatments or prescriptions, and ask for a signed, stamped doctor's report if an insurance claim is to be made. Visitors should also note that tipping doctors and nurses is still widespread (a relic of the Communist system).

Sign for a pharmacy

The Hungarian word for "pharmacy" or "chemist" is *patika*, although the German word *Apotheke* is also widely in use. Hungary's pharmacies are strictly regulated and by law have to be owned by their pharmacists. There are therefore no pharmacy chains, and finding a 24-hour pharmacy can be difficult. If the nearest pharmacy is closed, there should be a list displayed – either on the door or in the window – of all local chemists, including those who will be open on 24-hour emergency duty. In practice, however, the list is often missing. Tourinform or residents of the area should be able to help in such situations.

Most dental treatment is relatively cheap in Hungary, and, in fact, "dental tourism" from other countries is a growing industry. Visitors do not need any special vaccinations to travel to

Hungary, and there are no specific health risks associated with the country. Tap water is perfectly safe to drink, but bottled waters are cheap and of high quality. Food hygiene laws are strictly enforced, so food poisoning is now rare, but it never hurts to be circumspect when deciding to eat at smaller buffets or street food stands. Mosquitoes can be a problem in high summer, especially around Lake Tisza.

DIRECTORY

Emergencies

English-Language Emergency Hotline (Tourinform)
Tel (1) 438 80 80.

General Emergencies
Tel 112.

Embassies

Australian Embassy
Mattiellistrasse 2–4, Vienna, Austria.
Tel +43 (1) 50 67 40.

British Embassy
Harmincad utca 6, Budapest.
Tel (1) 266 28 88.
W www.gov.uk

Canadian Embassy
Ganz utca 12–14, Budapest.
Tel (1) 392 33 60.
W hungary.gc.ca

US Embassy
Szabadság tér 12, Budapest.
Tel (1) 475 44 00.
W hungary.usembassy.gov

Banking and Currency

Although a member of the European Union (EU) since 2004, Hungary has not yet joined the Eurozone. Hungary still uses its own currency, the forint (although many places will also accept dollars and euros). The banking system is generally excellent, and there are cash machines (ATMs) everywhere, as well as foreign exchange bureaux. It is advisable to change money in a bank, as exchange rates are better, and the commission is far lower. The use of credit and debit cards is widespread, and most banks will advance cash on Visa cards and MasterCards.

An ATM cash dispenser, typically found all over the country

Banks

There are plenty of banks in all cities and towns, all providing a good service. Many of the branches have been modernized and the staff are all courteous and helpful. Their opening times vary, but the normal hours are 9am–5pm. Banks do not close for lunch. Most banks are closed at weekends and on public holidays. The largest banks, with branches in all towns, are **UniCredit Bank**, **Erste Bank**, **Raiffeisen** and **OTP**.

UniCredit

Logo of the UniCredit Bank

Currency Exchange

Since Hungary joined the EU there have been no limits on the amount of foreign or local currency that can be brought in or taken out of the country. Visitors arriving with foreign currency should change this at a bank. Although independent exchange bureaux may appear to offer better rates of exchange, or lower commission, they usually advertise only their rates for buying local currency, not for selling. Most also charge additional fees ,which are not clearly signposted.

The easiest way to procure local cash is with a card in a cash machine. ATM machines are found everywhere and, although your card issuer will usually charge a small fee for every transaction, the rate of exchange is always the same as that of the National Bank of Hungary at the time of the transaction. This method of obtaining cash often works out far cheaper than using a bureau de change.

Credit and debit cards are almost universally accepted in Budapest. Traveller's cheques can usually only be changed at a bank, and then at high commission rates – they are best avoided. American Express cashes its own traveller's cheques free of charge.

There are also a number of Automatic Currency Exchange Machines, where foreign currency is inserted to obtain forints in exchange.

Visitors may occasionally be approached by locals, offering to exchange currency at a better rate than the banks. This is to be avoided in all circumstances – it is illegal and likely to involve faked banknotes or other kinds of fraud and deception.

Visitors should try to spend all their Hungarian coins before leaving the country.

DIRECTORY

Banks

Erste Bank
Népfürdő utca 24–6, Budapest.
Tel (1) 298 02 22.
W erstebank.hu

OTP
Nádor utca 6, Budapest.
Tel (1) 366 63 88 (from abroad).
W otpbank.hu

Raiffeisen Bank
Akadémia utca 6, Budapest.
Tel (1) 48 44 400 (from abroad).
W raiffeisen.hu

UniCredit Bank
Szabadság tér 5–6, Budapest.
Tel (1) 301 12 71 or
(1) 325 32 00 (from abroad).
W unicreditbank.hu

Credit Cards and Traveller's Cheques

American Express
Váci út 33, Budapest.
Tel (1) 235 43 00.

Discover Card
(lost/stolen cards and customer service)
Tel 00-1-801-902-3100
(toll-free in US).

MasterCard
(lost/stolen cards and customer service)
Tel (80) 01 25 17.

Visa
(lost/stolen cards and customer service)
Tel (80) 01 76 82.

Local branch of Erste Bank in Keszthely

Banknotes

Hungary's currency is the forint (Ft). Banknotes come in denominations of 500, 1,000, 2,000, 5,000, 10,000 and 20,000. It can be difficult to pay using Ft 10,000 and 20,000 banknotes, especially in small stores or taxis.

500 forints

1,000 forints

2,000 forints

5,000 forints

10,000 forints

20,000 forints

Coins

The forint is available in six coin denominations: 5, 10, 20, 50, 100 and 200 forints. All cash transactions are therefore rounded up or down to the nearest unit of 5 or 10, if necessary. The international currency code for the forint is HUF.

5 forints

10 forints

20 forints

50 forints

100 forints

200 forints

Communications and Media

The Hungarian landline telephone system is first class. There are a number of operators, including Magyar Telekom, part of Deutsche Telekom. Public telephones are operated by using coins or calling cards, although calls to the emergency services are free. Phone boxes no longer contain telephone directories. However, the telephone information system provides a directory enquiry service *(see Directory)*. In recent years, Hungary's landlines have been joined by several nationwide mobile telephone networks. All mobile telephone operators offer foreign-language information services. The country's postal service is efficient – priority mail sent within Hungary should arrive the next day – although post offices themselves can be frustrating to use.

Public telephone boxes are painted in a variety of colours

Making a Phone Call

To make a call from a public phone kiosk, using a calling card from an operator such as Neophone, Barangoló or Telecard is the best option, and usually gives you better international rates than when using coins. They are available in a number of denominations from post offices, street vendors, service stations and most newspaper kiosks. Coin-operated phone boxes take 10, 20, 50 and 100 forint coins, and you may occasionally find a public phone that accepts debit and credit cards. To make an international call, dial 00 and wait for the dialling tone, then dial the country code followed by the rest of the number. To phone a Hungarian number from abroad, the international access code is 36. To call long distance within Hungary, dial 06 followed by the city code. The area code for Budapest is 1. If you have dialled an out-of-date number, you will hear a message or an error tone.

Mobile Phones

Most Hungarians are mobile-crazy, and almost everyone has at least one. Coverage of the country is almost total, with only a few remote areas of the Northern Highlands not bene-fiting from the presence of at least one of the networks. Most European visitors can use their mobile phones in Hungary; US and Australian visitors who do

not have a GSM phone may not. To make sure you can use your mobile phone while in Hungary, you will need to ensure that you have roaming access enabled before you leave home. Once in Hungary most phones auto-matically search for the network with the strongest signal. If you want to use a particular network, which may have an agreement with your home network, thus offering reduced roaming charges, you should change your phone setting from automatic searching for networks to manual.

Even if you are from another EU country and hence benefit from roaming charge caps, it is wise to check with your provider before you travel. If you will be spending longer periods in Hungary, it may be worthwhile buying a local SIM card. All of the local networks sell them, and you can obtain them from post offices and newspaper kiosks as well as phone stores.

Internet, Wi-Fi and Fax

Most hotels, airports, train stations and large shopping centres offer internet services. There are cheap internet cafés around the country, and even the smallest village usually has at least one access point. In larger towns and cities, there are also Wi-Fi hotspots for those with laptops or other enabled devices, although you will need to ensure compatibility before leaving home. Ask at the tourist office or at your hotel for help in accessing the public, and often free, Wi-Fi network with your device. Alternatively, visit a café such as **Farger** in Budapest, with its free Wi-Fi service. If you want to access mobile internet using a local SIM card or by roaming, all operators offer good 3G coverage, and 4G networks are also expanding.

If you need to send a fax, any post office will be able to help, or your hotel, though it may charge you a high fee.

An internet café, now to be found even in the smallest village

Postal Services

The Hungarian postal service (Magyar Posta) is as bureaucratic and inefficient today as it was during Communist times. If you need to use a post office, therefore, set some time aside. Postage stamps can also often be purchased from newspaper kiosks and souvenir shops. Sending a postcard costs 260–340 forints (under or just over €1) depending on the destination. Most post offices are open Monday to Friday from 8am to 6pm and 8am to 2pm on Saturday. For urgent parcels, a courier service, such as **DHL** or **Federal Express**, will be more reliable.

Addresses in Hungary, written with the postcode first, can be confusing. See p297 for more information.

A Hungarian postbox, Budapest

TV and Radio

Almost every hotel room in Hungary – even in budget hotels – now has a television equipped to receive a variety of domestic, national, cable or satellite channels. The most popular Hungarian television station is the state-run MTV (not to be confused with the music channel), which operates two channels, while TV2 and RTL Klub are the largest and most popular private stations. All imported programmes in Hungary are dubbed into Hungarian, so visitors are more likely to be interested in BBC World, CNN and EuroNews, the three English-language news channels invariably carried by

Newspaper kiosk, selling newspapers, magazines and phone cards

all cable and satellite operators. There is also usually a variety of German-language news and entertainment channels.

There are literally hundreds of radio stations in Hungary. Most play a mix of international and local pop and rock music, but there are also stations dedicated to classical, jazz, folk music and more.

Newspapers and Magazines

Hungary's leading newspapers are the quality broadsheets *Népszabadság* and *Magyar Hírlap*, and the *Magyar Nemzet*, though there are hundreds of other newspapers published around the country, many of them regional.

There is one English-language Hungarian publication, the bi-weekly *Budapest Business Journal (BBJ)*, which provides financial and business news for Hungary. The Budapest *Timeout* guide is a monthly entertainments listing magazine. Major foreign publications can be bought at central newspaper kiosks, railway stations, the airport and at **House of the World Press** in Budapest. **Relay Székesfehérvár** and **Relay Debrecen** are two other suppliers. Foreign papers are less widely available outside the capital, apart from German newspapers and magazines, sometimes found in the Lake Balaton resorts during the high season summer holidays.

DIRECTORY

Communications

International Directory Enquiries
Tel 199.

Postal services

Post Office (Magyar Posta)
Dunavirág utca 2–6, Budapest.
Customer Service: **Tel** (40) 46 46
46. W posta.hu

Courier Services

DHL
Tel (40) 45 45 45.
W dhl.hu

Federal Express
Tel (40) 98 09 80.
W fedex.com/hu

Internet and Wi-Fi

Farger
Zoltán utca 18, Budapest.
Tel (20) 237 78 25.
W farger.hu

Foreign Newspapers

House of the World Press
Városház utca 3–5, Budapest.
Tel (1) 317 13 11.

Relay Debrecen
Debrecen Station, Petőfi tér 12,
Debrecen.

Relay Székesfehérvár
Székesfehérvár Station,
Béke tér 3, Székesfehérvár.

TRAVEL INFORMATION

Most visitors arrive in Hungary by air, at Budapest's only major airport, Ferenc Liszt International. A second international airport, known as Hévíz-Balaton, is located near Keszthely, and a third has opened in Debrecen. Hungary has borders with no less than seven countries, so there are numerous road and rail entry points. As a rule of thumb, crossing the border from EU countries (Austria, Romania, Slovakia, Croatia and Slovenia) is quick and problem-free, while crossing from the Ukraine or Serbia can often involve long queues. Visitors can also travel into Hungary along the Danube, on scheduled summer boat services from Bratislava and Vienna or hydrofoils from Vienna.

Arrival by Air

Budapest's **Ferenc Liszt International** airport is served by a large number of international airlines, including **British Airways**, Delta, KLM/ Northwest Airlines, Lufthansa, and several low-cost carriers. For travellers from the northern hemisphere, there are direct flights into Budapest from over 70 cities, including most European capitals.

Ferenc Liszt International has two terminals, but Terminal 1 is closed indefinitely. Terminal 2 serves both low-cost airlines and scheduled carriers, including **easyJet**, German Wings and **Wizzair**.

Hévíz-Balaton, at Sármellék near Keszthely, is served by **Ryanair** from London Stansted and German Wings from Berlin. Another way to get to Budapest and northwestern Hungary is via a flight to neighbouring Vienna or Bratislava. Northeastern Hungary can be accessed via Wizzair, which flies from London Luton to **Debrecen Airport**.

One of Budapest's official fleet of yellow taxis

Getting from and to the Airport

Ferenc Liszt International is located 16 km (10 miles) southeast of Budapest city centre and is served by a public bus service to Kőbánya-Kispest, Határ út and Bajcsy-Zsilinszky út metro station, the last stop of metro line 3 (from just after midnight to 3:30am, it connects with a city night bus into the centre). Tickets costing about 350 forints (€1) can be bought from newspaper stands at the airport. An Airport Minibus Service takes passengers to and from any address in the city centre for about 3,200 forints (€10; one way). There may be a wait until there are enough passengers heading in the same direction. All licensed taxis in Budapest are yellow and operate on a standard tariff. The fare to the city centre is typically 6,000–8,000 forints (€19–25).

At Hévíz-Balaton airport, Fly-Car minibuses and Zala Volán buses run to Keszthely and other villages in the region. There are also hire cars and cheap taxis.

Arrival by Train

Budapest has direct rail links with more than 25 other European cities, and several trains a day arrive here from Paris, Vienna, Bratislava, Munich, Bucharest and Sofia. The rail journey from London to Budapest is easy and takes just 24 hours, via Eurostar to Paris, Orient Express to Vienna and InterCity "Avala" to Budapest. There are also daily trains from Krakow, Warsaw, Minsk, Moscow and Kiev. Trains for most other cities in Hungary, such as Pécs, Debrecen, Győr and Miskolc, depart from Budapest. InterRail and **Eurail Passes** are valid in Hungary.

Budapest's Railway Stations

There are three main railway stations in Budapest – Keleti pu (east), Nyugati pu (west) and Déli pu (west). Most international trains operate to and from Keleti pu, the exception being rail traffic to and from Croatia (Déli pu).

Ferenc Liszt International airport, Budapest

The lofty ticket hall in the famous West Train Station, designed by Gustafe Eiffel, in Budapest

All three stations are on the Budapest metro system, and just a couple of stops from the city centre. The buildings are grand from the outside but unwelcoming inside, and potentially dangerous for lone travellers late at night.

Arrival by Coach

Volánbusz and **Eurolines Coach Services** travel to Budapest from 13 countries (including Great Britain, Belgium, France, Germany and Austria). They arrive at Népliget, Budapest's international coach station, from where the M3 metro line can be accessed. The international routes are served by luxury coaches with facilities such as air conditioning.

Arrival by Car

The driving distance from London to Budapest, using motorways, is 1,834 km (1,140 miles). The fastest route, via France, Brussels, Germany and Austria, would take about 17 hours if driving nonstop. Apart

from petrol, motorists need to budget for road tolls, overnight stops and motorway tax discs for Austria and Hungary.

Hungary has more than 100 road border crossings, although in practice many of these are unstaffed and not always open. The main and most frequently used border crossing is Nickelsdorf/Hegyeshalom from Vienna; Vienna also has the only direct motorway link to Budapest. Other major border points are at Schachendorf/Búcsú from Graz in Austria and Rusovce/Rajka from Bratislava in Slovakia.

To drive in Hungary, a valid driving licence with a photo or an international driving licence and adequate insurance are required (see also pp308–9).

Arrival by Ferry

Perhaps the most exotic way to arrive in Hungary is by boat, on the Danube: **Mahart PassNave** operates daily hydrofoil services from Vienna to Budapest (Apr–Oct). The downstream journey takes 5 hours 20 minutes; it's a little

longer heading the other way. The trip is fairly expensive: tickets cost 40,000 forints (€125) return for adults. The hydrofoil arrives and departs in Budapest from the jetty at Belgrád rakpart, on the Pest side of the river, halfway between Szabadság and Erzsébet bridges.

DIRECTORY

Airports

Debrecen Airport
Tel (52) 52 11 92.
W debrecenairport.com

Ferenc Liszt International
Tel (1) 296 70 00.
(flight information)
W bud.hu

Hévíz-Balaton Airport
Tel (83) 20 03 04.
(flight information)
W hevizairport.com

Airlines

Air Berlin
W airberlin.com

British Airways
W ba.com

easyJet
W easyjet.com

Ryanair
W ryanair.com

Wizzair
W wizzair.com

Low-cost airlines (all)
W flycheapo.com

Rail Travel

European Rail (Eurail) Passes
W raileurope.com

Hungarian Railways (MÁV)
Andrássy út 35. **Tel** (1) 444 44 99.
W mav.hu
(general information)
W elvira.hu
(timetable)

Coach Travel

Eurolines
W eurolines.com

Ferries

Mahart PassNave
Belgrád rakpart, Budapest.
Tel (1) 484 40 00.
W mahartpassnave.hu

Luxury coaches serve international destinations

Travelling Around Hungary

Hungary's excellent railway network makes it relatively easy to travel around. The train is probably the easiest mode of transport for longer distances as the fares are also fairly low. However, the road infrastructure is also rapidly expanding and improving (for information on driving in Hungary, *see pp308–9*). There are InterCity buses, but these are often slow and crowded, though undeniably cheap. During the summer many of the towns on the Danube Bend, north of Budapest, can be reached by ferry, a most enjoyable way of travelling. There are no internal flights in Hungary.

Travelling by Train

Virtually all trains in Hungary are operated by **MÁV** (Magyar Államvasutak), a state-owned company; one other company, GYSEV, which is co-owned by the Austrian and Hungarian governments, operates trains and maintains rails in parts of western Hungary. MÁV usually runs a very good, reliable service, which offers excellent value for money. Almost all of the country's major cities and towns are connected by train services, as are a surprisingly large number of smaller towns and villages. The one problem is that the network is very much focused on Budapest, and so often the quickest route from A to B involves a detour to the capital.

Ticket office at Déli Station, Budapest

There are five different types of train in Hungary, offering varying degrees of speed and comfort. The fastest and most luxurious trains are the international Express services (Ex),

requiring a seat reservation, which run to all corners of Europe. The best domestic trains are the InterCity (IC) services for which a supplement is levied. They are very quick and comfortable, but currently only serve a limited number of cities to and from Budapest, and stop at few – if any – places in between. Next in line are *sebesvonat* services, which are less comfortable and stop at more stations, while *gyorsvonat* (literally "fast" trains) services

stop even more frequently. The "slow trains", *személyvonat,* stop at every single town, village and hamlet. Painfully slow, they should be avoided unless the destination is not served by a faster train.

Tickets are priced according to distance travelled, and the type of train used. InterCity trains are the most expensive, *személyvonat* the cheapest. In addition to the ticket, a seat reservation is required whenever a service is marked with an R, as well as busy services (otherwise, you will travel standing up). For InterCity services, reservations are usually included in the ticket price.

Buying tickets and making reservations can be difficult outside of Budapest, as little English is spoken. It is therefore advisable to learn in advance how to pronounce the desired destination correctly. Almost all tickets are singles (*egy útra*), as the system of charging per kilometre makes the notion of returns redundant. Returns (*retúr*) can be bought to be sure of a reservation in advance, but the price will almost always be exactly double that of a single.

A good way of ensuring that you get the ticket and train service you require is to buy all tickets in advance in Budapest, at the main MÁV office. Here, English and German are spoken and you can buy tickets for every destination in Hungary, and make reservations for up to 60 days before departure. A useful service is also provided by **Wasteels**, the international rail ticketing agent, which has an office at Keleti Station *(see Directory)*.

At the stations it is important to know that *indulás* means "departures" and *érkezés* "arrivals". The Hungarian word for "platform" is *vágány*. The entire railway timetable for all routes in Hungary is also posted on the internet, in English, with full pricing and routing information.

Travelling by Bus

The state-owned **Volánbusz** company operates an extensive network of buses serving every

An Express train in Nyugati Station, Budapest

corner of Hungary. Its fleet of 1,000 buses reach parts of the country even *személyvonat* trains do not get to, and visitors intending to visit the more remote areas of the Great Plain or the Northern High lands can be certain that one of these buses will take them there.

Volánbusz services are usually prompt and reliable, but single-carriageway roads may, of course, slow them down. Though most of the fleet is modern and relatively comfortable, the buses themselves are often crowded. On longer journeys a refreshment stop of around 15 minutes will be scheduled. As with the train network, almost all services begin and end in Budapest at Népliget, Stadion or Árpád Bridge bus stations. These are easily reached via the metro network, but note that in some towns the coach station may be some distance outside the city centre.

Tickets generally cost less than the second-class train fare equivalent and can be obtained from the ticket offices at the bus stations. These are usually open 6am–8pm daily. Volánbusz also has a central agency in Budapest, where advance tickets can be purchased for any bus or

People waiting on one of the platforms at West Train Station, Budapest

coach journey in Hungary, as well as for **Eurolines** services. The Volánbusz timetable is available on the Internet.

Travelling by Boat

One of the most enjoyable ways of travelling around Hungary is by boat. During the summer **Mahart PassNave** operates daily services from Vigadó ter in Budapest to Szentendre, Vác, Visegrád, Esztergom and Százhalombatta, with additional services at weekends. The tickets are not cheap (from around 2,000–2,500 forints (€6–8) oneway for adults; children are half-price) but they do include

the services of a guide, who will point out any sights on the route, in several languages. There are additional cruises to popular places, such as Mohács, Solt-Révbérpuszta and Kalocsa.

River boat in Budapest, passing the Royal Palace

Travelling by Car

Hungary is a small country: north to south, the greatest distance is 268 km (167 miles); east to west it is 528 km (328 miles). Although the government has heavily invested in the motorway network, many towns remain connected by single-lane highways. Driving on these can be frustratingly slow, yet road surfaces are generally good, and traffic is not too heavy, except for the rush hour in Budapest. The capital is a very difficult city for a visitor to navigate, as there are numerous one-way systems, making it easy to get lost. There are also few places to park, so exploring the city on foot and by public transport are better ideas.

Clear directions to European and national roads, and a motorway

Road Standards

Hungary's road network is extensive, with more than 30,000 km (18,641 miles) of paved roads, of which 1,515 km (940 miles) are motorways. Most of Hungary's motorways (prefixed M) lead to and from Budapest. The M0 ringroad circumnavigates southern and eastern Budapest; M1 goes to Vienna via Győr; M3 goes to Miskolc, with branches to Debrecen (M35) and Nyíregyháza (M30); M5 goes to Szeged; M7 goes to Lake Balaton (South).

To drive on Hungary's motorways visitors need to purchase an e-card or e-vignette *(matrica)*

from a major petrol station (MOL, Shell or OMV), online, or by SMS (text message) using a local SIM card. These are available for periods of 10 days, one month and one year. A 10-day e-card for a family car costs around 3,000 forints (€94). Visitors caught driving on a motorway without an e-card can expect a fine of 14,875 forints (€47) if paid within 30 days. When buying your e-ticket, it is important that you supply your vehicle's exact registration number, as an effective and extensive camera system with number-plate recognition is operated to enforce toll payment.

One of the more unusual traffic signs

All Hungary's other roads – prefixed E for European roads or H for national roads – are toll-free.

Signposting in Hungary is generally of a high standard, with town names and road numbers clearly marked.

Rules of the Road

Visitors need to be 17 years old to drive in Hungary, and have a full photographic licence issued by their home country. If you have a driving licence without a photo, you will need an International Driving Licence.

Road safety is good, despite occasional severe weather conditions. In winter, visitors may be barred from entering Hungary unless their car is equipped with snow chains. **Útinform** advises on current road conditions. The law also obliges drivers to keep a first-aid kit and a warning triangle in the car.

There are several speed cameras, many equipped to monitor other offences (using a bus lane, crossing lanes when prohibited, etc.) and although the police may not stop you on site, they will still automatically fine you by sending a letter by post. The maximum permitted speed on motorways is 130 km/h (81 mph), 110 km/h (68 mph) on European roads, and 90 km/h (56 mph) on national roads. In built-up areas the limit is 50 km/h (30 mph). By law, all passengers must wear seatbelts, and children under the age of 12 are not allowed to ride in the front. Using a hand-held mobile phone while driving is illegal.

To drive legally, the alcohol level in the bloodstream must be zero mg – no drinking at all. The law is very strictly enforced and even first offenders risk prison for breaking it.

Hungarians drive on the right, and at roundabouts vehicles already on the roundabout have priority. Many rural junctions do not have traffic lights, so always stop when joining a main road, even if there is no stop sign. Where two minor roads meet and there are no signs or traffic lights, the car approaching from the right has priority. This rule also applies in cities when traffic lights are flashing amber continuously (as they often do late at night).

The M7 motorway from Nagykanizsa to Budapest

Road Signs

Hungarian road signs follow the European standard, and there are no solely Hungarian signs. All visitors should be aware of signs they may not be familiar with, however.

As in the rest of Europe, brown signs indicate recommended tourist areas, heritage sites, tourist areas and attractions along the road, such as national parks, leisure centres or historic buildings.

Parking

In most cities and towns there is a charge for parking anywhere near the city centre. Tickets must be bought from the vending machines and displayed behind the windscreen. The vending machines usually only accept 100-forint coins, so it is best to keep a good number to hand. Traffic wardens inspect tickets bought either at the parking meters or by mobile phone texting, and should you fail to pay or exceed the time period you prepaid for, they will leave a notice containing a hefty fine on your windscreen. Parking on streets where there are no public car parking spaces is free but risky – locals sometimes damage unfamiliar cars that are parked in their favourite spot.

Parking offences may result in being towed

A petrol station operated by MOL, the state-run company

Fuel and Services

There are plenty of service stations on major roads and in towns and cities, but they can be few and far between in rural areas. All offer unleaded petrol and diesel, and many stay open 24 hours. There are emergency telephones on the motorways, connected to the emergency services. If you break down elsewhere, call the **Magyar Autóklub** or **AI Assistance** for assistance. You will have to pay but may be able to recover this from your insurance.

Renting a Car

All major international car hire firms have offices in Hungary, but car hire here is relatively expensive. Drivers must be aged 21 or over, and have held a valid driving licence for at least one year. A deposit is usually required. Most major companies include unlimited mileage, though check that this is the case before signing a rental agreement. As well as the international companies, there are smaller, local firms. While they at first seem to be cheaper, hidden costs can hike up the price. They may also not be so reliable in case of accident or breakdown.

Cars can be prebooked at airports and major hotels, although dropping them off at a different point incurs a surcharge. Cars are usually delivered with a full tank of petrol, and should be returned in the same condition.

DIRECTORY

Vehicle Recovery

AI Vehicle Assistance and Recovery
Tel (1) 266 89 49.

Magyar Autóklub (MAK)
Tel 188.

Road Conditions

Útinform
Tel (1) 366 24 00/01/02/03.
W internet.kozut.hu

Car Rental

Avis
Arany János utca 26–28, Budapest. **Tel** (1) 318 42 40.
W avis.hu

Budget
Krisztina krt. 41–43, Budapest.
Tel (1) 214 04 20.
W budget.hu

Europcar
Erzsébet tér 9–10, Budapest.
Tel (1) 505 44 00.
W europcar.com

Hertz
Tel (1) 296 09 99 or 235 60 08.
W hertz.hu

Using a Parking Meter

2 When the display panel shows the time you require, press the green button to request a ticket.

1 Insert coins for the required time, or insert a parking card. The parking meter indicates the maximum and minimum parking charges.

3 To cancel and terminate your transaction press, the red button.

4 Your ticket appears here.

Travel in the Cities

Most of Hungary's cities have good public transport networks, making use of modern buses, trolleybuses, trams and – in Budapest – a metro system and a suburban railway network. Most city centres are also very pedestrian-friendly, with a growing number of streets in the city centres now being declared car-free. Budapest aside, most city centres are small, with many sights within easy walking distance of each other. Even in Budapest the excellent public transport makes getting around quick and easy.

Public Transport in Budapest

Budapest has four metro lines. The oldest line is the M1 line, which is also known as the Millennium line, as it was built for the Hungarian Millennium celebrations in 1894. The Budapest Metro was the first electric underground railway system in continental Europe. Its original stations, all wood and wrought iron, as well as its small trains, make it a sight in itself. The line serves central Pest, Andrássy út and Városliget. Metro line M2 was built in the 1970s, but has been modernized to cater for increased commuter levels. The high-tech M4 crosses the river between Buda and Pest, while M3, the longest of the lines, serves Pest only. Two important words to remember when using the metro are *bejárat*, meaning "entrance", and *kijárat*,

Signs for the M2 and M3 metro lines

meaning "exit". All metro stations display maps of the local area, and the route of each line hangs above the doors in each carriage. A recorded voice announces the name of the next station. The metro runs from around 4:30am until 11:30pm.

There are also 30 tram lines and over 200 bus routes in Budapest. Trams are yellow; buses, blue. Trams are a particularly efficient way of traversing the city, as they avoid road traffic and run very frequently. One ticket is valid on all forms of public transport in Budapest. Tickets can be purchased from metro stations and newspaper kiosks, and from ticket vending machines sited at several main junctions and stops. They can be bought (for cash only) on board some vehicles, but not all, so are best bought in advance. A single journey ticket costs 350 forints (€1). The ticket must be validated in machines located at the entrance to metro lines or on board buses and trams. For each new journey, a new ticket has to be stamped (but not when changing lines on the metro). Children under six travel free. Season tickets for 1, 3 or 7 days' travel and a range of passes are sold at metro stations and from vending machines, as are books of ten tickets for 3,000 forints (€10). The Budapest Card (Ft 4,500 (€14) for 24 hours, Ft 7,500 (€23) for 48 hours or Ft 8,900 (€28) for 72 hours) allows free use of public transport as well as giving various discounts in museums and at tourist sights.

A typical hév train carriage, serving suburban stations

The Hév

Budapest and its suburbs also benefit from hév trains, an efficient and reliable – if sometimes slow – suburban rail service. Trains serve all of Budapest's suburbs, as well as a number of towns further afield, including Szentendre, Gödöllő and Ráckeve. HÉV trains are green, and depart from Batthyány tér for Szentendre, from Örs vezér tere for Gödöllő and the Hungaroring Formula One circuit, and from Közvágóhíd for Ráckeve. Standard Budapest transport tickets and passes are valid for journeys on hév trains within Budapest, but for journeys beyond the city limits tickets costing from 250 forints (under €1) can be purchased at station entrances or automated kiosks. Information and timetables for travel on Budapest's metro and hév trains, as well as buses, can be obtained from **BKK** who run Budapest's transport system.

Close to a million journeys are made on Budapest's metro every day

Tram in Debrecen, with the Great Reformed Church in the background

Public Transport in Other Cities

While Budapest has the only metro network in Hungary, several large towns, including Debrecen, Miskolc and Szeged, have tram systems. Every town (and even some smaller villages) has bus services. As a rule, all tickets need to be purchased before boarding the means of transport, and then franked or validated once on board. Tickets can usually be bought from newspaper kiosks, and sometimes from ticket machines.

It is important to validate tickets, as there are many ticket inspectors, both in uniform and plain clothes, who are empowered to stop travellers and demand to see their tickets even after they have got off their trains or buses.

In many towns trams can double as cut-price city tours. In Debrecen, for instance, the only tram line runs from the railway station to the city's large thermal bath complex, passing through the centre and past most important sights on the way. In Miskolc trams 1 and 2 run from the train station to the city centre, and on to Diósgyőr Castle *(see p231)*. In Pécs there is a sightseeing tourist train which departs from opposite the Csontváry Museum *(see p190)*, while Szeged's tram No. 1 runs from the station into the town centre.

In Hungary passengers are allowed to carry one piece of luggage and a children's buggy on buses and trams, but the bag must not be too large. Ticket inspectors may demand an additional payment if a bag is too large, or if more than one bag is carried.

Taxis

As elsewhere in the world, visitors should be wary when getting into a taxi anywhere in Hungary, but especially in popular tourist places. While most taxis are safe, cheap and a good way of getting around cities, many turn out to be far more expensive than expected, and they have been known to prey on bewildered visitors.

In Budapest, all licensed taxis are yellow, and all should have a licence number issued by the city council clearly displayed. They should also post their tariffs, which are standardized, on the windscreen or side of the passenger door. These taxis must meet set standards of comfort and roadworthiness.

Outside the capital, most taxis are operated by authorized taxi companies, and will display the company name and telephone number prominently. These are the taxis that should always be used. Take extra care when getting into a taxi outside a railway station; it is always advisable to agree a price for the journey in advance with the driver. If this proves impossible, it may be better to look for another taxi, even if that means waiting.

Sign denoting a taxi rank

Taxis can be booked over the phone, which is slightly cheaper, or hailed in the street. The best place to find a cab is in the taxi ranks near major bus stations, squares, markets or railway stations. Most hotels and restaurants will be happy to phone for a taxi for their guests. In fact, this may be cheaper than hailing one.

Licensed yellow taxis on the streets of Budapest

General Index

Acknowledgments

Hachette Livre Polska would like to thank the following staff at Dorling Kindersley:

Publisher
Douglas Amrine

Publishing Managers
Anna Streiffert, Christine Stroyan

Managing Art Editor
Jane Ewart

Editors
Sylvia Goulding, Jacky Jackson, Michelle Crane

Designer
Kate Leonard

Translator
Magda Hannay

Map Co-Ordinator
Casper Morris

DTP Manager
Natasha Lu

Additional Picture Research
Rachel Barber, Ellen Root

Production Controller
Shane Higgins

Dorling Kindersley would like to thank all those whose contributions and assistance have made the preparation of this book possible:

Main Contributor
Craig Turp is a linguist by training, and has spent most of his adult life studying and writing about the languages and peoples of Central and Eastern Europe. He has written a number of guide books to the region, and lives in Bucharest, Romania.

Additional Text Steve Fallon

Factcheckers Szilvia Szőke, Judit Mihalcsik

Proofreader Stewart J Wild

Indexer Helen Peters

Additional Photography
Demetrio Carrasco, Eddie Gerald, Ian O'Leary, Piotr Ostrowski, Mirek Osip

Additional Illustrations
ichapel.co.uk

Cartography
Base mapping supplied by Cartographia Ltd., Budapest.

Revisions Team
Louise Abbott, Hilary Bird, Surya Deogun, Caroline Elliker, Rhiannon Furbear, Darren Longley, Mohammad Hassan, Krisztian Hildebrand, Claire Jones, Phoebe Lowndes, Hayley Maher, Lucy Mallows, Agnes Ordog, Animesh Pathak, Susie Peachey, Marianne Petrou, Susana Smith, Nikky Twyman, Conrad Van Dyk

Special Assistance
The Publishers would like to thank the staff at shops, museums, hotels, restaurants and other organizations in Hungary for their invaluable help. Particular thanks go to: the Ambassador for the Republic of Hungary in Warsaw; the Ambassador for the Republic of Poland in Budapest; Peter Hajnal at Europress; Csilla Pataky at Cartographia Ltd., Budapest; Vanda Tódor at the Budapest Festival Centre.

Photography Permissions
The Publishers would like to thank all those who gave permission to photograph at musuems, palaces, churches, restaurants, hotels, shops and other sights too numerous to list individually. Particular thanks go to: the Aquaticum Thermal Baths in Debrecen; Bacchus Borkereskedés; the Christian Museum in Esztergom; staff at Festetics Palace and Helikon Palace Museum, Keszthely; Loránd Bereczky at the Hungarian National Gallery; Gyula Fülöp at the Szent István Király Museum, Székesfehérvár; Ágnes Langer at the Zettl-Langer Collection, Sopron.

Boscolo Budapest Hotel: 265tr.
Budapest History Museum: 60tl.
Budapest Spa LLC: 109tr.
Budapest Tourist Office: 88t, 114bc.
Buddha-Bar Hotel: 100cl.
Centrum Panzio: 266tl.
Cephas Picture Library: 183b; Herbert Lehmann 32br.
Corbis: 51br; Barry Lewis 75tl, 273tl; Bettmann 46clb, 50br, 51tl, 294-295c; Walter Bibikow 196-197, 292tl, 293t; Zsolt Czegledi 35cra, 35bl, 36bl; Rose Hartman 27cra; Hulton-Deutsch Collection 49c, 50bl; Ira Nowinski 30c; Sylvain Sonnet 70, 195cra, 195bl; Swim Ink 2, LLC 27crb; Underwood & Underwood 47clb; Sandro Vannini 28br, 29tl; Zefa/Klaus Hackenberg 31bl.
Danubius Hotel Gellert: 75bl.
Dorling Kindersley: 20tl, 22cl, 24cla, 24cra, 24crb, 25cra, 25crb, 28tr, 32cl, 32c, 32fcl, 33tc, 33tr, 42br; Demetrio Carrasco 59br, 97t, 113tl, 116clb, 298b, 300tr; Eddie Gerald 21ca, 49bl; Ian O'Leary 272-273.
Dreamstime.com: Artzzz 304cra, 311bl; Yulia Babkina 12bl; Artur Bogacki 56; Dreamframer 140-141; Emicristea 80; Jorg Hackemann 305tl, 315tr; Ladiras81 52-53; Laraclarence 106; Llareggub 10br; Fabio Lotti 10cl; Markborbely 15br; Plotnikov 11tr; Stitchik 15tl; Tupungato 300bl; Nikoleta Vukovic 310bl; Zagorskid 13tr.
Eco Cafe: 279tl.
Erhardt: 281br.
Esztergom Basilica: 148tr.
Ethnographical Museum: 82tr.
Europress Fotougynokseg: 34cr, 36cr, 37bl, 50tl, 51crb, 67cr, 96bl, 115t, 195clb, 251tl, 251clb, 288b, 289b; Katalin Darnay 77tr; Tibor Szabu 97crb.
Ferenc Liszt International airport: 304bl.
Gabor Barka: 66cr, 67tl, 67br, 84cl, 84br, 85tl, 85cra, 85crb, 85bc, 91tl, 91tc, 91cra, 91crb, 91bc, 92cla, 92crb, 92br, 93tl, 93cra, 93crb, 93bc, 96cla, 270br.
Getty Images: aGinger 132c; Oliver Benn 19b; Karsten Bidstrup 248-249c; David Borland 14br; Attila Kisbenedek 234c; Chlaus Lotscher 284bl.
Grand Photo Agency: Koltai Andor 28cl; Molnar V. Attila 25cb, 26br; Zoltan Bagosi 24c, 25cla; Béla Budai 33bc; Katalin Darnay 33cr; Anita Huszti 24clb; Diósi Imre 24cb; György Kallus 31c; Kata Kovács 33br; Tibor Rigo 29cra, 32tr, 33clb; Tibor Szabó 33bl; Bagosi Zoltan 24bl.
Helikon Palace Museum: Zsolt Banko 202clb; Laszlo T. Meszaros 203tl.
hemis.fr: 311tl; Emilio Suetone 23tr.
House of Terror Museum: 105b.
Hungarian National Gallery: 38l, 42tr, 43bl, 44bc, 62tr, 62cl, 62bl, 62br, 63tl, 63tr, 63br, 63b, 189br.
Hungarian National Museum: 8-9, 39tc, 40bl, 40bc, 40br,

43cb, 44tl, 44cr, 45tc, 45bc, 45br, 102tr, 102cla, 102bl, 102fcl, 103cla, 103c, 103crb, 103bl, 187br.
Janus Atrium: 268tl.
Karolina Kavehaz: 282bl.
The Kobal Collection: Paramount 30cra.
Krizia: 277bl.
La Mareda: 280tl.
The Liszt Academy: Gabor Fejer 105tl.
Lonely Planet Images: Jonathan Smith 29cr.
Mary Evans Picture Library: 47bl, 48tl.
Menza Restaurant: 278br.
Museum of Applied Arts: 87clb.
Museum of Fine Arts: 108tr.
Museum of Fine Arts, Budapest: 110cb.
National Office of Cultural Heritage: 42-43.
National Széchényi Library: 42cl, 43tc.
NHPA/Photoshot: Bill Coster 24bc; Andy Rouse 25cl.
Pannonhalma Abbey: 181fbr.
Laszlo Papp: Laszlo Papp 121tl.
Photolibrary: Jon Arnold Images/Jon Arnold 24tr.
Piroska Csarda: 283tc.
Press Association Images: AP 30bc; AP/Arpad Hazafi 49crb; S&G 31tr.
Rex Features: 37cr.
Robert Harding Picture Library: Ellen Rooney 94c.
Rock Church: 76tl.
Szamos Marzipan Museum: 142tr.
Szechenyi National Library: 60bc.
The Art Archive: National Gallery Budapest/Dagli Orti 42bl.
The Office of the National Assembly: Gyorgy Kovacs 82cla, 84tr.
The Renaissance: 281tl.
Tiszavirag: 285tr.
TopFoto.co.uk: Topham Picturepoint 48bc.
Trattoria Pomo D'Oro: 277tr.
UniCredit Bank: 300c.
Vac Tourist Information: Andrea Ivor 137br.
Varkert Bazar: 78cl.
West-Balaton Tourism Nonprofit Ltd.: Meszaros T. Laszlo 200cl, 201tl.

Jacket Front and Spine Images: Robert Harding Picture Library: Image Broker.
Front Endpapers: **Alamy Images**: Danita Delimont Rtr; **AWL Images**: Ian Trower Lcla, Lbl; **Dreamstime.com**: Ladiras81 Ltr; **Getty Images**: aGinger Rbl, Attila Kisbenedek R.

All other images © Dorling Kindersley.
For further information see: www.dkimages.com

Special Editions of DK Travel Guides

DK Travel Guides can be purchased in bulk quantities at discounted prices for use in promotions or as premiums. We are also able to offer special editions and personalized jackets, corporate imprints, and excerpts from all of our books, tailored specifically to meet your own needs.

To find out more, please contact:
in the United States **SpecialSales@dk.com**
in the UK **travelspecialsales@uk.dk.com**
in Canada DK Special Sales at **general@ tourmaline.ca**
in Australia **business.development@pearson. com.au**

Phrase Book

Pronunciation

When reading the literal pronunciation given in the right-hand column of this phrase book, pronounce each syllable as if it formed part of an English word. Remember the points below, and your pronunciation will be even closer to correct Hungarian. The first syllable of each word should be stressed (and is shown in bold). When asking a question the pitch should be raised on the penultimate syllable. "R"s in Hungarian words are rolled.

a	as the long 'a' in father
ay	as in 'pay'
e	as in 'Ted'
ew	similar to the sound in 'hew'
g	always as in 'goat'
i	as in 'bit'
o	as in the 'ou' in 'ought'
u	as in 'tuck'
y	always as in 'yes' (except as in ay above)
yuh	as the 'yo' in 'canyon'
zh	like the 's' in leisure

In Emergency

Help!	Segítség!	shegeetshayg!
Stop!	Stop!	shtop!
Look out!	Tessék vigyázni!	teshayk vidyahzni!
Call a doctor	Hívjon orvost!	heevyon orvosht!
Call an ambulance!	Hívjon mentőt!	heevyon menturt!
Call the police!	Hívja a rendőrséget!	heevya a rendur shayget!
Call the fire department!	Hívja a tűzoltókat!	heevya a tewzoltowkot!
Where is the nearest telephone?	Hol van a legközelebbi telefon?	hol von a legkurze-lebbi telefon?
Where is the nearest hospital?	Hol van a legközelebbi kórház?	hol von a legkurze lebbi koorhahz?

Communications Essentials

Yes/No	Igen/Nem	igen/nem
Please (offering)	Tessék	teshayk
Please (asking)	Kérem	kayrem
Thank you	Köszönöm	kurssurnurm
No, thank you	Köszönöm nem	kurssurnurm nem
Excuse me, please	Bocsánatot kérek	bochanutot kayrek
Hello	Jó napot	yow nopot
Goodbye	Viszontlátásra	vissontlatashruh
Good night	Jó éjszakát/jó éjt	yaw-ayssukat/yaw-ayt
morning (4–9 am)	reggel	reggel
morning (9am–noon)	délelőtt	daylelurt
morning (midnight–4am)	éjjel	ay-yel
afternoon	délután	daylootan
evening	este	eshteh
yesterday	tegnap	tegnup
today	ma	muh
tomorrow	holnap	holnup
here	itt	it
there	ott	ot
What?	mi?	mi
When?	mikor?	mikor?
Why?	miért?	miayrt?
Where?	hol?	hol?

Useful Phrases

How are you?	Hogy van?	hod-yuh vun?
Very well, thank you	köszönöm nagyon jól	kurssurnurm nojjon yowl
Pleased to meet you	Örülök hogy megismerhettem	ur-rewluk hod-yuh megishmerhettem
See you soon!	Szia!	seeyuh!
Excellent!	Nagyszerű!	nud-yusserew!
Is there ... here?	Van itt ... ?	vun itt?
Where can I get ...?	Hol kaphatok ...-t?	hol kuphutok ...-t?
How do you get to?	Hogy lehet ...-ba eljutni?	hod-yuh lehet ...-buh el-yootni?
How far is ...?	milyen messze van ...?	meeyen messeh van ...?
Do you speak English?	Beszél angolul?	bessayl ungolool?
I can't speak Hungarian	Nem beszélek magyarul	nem bessaylek mud-yarool
I don't understand	Nem értem	nem ayrtem
Can you help me?	Kérhetem a segítségét?	kayrhetem uh shegeechaygayt?
Please speak slowly	Tessék lassabban beszélni	teshayk lushubbun bessaylni
Sorry!	Elnézést!	elnayzaysht!

Useful Words

big	nagy	noj
small	kicsi	kichi
hot	forró	meleg
cold	hideg	hideg
good	jó	yow
bad	rossz	ross
enough	elég	elayg
well	jól	yowl
open	nyitva	nyitva
closed	zárva	zarva
left	bal	bol
right	jobb	yob
straight on	egyenesen	ejeneshen
near	közel	kurzel
far	messze	messeh
up	fel	fel
down	le	leh
early	korán	koran
late	késő	kayshur
entrance	bejárat	beh-yarut
exit	kijárat	ki-yarut
toilet	WC	vaytsay
free/unoccupied	szabad	sobbod
free/no charge	ingyen	injen

Making a Telephone Call

Can I call abroad from here?	Telefonálhatok innen külföldre?	telefonalhutokinen kewlfurldreh?
I would like to call collect	Szeretnék egy R-beszélgetést lebonyolítani	seretnayk ed-yuh er-bessaylgetaysht lebon-yoleetuni
local call	helyi beszélgetés	hayee bessaylgetaysht
I'll ring back later	Visszahívom később	vissuh-heevom kayshurb
Could I leave a message?	Hagyhatnék egy üzenetet?	hud-yuhutnayk ed-yuh ewzenetet
Hold on!	Várjon!	vahr-yon
Could you speak up a little, please?	kicsit hangosabban, kérem!	kichit hungosh-shob-bon kayrem

Shopping

How much is this?	Ez mennyibe kerül?	ez menn-yibeh kerewl?
I would like ...	Szeretnék egy ...-t	seretnayk ed-yuh ...-t
Do you have ...?	Kaphatό önöknél ...?	kuphutsav urnurtknayl...?
I'm just looking	Csak körülnézek	chuk kur-rewlnayzek
Do you take credit cards?	Elfogadják a hitelkártyákat?	elfogud-yak uh hitelkart-yakut?
What time do you open?	Hánykor nyitnak?	Hahnkor nyitnak?
What time do you close?	Hánykor zárnak?	Hahnkor zárnak?
this one	ez	ez
that one	az	oz
expensive	drága	drahga
cheap	olcsó	olchow
size	méret	mayret
white	fehér	feheer
black	fekete	feketeh
red	piros	pirosh
yellow	sárga	sharga
green	zöld	zurld
blue	kék	cake
brown	barna	borna

Types of Shop

antique dealer	antikvárius	ontikvahrioosh
baker's	pékség	paykshayg
bank	bank	bonk
bookshop	könyvesbolt	kurn-yuveshbolt
cake shop	cukrászda	tsookrassduh
chemist	patika	putikuh
department store	áruház	aroo-haz
florist	virágüzlet	vi rag-ewzlet
greengrocer	zöldséges	zurld-shaygesh
market	piac	pi-uts
newsagent	újságos	oo-yushagosh
post office	postahivatal	poshta-hivatal
shoe shop	cipőbolt	tsipurbolt
souvenir shop	ajándékbolt	uy-yandaykbolt
supermarket	ábécé/ABC	abaytsay
travel agent	utazási iroda	ootuzashi iroduh

Staying in a Hotel

Have you any vacancies?	**Van kiadó szobájuk?**	vun *ki-udaw soba-yook*
double room with double bed	**francia-ágyas szoba**	*frontsia-ahjosh sobuh*
twin room	**kétágyas szoba**	*kaytad-yush sobuh*
single room	**egyágyas szoba**	*ed-yad-yush sobuh*
room with a bath/shower	**fürdőszobás/ zuhanyzós szoba**	*fewrdur-sobahsh/ zoohonzahsh soba*
porter	**portás**	*portahsh*
key	**kulcs**	*koolch*
I have a reservation	**Foglaltam egy szobát**	*foglultum ed-yuh sobat*

Sightseeing

bus	**autóbusz/busz**	*owtawbooss/booss*
tram	**villamos**	*villumosh*
trolley bus	**troli(busz)**	*troli(booss)*
train	**vonat**	*vonut*
underground	**metró**	*metraw*
bus stop	**buszmegálló**	*boossmegallaw*
tram stop	**villamosmegálló**	*villomosh-megahllaw*
art gallery	**képcsarnok**	*kayp-chornok*
palace	**palota**	*polola*
cathedral	**székesegyház**	*saykesh-ejhajz*
church	**templom**	*templom*
garden	**kert**	*kert*
library	**könyvtár**	*kurnvtar*
museum	**múzeum**	*moozayoom*
tourist information	**turista információ**	*toorishta informatzeeo*
closed for public holiday	**ünnepnap zárva**	*ewn-nepnap zarva*

Eating Out

A table for … please	**Egy asztalt szeretnék… személyre**	*ed-yuh usstult seretnayk … semayreh*
I want to reserve a table	**Szeretnék egy asztalt foglalni**	*seretnayked-yuh usstultfoglolni*
The bill, please	**Kérem a számlát**	*kayrem uh samlat*
I am a vegetarian	**Vegetáriánus vagyok**	*vegetari-ahnoosh vojok*
I'd like …	**Szeret nék egy …-t**	*seret nayk ed-yuh …-t*
waiter/waitress	**pincér/pincérnő**	*pintsayr/pintsayrnur*
menu	**étlap**	*aytlup*
wine list	**itallap**	*itullup*
chef's special	**konyhafőnök ajánlata**	*konha-furnurt oyahu-lotta*
tip	**borravaló**	*borovolo*
glass	**pohár**	*pohar*
bottle	**üveg**	*ewveg*
knife	**kés**	*kaysh*
fork	**villa**	*villuh*
spoon	**kanál**	*kunal*
breakfast	**reggeli**	*reg-geli*
lunch	**ebéd**	*ebayd*
dinner	**vacsora**	*vochora*
main courses	**főételek**	*fur-aytelek*
starters	**előételek**	*elur-aytelek*
vegetables	**zöldség**	*zurld-shayg*
desserts	**édességek**	*aydesh-shaydek*
rare	**angolosan**	*ongoloshan*
well done	**átsütve**	*ahtshewtveh*

Menu Decoder

alma	*olma*	apple
ásványvíz	*ahshvahnveez*	mineral water
bab	*bob*	beans
banán	*bonahn*	banana
barack	*borotsk*	apricot
bárány	*bahrahn*	lamb
bors	*borsh*	pepper
csirke	*cheerkeh*	chicken
csokoládé	*chokolahday*	chocolate
cukor	*tsookor*	sugar
ecet	*etset*	vinegar
fagylalt	*fodyuhloot*	ice cream
fehérbor	*feheerbor*	white wine
fokhagyma	*fokhodyuhma*	garlic
főtt	*furt*	boiled
gomba	*gomba*	mushrooms
gulyás	*gooyahsh*	goulash
gyümölcs	*dyewmurlch*	fruit
gyümölcslé	*dyewmurlch-lay*	fruit juice
hagyma	*hojma*	onions
hal	*hol*	fish
hús	*hoosh*	meat
kávé	*kavay*	coffee
kenyér	*ken-yeer*	bread
krumpli	*kroompli*	potatoes

kolbász	*kolbahss*	sausage
leves	*levesh*	soup
máj	*my*	liver
marha	*marha*	beef
mustár	*mooshtahr*	mustard
narancs	*noronch*	orange
olaj	*oloy*	oil
paradicsom	*porodichom*	tomatoes
párolt	*pahrolt*	steamed
pite	*piteh*	pie
sertéshús	*shertaysh-hoosh*	pork
rántott	*rahntsott*	fried in batter
rizs	*rizh*	rice
rostélyos szelet	*bifstek*	steak
roston	*roshton-*	grilled
sajt	*shoyt*	cheese
saláta	*sholahta*	salad
só	*shaw*	salt
sonka	*shonka*	ham
sör	*shur*	beer
sült	*shewlt*	fried/roasted
sült burgonya	*shewlt boorgonya*	fried potatoes/chips
sütemény	*shewtemayn-yuh*	cake, pastry
szendvics	*sendvich*	sandwich
szósz	*sowss*	sauce
tea	*tay-uh*	tea
tej	*tay*	milk
tejszín	*taysseen*	cream
tengeri hal	*tengeri hol*	seafood
tojás	*toyahsh*	egg
töltött	*turlturt*	stuffed
vörösbor	*vur-rurshbor*	red wine
zsemle	*zhemleh*	roll
zsemlegombóc	*zhemleh-gombowts*	dumplings

Numbers

0	**nulla**	*noolluh*
1	**egy**	*ed-yuh*
2	**kettő, két**	*kettur, kayt*
3	**három**	*harom*
4	**négy**	*nayd-yuh*
5	**öt**	*urt*
6	**hat**	*hut*
7	**hét**	*hayt*
8	**nyolc**	*n-yolts*
9	**kilenc**	*kilents*
10	**tíz**	*teez*
11	**tizenegy**	*tizened-yuh*
12	**tizenkettő**	*tizenkettur*
13	**tizenhárom**	*tizenharom*
14	**tizennégy**	*tizen-nayd-yuh*
15	**tizenöt**	*tizenurt*
16	**tizenhat**	*tizenhut*
17	**tizenhét**	*tizenhayt*
18	**tizennyolc**	*tizenn-yolts*
19	**tizenkilenc**	*tizenkilents*
20	**húsz**	*hooss*
21	**huszonegy**	*hoossoned-yuh*
22	**huszonkettő**	*hoossonkettur*
30	**harminc**	*hurmints*
31	**harmincegy**	*hurmintsed-yuh*
32	**harminckettő**	*hurmintskettur*
40	**negyven**	*ned-yuven*
50	**ötven**	*urtven*
60	**hatvan**	*hutvun*
70	**hetven**	*hetven*
80	**nyolcvan**	*n-yoltsvun*
90	**kilencven**	*kilentsven*
100	**száz**	*saz*
110	**száztíz**	*sazteez*
200	**kétszáz**	*kayt-saz*
300	**háromszáz**	*haromsaz*
1000	**ezer**	*ezer*
10,000	**tízezer**	*teezezer*
1,000,000	**millió**	*milliaw*

Time

one minute	**egy perc**	*ed-yuh perts*
hour	**óra**	*awruh*
half an hour	**félóra**	*faylawruh*
Sunday	**vasárnap**	*vusharnup*
Monday	**hétfő**	*haytfur*
Tuesday	**kedd**	*kedd*
Wednesday	**szerda**	*serduh*
Thursday	**csütörtök**	*chewturturk*
Friday	**péntek**	*payntek*
Saturday	**szombat**	*sombut*

Road Map of Hungary

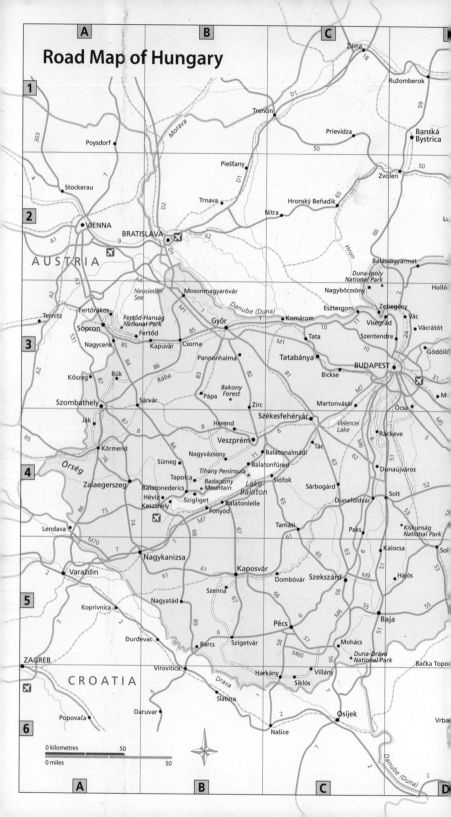